HEIDEGGER'S *BEING AND TIME*

Martin Heidegger's *Being and Time*, published in 1927, is widely regarded as his most important work and it has had a profound influence on twentieth-century philosophy. This Critical Guide draws on recently translated and published primary sources as well as the latest developments in Heidegger scholarship to provide a series of in-depth studies of this influential text. Twelve newly written essays examine the unity of *Being and Time*, the nature of human communication, truth as a catalyst of cultural transformation, feminist approaches to *Being and Time*, the essence of authenticity, curiosity as an epistemic vice, the nature of rationality, realism and idealism, the ontological difference, the origin of time, the possibility of death, and the failure of the *Being and Time* project. This volume will be particularly valuable to students and scholars interested in phenomenology, existentialism, hermeneutics, metaphysics, epistemology, feminism, and ethics.

AARON JAMES WENDLAND is Vision Fellow in Public Philosophy at King's College, London, and a Senior Research Fellow at Massey College, Toronto. He is co-editor of *Wittgenstein and Heidegger* (2013) and *Heidegger on Technology* (2019).

TOBIAS KEILING is Associate Professor of Philosophy at the University of Warwick. He is the co-editor of *The Routledge Handbook of the Phenomenology of Agency* (2020) and the editor of the *Oxford Bibliographies* (2021) for Heidegger's middle and later works.

CAMBRIDGE CRITICAL GUIDES

Titles published in this series:

Heidegger's *Being and Time*
EDITED BY AARON JAMES WENDLAND AND TOBIAS KEILING
Hume's Essays
EDITED BY MAX SKJÖNSBERG AND FELIX WALDMANN
Hegel's Philosophy of Nature
EDITED BY MARINA BYKOVA
Plato's Gorgias
EDITED BY J. CLERK SHAW
Boethius' Consolation of Philosophy
EDITED BY MICHAEL WIITALA
Wittgenstein's Tractatus Logico-Philosophicus
EDITED BY JOSÉ ZALABARDO
Kierkegaard's *Either/Or A Critical Guide*
EDITED BY RYAN S. KEMP AND WALTER WIETZKE
Cicero's *De Officiis*
EDITED BY RAPHAEL WOOLF
Kierkegaard's *The Sickness unto Death*
EDITED BY JEFFREY HANSON AND SHARON KRISHEK
Nietzsche's *Thus Spoke Zarathustra*
EDITED BY KEITH ANSELL-PEARSON AND PAUL S. LOEB
Aristotle's *On the Soul*
EDITED BY CALEB M. COHOE
Schopenhauer's *World as Will and Representation*
EDITED BY JUDITH NORMAN AND ALISTAIR WELCHMAN
Kant's *Prolegomena*
EDITED BY PETER THIELKE
Hegel's *Encyclopedia of the Philosophical Sciences*
EDITED BY SEBASTIAN STEIN AND JOSHUA WRETZEL
Maimonides' *Guide of the Perplexed*
EDITED BY DANIEL FRANK AND AARON SEGAL
Fichte's *System of Ethics*
EDITED BY STEFANO BACIN AND OWEN WARE
Hume's *An Enquiry Concerning the Principles of Morals*
EDITED BY ESTHER ENGELS KROEKER AND WILLEM LEMMENS
Hobbes's *On the Citizen*
EDITED BY ROBIN DOUGLASS AND JOHANN OLSTHOORN
Hegel's *Philosophy of Spirit*
EDITED BY MARINA F. BYKOVA
Kant's *Lectures on Metaphysics*
EDITED BY COURTNEY D. FUGATE
Spinoza's *Political Treatise*
EDITED BY YITZHAK Y. MELAMED AND HASANA SHARP
Aquinas's *Summa Theologiae*
EDITED BY JEFFREY HAUSE

Aristotle's *Generation of Animals*
EDITED BY ANDREA FALCON AND DAVID LEFEBVRE
Hegel's *Elements of the Philosophy of Right*
EDITED BY DAVID JAMES
Kant's *Critique of Pure Reason*
EDITED BY JAMES R. O'SHEA
Spinoza's *Ethics*
EDITED BY YITZHAK Y. MELAMED
Plato's *Symposium*
EDITED BY PIERRE DESTRÉE AND ZINA GIANNOPOULOU
Fichte's *Foundations of Natural Right*
EDITED BY GABRIEL GOTTLIEB
Aquinas's *Disputed Questions on Evil*
EDITED BY M. V. DOUGHERTY
Aristotle's *Politics*
EDITED BY THORNTON LOCKWOOD AND THANASSIS SAMARAS
Aristotle's *Physics*
EDITED BY MARISKA LEUNISSEN
Kant's *Lectures on Ethics*
EDITED BY LARA DENIS AND OLIVER SENSEN
Kierkegaard's *Fear and Trembling*
EDITED BY DANIEL CONWAY
Kant's *Lectures on Anthropology*
EDITED BY ALIX COHEN
Kant's *Religion within the Boundaries of Mere Reason*
EDITED BY GORDON MICHALSON
Descartes' *Meditations*
EDITED BY KAREN DETLEFSEN
Augustine's *City of God*
EDITED BY JAMES WETZEL
Kant's *Observations and Remarks*
EDITED BY RICHARD VELKLEY AND SUSAN SHELL
Nietzsche's *On the Genealogy of Morality*
EDITED BY SIMON MAY
Aristotle's *Nicomachean Ethics*
EDITED BY JON MILLER

Continued after the Index

HEIDEGGER'S
BEING AND TIME
A Critical Guide

EDITED BY

AARON JAMES WENDLAND
King's College, London

TOBIAS KEILING
University of Warwick

Shaftesbury Road, Cambridge CB2 8EA, United Kingdom

One Liberty Plaza, 20th Floor, New York, NY 10006, USA

477 Williamstown Road, Port Melbourne, VIC 3207, Australia

314–321, 3rd Floor, Plot 3, Splendor Forum, Jasola District Centre, New Delhi – 110025, India

103 Penang Road, #05–06/07, Visioncrest Commercial, Singapore 238467

Cambridge University Press is part of Cambridge University Press & Assessment, a department of the University of Cambridge.

We share the University's mission to contribute to society through the pursuit of education, learning and research at the highest international levels of excellence.

www.cambridge.org
Information on this title: www.cambridge.org/9781108496001

DOI: 10.1017/9781108865579

© Cambridge University Press 2025

This publication is in copyright. Subject to statutory exception and to the provisions of relevant collective licensing agreements, no reproduction of any part may take place without the written permission of Cambridge University Press & Assessment.

When citing this work, please include a reference to the DOI 10.1017/9781108865579

First published 2025

A catalogue record for this publication is available from the British Library

A Cataloging-in-Publication data record for this book is available from the Library of Congress

ISBN 978-1-108-49600-1 Hardback

Cambridge University Press & Assessment has no responsibility for the persistence or accuracy of URLs for external or third-party internet websites referred to in this publication and does not guarantee that any content on such websites is, or will remain, accurate or appropriate.

Contents

List of Contributors	*page* ix
Acknowledgements	xi
List of Abbreviations	xii

	Introduction: The Circle of Understanding Aaron James Wendland and Tobias Keiling	1
1	*Being and Time* as a Whole: From Pragmatism, to Existentialism, to a Philosophy of Being, via the Good Denis McManus	7
2	The Trouble with the Ontological Difference Katherine Withy	31
3	Heidegger's Evenhanded Approach to Realism and Idealism David R. Cerbone	49
4	Discourse as Communicative Expression Taylor Carman	71
5	On Curiosity as Epistemic Vice Irene McMullin	84
6	Rethinking *Being and Time* as a Resource for Feminist Philosophy Charlotte Knowles	103
7	Authenticity, Truth, and Cultural Transformation Aaron James Wendland	125
8	What Does Authenticity Do in *Being and Time*? Sacha Golob	158

9	Why Ask Why? Retrieving Reason in *Being and Time* *Steven Crowell*	177
10	Time's Origin *Daniel Dahlstrom*	198
11	The Possibility of Death *Mark A. Wrathall*	217
12	Heidegger on the Failure of *Being and Time* *Tobias Keiling*	248

Bibliography 274
Index 289

Contributors

TAYLOR CARMAN is Professor of Philosophy at Barnard College, Columbia University. He is the author of *Heidegger's Analytic* (2003) and *Merleau-Ponty* (2008).

DAVID CERBONE is Professor of Philosophy at West Virginia University. He is the author of *Understanding Phenomenology* (2006) and *Existentialism: All That Matters* (2015).

STEVEN CROWELL is Emeritus Professor of Philosophy at Rice University. He is the author of *Normativity and Phenomenology in Husserl and Heidegger* (2013) and the editor of *The Cambridge Companion to Existentialism* (2012).

DANIEL DAHLSTROM is John R. Silber Professor of Philosophy at Boston University. He is the author of *Heidegger's Concept of Truth* (2001) and *The Heidegger Dictionary* (2013).

SACHA GOLOB is Professor of Philosophy at King's College, London. He is the author of *Heidegger on Concepts, Freedom, and Normativity* (2014) and the co-editor of *The Cambridge History of Moral Philosophy* (2017).

TOBIAS KEILING is Associate Professor of Philosophy at the University of Warwick. He is the co-editor of *The Routledge Handbook of the Phenomenology of Agency* (2020) and the editor of the *Oxford Bibliographies* (2021) for Heidegger's middle and later works.

CHARLOTTE KNOWLES is Assistant Professor of Philosophy at the University of Groningen. She has published on Heidegger in *The Monist* and sits on the editorial board of *Hypatia: A Journal of Feminist Philosophy*.

DENIS MCMANUS is Professor of Philosophy at the University of Southampton. He is the author of *Heidegger and the Measure of Truth* (2012) and the editor of *Heidegger, Authenticity and the Self* (2015).

IRENE MCMULLIN is Professor of Philosophy at the University of Essex. She is the author of *Time and the Shared World: Heidegger on Social Relations* (2013) and *Existential Flourishing: A Phenomenology of the Virtues* (2018).

AARON JAMES WENDLAND is Vision Fellow in Public Philosophy at King's College, London, and a Senior Research Fellow at Massey College, Toronto. He is the co-editor of *Wittgenstein and Heidegger* (2013) and *Heidegger on Technology* (2018).

KATHERINE WITHY is Professor of Philosophy at Georgetown University. She is the author of *Heidegger on Being Uncanny* (2015) and *Heidegger on Being Self-Concealing* (2022).

MARK WRATHALL is Professor of Philosophy at the University of Oxford. He is the author of *Heidegger and Unconcealment: Truth, Language and History* (2010) and the editor of *The Cambridge Companion to Heidegger's Being and Time* (2013).

Acknowledgements

We editors would like to thank Hilary Gaskin at Cambridge University Press for believing in this project. Many thanks are also due to our contributors for their excellent essays. This book was commissioned shortly before the outbreak of the COVID-19 pandemic. Those who lived through this plague know it disrupted daily life and presented serious challenges to academic research. So, we appreciate the patience Hilary and our contributors showed as we brought this volume to completion. Finally, we editors are grateful for Pauline Mitschack's help as a copyeditor.

Aaron James Wendland's work on this collection was completed while he was reporting on the Russo-Ukrainian war for *The Toronto Star* and working from Kyiv to generate international support for the Ukrainian academy. Aaron is thus indebted to the Armed Forces of Ukraine and the coalition providing air defences around Kyiv for making all his efforts in Ukraine possible. Aaron also appreciates the institutional support he received from King's College, London, and Massey College, Toronto over the course of this project, and he values the hard work of his co-editor. Most importantly, Aaron dedicates this book to his daughter, Sienna Aino. Sienna was born in February 2023, and she is a great joy in what any newspaper will tell you is a dark and disconcerting world.

Tobias Keiling joined as an editor of this collection when work was already well underway, and he is indebted to his co-editor for the initiative, for the invitation to contribute, and for his editorial work. Tobias is also grateful for the institutional support he received from the University of Warwick while editing this volume.

Abbreviations

AM: *Aristotle's Metaphysics Θ 1–3: On the Essence and Actuality of Force*. Trans. Walter Brogan and Peter Warnek. Bloomington, IN: Indiana University Press, 1995.

Basic: *Basic Concepts*. Trans. Gary E. Aylesworth. Bloomington, IN: Indiana University Press, 1993.

BaT: *Being and Truth*. Trans. Gregory Fried and Richard Polt. Bloomington, IN: Indiana University Press, 2010.

BCAP: *Basic Concepts of Aristotelian Philosophy*. Trans. Robert D. Metcalf and Mark B. Tanzer. Bloomington, IN: Indiana University Press, 2009.

BFL: *Bremen and Freiburg Lectures. Insight Into That Which Is and Basic Principles of Thinking*. Trans. Andrew J. Mitchell. Bloomington, IN: Indiana University Press, 2012.

BH: *Becoming Heidegger: On the Trail of His Early Occasional Writings, 1910–1927*. Ed. Theodore Kisiel and Thomas Sheehan. Evanston, IL: Northwestern University Press, 2007.

BN: *Ponderings II–VI: Black Notebooks 1931–1938*. Trans. Richard Rojcewicz. Bloomington, IN: Indiana University Press, 2016.

BN2:   *Ponderings VII–XI: Black Notebooks 1938–1939*. Trans. Richard Rojcewicz. Bloomington, IN: Indiana University Press, 2017.

BP: *The Basic Problems of Phenomenology*. Rev. ed. Albert Hofstadter. Bloomington, IN: Indiana University Press, 1988.

BQ: *Basic Questions of Philosophy: Selected "Problems" of "Logic"*. Trans. Richard Rojcewicz and André Schuwer. Bloomington, IN: Indiana University Press, 1994.

BT: *Being and Time*. Trans. John Macquarrie and Edward Robinson. New York, NY: Harper & Row, 1962. The page numbers from the Macquarrie and Robinson translation are followed by the page numbers from the standard German

edition: Heidegger, M. *Sein und Zeit*. Tübingen: Max Niemeyer Verlag, 1953.
BW: *Basic Writings*. Ed. David Farrell Krell. New York, NY: HarperCollins, 1993.
CP: *Contributions to Philosophy (From Enoknowning)*. Trans. Parvis Emad and Kenneth Maly. Bloomington, IN: Indiana University Press, 1999.
CP: *Contributions to Philosophy (of the Event)*. Trans. Daniela Vallegae-Neu and Richard Rojcewicz. Bloomington, IN: Indiana University Press, 2012.
CPC: *Country Path Conversations*. Trans. Bret W. Davis. Bloomington, IN: Indiana University Press, 2010.
CT: *The Concept of Time*. Trans. Ingo Farin. London/New York: Continuum. 2011.
D: *Denkerfahrungen: 1910–1976*. Frankfurt am Main: Vittorio Klostermann, 1983.
DS: *Duns Scotus's Doctrine of Categories and Meaning*. Trans. Joydeep Bagchee and Jeffrey D. Gower. Bloomington, IN: Indiana University Press, 2022.
DT: *Discourse on Thinking*. Trans. John M. Anderson and E. Hans Freund. New York, NY: Harper & Row, 1966.
E: *The Event*. Trans. Richard Rojcewicz. Bloomington, IN: Indiana University Press, 2013.
EF: *The Essence of Human Freedom: An Introduction to Philosophy*. Trans. by Ted Sadler. London/New York: Continuum, 2002.
EGT: *Early Greek Thinking: The Dawn of Western Philosophy*. Trans. David Farrell Krell and Frank A. Capuzzi. New York, NY: Harper & Row, 1975.
EHP: *Elucidations of Hölderlin's Poetry*. Trans. Keith Hoeller. Amherst, NY: Humanity Books, 2000.
EP: *The End of Philosophy*. Trans. Joan Stambaugh. Chicago, IL: University of Chicago Press, 1973.
ET: *The Essence of Truth: On Plato's Parable of the Cave Allegory and Theaetetus*. Trans. Ted Sadler. London: Continuum, 2002.
FCM: *The Fundamental Concepts of Metaphysics: World, Finitude, Solitude*. Trans. William McNeill and Nicholas Walker. Bloomington, IN: Indiana University Press, 1995.
FS: *Four Seminars*. Trans. Andrew Mitchell and François Raffoul. Bloomington, IN: Indiana University Press, 2003.

GA: Gesamtausgabe (102 vols., volume number indicated by Arabic numerals). Frankfurt am Main: Vittorio Klostermann, 1975–present.

> GA 1: *Frühe Schriften. 1912–16*. Frankfurt am Main: Vittorio Klostermann, 1978.
> GA 4: *Erläuterungen zu Hölderlins Dichtung*. Frankfurt am Main: Vittorio Klostermann, 1981. Translated as: *Elucidations of Hölderlin's Poetry*, see *EHP*.
> GA 5: *Holzwege*. Frankfurt am Main: Vittorio Klostermann, 1977. Translated as: *Off the Beaten Track*, see *OBT*.
> GA 9: *Wegmarken*. Frankfurt am Main: Vittorio Klostermann, 1976. Translated as: *Pathmarks*, see *PM*.
> GA 14: *Zur Sache des Denkens*. Frankfurt am Main: Vittorio Klostermann, 2007. Translated as: *On Time and Being*, see *TB*.
> GA 15: *Seminare*. Frankfurt am Main: Vittorio Klostermann, 1986. First part (9–263) translated as: *Heraclitus Seminar*, see *H*. Second part (270–400) translated as: *Four Seminars*, see *FS*.
> GA 18: *Grundbegriffe der Aristotelischen Philosophie*. Frankfurt am Main: Vittorio Klostermann, 2002. Translated as: *The Basic Concepts of Aristotelian Philosophy*, see *BCAP*.
> GA 20: *Prolegomena zur Geschichte des Zeitbegriffs*. Frankfurt am Main: Vittorio Klostermann, 1979. Translated as: *History of the Concept of Time: Prolegomena*, see *HCT*.
> GA 21: *Logik: Die Frage nach der Wahrheit*. Frankfurt am Main: Vittorio Klostermann, 1976. Translated as: *Logic: The Question of Truth*, see *LQT*.
> GA 26: *Metaphysische Anfangsgründe der Logik im Ausgang von Leibniz*. Frankfurt am Main: Vittorio Klostermann, 1978. Translated as: *The Metaphysical Foundations of Logic*, see *MFL*.
> GA 27: *Einleitung in die Philosophie*. Frankfurt am Main: Vittorio Klostermann, 1996. Translated as: *Introduction to Philosophy*, see *IP*.
> GA 29/30: *Die Grundbegriffe der Metaphysik. Welt – Endlichkeit – Einsamkeit*. Frankfurt am Main: Vittorio

List of Abbreviations

Klostermann, 1992. Translated as: *The Fundamental Concepts of Metaphysics*, see *FCM*.

GA 40: *Einführung in die Metaphysik.* Frankfurt am Main: Vittorio Klostermann, 1983. Translated as: *Introduction to Metaphysics*, see *IM*.

GA 45: *Grundfragen der Philosophie. Ausgewählte "Probleme" der "Logik".* Frankfurt am Main: Vittorio Klostermann, 1984. Translated as: *Basic Questions of Philosophy*, see *BQ*.

GA 58: *Grundprobleme der Phänomenologie.* Frankfurt am Main: Vittorio Klostermann, 1993. Translated as: *Basic Problems of Phenomenology*, see *BP*.

GA 60: *Phänomenologie des religiösen Lebens.* Frankfurt am Main: Vittorio Klostermann, 1995. Translated as: *The Phenomenology of Religious Life*, see *PRL*.

GA 62: *Phänomenologische Interpretationen ausgewählter Abhandlungen des Aristoteles zur Ontologie und Logik.* Frankfurt am Main: Vittorio Klostermann, 2005.

GA 64: *Der Begriff der Zeit.* Frankfurt am Main: Vittorio Klostermann, 2004. First part (7–104) translated as: *The Concept of Time*, see *CT*. Second part translated as: *The Concept of Time*, trans. William McNeill (Oxford: Blackwell, 1992).

GA 80.1: *Vorträge, Teil 1: 1915–1932.* Frankfurt am Main: Vittorio Klostermann, 2016.

GA 82: *Zu eigenen Veröffentlichungen.* Frankfurt am Main: Vittorio Klostermann, 2018.

GA 94: *Überlegungen II-VI ("Schwarze Hefte" 1931–1938).* Frankfurt am Main: Vittorio Klostermann, 2014. Translated as *Ponderings*, see *BN*.

H: *Heraclitus Seminar.* Trans. Charles H. Seibert. Evanston, IL: Northwestern University Press, 1993.

HC: *The Heidegger Controversy: A Critical Reader.* Ed. Richard Wolin. Cambridge, MA: The MIT Press, 1993.

HCT: *History of the Concept of Time: Prolegomena.* Trans. Theodore Kisiel. Bloomington, IN: Indiana University Press, 1985.

List of Abbreviations

HDL: *Heraclitus: The Inception of Occidental Thinking and Logic. Heraclitus' Doctrine of the Logos.* Trans. Julia Goesser and S. Montgomery Ewegen. London: Bloomsbury, 2018.

HH: *Hölderlin's Hymn "The Ister".* Trans. William McNeill and Julia Davis. Bloomington, IN: Indiana University Press, 1996.

HIS: "Phenomenological Interpretations with Respect to Aristotle: Indication of the Hermeneutical Situation". In *Becoming Heidegger: On the Trail of His Early Occasional Writings, 1910–1927*, eds. Theodore Kisiel and Thomas Sheehan, 155–184, 477–480. Evanston, IL: Northwestern University Press, 2007.

HPS: *Hegel's "Phenomenology of Spirit".* Trans. Parvis Emad and Kenneth May. Bloomington, IN: Indiana University Press, 1988.

HR: *The Heidegger Reader.* Ed. Günter Figal, Trans. Jerome Veith. Bloomington, IN: Indiana University Press, 2009.

ID: *Identity and Difference.* Trans. Joan Stambaugh. New York, NY: Harper & Row, 1969.

IM: *An Introduction to Metaphysics.* Trans. Gregory Fried and Richard Polt. New Haven, CT: Yale University Press, 2000.

IP: *Introduction to Philosophy.* Trans. William McNaill. Bloomington, IN: Indiana University Press, forthcoming.

IPR: *An Introduction to Phenomenological Research.* Trans. Daniel O. Dahlstrom. Bloomington, IN: Indiana University Press, 2005.

ITP: *Introduction to Philosophy – Thinking and Poetizing.* Trans. Phillip Jacques Braunstein. Bloomington, IN: Indiana University Press, 2011.

KPM: *Kant and the Problem of Metaphysics*, 5th ed. Trans. Richard Taft. Bloomington, IN: Indiana University Press, 1990.

LEL: *Logic as the Question Concerning the Essence of Language.* Trans. Wanda Torres Gregory and Yvonne Unna. Bloomington, IN: Indiana University Press, 2009.

LQT: *Logic: The Question of Truth.* Trans. Thomas Sheehan. Bloomington, IN: Indiana University Press, 2010.

M: *Mindfulness.* Trans. Parvis Emad and Thomas Kalary. London: Continuum, 2006.

MHC: *Martin Heidegger in Conversation.* Trans. B. Srinivasa Murthy. New Delhi: Arnold-Heinemann Publishers, 1977.

MFL: *The Metaphysical Foundations of Logic.* Trans. Michael Heim. Bloomington, IN: Indiana University Press, 1992.

List of Abbreviations

N:	*Nietzsche* (4 vols., volume number indicated by Roman numerals). Trans. David Farrell Krell. New York, NY: Harper & Row, 1979–1987.
OBT:	*Off the Beaten Track.* Ed. and Trans. Julian Young and Kenneth Haynes. Cambridge: Cambridge University Press, 2002.
OHF:	*Ontology – The Hermeneutics of Facticity.* Trans. John van Buren. Bloomington, IN: Indiana University Press, 2008.
OWL:	*On the Way to Language.* Trans. Peter D. Hertz. New York, NY: Harper & Row, 1971.
P:	*Parmenides.* Trans. André Schuwer and Richard Rojcewicz. Bloomington, IN: Indiana University Press, 1992.
PIA:	*Phenomenological Interpretations of Aristotle.* Trans. Richard Rojcewicz. Bloomington, IN: Indiana University Press, 2008.
PIE:	*Phenomenology of Intuition and Expression.* Trans. Tracy Colony. New York: Continuum, 2010.
PIK:	*Phenomenological Interpretation of Kant's* Critique of Pure Reason. Trans. Parvis Emad and Kenneth Maly. Bloomington, IN: Indiana University Press, 1997.
PLT:	*Poetry, Language, Thought.* Trans. Albert Hofstadter. New York, NY: Harper & Row, 1971.
PM:	*Pathmarks.* Trans. William McNeill. Cambridge: Cambridge University Press, 1998.
PR:	*The Principle of Reason.* Trans. Reginald Lilly. Bloomington, IN: Indiana University Press, 1991.
PRL:	*The Phenomenology of Religious Life.* Trans. Matthias Frisch and Jennifer Anna Gosetti-Ferencei. Bloomington, IN: Indiana University Press, 2004.
PS:	*Plato's Sophist.* Trans. Richard Rojcewicz and André Schuwer. Bloomington, IN: Indiana University Press, 1997.
PT:	*The Piety of Thinking.* Trans. James C. Hart and John C. Maraldo. Bloomington, IN: Indiana University Press, 1976.
QT:	*The Question Concerning Technology and Other Essays.* Trans. William Lovitt. New York, NY: Harper & Row, 1977.
SA:	The Self-Assertion of the German University. In *The Heidegger Controversy: A Critical Reader*, ed. Richard Wolin, 29–40. Cambridge, MA: MIT Press, 1993.
STF:	*Schelling's Treatise on the Essence of Human Freedom.* Trans. Joan Stambaugh. Athens, OH: Ohio University Press, 1985.

Supp:	*Supplements: From the Earliest Essays to* Being and Time *and Beyond*. Ed. John van Buren. Albany, NY: State University of New York Press, 2002.
TB:	*On Time and Being*. Trans. Joan Stambaugh. New York, NY: Harper & Row, 1972.
TDP:	*Towards the Definition of Philosophy*. London/New York: Continuum, 2000.
WCT:	*What is Called Thinking?* Trans. J. Glenn Gray. New York, NY: Harper & Row, 1968.
WIP:	*What is Philosophy?* Trans. Jean T. Wilde and William Kluback. New Haven, CT: College & University Press, 1956.
WP:	Why Do I Stay in the Provinces? In *Heidegger: The Man and the Thinker*, ed. Thomas Sheehan, 27–30. New Brunswick, NJ: Transaction Publishers.
WT:	*What is a Thing?* Trans. W. B. Barton, Jr. and Vera Deutsch. Chicago, IL: Henry Regnery, 1967.
Zo:	*Zollikon Seminars: Protocols – Conversations – Letters*. Ed. Medard Boss, Trans. Franz Mayr and Richard Askay. Evanston, IL: Northwestern University Press, 2001.

Introduction: The Circle of Understanding

Aaron James Wendland and Tobias Keiling

Martin Heidegger's *Being and Time* was published in 1927, and the text has been intensely discussed and studied ever since. Despite long-standing and unfolding controversies around Heidegger's affiliation with the Nazis, Heidegger scholarship is ubiquitous. New editions and translations of Heidegger's work appear regularly. Journals are dedicated exclusively to his philosophy. And countless papers and monographs draw on and address various themes in Heidegger's writings. Why then another book on Heidegger's philosophy? Why consider anew Heidegger's *magnum opus*, about which so much ink has already been spilled?

Answers to these questions can be found in *Being and Time* itself. As Heidegger emphasizes, we are not anonymous "subjects" who analyze and engage with independent "objects." Instead, we interact with an evolving world from a human standpoint, even when we engage in research. This means our understanding takes place within a specific sociohistorical context: It draws from the questions and answers of a particular time and place; it is both path-dependent and expectation-driven.

Heidegger famously describes the basic structure of our understanding in terms of a hermeneutic circle: that is, the "circle of understanding" (*BT* 195/153). This circle of understanding is not vicious; on the contrary, Heidegger claims the path-dependency and expectation-driven character of human understanding harbors the "positive possibility of the most primordial kind of knowing" (*BT* 195/153).

The idea is quite simple. Since "an interpretation is never a presuppositionless apprehending of something presented to us" (*BT* 191–192/150), whoever engages in research inherits work that has been done in the past. Whenever we turn to a specific topic, raise a particular question, conduct a set of experiments, or read and re-read a book, we do so with some sense of what we are trying to understand. In short, whenever we set out to understand something, we've already been engaged in understanding.

Put like this, Heidegger's idea is not very interesting. Understanding followed by understanding seems to suggest endlessly repeating the same operation. However, this is not what Heidegger means. There is a qualitative difference between what we initially know about a given subject and what we come to know by interpreting it in a specific way. Research is not only dependent on its *past*; it is also driven by *future* expectation in our *current* context. These three temporal orientations are crucial features of human understanding and our ability to interpret the world around us.

Heidegger calls the first feature our "fore-conception" (*Vor-griff*, BT 191/150): the "state of the art" in a particular field, or our current understanding of what something is to the best of our knowledge up to this point in history. But our current understanding isn't fully determined by the past, precisely because it is shaped by the questions raised by previous research and our anticipated answers to those questions.

As Heidegger says, understanding requires that there is "*something we see in advance*," and he calls the second feature of human understanding our "fore-sight" (*Vor-sicht*, BT 191/150). When it comes to academic inquiry, fore-sight is something like a conjecture we are trying to prove, a theory we are aiming to confirm via the accuracy of its predictions, or a set of criteria we are trying to meet to successfully answer a research question.

Yet if the circle of understanding simply hovered between the sediments of past understanding and the anticipation of a better understanding in the future, it would be spinning in a void. Heidegger therefore calls the third feature of human understanding our "fore-having" (*Vor-habe*, BT 191/150), and it indicates that our understanding is always anchored in our present practices. In the case of research, "fore-having" often takes the form of a particular experiment, project, or paper through which we actively appropriate our prior understanding of a given field and attempt to improve upon it by positing various hypotheses and conjectures that guide our current work.

Taken together, Heidegger's account of fore-conception, fore-sight, and fore-having illustrates that human understanding unfolds and evolves through time, and this means we are always able to advance and enhance our understanding of the history of philosophy, including *Being and Time*. Heidegger's version of human understanding is also consistent with the aims of the *Critical Guide* series, that is, to offer cutting-edge research on key texts in philosophy.

The chapters in this collection are accordingly written by renowned researchers who are well-versed in Heidegger scholarship and who are well-placed to offer innovative interpretations of Heidegger's *magnum opus*.

Introduction: The Circle of Understanding

And since human understanding always takes place within a specific sociohistorical context, the chapters in this book promise not only to advance our understanding of Heidegger's philosophy but also enhance our understanding of our time and place, generally.

Denis McManus' "*Being and Time* as a Whole: From Pragmatism, to Existentialism, to a Philosophy of Being, via the Good" notes that the commitments of Heidegger the pragmatist, Heidegger the existentialist, and Heidegger the philosopher of being can seem disparate or even incompatible. But according to McManus, seeing how our openness to our concerns as a whole is both necessary for authenticity and reveals a unified horizon against which entities with different ways of being show themselves, dissipates this apparent tension. As recognition of the mediating role played by a conception of the good that Heidegger's reading of Aristotle and Augustine inspired makes most clear, authenticity is both compatible with the practical embeddedness of our concerns and reveals a form of understanding necessary for ontology to be possible.

In "The Trouble with the Ontological Difference," **Katherine Withy** examines arguments that have been or might be used to establish or defend the distinction that Heidegger draws between entities (things that *are*) and the being of entities (that by virtue of which those things are). Withy finds these arguments for the ontological difference to fail – due largely to the self-concealing nature of being, which makes it difficult to distinguish being from entities. At the same time, Withy sees something positive in these troubles for the ontological difference, that is, they serve as prompts to question the meaning of being.

David R. Cerbone's essay, "Heidegger's Evenhanded Approach to Realism and Idealism," explains why Heidegger rejects the traditional metaphysical distinction between realism and idealism. Although Heidegger's evenhandedness seems similar to Kant's commitment to empirical realism and transcendental idealism, Cerbone argues that Heidegger's position does not map onto the empirical vs. transcendental distinction. And in view of Heidegger's affirmation that entities are independent from Dasein, Cerbone claims Heidegger's position needs to be understood as more robustly realist, closer to Quine's naturalism than to contemporaneous idealists such as Fink.

In "Discourse as Communicative Expression," **Taylor Carman** discusses Heidegger's philosophy of language in *Being and Time*. Carman's focus is on the notion of discourse (*Rede*) and Heidegger's claim that discourse cannot be equated with speech or verbal communication. Discourse is not language but what makes language possible: Dasein's expressive and communicative practices and comportments. Carman defends this view against readings that take discourse to be inherently conceptual, highlighting phenomena that Heidegger associates with discourse that are crucially noncognitive and nonlinguistic: the call of conscience and the practice of remaining silent.

Irene McMullin's chapter, "On Curiosity as Epistemic Vice," elucidates Heidegger's counterintuitive view that curiosity is problematic. On McMullin's reading, Heideggerian virtues are best understood as tendencies to cope well with existential obstacles to flourishing. And based on this reading, McMullin argues that Heidegger believes that curiosity involves an epistemically vicious misunderstanding of both self and world that arises from our tendencies toward impatience, arrogance, and fear.

In "Rethinking *Being and Time* as a Resource for Feminist Philosophy," **Charlotte Knowles** responds to three standard feminist objections to Heidegger's work in *Being and Time*: his structural analysis of Dasein is masculine; he neutralizes gender at the ontological level; and his account of our authentic existence extirpates individuals from their social world. Specifically, Knowles argues that Heidegger's analysis of Dasein can be profitably used for feminist purposes, his ontological neutrality speaks to an anti-essentialist critique of binary gender, and that leading an authentic existence can contribute to the formation of a collective "feminist consciousness."

Aaron James Wendland's essay, "Authenticity, Truth, and Cultural Transformation," explores the connection between Heidegger's existentialism and fundamental ontology. Specifically, and *contra* Haugeland who argues that existentialism is a key feature of fundamental ontology insofar as taking responsibility for our existence entails getting the being of entities right, Wendland claims that taking responsibility for our existence explicitly exhibits the temporal horizon that is fundamental for all our purposive activities and our understanding of entities, generally.

In "What Does Authenticity Do in *Being and Time*?," **Sacha Golob** considers three distinct readings of the function of authenticity in *Being and Time*. On a transcendental reading, authenticity is what allows us to first recognize reasons as such and act in light of norms at all. On what Golob calls a unity reading, authenticity unifies Dasein's commitments, and thereby grants a novel and genuinely existential unity to who I am. Finally, on the structural reading Golob advocates, authenticity is an inchoate awareness of the structural features of normative space and of Dasein's own way of being.

Introduction: The Circle of Understanding 5

Steven Crowell's essay, "Why Ask Why? Retrieving Reason in *Being and Time*," explains how *Being and Time* can be read as a work that theorizes normativity. Crowell's focus is on the notion of care (*Sorge*). When Heidegger takes care to constitute the being of Dasein, Crowell argues, he is not rejecting the idea that humans are rational beings. Rather, he reconceives reason as reason-*giving*, a practice demanded of us by our being as care. Drawing from Heidegger's interpretation of Kant and his essay "The Principle of Reason," Crowell argues that *Being and Time* develops a phenomenology of human, finite reason through his discussion of conscience, guilt, and death.

Daniel Dahlstrom's chapter, "Time's Origin," offers a defense of Heidegger's account of Dasein's temporality or timeliness (*Zeitlichkeit*) in *Being and Time*. For Heidegger, both the vulgar time shown on the clock and the world-time of our shared practices are derivative of a more fundamental or original way in which each Dasein is temporal: We live in the three ecstasies of the past, present, and future, privileging not the now of the present moment but our open future. Dahlstrom provides a detailed account of these temporal phenomena and defends the priority Heidegger establishes. And *pace* Ernst Tugendhat, Dahlstrom claims Heidegger does not help himself to an understanding of time as a continuous sequence when arguing for the priority of timeliness over the other forms of time.

In "The Possibility of Death," **Mark A. Wrathall** states that any adequate account of "death" in *Being and Time* must clear three hurdles: It must explain the distinction between death and demise, illustrate the existential import of death, and elucidate the methodological role death plays in Heidegger's *magnum opus*. Wrathall considers the most promising account of death developed to date, the "existential death interpretation," in which death refers to the loss of a meaningful world. This account clears the first hurdle, but Wrathall claims it fails as an adequate reading of *Being and Time* for philosophical and textual reasons. So, Wrathall develops a "modal interpretation" of death in which the distinction between death and demise is based on the distinction between possibilities and the events that actualize those possibilities, and the import of death is found in the way death modalizes all our other possibilities.

Finally, in "Heidegger on the Failure of *Being and Time*," **Tobias Keiling** discusses Heidegger's retrospective critique of his *magnum opus*. In public writings, Heidegger repeatedly explained the incompleteness of *Being and Time* as a failure necessary for further progress in thinking, a turn (*Kehre*) on the path of thought. After discussing the idea of the turn,

Keiling examines a recently published set of private notes on *Being and Time*, which includes Heidegger's most extensive, detailed, and severe critique of his own work and shows that the turn narrative downplays the philosophical problems with *Being and Time*. Although Heidegger takes issue with several methodological and substantial commitments of the book, *Being and Time*'s crucial problem is in the aim it sets for itself: to *answer* the question of being with respect to time.

CHAPTER 1

Being and Time *as a Whole: From Pragmatism, to Existentialism, to a Philosophy of Being, via the Good*

Denis McManus

> If the question of being had been grasped, even if only in a crude way, ... then *Being and Time* could not have been misinterpreted and misused as an anthropology or a 'philosophy of existence' ... [T]he individuality of the existing individual is not the problem but is only a contingent passageway to the alone-ness [*Allein-heit*] of Dasein, wherein the all-oneness [*All-einheit*] of being happens.
> (*BN* 17)

Part of the fascination of *Being and Time* is that it seeks to weave together so many different strands of thought, the deepest insights – Heidegger believes – of so many key figures in the Western tradition. Its writing came at the end of a decade in which Heidegger taught courses on Plato, Aristotle, St Paul, St Augustine, Aquinas, Descartes, Kant, Hegel, Dilthey, and Husserl, while also studying Duns Scotus, Meister Eckhart, Luther, Kierkegaard, Nietzsche, Schleiermacher, Lask, Jaspers, and Scheler. But unsurprisingly, its readers also worry that a work that pulls so many strands of thought together must subject itself to such strain that ultimately it must unravel.

Key tensions are between the outlooks of three figures: Heidegger the pragmatist, Heidegger the existentialist, and Heidegger the philosopher of being. The first insists that our engagement with the world is through specific, shared, and historically and culturally located practices, but this might seem to clash with the ambitions of the second – who espouses an authentic, autonomous, 'individualised' life (*BT* 369/322) that is, in some sense, distinctively one's own – and the third – who seems to seek a brand of universal, transhistorical, and transcultural truth about the nature of reality.

Hence, one might wonder whether Heidegger the philosopher of being wants what Heidegger the pragmatist says he cannot have: as Sheehan (1984, 198) puts it, '[h]ow can a systematic ontology be reconciled with the historicity of human existence?'.[1] Or one might wonder with Hannah Arendt and David Cooper, whether Heidegger the existentialist calls on us to perform a 'Promethean extrication' from the practices in which we are embedded (Cooper 1997, 110) and, hence, to 'escape' from 'structures' that Heidegger the pragmatist depicts as 'inherent in the human condition as such' (Arendt 1994, 433). Not that the existentialist and the philosopher of being are obviously happy bedfellows either: as John Haugeland asks of *Being and Time*, if '[t]he official and abiding aim of the work as a whole is to "reawaken the question of the sense of being"', 'what is all that "existentialism" doing in there?' (Haugeland 2000, 188 and 2013c, 44).

To use an expression to which we will return, this chapter will identify a 'guiding connectedness' in the thought of our three Heideggers, such that we can see that they are one and the same, and one way we see this 'connectedness' best is in light of two of Heidegger's most powerful influences: Aristotle and Augustine.

Section 1.1 of the chapter identifies which 'questions of being' concern Heidegger: key is whether we have a grasp on a unity that holds together the many ways in which entities are, ways which ontology – Aristotle's (1984a, 1003b15–16)[2] 'science of being *qua* being' – might then articulate. Section 1.2 demonstrates how a well-known discussion in *Being and Time* that is key to his perception as first and foremost a pragmatist originates in his reading of Aristotle and Augustine, though one also finds there a vision of a possible 'entanglement' (*BT* 223/179) in our practical world. We become 'distracted by' or 'lost in' merely 'closest concerns' (*BT* 264/222, 387/338) – in 'things of minor importance' – becoming 'slaves' of 'everyday importunities' (*PS* 36, 89), and this vision provides Heidegger the existentialist with a vision of inauthenticity.

But what then is the freedom with which such 'slavery' contrasts? Augustine sees that as our orienting our lives to the *summum bonum*, 'the good'. This raises the philosophical question of why *that* should render one free, but also the interpretive question of what – if anything – corresponds to such freedom in Heidegger. Section 1.3 shows that the same abstract logic that leads Augustine to the good can indeed be found in Heidegger too, though it leads us to puzzling places: there we find the *Worumwillen* – the 'for-the-sake-of-which' – and Heidegger identifies this

---

[1] Cf. Husserl's accusation that Heidegger's 'anthropologism' robs philosophy of the 'methodological grounding' it needs (Husserl 1997, 486).
[2] I generally follow the translations of Aristotle in Barnes' *The Complete Works* (Aristotle 1984) and of Augustine at www.newadvent.org/fathers/.

'good' with both 'Dasein's very being' (*BT* 116–117/84) and with Dasein's world. The former identification can suggest an 'extreme egoism' (*MFL* 186), while the latter identification seems simply baffling, as is how these two identifications can be of one and the same thing.

To resolve these puzzles, we must return to Heidegger's reading of Aristotle. Section 1.4 traces there too a path that leads to the postulation of the good – the *agathon* – focusing here on how that good provides a unity to our lives, a 'guiding connectedness' to our 'manifold of concerns', without which they are 'a mere heap' (*BCAP* 49, 50). But what then is *this* good? Some commentators see in Aristotle's work what Broadie (1991, 198) has called a vision of a 'grand end', a 'comprehensive, substantial vision' of a flourishing human life. But Section 1.5 identifies another notion of the good at work there that is far more formal or abstract: 'what is best' or 'what matters most', by which we identify 'the thing to do'. But why then should we concern ourselves with this thin, abstract 'good'? And again, what – if anything – corresponds to it in Heidegger?

As Section 1.6 explains, Section 1.2 has already answered the first of these questions: we sometimes do *not* direct our will to what is best but instead allow ourselves to become 'entangled' in 'things of minor importance'. In Aristotle, the capacity of ours which engages 'in a constant struggle against [this] tendency' is *phronesis* (*PS* 36–37). This guides action not with regard merely to particular goals – 'promot[ing] health or strength, for instance' (Aristotle 1984b, 1140a25–31) – but instead with regard to how Dasein should act 'as such and as a whole' (*PS* 34), and in answer to the previous paragraph's second concluding question, it is in his interpretation of this notion that we find, I argue, the inspiration for Heidegger's identification of 'the sole authentic "for-the-sake-of-which"' (*BT* 116–117/84) as 'Dasein's very being', as '[t]he *telos* in *phronesis* is the *anthropos* himself' (*PS* 35) . Rather than a brand of egoism, this is a species of 'self-concern' (*PRL* 183), Section 1.7 goes on to explain, where the salient contrast is not focusing on one's own being rather than on that of others, but a focus on one's being as such rather than some mere aspect of one's being – one's being a mother, a friend, an employee, a pursuer of health or strength, say.

Focusing simply on such an aspect will be recognizably a failure to make one's life one's own: a failure of self-knowledge – in 'dimming down' (*BT* 239/195) other aspects of one's own life – and of self-expression – in failing to bring to bear on one's life one's own overall sense of what matters most. Our instead bringing that sense to bear is also recognizably a brand of freedom – of self-determination – in which one acts on one's own best judgment, rather than subjecting one's life merely to the demands of some one role that one happens to occupy or some one goal that one happens to pursue. Moreover, Heidegger's *Worumwillen* shows its other face here too, as orienting oneself to one's being as such is to be open to one's world as a whole: the salient contrast here is with openness merely to those aspects of one's world that bear on one's life as a mother, a friend, an employee, etc., aspects that may matter but may be in any particular here and now 'things of minor importance'. Section 1.8 takes stock in spelling out explicitly how the supposed splits in Heidegger's philosophical personality that we identified in opening appear in light of the reading offered. That reading shows that Heidegger the existentialist understands authenticity not as a Promethean extrication from the demands of the shared practices in which our lives are embedded, but instead as our each engaging with those demands grasped as a whole. In doing so one is also open to one's world as a whole, the entities that populate that world presenting themselves there together, despite their diverse modes of being. The diversity and unity of being is then – to use a Heideggerian expression – always already an existential challenge for Dasein, and, in answer to the questions of Heidegger the philosopher of being, it is our capacity for such openness that equips us to be ontologists. As Heidegger the pragmatist makes clear, we can achieve such an openness only thanks to our historically and culturally located practices, but what makes all such instances instances of such openness are transhistorical, transcultural features those instances share, and key amongst those, Heidegger comes to believe, is a certain openness to time. Our reading gives that belief some plausibility too, as Section 1.9 shows. But I end by pointing to reasons why Heidegger's overarching project may still have been doomed to fail, reasons which Section 1.10 shows have their roots too in antiquity's reflections on the good.

1.1 Questions of Being

Idea of a science of being: unity of the topic; where and how is being in general accessible.

(*BCAP* 162)

It is difficult to precisely identify Heidegger's 'official aims' for *Being and Time* because he did not complete the book.[3] But three 'questions of

---

[3] For debate concerning what he did complete, see the essays in Braver (2015).

being' seem central. The first is '[t]he question of the possible *multiplicity of being*' (*BP* 120). Heidegger challenges 'the domination of the ontology of the "substantial"' (*BT* 469n.xix/320), proposing what has become known as an 'ontological pluralism'.[4] Rather than assimilating 'history, Nature, space, life, Dasein, language', etc., to a generic category of 'substances' or 'things', such a pluralism maintains that they instantiate multiple and different ways of being (*BT* 29/9).

A key inspiration here is Aristotle and his remark that 'being is said in many ways' (Aristotle 2001, 1003a33). But Heidegger claims that he also found 'concealed' in that remark a second 'urgent' question, that of 'the *unity of the concept of being in general*' (Richardson 1963, x; *BP* 120).[5] It is urgent because it raises an objection to the very possibility of ontology. There being no such unity might seem to confirm ontological pluralism. But it would not, in that, if there were no 'single unifying concept of being in general that would justify calling these different ways of being ways of *being*' (*BP* 176), then whatever distinctions such pluralists might be marking, they would not be entitled to label them '*ontological* distinctions', identifying different ways of achieving some singular feat, 'being'. 'Being' would then be 'said in many ways' but as 'bank' and 'lock' are. There would be no 'unity of the topic' (*BCAP* 162) of ontology – the 'science . . . [that] stud[ies] all things that are, *qua* being' (Aristotle 1984a, 1003b15–16) – any more than there is of 'bankology' – the 'science' of financial institutions and riversides – or 'lockology' – the 'science' of small quantities of hair, some door fastenings, and gates and sluices used to change the water level of canals. Thus, in setting himself the task of identifying a 'horizon for any understanding whatsoever of being' (*BT* 19/1), Heidegger is seeking to defend 'the possibility . . . of ontology as such' (*BP* 228), there being a subject-matter of which this -ology could be a *logos*, an account.

But 'the question of the being of beings' 'is at the same time a question about the way in which the sense of being can be experienced' (*BH* 273). Just as our first question raises at the same time our second, so too the second raises a third: 'where and how is being in general accessible?' (*BCAP* 162). If ontology *is* possible, then there must be a 'horizon' against which the multiple ways in which entities are present themselves together; and if ontology is possible for *us*, then we must have an 'experience' in some

---

[4] See Turner (2010).
[5] I will not concern myself here with how reliable Heidegger's readings of Aristotle and Augustine might be but only with how those readings may have shaped his thought.

sense of such a horizon. Against such a horizon, a science of being *qua* being might identify 'what is common to [all] beings' and 'the specific wholeness of [being's] principal divisions' (*KPM* 6).[6] So, do we have an 'experience' of such a horizon, such that we might pursue such a science? If we do, what is that 'experience'?

Heidegger does give us a further clue. While the 'object of first philosophy' is 'taking all possible beings together in the fundamental question of being as such' (*BCAP* 138) – 'mak[ing] entities thematic in their totality' (*MFL* 157) – Heidegger insists that

> we must not permit ourselves to speak of the totality of beings as if this were a collection [*Ansammlung*] of certain realms or other. Accordingly, the *manifoldness* of the various *specific manners of being* with respect to their possible *unity* poses a quite specific problem, one that can only be tackled as a problem once we have developed a satisfactory concept of *world*. (*FCM* 279)

The 'so-called regions of being' are not then a mere collection – to use an expression to which we will return, a 'heap' – 'arrayed alongside one another or above or behind one another', nor are they 'lined up alongside one another in a vacuum'; instead they 'are what they are only *within and out of a prevailing of world*' (*FCM* 354). Quite why we might think so is an issue in what follows. But for now, this does at least suggest a refinement of our third question: 'where and how is the *prevailing of world* accessible to us?'

I propose that Heidegger's answer, which also lies 'concealed' in Aristotle, is 'In the lives of the authentic'. But to see this, we must begin with one of the discussions in *Being and Time* that has done most to promote a vision of Heidegger as first and foremost a pragmatist.

1.2 The Conducive, the Perverse, and Entanglement in the Mundane

Chapter Three of Division One of *Being and Time* presents a vision of the 'world of everyday Dasein' and the entities that it encounters therein (*BT* 94/66). The latter reveal themselves 'not [to] a bare perceptual cognition' but rather in our 'dealings [*Umgang*]', 'that kind of concern which manipulates entities and puts them to use' (*BT* 95/66–67). Heidegger proposes that such entities, which he dubs 'equipment [*Zeug*]', are

---

[6] For further discussion, see McManus (2013) and (2022b).

'constituted by' being – and are 'essentially' – 'something in-order-to [*etwas um-zu*]'; in this 'structure there lies a reference' – a *Verweisung* – 'of something to something', and more specifically, a 'serviceability, conduciveness [*Beiträglichkeit*], usability [*Verwendbarkeit*], manipulability' for ... (*BT* 97/67–68).

This vision has its roots in lectures earlier in the 1920s. In his Aristotle lectures, Heidegger states that 'the world in which human beings move themselves is encountered ... in the character of the *sumpheron*' – which Heidegger translates as the *Beiträgliche,* and his translators as 'the conducive' (*BCAP* 41).[7] Heidegger stresses that '*[s]omething that is conducive* is, in itself, a being that has a *reference to something* [Verweisung ... auf etwas]', '[t]his conduciveness [*Beiträglichkeit*], its usability [*Verwendbarkeit*], constitut[ing] its existence', and he draws on a familiar example, '[t]he hammer is ... in such a way that I can hammer a nail with it' (*BCAP* 41, 63).

This same pattern of thought appears in Heidegger's earlier lectures on Augustine, who distinguishes 'use' from 'enjoyment' – *uti* from *frui* – where that which we use is used 'for the sake of something else', while that which we enjoy we 'love ... for its own sake' (*PRL* 204). Here Augustine introduces a theme that will be crucial for us. The *Verweisungen* that characterise equipment form chains. '[T]he work ... produced' – 'the "*towards-which*" of such things as the hammer' – 'likewise has the kind of being that belongs to equipment': for example, '[t]he shoe which [our use of our hammer] produced' is '*Schuhzeug*', something 'for wearing' (*BT* 99/70). But this raises the question of whether and where such chains end. Augustine identifies such an end in two ways – abstractly and concretely, as one might put it. We will return to the latter, but we have encountered the former already, his identification of that end as the object of a distinctive relation that we bear to it: we enjoy it, 'loving it for its own sake', it 'giv[ing] delight in itself, not by reference to something else' (*PRL* 204).[8]

Or rather – bringing us to another theme that will be crucial – that is how things *should* be. '[A]ll human perversion', Augustine proposes, is 'the will to use for the sake of enjoyment, and to enjoy for the sake of use', rather than 'enjoy[ing] for the sake of enjoyment, and us[ing] for the sake of use' (Augustine 1982, qu. 30, quoted at *PRL* 204). A key form this 'perversion' takes is a tendency to 'take the current object of [our] efforts as

---

[7] Cf. Heidegger's use of the contrasting *Abträglichkeit* at, e.g. *BT* 114/83, 179–80/140–41, 184/144, 230–31/185–86, and 391/341.
[8] Cf. Augustine (1887a, XI 25, and 1887b, VII 9), quoted at *PRL* 144 and 203.

the most important thing': we 'fall back upon ... what is at [our] disposal in the moment, what is conveniently attainable for' us (*PRL* 150, 145). When we succumb to this '*temptation* of *uti*', we let that which we should use be 'experienced in such a way that it suffices for itself, by itself' (*PRL* 193, 163). 'Perversely', we see the call it makes on us to act as significant in itself rather than as significant only in light of its serving further ends.

We see this theme in the Aristotle lectures too: an agent allows herself to become 'concerned' 'with things of minor importance [*nebensächliche Dinge*]' – 'a slave of circumstances and of everyday importunities' – as she 'take[s] easy refuge in ... the supposedly indispensable resolution' of 'some pressing mundane task or other' (*PS* 36, 89; *PIA* 92). Similarly, *Being and Time* describes a life in which the agent 'understands himself in terms of those very closest [*nächste*] events and be-fallings which he encounters ... and which thrust themselves upon him'; he 'abandon[s] [him]self to whatever the day may bring', 'cling[ing]' to 'what is proximally at [his] everyday disposal', 'distracted by' – 'entangled in', 'lost in' – 'the objects of [his] closest concern' (*BT* 463/410, 396/345, 235/191, 239/194, 477/424, 387/338; *HCT* 281).

This 'entanglement' Heidegger identifies with the life of the inauthentic. It is a 'slavery' in which Dasein 'abandons' itself to being 'lived by whatever it happens to be occupied with' (*CT* 45; cf. *BT* 240/195), and this 'turns the will into a servant' (*PRL* 189). But in what sense? And what would it be to escape this condition? Augustine argues that '[i]nsofar as the will is directed at the highest good [*höchste Gut*]' – the *summum bonum* that is the proper object of our love, our enjoyment – then it is free: it is 'not subject to a *servitudo* [servitude]' (*IPR* 113). '[B]eing-free' is not then 'an *absentia coactionis et determinationis*', an absence of "being forced and determined" of the sort that a decisionist existentialist – with whom Heidegger has been so often identified – champions; rather it is '*determinatio in summum bonum*' – determination of one's will towards the highest good (*IPR* 110–111). But this raises several questions. Why must there be a *summum bonum*? If there is, what is it? Why should directing one's will at it make one free? And what does any of this have to do with *Being and Time*?

1.3 Dasein and Its World as the *Worumwillen*

I talked above of Augustine identifying the *summum bonum* both abstractly and concretely, and the concrete form that Augustine believes the *summum bonum* takes is 'the enjoyment of God': 'life eternal is the supreme good' (Augustine 1887a, XIX 4, VIII 8). There is no sign of that in *Being and Time*, but we do see at work there the same abstract 'logic' leading to a *summum bonum*, though what we find there is puzzling. With a hammer,

> there is an involvement in hammering; with hammering, there is an involvement in making something fast; with making something fast, there is an involvement in protection against bad weather; and this protection 'is' for the sake of [*um-willen*] providing shelter for Dasein – that is to say, for the sake of a possibility of Dasein's being. (*BT* 116/84)

Heidegger proposes that 'the totality of [such] involvements itself goes back ultimately to a "towards-which" in which there is no further involvement' (*BT* 116/84) – something at which our will is directed then not 'for the sake of something else', but 'for its own sake'. He labels this 'primary towards-which' a '*Worumwillen*' – a 'for-the-sake-of-which' – and declares that 'the sole authentic "for-the-sake-of-which"' is 'Dasein's very being' (*BT* 116–117/84).

For many first-time readers of *Being and Time*, this comes as a shock, made worse when Heidegger then declares 'for the present, however, we shall pursue this no further'.[9] As he himself later articulates this shock, does he not seem here to promote 'an extreme egoism', a 'narcissism' according to which 'all entities ... exist only' as 'instruments' 'for the individual human being and his egotistic goals' (*MFL* 186; *PM* 122; *BP* 296)? Where Augustine places God, Heidegger here seems to place Dasein.

A further puzzle is that there seems to be a second candidate for that which lies at the end of our chains of *Verweisungen*. These chains are 'bound up with one another as a primordial totality' which 'makes up the structure of the world – the structure of that wherein Dasein as such already is' (*BT* 120/87; cf. *BT* 236/192, 344/297, and 118/85). Thus, while Heidegger states that 'Dasein is in such a way that it exists *for the sake of itself*', he also states that the 'world shows itself to be that for the sake of which Dasein exists' (*PM* 121). But what would it mean to exist 'for the sake of' the 'primordial totality' that is one's world? And how can Dasein and its world *both* be the *Worumwillen*?

To answer these questions and those with which the previous section closed, let us switch scenes in the next three sections back once again to the

---

[9] In a discussion that brings us to this same puzzling point, Dahlstrom (2009, 264) observes that, as Heidegger 'is clearly appropriating' into 'the existential analytic in *Being and Time*' 'Augustinian themes that suppose a conception of the good', 'we are left to ask whether some conception of the good implicitly informs the existential analysis'.

Aristotle lectures. '*Worumwillen*' first enters Heidegger's lexicon as a translation of Aristotle's '*hou heneka*', and Heidegger identifies this, in turn, precisely with the *agathon*, which is standardly translated as 'the good': '[a]*gathon* is ... that which is "graspable in itself and for its own sake"', the '*hou heneka*, "for-the-sake-of-which [*Worum-willen*]"' (*BCAP* 28 and 43, citing Aristotle 1984a, 1022a8 and 1984c, 1362a22, respectively. Cf. *BCAP* 116; *PS* 35, 101; and *GA* 27, 172). As we have already seen, the Aristotle lectures depict a world revealed as 'conducive', and the following section will identify an argument why chains of 'conduciveness' must lead to 'a *telos* that is *di auto*' – a goal or end 'with which we are concerned "for its own sake"' (*BCAP* 51) – and a singular such *telos* at that. However, we will find in Section 1.5 a very distinctive construal of just what kind of thing this *summum bonum* is.[10]

We also find in Heidegger's discussion of Aristotle's concept of '*phronesis*' – 'the *telos*' of which is 'a "for-the-sake-of-which"' (*PS* 35) – the roots of his puzzling insistence that 'the sole authentic "for-the-sake-of-which"' is 'Dasein's very being'. Those roots lie, Section 1.6 will propose, in a contrast between *phronesis*, on the one hand, and, on the other, *poiesis* and *techne* – production or making, and skill. 'In the case of *poiesis*, the *telos* is something other, a worldly entity over and against Dasein', and 'the deliberation of *techne* relates simply to what contributes to the production of something else', the thing one is aiming to make (*PS* 36, 34). But '[t]he *telos* in *phronesis* is the *anthropos* himself': '[i]n the deliberation of the *phronimos*, what he has in view is himself and his own acting' (*PS* 35–36. Cf. *BH* 179; *BCAP* 123; and *GA* 27: 172). Here we will also find an understanding of why directing one's will at Heidegger's Aristotelian *summum bonum* renders one free.

1.4 A Single, Encompassing *agathon*

Heidegger's Aristotle argues that '[i]t is impossible that we, within the circle of all possible concerns in relation to one another, "take hold of one on account of another"', as, if we did, our concern would 'become[] ... empty and vain [*leer und eitel*]' (*BCAP* 64, 51, quoting Aristotle 1984b 1094a19–21). Only if our chains of *Verweisungen* reach a '*telos* that is *di auto*' will our concern not be left 'grasping at thin air' – *ins Leere greifen*; '[o]nly in this way' is 'the consummation [*Vollzug*]' of our concern

---

[10] For a fuller account of these themes, see McManus (2020 and 2022a).

'possible' – 'is it possible for a concern in general to come into its being' (*BCAP* 51).

A way to understand this demand is that, without a terminating *agathon*, the significance of any such conduciveness remains moot: '*x* may well be conducive to *y* . . . but so what?' A concern fails to 'come into being' until we have reason to think we should pursue *y*, where that reason must present *y* as 'a *telos* with which we are concerned "for its own sake"' (*BCAP* 51) if it too is not to be met with a further 'So what?' Without that, the significance of the claim upon us of any such conduciveness remains indeterminate, leaving us grasping at thin air.

A reason why such chains of conduciveness should lead to *a single* terminating *telos* emerges when Heidegger's Aristotle identifies a second function for the *agathon*. *Being and Time* stresses that our 'dealings' 'disperse themselves into manifold ways of concern' (*BT* 95/67). Augustine stresses this too,[11] and so does Aristotle: for human beings, 'a *manifoldness of concerns* is given' and, 'with this manifoldness of concerns, there will also be a *manifoldness of tele* at which concern reaches its end' (*BCAP* 49).[12] But for this manifold to be 'not a mere aggregate' or 'heap [*Menge*]', it must be the case, Heidegger's Aristotle tells us, that 'among these concerns a certain *guiding* appears' (*BCAP* 49, 50, cf. 63). '[A] *guiding connectedness* is presupposed by the manifold of concerns' such that, with it in place, 'there is thus one whole manifoldness [*eine ganze Mannigfaltigkeit*] of concern' (*BCAP* 50). If instead separate chains of conduciveness terminated in a 'heap' of *tele*, the claim that a particular act is conducive to one such *telos* would invite the 'So what?' response, as achieving that *telos* might be incompatible with the achievement of others in the heap. A chain of conduciveness may lead, as in *BT* 116/84's example, from my use of a hammer to maintaining my health, but attaining that *telos* might clash with my fulfilling my obligations to others, nurturing my talents, etc. So a determinate sense of what I should do depends on bringing these *tele* too together, in an ordering or 'guiding connectedness' which will settle which ought to be pursued at the expense of the rest.

In this way, we may then seem to be driven towards a *summum bonum*. If a concern is to 'come into being', some overarching *telos* must provide a 'horizon' in light of which we can gather together and weigh the *tele* we pursue: 'Aristotle says that there must be, in this manifoldness of concerns,

---

[11] See, e.g. *PRL* 153 on 'the many significances in which I live'.
[12] Cf. Aristotle 1984b, 1094a6 ff, to which Heidegger is alluding; see *BCAP* 50.

such a *telos* that is *di auto'* and which 'encompasses the others, encloses them in itself' (*BCAP* 51, cf. Aristotle 1984b, 1094b6).[13]

1.5 Identifying the *agathon* – Abstract and Concrete

But what then is this overarching, all-encompassing good? As Augustine sets here 'the enjoyment of God', Aristotle too has been seen as identifying – as Broadie (1991, 198) puts it – a 'grand aim', in reflections on *eudaimonia*, contemplation, 'the mean', or a supposed defining *ergon* of human beings.[14] But Heidegger strikingly declares that 'Aristotle comes to the conclusion that there cannot be a good in itself', that 'a "good in general [*Gutes überhaupt*]"' makes no sense (*BCAP* 207, 55. Cf. *BCAP* 27, 49, 55, and 252). Heidegger also elaborates on these puzzling claims in puzzling ways. He says of a 'good in general', 'if there were such a thing, it would not settle anything': 'Useless!', he adds (*BCAP* 253). In contemplating some 'good that hovers over being', 'there would be nothing there for *praxis*' – action – 'to be concerned about', because 'the view of *praxis* goes right to ... the 'here and now' under such and such circumstances' (*BCAP* 207, 208. Cf. *BCAP* 55, 95 and *PS* 96).

To understand how this can be squared with the previous section's argument for the necessity of an overarching and orienting *agathon*, we must recognize just what *kind* of *telos* such a good is, and focus on an aspect of the Aristotelian view of our normative predicament which I believe Heidegger inherits but on which we have so far merely touched: as McDowell (1998, 41) expresses it, 'practical worthwhileness is multi-dimensional'. Human lives are subject to multiple normative demands interacting in complex ways, with some trumping others in some situations and being trumped by others in others; as a result, it is 'hardly plausible that a conception of how a human being should live could be fully captured in terms of ... universal prohibitions' (McDowell 1998, 27n9), or prescriptions: as Heidegger would seem to make the point, '[f]or our being, ... no unique and absolute norm can be given' (*BCAP* 126, cf. *MFL* 185). In this light, in each here and now in which we find ourselves,

---

[13] On a popular reading, Heidegger's 'for-the-sake-of corresponds to practical identity' (Crowell 2013c, 245), such that 'I write on the blackboard in a classroom, with a piece of chalk, in order to draw a chart, as a step towards explaining Heidegger, for the sake of my being a good teacher' (Dreyfus 1991, 92). But the reading I am offering here suggests that, in still inviting the question, 'So what?', such a *Worumwillen* cannot perform the function that the *Worumwillen* was assigned.

[14] Heidegger's reading of Aristotle has a place for some of these notions. See, e.g. *BCAP* 114, 115, 121, 126, and 128 on 'the mean'.

there will be 'given' a *'manifoldness of concerns'* – *'of tele'* – our challenge being to weigh these multiple, competing demands in order to establish which matters most.

This points us to an altogether more abstract or formal *agathon*: 'what matters most' or 'is best here and now'. This is no concrete 'grand end', a 'comprehensive, substantial vision' of 'the good' (Broadie 1991, 198). But it is 'a *telos* that is *di auto*' because – to adapt a related thought of Wiggins (1987, 223) – 'nothing suitable by way of practical or ethical concern ... would be left over (outside the ambit of [this *telos*])'. If any concern were to challenge what we take to be best here and now, that would serve not to question whether we should take doing what is best here and now as our *telos* but rather our identification of what concretely here and now is, in fact, best.

As Price (2011, 4) articulates a similar distinction that he finds in Aristotle, in pursuing the abstract goal of 'living well' or 'acting well', the agent tries 'in deliberating ... to identify what, for him then and there, is *the thing to do*', where what that is – 'what *counts as*' acting well – 'is concrete and variable' 'from context to context'. Directing one's will at the abstract goal 'does not itself place any restriction upon the range of relevant considerations' the agent should weigh (Price 2011, 39, 68), other than that 'nothing suitable by way of practical or ethical concern' is 'left over' 'outside the ambit' of one's deliberations.

Similarly, Heidegger believes that Aristotle's discussion of the *agathon* 'provides no specific determination whatsoever with respect to what the *telos* of human beings is', and that this is a consequence of the 'type of consideration' this discussion embodies: it is a 'formal consideration of structure' (*BCAP* 63, 51), a theme that the following two sections will develop further. They will also address an obvious concern that the *summum bonum* identified here raises. It is no 'grand end' because, although it is 'comprehensive', it is not 'substantial', concrete. But why then would one be interested in this 'bare abstraction' (Price 2011, 5)? More specifically, and in light of our overarching concerns, why would it interest Heidegger the existentialist and the philosopher of being?

1.6 The *Telos* of Judging the *agathon* is the Judge Herself

In Heidegger's discussions of *phronesis*, we encounter again Section 1.2's logic of 'conduciveness', Section 1.4's '*telos* that is *di auto*' and that 'encompasses the others', and Section 1.5's more precise – if more abstract – specification of that *telos*. *Phronesis* guides action in the light of an understanding not of particular goals – of 'what sorts of things promote health or strength, for instance' (Aristotle 1984b, 1140a25–31, cf. 1139b1–4), or, as Heidegger puts it, 'particular *Beiträglichkeiten* which promote Dasein in a particular regard' – but instead with regard to how Dasein should act 'as such and as a whole [*als solches im Ganzen*]' (*PS* 34). Doing that requires the *phronimos* to 'disclos[e] the concrete individual possibilities of the being of Dasein' – the many courses of action its situation's *Beiträglichkeiten* solicit – with a view to uncovering 'what is best among th[ose] possible actions' (*PS* 96, 95). In Price's terms, *phronesis* identifies for the agent 'what, for him then and there, is *the thing to do*', and this explains, I believe, why '[t]he *telos* in *phronesis* is the *anthropos* himself', why 'the deliberation of the *phronimos*' has 'in view ... himself and his own acting'.

The inspiration for these remarks – and, I am arguing, Heidegger's identification of 'the sole authentic "for-the-sake-of-which"' as 'Dasein's very being' – are remarks of Aristotle's such as that, '[w]hile *poiesis* has an end other than itself', 'good action is itself its end', our performing such acts 'for the sake of the acts themselves' (Airstoteles 1984b, 1140b5–7, 1144a19–20). But identifying these sources will not explain Heidegger's view if they are themselves puzzling. For instance, as Whiting (2002, 273) asks, don't 'virtuous actions typically aim at ends beyond themselves', 'generous actions ... at ends like providing shelter to the homeless' and 'courageous actions ... at ends like securing the safety of one's *polis* or fellow citizens'?[15] Heidegger's discussion suggests a response, one which also explains why he is not espousing an 'extreme egoism', and why we might be interested in the 'bare abstraction' that is 'what is best', '*the thing to do*'.

One reason is that, as Section 1.2 noted, we sometimes do *not* direct our will at that *telos*. Instead, we satisfy ourselves with *a* thing to do, 'perversely' taking some 'closest concern' – the 'resolution' of some 'mundane task or other' – to 'suffice for itself, by itself', and Heidegger precisely identifies *phronesis* as engaged 'in a constant struggle against [this] tendency to concealment residing at the heart of Dasein' – this tendency to become 'concerned' 'with things of minor importance' (*PS* 36–37). So one's act may 'promote health or strength', but the question remains whether those feats are of 'minor importance' compared to those that other

---

[15] Aristotle says as much (1984b, 1094b5, 1099b38, and 1101b15). Interwoven in complex ways with this issue is the accusation that Aristotle's own view is fundamentally egoistic too. See Angier (2018).

acts one's situation makes available might achieve. Promoting such concrete goods will figure in an explanation of what *counts as* doing what is best here and now, but if one is guided solely by such considerations – by the 'production' of such ends – one is closed to the question, 'What is best here and now?'

Nor do such concrete goods compete – so to speak – with that abstract *telos*. So when Heidegger proposes that 'the sole authentic "for-the-sake-of-which"' is 'Dasein's very being', and Heidegger's Aristotle that '[t]he *telos* in *phronesis* is the *anthropos* himself', they are not then identifying a *telos* that clashes with shelter, safety, strength, or health or, for that matter, one that endorses egoism. Pursuit of a particular concrete good may be ruled out as not here and now what is best, but if so, that will be because other concrete goods matter more. As touched on above, one may raise a concrete concern to challenge what we take to be best here and now, but that serves not to question whether we should take doing what is best here and now as a *telos* but rather just what is, as a matter of 'concrete and variable' fact, best here and now.

As Heidegger puts it then, that '[t]his primary "towards-which"' – this '*formal* "for-the-sake-of-which"' – 'is not just another "towards-this"', and for this reason, it cannot 'be "refuted", for instance, by pointing out that many human beings sacrifice themselves *for others*' (*BT* 116/84; *MFL* 186; *PM* 122, first italics added; cf. *PM* 126 and *EGT* 126). '[S]uch a correction would correct something it cannot correct' (*MFL* 186), a concrete claim about what might be best here and now 'correcting' – competing with – the abstract imperative to do what is best. As the following section will spell out, the demand that the latter places upon one is to be open to oneself as a whole and to one's world as a whole, though in such receptivity, one is also, in a recognizable sense, spontaneous – free.

1.7 'Self-Concern', 'Self-Expression', and Openness to One's Concrete World

Heidegger aligns his claim that 'the sole authentic "for-the-sake-of-which"' is 'Dasein's very being' with his claim early in *Being and Time* that, 'in its very being', Dasein's own being 'is an issue for it' (*BT* 32/12), that 'it belongs to Dasein's essence to be concerned about its own being [*um sein eigenes Sein geht*]' (*MFL* 186. Cf. *BT* 67/42, 160/123, 143/182–183; *BCAP* 116; and *BP* 170 and 295). We can trace this notion of 'self-concern' back to the Augustine lectures – 'our life must somehow *concern* [*angehen*] us ourselves' (*PRL* 183) – though here Heidegger distinguishes two forms that this 'self-concern' can take:

> [S]elf-concern [*Selbstbekümmerung*] appears easy and convenient, interesting and superior as "egoism", at the same time destructive of the "general good", a dangerous individualism. Really: self-concern is precisely the most difficult, taking oneself to be less and less important [*immer weniger wichtig*] by engaging oneself all the more. (*PRL* 180)

The former 'love of oneself [*Eigenliebe*]' is a '*self-importance* [*Selbstwichtignahme*]' through which one 'desire[s] to validate oneself', 'to rescue and justify [one]self', 'to secure one's own being' (*PRL* 221, 173). But because I may be 'liv[ing] in joys about which I should weep, and sorrows about which I should rejoice', this "self-love" is really self-hate' (*PRL* 187, 221). True 'self-concern' requires instead that one 'radically appropriates' – acknowledges or confesses – the truth about oneself: 'what is ... demanded is *iustitia* [justice]', with the possible consequence that, rather than 'securing' or 'validating oneself', one may find oneself 'shaken up', 'question[ing one's] own ... existence' (*PRL* 148, 177). As Heidegger later says of authenticity, such 'self-concern' may 'shatter[] all one's clinging to [*Versteifung auf*] whatever existence one has in each case attained', 'the comfortableness of the accustomed' (*BT* 308/264, 422/370). '[T]he most decisive and purest concern for oneself' (*PRL* 180) is one in which 'I am myself co-concerned only for the *bonum* as such' (*PRL* 177).

We see emerging here a sense in which, when 'a genuine appreciation of the *bonum* is enacted' and one asks what one must do 'as such and as a whole', 'the self always sees itself before itself' (*PRL* 180). In contrast, the 'person' who is 'concerned' 'with things of minor importance' – only with 'producing' some particular concrete good, such as perhaps meeting some selfish need or indeed, for that matter, making some particular sacrifice for others – is 'so wrapped up in himself that he does not genuinely see himself' (*PS* 36). This vision of self-knowledge and its loss also identifies a vision of self-expression and its failure, one which – to return to another of Section 1.2's closing questions – identifies a sense in which freedom is '*determinatio in summum bonum*': the *phronimos*, who directs her will towards what is best here and now, expresses her own judgment, decides herself how to act, and is, hence, self-determining.

In a passage inspired by Aristotle's *Rhetoric*, Heidegger spells this out, asking what it takes for us 'as hearers [to] take [a] speaker to be *himself* bearing witness to the matter that he represents', 'the speaker speak[ing] for the matter *with his person* [*mit seiner Person*]' (*BCAP* 112, cf. Aristotle

1984c, 2.1 1378a). Heidegger proposes that if, '[i]n the counsel he delivers', the speaker 'holds back what his *phronesis* makes available to him' and instead only 'recommend[s] something as *sumpheron* – *beiträglich* – then the speaker 'screens his own position' (*BCAP* 112). Familiar questions show why. To his recommendation, we can reply 'So what? What do *you* think ought to be done?' But there would be something akin to Moore's paradox in a speaker who 'bring[s] himself to say what is best' (*BCAP* 112) then adding '... though that is not what *I* think ought to be done'. A recommendation of the *Beiträgliche* still leaves room, so to speak, for such a further clause, because its utterer 'does not say everything' and 'knows still more' (*BCAP* 112), has further thoughts and valuations. Such a speaker may be sincere – 'recommend[ing] something as *sumpheron* that he believes is *sumpheron*' – and honestly expresses a belief or desire of his; but he does not express *himself*: only if he 'bring[s] himself to say what is best' does he 'present himself in what he says' (*BCAP* 112).

A superficial form of such 'screening' hides from others what I think is best. But a deeper form, in which I hide from myself too, is a failure to *settle* what I myself think – to direct myself to the question of what is best. Instead, I 'distract' myself with 'things of minor importance', 'a serious proposal, though not the best' (*BCAP* 112). The multi-dimensional 'practical worthwhileness of the entities I encounter around me' is their 'conducive' solicitation of multiple different actions for which my occupation of multiple roles – father, son, teacher, etc. – and pursuit of multiple goals – strength, health, safety, etc. – call. But when I 'lose' myself in some 'everyday importunity', I am 'entangled in [my]self' (*BT* 223/178, cf. *IPR* 91; *CT* 31), as a concern of mine – some fragment of myself – subjugates my other concerns and I act merely as an occupant of role *x* or pursuer of goal *y*. The *phronimos* instead sees herself as a whole, but also *for* herself as a whole. She judges and acts as all of what she is, as all her concerns have a voice, even if only in her judging which of these matters most here and now. In this sense then, only with phronetic openness do we see 'the bursting forth of the acting person as such' (*PS* 103), a person truly 'act[ing] from out of himself' (*BCAP* 123).

As should now be clear, this openness to oneself as a whole requires an openness to one's world and it as a whole, and this resolves the apparent tension that Section 1.3 noted between Heidegger's identification of two *summa bona*. 'Dasein is in such a way that it exists *for the sake of itself*' and the 'world shows itself to be that for the sake of which Dasein exists', because genuine 'self-concern' requires openness to 'the wholeness' of 'that wherein Dasein as such already is'. 'It is entirely lop-sided to represent

[this] radical self-possession as a hyper-reflected solipsism' because 'the self' is 'the self in its world, with that in which it lives' (*PRL* 191). The *phronimos* acts not merely as a father (or a teacher, say), considering what fathers (or teachers) should do in light of aspects of the world that have a place in the life of fathers (or teachers). Rather the *phronimos* 'act[s] in the full situation within which [he] act[s]' – in light of 'the situation in the largest sense' – and also thereby 'become[s] transparent to himself' (*PS* 101, 36) as the full individual that he is. As Heidegger puts the point later, authenticity 'individualizes Dasein and thus discloses it as "*solus ipse*"',

> But this existential "solipsism" is so far from the displacement of putting an isolated subject-Thing into the innocuous emptiness of a worldless occurring, that in an extreme sense what it does is precisely to bring Dasein face to face with its world as world, and thus bring it face to face with itself as being-in-the-world. (*BT* 233/188)

1.8 'The Alone-ness of Dasein, Wherein the All-Oneness of Being Happens'

Much more needs to be said to defend the intelligibility of the feat of openness described above and the notion that it can indeed be Heideggerian authenticity.[16] But I have endeavoured to show that the feat is plausibly one of self-expression, self-knowledge, and self-determination, which intuitively all seem key elements in the (admittedly hazy) notion of 'being oneself', of living an authentic life that one makes one's own. We are also now in a position to return to the worries with which this chapter began, and to the questions that Section 1.1 identified. There we asked whether we have an 'experience' in which the many ways in which entities might be present themselves to us together against a single, unified 'horizon'? – to use an expression of Chang's (2004, 11), 'on the same page'? We noted that Heidegger sees the concept of 'world' as key here and I propose that the kind of horizon that Heidegger the philosopher of being needs is the horizon to which, as we have seen, Heidegger the pragmatist is led along converging chains of *Verweisungen* and that Heidegger the existentialist argues is 'disclose[d], primordially and directly' only to the authentic (*BT* 232/187).

---

[16] McManus (2019, 2020, and 2022a) discusses some of the previous section's themes and how they relate to *phronesis*. This reading grew out of an interpretation of Heidegger's discussion of 'being-towards-death' in McManus (2015).

That authenticity, world, and being as a whole should align in this way is not unintuitive. As Heidegger the pragmatist describes, we live in a world in such a way that the entities we encounter there solicit action from us. But they in their multiplicity solicit action from us in multiple ways, and the significance of any such solicitation remains moot – its claim on us 'grasping at thin air' – until we gather them together in assessment of what here and now is best. We then draw together into a 'guiding connectedness' our diverse reasons for acting – epistemic, moral, aesthetic, prudential, religious, political, etc. – with which the many different kinds of entities we find around us – and the diverse states of affairs in which they figure – present us, understood through the many roles we occupy and the many goals we pursue. But as Heidegger the existentialist describes, that gathering is a task that we may shirk or embrace and, in doing so, we shirk or embrace self-knowledge, self-expression, and self-determination.

The challenge is not that of a Promethean extrication from the entities I find around me and from the claims that they make upon me through the practices in which my life is embedded. Instead it is one of opening myself up to those entities as a whole – to my *world*, those entities together in their diverse ways of being '*within and out of a prevailing of world*'. When inauthentic, Dasein 'immerses' itself in 'objects of closest concern'; they alone then 'become[] the "real world"' and Dasein is itself 'less than whole' (*BT* 276/233, 240/195) – '*als unganzes*', fragmentary, as Joan Stambaugh puts it. But when instead I 'act in the full situation within which [I] act', then I live not just as a father, or a teacher, say, but as the whole, multi-dimensional individual I am – asking what is best in light of *all* the roles I occupy and *all* the goals I pursue; then I come 'face to face with myself' and with my 'world as world'. Thus, this authentic 'individualization' returns us to the passage with which this chapter began: 'the alone-ness of Dasein' – its *Allein-heit* – is that 'wherein the all-oneness of being' – its *All-einheit* – 'happens'.

This provides Heidegger the philosopher of being with responses he needs in trying to fathom 'where and how being in general is accessible' to us. What equips us to be ontologists is the fact that we always already face the existential challenge of authenticity. The diversity of being is always already an existential challenge for Dasein, in light of which we may 'fragment' or 'be-whole';[17] and taking in being as a unity is always already

---

[17] Heidegger's vision of authenticity as being-whole and inauthenticity as 'fragmentary' (cf. *BT* 422/371 and 442/390) also seems to have roots in Augustine and his contrast of *continentia* with *defluxus* (see *PRL* 151–154, 177, 187, 203, 206, and 212).

an existential feat, which Dasein achieves when it is authentic – when it itself achieves unity. The horizon to which we need access to conduct a science of being *qua* being is the horizon that we take in as a unity when authentic; so if we can understand the latter feat and what it distinctively grasps, we can understand the former and account for 'the possibility of ontology as such'. So in answer to Haugeland's (2000, 187, 188 and 2013c, 44) question, that, I propose, is 'what ... all that "existentialism" [is] doing in there', in the 'technical treatise on the question of being' that *Being and Time* is.

But what of Sheehan's question? To approach this, let us note that there is an obvious sense in which a horizon that allows me to judge what is best here and now does *not* allow me to 'take [in] all possible beings together' (*BCAP* 138, quoted in Section 1.1). As the Aristotle lectures put it, Dasein 'moves in each case within a definite surrounding world', '[t]he circumstances, the givens, the times, and the people' 'in every case different' (*PS* 100, 101). So there certainly is one sense in which, if 'first philosophy' requires 'taking [in] all possible beings together', then Dasein cannot pursue it, and we return to Sheehan's worry: are Heidegger's philosophical ambitions consistent with his own stress on our finitude?[18] We must assume that Heidegger *believed* they were, and the *way* in which his exploration of the authentic agent's openness to her world develops does suggest how he may have believed it.

1.9 Time as a 'Clue' and 'The Basic Determination' of 'The Primary Bearer' of 'All That Belongs Together'

While Dasein is 'an entity that finds itself situated *in the midst* of entities' – so incapable of occupying some God's eye's view – 'in so doing [it] exists in such a way that entities are always manifest as a whole': each such openness grasps diverse kinds of entities together – 'on the same page' – as elements within a 'world as a wholeness' (*PM* 121). Even as these entities as *beiträglich* call on us for incompatible responses, they do so, nonetheless, in a 'connectedness' – 'one whole manifoldness of concern' – to be open to which is to be open to the challenge of doing 'what is best'. 'The idea of the good', Heidegger proposes, is 'the basic determination of ... all that

---

[18] I will not address here two other worries that Heidegger's project thus envisaged might face: firstly, whether 'purpose-free' entities, such as those that *prima facie* the natural sciences reveal, 'also root ... in the for-the-sake-of-which' (as *BP* 295 claims), and, secondly, whether the unity this project promises can be of being in general and not just of our *understanding* of being in general. For relevant discussion, see McManus (2012) and (2017), respectively.

belongs together' – 'the primary bearer of this coherence' (*MFL* 116), and Heidegger hopes to see what it is that the authentic – in their distinctive openness to 'what is best' – distinctively grasp such that they can grasp entities in such 'connectedness', 'the basic determination' of entities such that they can be understood 'belonging together'.

To identify what the authentic distinctively grasp – this sought-after 'primary bearer of coherence' – our concern is not with the contents that particular concrete instances of such openness can reveal, as that is 'in every case different'; the distinctive openness to the world that authentic Dasein achieves does indeed take historically and culturally diverse forms. But what makes all of these concrete instances of such openness are abstract, transhistorical and transcultural features. Identifying those requires again a 'formal consideration of structure', of that which is in every case the same, and what Heidegger believes he uncovers is that key amongst those features is all such instances sharing in a distinctive openness to time. We cannot penetrate deeply here into what Blattner (2014, 129) has called 'the bog of Heidegger's account of temporality'. But our discussion of 'perversity' shows us the first steps, I believe.

The inauthentic 'live always in' – 'entangled in', 'clinging to' – 'the present' (*BH* 267, 211; *CT* 55) and that, I suggest, is best understood as another face of our 'entanglement' with, and 'clinging to', 'objects of closest concern'. The inauthentic distinctively 'await' the future, as Heidegger puts it, in relating to it as no more than a repository of opportunities for, or threats to, their present 'closest concern'. Dasein 'understands itself in terms of that potentiality-for-being which confronts it as coming from its possible success or failure with regard to whatever its object of concern may be' (*BT* 386–387/337), and the future being '*pulled into the present time*' (*CT* 55) is at the same time a specific way of relating to our past: we 'forget', as Heidegger puts it, how we came to find ourselves 'absorbed' in this 'closest concern', which 'loses its character of having-become what it is' (*BH* 267).

When authentic, Dasein instead '[c]omes back resolutely to itself'; the authentic person's relation to her past is 'repetition' – a *Wiederholen*, a 'taking back' or 'again', of concerns one otherwise 'falls back behind' (*BT* 448/396, 308/264). One sees them not as givens – as 'simply there [*einfach da*]' (*BH* 267), sufficing for themselves, by themselves – but recognizes one's engagement with them as instead expressive of a judgment, a choice. '[A]uthentically seized pastness reveals [one's] range of choices clearly' in an 'anticipation' of – a *Vorlaufen* or running-ahead towards – 'all the possibilities that lie ahead' (*BT* 309/264). In this openness to past and future in 'full possibility' (*CT* 45), Dasein is 'free for the factical possibilities of existence in its present instant' (*BP* 288), free then to 'question' its present 'existence', 'closest concerns' to which it might otherwise 'cling', and what may be their 'joys about which [it] should weep, and sorrows about which [it] should rejoice'. In this way, openness to one's world as a whole – and its unified grasping-together of the diverse entities one finds there – requires an openness to one's past, present, and future as the wholes that they are, the latter openness collapsing when inauthentic Dasein instead collapses its world into some 'closest concern'.

In hoping to find a recognition of that 'basic determination' of entities such that, despite their diversity, they can 'belong together' in a 'world as a wholeness', is it obvious that it is the *temporal* structure of openness to such wholes that will prove to be the key? Time has 'long functioned' as an '"index" for the differentiation and delimitation of domains of being as such' (*BT* 39/18; *HCT* 5; cf. *BP* 303). But Heidegger labels this only a 'clue' (*BT* 63/39), and I will go no further here into the 'bog' into which it leads him, and in which the path that *Being and Time* was to have taken vanishes. Fascinating thought though it is, that the form of understanding that we distinctively exhibit when self-determining, self-expressive, and self-knowing might be where 'the path to philosophy' begins and 'is made possible' (*PRL* 8), there are many steps that remain for Heidegger to take from the above temporal horizon of the authentic agent's openness to her world as world to his realising his 'aim' of 'interpreting' this 'as the possible horizon for any understanding whatsoever of being' (*BT* 19/1). Chapters 4 and 6 of Division Two might take some of those steps, but presumably the never-published and quite possibly never-written Division Three was to complete the journey somewhere deep within 'the bog'.[19]

I have also argued elsewhere (McManus 2013 and 2022b) that there may be paradoxes lurking there. Hanging over the question of how Heidegger's hopes for 'primordial temporality' (*BT* 376/328) might have worked out in detail are systematic reasons why his overarching project may have been doomed to fail, and I will end by noting how our discussion points us in that direction too.

---

[19] I have also said nothing about the book's projected Part Two and its promised reading of Aristotle, Descartes, and Kant. If Heidegger's 'question of being' is indeed 'the basic theme of philosophy' (*BT* 62/38) – 'the inner and hidden life of the basic movement of Western philosophy' (*MFL* 154) – that is a claim the substantiation of which clearly gives Heidegger the historian of philosophy work to do too.

1.10 On 'The Ground and Origin of All'

If there seems something odd about the notion that 'the good' might 'play a fundamental role in the clarification of being' (*BCAP* 213), it would not seem to have struck Plato: 'not only do the objects of knowledge owe their being known to the good, but their being is also due to it' (Plato 1997, 509b). In many of his discussions of Plato, Heidegger comments on this 'close conjunction' of 'the idea of the good ... with the idea of being in general' (*MFL* 116–117), 'the *agathon*' as 'the principle of all beings and of all truth about beings' (*BCAP* 200. Cf. *BCAP* 94, 200–201; *BP* 283; *PM* 175–176; and *ET* 78–79). But hugely influential though it is, the above remark of Plato's is amongst those through which 'Plato's good ... became a byword for obscurity' (Annas 1981, 246). Heidegger could then be seen as trying to see the truth in Plato's claim.

In the best Aristotelian tradition, and in contrast with what Heidegger sees as Augustine's lingering Platonism,[20] our discussion has brought the good down to earth. No longer an 'everlasting entity' (*PM* 125) 'hovering over being', it is a horizon against which all that is manifests itself as realising the common feat of being, despite doing so in a variety of different ways. One might wonder whether this 'horizon' is still recognizable as a *good*. As we saw above, the 'primary "towards-which" is not just another "towards-this"', not a good of which I can take possession like comfortable shoes. But it does share with such more prosaic ends the character of being something by reference to which an activity on Dasein's part makes sense and entities can take on a certain character. Hammering is what it is and hammers are what they are in light of that which can be made through it and using them. Similarly, authenticity – being oneself – is what it is as an opening of oneself up to the question of what is best, and what would otherwise embody a 'heap' of entities can constitute a 'world as a wholeness' – 'one whole manifoldness' 'on the same page' – in light of this horizon's 'guiding connectedness'. In as much as self-knowledge, self-expression, and self-determination are valuable, then that 'horizon' in light of which the authentic distinctively live can also then be seen as a good, though living that way is '*not a solid possession*' (*LQT* 195) – again unlike my comfortable shoes – but rather a standard up to which I constantly match or fail to match.

However, there is perhaps a deeper question that looms here of which there are intimations in Heidegger's discussions of 'the good'. The horizon

---

[20] See e.g. *PRL* 115, 212, and 216.

sought is 'for any understanding whatsoever of being', for any way in which things might be. But how then is *it*? Must there not be a further horizon beyond it and in virtue of which it can be as it is 'on the same page' as all else that is and might be? – not that any imagined 'further horizon' will escape this same question. Perhaps we must deny that this horizon is itself an entity, as Heidegger insists that 'world is not an entity' (*PM* 122), and that neither being nor 'primordial temporality' are either (*BT* 26/6, 376/328). But in seeking such a horizon, are we not seeking – as Heidegger says precisely of the good – something that is 'higher than being itself, which, moreover, still is being itself' (*BCAP* 116), as it must if it is both to be a 'horizon' for being and still itself something that is thus-and-so, something that is in *some* way or other? Are we not left wondering then not only what '"[t]he ground and origin of all", of both beings and being' (*BCAP* 87), is but also whether we can make sense of the idea *that* it is, there being such a thing – there being, so to speak, room for it to be any way at all? Might we not glimpse here – as Heidegger also says precisely of the good – '[t]he limit of philosophy' (*ET* 77, cf. 80), 'the extreme boundary of philosophical inquiry, the beginning and end of philosophy', a light that '[a]ll vision needs' but which 'is not itself seen' (*BP* 284)?

CHAPTER 2

The Trouble with the Ontological Difference
Katherine Withy

The ontological difference is the difference or distinction between entities (things that *are*) and being (that by virtue of which entities are). Although it was not named until 1927's *The Basic Problems of Phenomenology* (*BP* 17; *GA* 24: 22), the ontological difference is a basic principle of Heidegger's philosophy. In *Being and Time*, he invokes it when he claims that '[t]he being of entities "is" not itself an entity' (*BT* 26/6), given that this 'not' plausibly distinguishes being and entities (as Heidegger claims later: '[t]he ontological difference is the "not" between entities and being' (*PM* 97; *GA* 9: 123)).[1] Much of *Being and Time* relies on distinctions Heidegger draws on the basis of the ontological difference – distinctions between science and ontology, the existentiell and the existential, the ontic and the ontological. It is for this reason that '[t]he possibility of ontology, of philosophy as a science, stands and falls with the possibility of a sufficiently clear accomplishment of th[e] differentiation between being and entities' (*BP* 227; *GA* 24: 322). Yet, shortly after *Being and Time*, the ontological difference comes to seem deeply problematic to Heidegger. In his 1929/1930 lectures *The Fundamental Concepts of Metaphysics*, he says that 'this distinction as a whole is in its essence a *completely obscure distinction*. Only if we endure this obscurity will we become sensitive to what is problematic, and thereby reach a position from which we can develop the central problem inherent in this distinction' (*FCM* 356; *GA* 29/30: 518). In the late 1930s, the ontological difference remains 'tormenting and discordant' (*CP* 197; *GA* 65: 250).

In order to understand the ontological difference, on which Heidegger's philosophy is built, we must come to be similarly troubled by it. We must 'try to set out what is problematic about this distinction . . . in order to

---
[1] In quoting English translations of Heidegger's texts, I transliterate all Greek terms, replace *beings* with *entities*, and decapitalise *Being*. In quoting from *BP*, I remove the article from the translator's *a/ the Dasein*.

gain a foothold in the problem: not so much to solve it, but in order to have an opportunity to continually bring closer to us what is enigmatic about this issue that is the most self-evident of everything self-evident' (*FCM* 356–357; *GA* 29/30: 518). I will do this by trying to identify what reason or reasons there might be for holding that there is a distinction between entities and being. Trying to understand why we should distinguish between being and entities will also allow me to articulate more precisely what lies on each side of the distinction. I begin by considering the formal indications of being with which Heidegger begins *Being and Time* and asking whether and how these establish a difference between being and entities.

2.1 Being and Entities

The ontological difference distinguishes being from entities. The entity (*das Seiende*) is that which is, so 'entities' includes everything that is. To reach being, ask: what makes it such that the entity or some entity *is*? This question is grammatically (but not ontologically) analogous to the question: what makes it such that the climber or some climber is a climber? The answer is: (their) climbing. What makes that which *is* something that is? The answer is: (its) is-ing, or be-ing. Being thus answers the question: what makes an entity be an entity? Being is 'that which determines entities as entities' (*BT* 25/6). This is a first formal indication of being.

We can also ask: what makes it such that the entity or some entity *is there* (rather than not), and what makes it such that the entity or some entity *is what it is* (rather than some other kind of thing)? The former asks after the existing or that-being of the entity and the latter asks after the essencing or what-being of the entity. It is as their that-being and what-being that being determines entities, as that and what they are.

Entities are that and what they are insofar as they show themselves as that and what they are. Because they are self-showing, entities are *ta phainomena*: that which show themselves, as they are, from themselves (*BT* 51/28). This is not to say that all entities are perceivable but that all entities are meaningful: they show up meaningfully as that and what they are. Further, they show up meaningfully *to someone*. This essential dative position is occupied by us, and we – whoever 'we' are – are cases of what Heidegger calls 'Dasein'. Dasein allows entities to show up to it as that and what they are by understanding those entities in their being. More strictly, we understand them *on the basis of* their being. Being is thus 'that on the basis of [*woraufhin*] which entities are already understood' (*BT* 25–26/6). This is a second formal indication of being.

We might think that we already have enough to establish the ontological difference on the basis of this second formal indication. For if being is that on the basis of which entities are understood, then an entity and its being must be logically distinct. Some commentators take this to be the ontological difference, as is implied by the way that they formulate the difference. Thus Crowell (1984, 37): 'the Ontological Difference – at least as it appears in *Being and Time* – is best understood as the "difference" between an entity and "its" meaning'.[2] And Polt (2011, 32): 'The being of an entity, as its essence or meaning, is not itself that entity'. One way of hearing these formulations (and I will offer another in a moment) is as saying that an entity and its meaning or being must be two distinct items. Is this not the ontological difference?

A second but similar approach extends the intuition by holding that being and entities must be logically distinct items because they play different functional roles. Some readers of Heidegger hold that being, as that *on the basis of which* entities are understood, is or is like the 'background' to the 'foreground' of entities.[3] The appeal is to gestalt psychology, which understands perception as setting a figure or a foreground off from a perceptual background. The perceptual objects in the background play a different role in perception than do those in the foreground, as is clear from the fact that we cannot foreground them *qua* backgrounded. Foregrounding a perceptual object forces it to lose its backgrounded character, and this shows that (being in) the background is fundamentally different from (being in) the foreground. So too, we might think, for being as that which determines entities as entities. As something like the background against which entities show up, being must be fundamentally distinct from entities.

But the analogy with perception does not guarantee what the ontological difference is supposed to guarantee – namely, that being is not an entity. Notice that in the perceptual case, what is in the background and what is in the foreground are, *ex hypothesi*, the same sorts of things:

---

[2] Crowell finishes the quoted sentence with a parenthetical 'or meaning as such'. My point holds even more clearly if we substitute *meaning as such* for *an entity's meaning*, since a given entity is necessarily distinct from meaning as such (unless, perhaps, that entity is the world). But, as I will argue, this is not the ontological difference.

[3] Polt (2006, 144) claims that be-ing is 'the background to all presentation and representation'. Dreyfus (1991) holds that Dasein's *understanding* of being is a background to its engaging with entities, and that being is intelligibility, which plausibly entails that being is a background intelligibility.

perceivable objects. Their status as background or foreground is not a difference in kind but only in contingent status. So too for that on the basis of which an entity is understood. It might be some other entity, playing the role of *that on the basis of*. Nothing yet guarantees that what plays this role must be other than and different to entities.

Similarly for the intuition that an entity and that on the basis of which it is understood must be logically distinct. This may be true, but it does not guarantee what the ontological difference is supposed to guarantee. That being is not an entity does not follow from the distinctness of an entity and its meaning or being. (Compare: that a mother must be distinct from her daughter does not entail that mothers are not daughters, that daughters are not mothers, that a mother is not also a daughter, or that a daughter is not also a mother.) The problem is that this sort of distinction is a token distinction rather than a type distinction. To guarantee that being is not an entity, we need to show not merely that two items are distinct tokens but that they cannot belong to the same ontological type.

Neither of the interpretations that I have considered so far captures the ontological difference because neither makes the distinction one of type. The first distinguishes the entity from its being or meaning, and in doing so, distinguishes between tokens rather than types. The second distinguishes foreground and background, which are different functional roles that can be taken up, but which need not be taken up by things of different ontological types. A functional distinction, however, *would* amount to a type distinction if the function were not merely a contingent role taken up but integral to what a thing is. To return to gestalt psychology, this would be a background that cannot be foregrounded. Being-the-background would not be a status that perceivable objects could take up and then relinquish but something that is fixed in any act of perceiving *as such*. If there is such a universal perceptual background, then there would be a sharp distinction between background and foreground that would entail that the background can never be foregrounded. To guarantee that being is not an entity, being would need to be a universal background of *this* sort.

According to Plato, the universal *visual-perceptual* background is light (Plato 1997, 1128). Light is a necessary condition of possibility of seeing anything at all, and it is essentially backgrounded: we can never perceive the light as such but can perceive only perceivable objects illuminated by the light. In order to be a background of this sort, being must likewise be the necessary condition of possibility of anything being (meaningful) at all, which can never be meaningful for us and which we can access only through meaningful entities. The ontological difference would be, as Carman (2013, 94) has it, the 'distinction between horizons of intelligibility and what those horizons embrace'. And being, as this horizon, would be 'the *transcendens* pure and simple' (*BT* 62/38; original italicized), lying 'beyond every entity and every possible character which an entity may possess' (*BT* 62/38).[4]

This interpretation helps us to make sense of something else that Heidegger tells us about being at the outset of *Being and Time*. Recall that entities are phenomena and so show up meaningfully to us. If being is not an entity, then it would seem to follow that being cannot be a phenomenon and so cannot show up meaningfully to us. But being *is* a phenomenon and it *does* show up to us; it is in fact the privileged object of phenomenology (*BT* 59/35). We can resolve the contradiction if being is to entities as light is to perceivable objects: like light, being appears, but in a manner that is 'fundamentally different' from how entities appear (*BP* 281; *GA* 24: 398). Indeed, what makes being the privileged object of phenomenology is that it appears precisely in a self-effacing, backgrounding way. Being appears in the same way that light is visible: as an 'inconspicuous shining [*unscheinbare Scheinen*]' (*HDL* 109; *GA* 55: 144).

That being is a universal background is plausibly the sort of thing that Crowell and Polt were intending to say: being is that on the basis of which *entities* are understood, and as such it must be something further than and different from not only *the* entity for which it is the basis but *all* entities.[5] In that case, however, each was mistaken in expressing the ontological difference as a distinction between *an* entity and *its* being. This point is not marked in Heidegger's German: his *das Seiende* (*that which is*) can refer either singularly to *an* or *the* entity or collectively to *all* entities. To clarify Heidegger's point, then, we should hear his '*die Scheidung zwischen Sein und Seiendem*' (*GA* 24: 22) just as the English translator has it: 'the differentiation between being and entities' (*BP* 17) in the plural.

Similarly for the 'being' side of the ontological difference: it cannot refer to the way of being of any particular region of entities, such as the

---

[4] Heidegger does not often speak this way (except at *N* IV 157ff; *GA* 6.2: 212–213ff), but we could put the same point by saying that being is the a priori.

[5] Thus Crowell (1984, 37, 38): '"Meaning" (*Sinn*) is the specific theme of philosophical, that is to say reflective, inquiry into "what is" as such; it is therefore not an object for cognition, but the latter's *condition*', and 'this relation is structurally similar to the Ontological Difference between an entity and the Being of that entity'. And Polt (2011, 32): 'A shoe is not the meaning of a shoe; the meaning of a shoe permits the shoe to show itself both as meaningful and as exceeding meaning. If there were no shoe to be found, then the horizons within which we interpret shoes would be, in Husserlian terms, unfulfilled intentions – meanings without anything that showed up in their light'.

readying-to-hand of equipment or the being-captivated of the animal. This is for the reason I gave earlier: any particular way of being is not guaranteed to be a universal background but could, in principle, be understood on some further basis. That, for instance, I understand tools as ready-to-hand on the basis of the way of being of readying-to-hand still permits readying-to-hand itself to be understood on some other basis. (In terms of the analogy with light, I suppose that the point would be that we can perfectly well come to see the localised illumination of a lamp; it is only sunlight that necessarily shines inconspicuously.) The point should hold not only for the different ways of being corresponding to different regions of entities but also for that-being and what-being. What belongs on the 'being' side of the ontological difference is not one, some, or all of these. It must be *being as such*.

More precisely formulated, then, the ontological difference is the distinction between entities *as a whole* and being *as such*.[6] And because being as such is the being of the entity *as such*, we can say that the ontological difference must be between *entities as a whole and as such*, or *the entity as such*, and *being as such*.

2.2 The Third-Man Regress

Now that we know what the ontological difference is supposed to be the difference between, we can ask why we should think that there is such a difference. Why posit, beyond entities, a universal background on the basis of which entities are intelligible but which is not itself an entity? The reason that I have until recently given when I teach *Being and Time* is that otherwise Heidegger will have a third-man-style regress on his hands.[7] The argument takes the form of a *reductio*. The basic idea is that were being as such *not* distinct from entities as such and as a whole, then being would be an entity and something *further* would have to be posited as that on the basis of which *that* entity is intelligible – being$_2$, which if it itself were an entity would then require a further basis of intelligibility in being$_3$, and so on through the regress. Insofar as that is an absurd outcome, we must reject our original supposition. Being as such must be distinct from entities as such and as a whole.

---

[6] A regionalised version of the ontological difference will also obtain between the totality of entities in some realm and their being.

[7] Others also use the regress to establish the ontological difference: e.g. Thomson (2005, 19) and Haugeland (2013, 193). Carman (2013, 91) discusses the regress in a slightly different but related context, as does McManus (2013, 667).

Here is the argument presented more formally, adapted from Vlastos's (1954, 320ff) reconstruction of the argument given in Plato's *Parmenides*.[8] Posit being as a universal background:

(1) If a number of things, *a, b, c,* all are, there must be a single, unified phenomenon – being (are-ing, is-ing) – by virtue of which those entities are and on the basis of which they are understood as being.

Now posit, with Polt and Crowell, that any entity must be logically distinct from its meaning (which may be true, even if it is not the ontological difference):

(2) If anything *is*, then it cannot be identical with the *being* or *is-ing* by virtue of which it is.

Now, posit that being is an entity:

(3) Being, that by virtue of which entities *are*, itself *is*.

These three premises together generate a version of Plato's third-man regress:

(4) If *a, b, c,* and *being* are all entities, then there must be some other thing, being$_1$, in virtue of which *a, b, c,* and *being* are all entities and are understood as such.

To avoid the regress, we reject the third premise, which holds that being is an entity and is the antecedent of the regress-generating conditional in (4). *Voilà!* Being is not an entity. The *not* of the ontological difference has been established.

The regress is a problem for Heidegger for the same reason that it is a problem for Plato. Plato's forms cause the properties of sensible things (via participating) and are that by virtue of which we grasp the properties of sensible things (via recollecting). So too, Heidegger's being is supposed to be that which 'makes' entities be entities or determines them as such, and it is 'that on the basis of [*woraufhin*] which entities are already understood' (*BT* 25–26/6). The explanatory work that both being and the forms are supposed to do is undermined by the regress, because the regress indefinitely defers that which would do the explaining – not being but being$_1$,

---

[8] Vlastos (1954, 330) interprets the statement of the argument in *Parmenides* 132a1–b2, arguing that the version of the argument given in *Parmenides* 132d1–133a6 'is similar in logical structure to his first and presupposes both of the inconsistent premises presupposed by the first'.

and then being$_2$, and so on. In the face of such a regress, we would have not an ontological difference but ontological *différance*.

So, Heidegger needs to avoid the regress by rejecting one of its premises. He appears to reject the third premise when he claims that '[t]he being of entities "is" not itself an entity' (*BT* 26/6). But he does not give us a reason to reject this premise rather than, say, the second premise. The second premise holds that an entity must be distinct from its meaning or being. It might seem unwise to reject this premise, inasmuch as it is implausible to think that things are identical to what accounts for them – in this case, that entities are (meaningful) by virtue of themselves. But we do not need to hold precisely this in order to reject the second premise. We need hold only that there is *one* thing that is as it is by virtue of itself. This would be a special entity, quite unlike other entities. It would be God, in the sense of an Aristotelian unmoved mover or self-caused final cause.

This strategy might seem denied to a Heideggerian because it puts us in the company of those philosophers whom Heidegger accuses of 'ontotheology': holding an ontology that identifies being with some special, highest entity. Heidegger thinks that ontotheological moves are mistaken: '[i]f we are to understand the problem of being, our first philosophical step consists in not *muthon tina diēgeisthai*, in not "telling a story" – that is to say, in not defining entities as entities by tracing them back in their origin to some other entities, as if being had the character of some possible entity' (*BT* 26/6). Why is this a mistake? The *ontological* dimension of ontotheology asks about what makes for entities (namely, being), whereas the *theological* dimension of ontotheology answers that question by identifying the highest entity, God. The problem is that an inquiry into being is conflated with an inquiry into an entity, and this violates the ontological difference.

So, only if we already subscribe to the ontological difference do we have reason not to solve the regress by rejecting the second premise. And in the absence of a positive reason to reject the third premise instead, it is unclear why we should follow Heidegger in doing so. *That* Heidegger rejects the third premise is reasonably clear – or rather, that he *would* do so is clear. For Heidegger never seems to worry about a third-man-style regress and he never uses it to establish the ontological difference.[9] As a matter of textual interpretation, then, we cannot say that Heidegger bases the ontological difference on this solution to the regress. And if we ourselves want to

---

[9] Thanks to Filippo Casati for reminding me that Heidegger does mention a third-man-style regress with regard to asking for a reason for the principle of reason (*PR* 12; *GA* 10: 17).

motivate the ontological difference by appeal to the regress, then we will need some reason to reject the third premise rather than the second.

2.3 Our Pre-Ontological Understanding of Being

Heidegger does not begin any of his books or lectures with arguments designed to establish the ontological difference. In fact, Heidegger does not expect us to begin with a clear understanding of the ontological difference at all, because something else needs to be accomplished first:

> It is easily seen that the ontological difference can be cleared up and carried out unambiguously for ontological inquiry only if and when the meaning of being in general has been explicitly brought to light, that is to say, only when it has been shown how temporality makes possible the distinguishability between being and entities. (*BP* 17–18; *GA* 24: 23)

We can get a good grip on the ontological difference only at the *end* of the inquiry, after the meaning of being has been identified as time. This is presumably because time will serve as the common horizon or context against which being can be differentiated from entities. (A higher commonality or unity (*sunthesis*) is always required if we wish to draw a distinction between two things (*diairesis*)). Until we understand time – or something like it – as the meaning of being (which Heidegger does not succeed at), we will not know how to approach the ontological difference. Having not 'attain[ed] the field or *dimension* in which to make the distinction', we will be 'unsure and at a loss to begin with' (*FCM* 356; *GA* 29/30: 518).[10]

If this is our hermeneutic situation, we should not expect to begin with a clear, philosophical justification of the ontological difference. But we must begin with something. Even if we are unsure and at a loss, we must have some sort of access to that which we seek – some sort of access to the distinguishing of being and entities.

In his lectures, when Heidegger is trying to get intuitive buy-in from his auditors for his talk of being, he typically invokes features of our everyday experience for our reflection. First, because being is the being *of* entities (*BT* 26/6), we encounter it in all the entities to which we are open, the that-being and what-being of which make a difference to us (e.g. *N* IV 193; *GA* 6.2: 251). Or, Heidegger might point out, second, the range of

---

[10] Later, Heidegger will worry that the 'horizon' for the ontological difference, as something beyond being, 'cannot appear as an explicit theme for ontology' (*FS* 25, *GA* 15: 310).

different things that we might mean when we say that something *is* (e.g. *IM* 37f; *GA* 40: 26f), which shows not only the variety of different ways of being but also being's close connection to language. In *Being and Time*, he draws our attention to the fact that we always operate with a sense of what it is to say that something *is* (*BT* 25/5) – that we already have some 'vague average understanding of being' (*BT* 25/5; original italicized) – but that when we turn to the history of philosophy, we find that it has not given any account of being that does not, upon interrogation, unfold into a perplexity about being (*BT* 22–23/3–4). These strategies serve to motivate the question of being and orient us towards our pre-ontological understanding of being. They do not draw a distinction between being and entities, but they do suggest that we should look to our experience for a reason to draw that distinction.

Nicholson (1996) purports to recognize it in our everyday sense that *what* I am differs from my *being* what I am. As an artist, for example, I have access to the social role of *artist*, but I also grasp my *being* an artist as something distinct from that. The distinction between the social role and my inhabiting it shows up to me in the fact that something changes when I become an artist, in the fact that my *being* an artist matters to me, in the fact that I am open to the possibility of *not* being an artist, and in the fact that all I shall be is not necessarily settled. Thus 'as the writing of *any* play differs from the play; and as the playing of *any* character differs from the character, so does being an artist or doctor differ from art or medicine. And our awareness is accordingly divided' (Nicholson 1996, 372). Is this our pre-ontological awareness of the ontological difference?

In distinguishing a social role from our inhabiting it, Nicholson treats the social role as something like a property or a predicate and our inhabiting it as a way of possessing that property. Thus, the ontological difference, as Nicholson (1996, 367, 373) understands it, is '[t]he separation between the role or the predicate, artist or art, and the factor of being' which is expressed in the copula: '[t]hroughout this paper, it was the predicating gerund that referred to being, *das Sein*, and it was the predicate terms, "artist", "doctor", etc., that signified beings, *das Seiende*'. But the difference between being and entities does not map onto the difference between copula and predicate. Notice, first, that this formulation of the ontological difference does not entail that being is not an entity but only that it is not a particular *type* of entity: '*das Sein* is no form or type or species at all' (Nicholson 1996, 372). This is because, second, 'entity' is not coextensive with 'predicate'. (The subject, for example, is an entity that is not a predicate.) Indeed, and third, I do not see any reason to think that instantiating a property or inhabiting a social role is not an entity or something that *is*. Nicholson (1996, 371) suggests that inhabiting a social role is a matter of acquiring an Aristotelian *hexis* (disposition, habit), and (acquiring) a *hexis* is certainly something that *is*. Living out a life as an artist seems no different in this regard than writing a play: they are both rather complicated things that we *do*, and as human activities, they are things that *are*. That they are expressed with verbs rather than nouns or adjectives does not mean that they are not entities.

Although Nicholson does not get to the ontological difference, he does draw our attention to the fact that who I am *matters* to me. He says that 'our own existence, our own identity, and whatever we may predicate of ourselves, are uniquely momentous for every human being' (Nicholson 1996, 363). I take it that Nicholson is glossing Heidegger's point that our being is an *issue* for us (*BT* 32/12). This brings out another potential dimension of Nicholson's argument: perhaps it is in being an issue for us that (our) being is experienced pre-ontologically as distinct from entities.

But Nicholson's interpretation of what it is for our being to be at issue is too trivial. Being an artist is at issue not only in the sense that it matters to me whether or not I am an artist but also in the sense that what it is to be an artist is constantly at stake as I go about being one. This is because a social role such as 'artist' *both* sets the standards for what it takes to inhabit the social role (to be an artist, one must do *this*) *and* reflects, in those standards, what those inhabiting the social role actually do (those who are artists do *this*). So, how I go about being an artist contributes to shaping what it is to be an artist, which means that the standards for being an artist are at issue or at stake in how I live out my life as an artist. Further, what it takes to be *art* will be at stake – as will what it takes to be an *installation* and a *paintbrush* and so on. The standards governing *what* other entities can *be* are at issue because those standards are derived from the standards governing what it takes to be a certain sort of person and so inherit their being-at-issue from them.

The suggestion is that in such being-at-issue, we are open pre-ontologically to the differentiating of being and entities, because this being-at-issue is distinctively ontological and different from ontic being-at-issue. Ontic being-at-issue has to do with the facts of whether, what, and how things are (e.g. 'Is this a painting?'). Ontological being-at-issue presumably has to do with what it *means* or *takes* to be this or that sort of thing (e.g. 'What is a painting?'). Because it concerns the constitutive standards for counting as this or that, ontological being-at-issue is normative being-at-issue.

But normative being-at-issue is only superficially different in kind from ontic being-at-issue. 'What is a painting?' might seem to be an importantly different kind of question from 'Is this a painting?', but it is re-expressed without loss as 'What are the standards for counting as a painting?', or 'Is this the standard for counting as a painting?'. These are ontic questions about entities. Norms might be entities unlike paintings and power stations, and so their being-at-issue might be distinctive. But this distinction does not appear to be that of the ontological in contrast to the ontic.

2.4 Angst

Perhaps we should look for the ontological difference not in our everyday experience of ourselves and entities but in some special, philosophical experience of being. Our philosophical access to being as 'the *transcendens* pure and simple' (*BT* 62/38; original italicized), beyond all entities, is through the mood of angst. In angst, everyday concerns slip away, and along with them, the entities with which we are ordinarily engaged (*BT* 231/186; *PM* 88). Heidegger interprets this experience in a distinctly ontological light, saying that, in angst, Dasein 'is in each case already beyond entities as a whole. Such being beyond entities we call *transcendence*' (*PM* 91; *GA* 9: 115). If being is the *transcendens* and angst is Dasein's experience of transcendence, then perhaps it is in angst that Dasein experiences the distinguishing of being and entities.

But there is no mention of the ontological difference in Heidegger's analyses of angst in *Being and Time* or 'What is Metaphysics?'. In 'What is Metaphysics?', Dasein experiences entities as a whole as 'radically other' not than being but than the nothing (*PM* 90; *GA* 9: 114). The nothing is the alternative to all that there is – a sort of cosmic emptiness. In angst, it strikes us that it is strange that there is all the stuff that there is, rather than nothing instead (*PM* 90; *GA* 9: 114). In grasping entities as radically contrasted to nothing, we are thereby open to the very fact that they, as a whole, are – to their being *as such*. So, in angst, we experience both entities as a whole and as such, and we experience their being as such.[11]

---

[11] This is what Heidegger has in mind when he says that the nothing 'does not remain the indeterminate opposite of entities but unveils itself as belonging to the being of entities' (*PM* 94; *GA* 9: 120). He gives his reasoning: 'being itself is essentially finite and manifests itself only in the transcendence of a Dasein that is held out into the nothing' (*PM* 95; *GA* 9: 120). The claim is that Dasein is open to being only through the process of being exposed to (i) entities as a whole (ii) in contrast to nothing, and so to (iii) entities as such and thus to (iv) being. Being cannot manifest itself without the nothing and so is finite and must encompass the nothing, *qua* nothingness. This

These are the two sides of the ontological difference. But we do not, as far as I can tell, experience the ontological difference. As Heidegger puts it in a different context: '[t]hough the two elements of the difference, that which is present [i.e. entities] and presencing [i.e. being], disclose themselves, they do not do so *as* different' (*OBT* 275; *GA* 5: 364–365). Experiencing them *as* different would require experiencing the *distinguishing* of entities as a whole from being as such. And there is no reason, textual or philosophical, to think that this distinguishing is part of what is experienced in angst.

Being and Time gives a slightly different account of the experience of angst, because there 'the nothing' does not refer to cosmic emptiness but instead to the world as such, in its worldhood (*BT* 231/186).[12] Like the nothing, however, the world is experienced in angst as quite other than entities: it is *no thing*, in the sense that it is not an innerworldly entity but instead that on the basis of which innerworldly entities are (meaningful). But the experience of this is also not an experience of being as distinguished from entities. For, although world (like being) is a that-on-the-basis-of-which (*Woraufhin*) (*BT* 119/86), it is an entity (*BT* 93/65, 141/106).[13] In angst, this entity is manifest in its being: the world in its worldhood. This is crucial to how the world as no-thing factors into angst's disclosing of Dasein's being. For when world shows up in its worldhood, it shows up as essentially referring to Dasein's ability-to-be as the world's organising for-the-sake-of-which, which reveals that Dasein and world are ontologically connected. So, on the basis of its openness to an entity that is no innerworldly thing, Dasein is disclosed to itself as being-in-the-world. Thus open to its own being, Dasein has seen something about itself. It is on the way to becoming authentic. But neither its own being, nor being as such, has been distinguished from entities.

2.5 Our Pre-Ontological Self-Understanding

Perhaps the reason to distinguish being from entities lies not only deeper than argument but deeper than any contingent experience such as a mood.

---

says: for entities to be meaningful includes that they show up as other than non-meaning (not-non-meaning).

[12] *The nothing* in 'What is Metaphysics?' could also be read this way.
[13] '"World" can be understood in another ontical sense ... as that "*wherein*" a factical Dasein as such can be said to "live"' (*BT* 93/65, 140–141/106). This entity has its being in worldhood (*BT* 93/65, 140–141/106). Of course, Heidegger does sometimes deny that world is an entity. I discuss the issue in Withy (2022, §7).

Perhaps we find it in our very being. Heidegger describes us as 'stand[ing] in the differentiation of entities and being' (*N* IV 153; *GA* 6.2: 207; original italicized), in which our essence is 'maintained' and 'sustained' (*N* IV 184; *GA* 6.2: 242). More fully:

> The distinction between being and entities *is there* [*ist da*], latent in Dasein and its existence, even if not in explicit awareness. The distinction *is there, ist da* [i.e. *exists*] [sic]; that is to say, it has the mode of being of Dasein: it belongs to existence. Existence means, as it were, "to be in the performance of this distinction" ... The distinction between being and entities is *pre-ontologically* there, without an explicit concept of being, *latent in Dasein's existence*. As such it can become *an explicitly understood difference* ... [W]e call the distinction between being and entities, when it is carried out explicitly, the *ontological difference*. (*BP* 319; *GA* 24: 454)

To say that the ontological difference is '*pre-ontologically* there' is to say that it belongs to us prior to any explicitly developed ontology. 'It prevails, without our being aware of it' (*N* IV 153; *GA* 6.2: 207). Still, its prevailing belongs to our being.

Heidegger describes this (as it were) 'pre-ontological difference' as 'a, indeed *the*, "basic structure" of Da-sein itself' (*CP* 369; *GA* 65: 469; cf. *N* IV 184; *GA* 6.2: 242), and he identifies it with Dasein's transcendence (*PM* 106; *GA* 9: 135). But it is misleading to think of it as a structure, just as it is misleading to think of Dasein's being or is-ing as existence rather than exist*ing*, or as transcendence rather than transcend*ing*. If it belongs to Dasein's be-ing, then the pre-ontological difference is not a structure but something that happens, as it were – something performed. We might call it 'the pre-ontological differentia*ting*'. This differentiating is not something that we ourselves perform (cf. *N* IV 156; *GA* 6.2: 210), or something that contingently or occasionally happens in or to us. '[W]e are always already moving *within* the *distinction as it occurs*. It is not *we* who make it, rather *it* happens *to us* as the fundamental occurrence of our Dasein ... *fundamentally* and constantly' (*FCM* 357; *GA* 29/30: 519). The pre-ontological differentiating *is* our being. It is that happening by virtue of which we *are*, and on the basis of which we are understood.[14]

If the pre-ontological differentiating of being and entities is our being, by virtue of which we are what we are, and if we have some implicit openness to and understanding of our being, then we must also have an

---

[14] Heidegger also attributes the differentiating of the ontological difference to beyng (*CP* 366; *GA* 65: 465).

The Trouble with the Ontological Difference 45

implicit openness to the distinguishing of being and entities.[15] We have to have some working sense of this distinction. If we want to understand the ontological difference, then, we need only to direct our attention towards the sense for the ontological distinguishing that we already have. Where in our pre-ontological self-understanding do we find being distinguished from entities?[16]

Recall the idea with which I concluded Section 2.1: being is the universal background to the appearing of entities, which show up in the foreground. We plausibly tell entities apart from being by distinguishing the foreground from the background. To see how this happens in our pre-ontological self-understanding, consider Dreyfus's take on the intellectual origin of Heidegger's ontological difference:

> Heidegger conceptualizes the difference between specific coping (ontic transcendence) and world-disclosing background coping (originary transcendence) as the difference between our relation to beings and our understanding of being. This is presumably the original version of the famous *ontological difference*. (Dreyfus 1991, 107)

We can work this idea up into an account of how being and entities are distinguished in our being, as follows. There are two different things that we essentially do: (i) comporting towards entities or ontic transcending, which is our being-oriented towards the foreground, and (ii) originary transcending, or disclosing ourselves and world, which is our being-oriented towards the background. Our pre-ontological self-understanding is open to the difference between these two dimensions of our being, and in being so open distinguishes being from entities. Being is distinguished from entities insofar as ontic transcending relates to entities and is distinguished from originary transcending, which relates to being.

---

[15] In *Basic Problems of Phenomenology*, Heidegger tries to found the ontological difference by temporally analysing not our pre-ontological self-understanding but our pre-ontological understanding of being generally. In our everyday understanding of the being of entities other than ourselves, we can see our grasp of the distinction between entities and being (*BP* 13–14; *GA* 24: 18). But Heidegger never connects the temporal analysis of our understanding of being back to the ontological difference, so he does not make clear precisely where in our pre-ontological understanding of being the pre-ontological differentiating takes place.

[16] In the final hours of his lecture course, *The Fundamental Concepts of Metaphysics*, Heidegger attempts to 'transpos[e] [us] into the *occurrence of this distinguishing*' (*FCM* 361; *GA* 29/30: 524): to give us an experience of ourselves in which we can access the pre-ontological distinguishing of being and entities, which we ourselves are. It is the only time that he attempts this, as far as I am aware. It thus saddens me to report that working through this text has not (yet) succeeded in transposing me into the differentiating of being and entities. Heidegger's analysis is dense, difficult, and underdeveloped. One would have thought that, if the pre-ontological differentiating of being and entities is our very being, it would be a fair bit easier to recognise.

Unfortunately, the two distinctions do not map onto one another.[17] Originary transcending is our disclosive being-in (*BT* 120/87; *MFL* 135; *GA* 26: 170). As Heidegger analyses it in *Being and Time*, it involves finding ourselves, projecting onto an ability-to-be, and discoursing with others (*BT* 169–224/130–180). In such finding and discursive projecting, Dasein sets up a for-the-sake-of-which that organises a world of meaning, on the basis of which it makes sense of entities in comporting. This 'setting up' and 'organising' is what Heidegger calls 'signifying' (*BT* 120/87), and it is the worlding of the world. In originary transcending, then, Dasein discloses itself and in doing so discloses the world. The world disclosed in originary transcending is *entities as such and as a whole*, understood as the totality of the ready-to-hand or the manifestness of entities as such: '*everything* [jedes] ready-to-hand as ready-to-hand' (*BT* 117/85); 'the possibility of the ready-to-hand in general' (*BT* 231/187); 'the manifestness of entities as such as a whole' (*FCM* 353; *GA* 29/30: 512); 'all those entities that are accessible in each case, ourselves included, are embraced by this whole [*Ganzen*]' (*FCM* 353; *GA* 29/30: 513). The worlding of the world, or signifying, is the being of entities as such and as a whole. But these are the two sides of the ontological difference: entities as such and as a whole, and the being of entities as such and as a whole (i.e. being as such). Both sides of the distinction belong to originary transcending.

Ontic transcending does not capture the 'ontic' side of the ontological difference because it concerns not entities as such and as a whole but particular entities to which a case of Dasein is intentionally directed in comporting (*BT* 116/84; *MFL* 135; *GA* 26: 169). The distinction between ontic transcending and originary transcending is the difference between being intentionally directed to a particular entity, on the one hand, and world- and self-disclosing, on the other. Because this latter contains both sides of the ontological difference, the ontological difference must be a distinction *within* originary transcending.

But it is not that simple. If *world* names entities as such and as a whole, and if entities as such and as a whole is what is named by the 'entities' side of the difference, then the ontological difference can be expressed as a distinction between world and being. (This is perhaps why Heidegger associates the problem of the ontological difference with the 'problem of world' (*FCM* 356; *GA* 29/30: 518).) But world is a sort of background to our experience of entities (*BT* 119/86) and the 'entities' side of the

---

[17] For more on the distinction between ontic transcending and originary transcending, see Withy (2022, §11).

ontological difference was supposed to be a sort of foreground. Indeed, the status of world vis-à-vis the ontological difference is thoroughly ambiguous in Heidegger's corpus. Heidegger does frequently take world as an ontic totality (e.g. *BT* 93/65), but he also positions it on the 'being' side of the ontological difference: 'world is not an entity' (*PM* 122; *GA* 9: 158) and, just as being 'is' not, '[w]orld never *is*, but *worlds*' (*PM* 126; *GA* 9: 164). So, the attempt to situate the ontological difference within Dasein's originary transcending runs into the problem of the status of world vis-à-vis the ontological difference.[18]

To avoid this problem and save the Dreyfusian interpretation, we would need to revisit the original argument in Section 2.1 that the 'entities' side of the ontological difference houses entities as such and as a whole rather than any particular entity that we engage with. At this point, then, we are troubled not only by the question of what being 'is' if it is distinguished from entities, but also by the question of what *entities* are, if they are distinguished from being.

2.6 The Trouble

The ontological difference has been nothing but trouble, but I think that we can now see why.

Let us accept that being is something like a background to our foreground experience of entities, and so that the ontological difference is something like the difference between a background and a foreground. It remains to figure out what this could mean beyond the perceptual metaphor. One option lies in Heidegger's interpretation of the principle of sufficient reason, which suggests that *entities* names everything that has a ground (*PR* 44) and being is that which is a ground but has no ground (*PR* 51; *GA* 10: 76–77).[19] *Having a ground* would replace the *being foregrounded* of entities, and *grounding but having no ground* would be what it means to say that being is the background. The distinction between having a ground and not having a ground would still be a

---

[18] The problem is compounded, but perhaps ultimately helped, by introducing the notion of beingness (*Seiendheit*). Caputo reports that 'Max Müller reports a first draft of "Time and Being" which distinguishes *two* forms of the ontological difference: (1) "the "*transcendental*" or ontological difference in the narrow sense: the difference of beings from their beingness [*Seiendheit*, abstracted, universalized is-ness]"; (2) "the "*transcendentish*" (*transcendenzhafte*) or ontological difference in the wider sense: the difference of beings *and* their beingness from Being itself" (Caputo 2020, 26). Caputo gives the following reference: Max Müller, *Existenzphilosophie im Geistigen Leben der Gegenwart* (Heidelberg: Kerle Verlag, 1964), 67.
[19] Thanks to Filippo Casati for sharing this insight.

distinction that happens in and along with our being as disclosing, inasmuch as we are entities who ground things – and so also, who uncover lacks of grounds.

But notice that if being has no ground, it in some sense escapes intelligibility. It will show up to our disclosing as concealed from it.[20] We saw this already when considering being as backgrounded: being backgrounded is a way of being concealed, of shining only inconspicuously. One side of the ontological difference is concealed. Indeed, we might say that the very distinguishing between entities and being serves to conceal being. (Not that there would be any alternative, of course.) But concealing one of its terms also conceals the ontological difference itself; a difference is nothing if not the relationship between its terms. Thus Heidegger: '[B]eing, together with its essence, its difference from the entity, keeps to itself. The difference collapses. It remains forgotten' (*OBT* 275; *GA* 5: 364). It follows that 'the oblivion of being is oblivion to the difference between being and the entity' (*OBT* 275; *GA* 5: 364). Because the differentiating of entities and being conceals being, it conceals itself. The ontological difference is self-concealing.

This, I suggest, is the trouble with the ontological difference, and why it has been such trouble to pin down. That it is shot through with concealing is why the ontological difference is 'the unknown and ungrounded ground of all metaphysics' (*N* IV 155; *GA* 6.2: 210), for which it 'appears to be a differentiation whose differences are not differentiated by anyone, a differentiation for which no differentiator "is there" and no region of differentiation is constituted, let alone experienced' (*N* IV 153–154; *GA* 6.2: 207–208). That it is self-concealing is why, even for a thinking that goes beyond metaphysics in attempting to interrogate the ontological difference, it is not even obvious whether the phenomenon in question is a differentiation (*N* IV 156; *GA* 6.2: 210). If being is both *not* an entity (*BT* 26/6) and yet *of* entities (*BT* 26/6), then what sort of relationship obtains between being and entities? '[I]f the two are fundamentally different, then nevertheless they are still *related to one another in this distinction*: the bridge between the two is the "and"' (*FCM* 356; *GA* 29/30: 518). We question, in the end, whether there is a difference at all.[21]

---

[20] I argue in Withy (2015) that Heidegger both recognises and neglects this self-concealing of being in *Being and Time*.

[21] Earlier versions of this paper were delivered at Temple University in the Department of Philosophy and at the 2018 annual meeting of the International Society for Phenomenological Studies. I thank audiences at both for their comments, and I thank David Cerbone and the editors of this volume for helpful feedback on a draft of this paper.

CHAPTER 3

Heidegger's Evenhanded Approach to Realism and Idealism

David R. Cerbone

3.1 The Truman Show

There is a well-traveled story – perhaps apocryphal – about United States President Harry Truman, wherein he is said to have demanded in a moment of frustration a "one-handed economist." Truman's frustration stemmed from being presented with economic reports whose signals and indicators could be interpreted in more than one way: on the one hand, they suggested X, while on the other hand, they might mean Y. For a president at whom the "buck stops," such reports hardly sufficed to determine a single course of action. Hence Truman's exasperated demand.

Such two-handedness is hardly unique to economics and presidential politics, nor is the frustration it can generate. Chapter 6 of Division One of *Being and Time* is arguably apt to provoke Truman-like frustration, since there Heidegger tells us that (on the one hand) *entities* do not depend on Dasein, while (on the other hand) *being* does depend on Dasein:

> Entities *are*, quite independently of the experience by which they are disclosed, the acquaintance in which they are discovered, and the grasping in which their nature is ascertained. But being 'is' only in the understanding of those entities to whose being something like an understanding of being belongs. Hence being can be something unconceptualized, but it never completely fails to be understood. (*BT* 228/183)

Readers eager to align Heidegger's philosophy with some form of realism will seize upon the first sentence in this passage. Indeed, had Heidegger stopped with just the first sentence, one-handedly as it were, then it would be difficult *not* to understand Heidegger's philosophy as at least compatible with – if not outright endorsing – realism about entities.

What dampens the enthusiasm of the would-be realist is that Heidegger (obviously) did not stop with just the first sentence, but, as if to provoke the Trumans of the philosophical world, offered another hand to consider.

This second hand proffers the dependence not of entities – of *beings* – but of *being* on Dasein. The difficulty here concerns how these two "hands" work together in a manner that allows for the retention of what each one offers, rather than being a matter of giving with one hand and taking away with the other. A suspicion that something like the latter is happening can be provoked by pondering the first – and italicized – occurrence of "are" in this passage: "Entities *are* . . . ." The verb "are" is a form of the verb "to be," and so points back to the idea of *being*. But how, we might ask, can entities *be* in any way "quite independently," if, as the second part of the passage tells us, "being 'is' only in the understanding of those entities to whose being something like an understanding of being belongs," that is, to Dasein? If entities *are*, then they must (mustn't they?) *be* in some way or other, but if their being in some way or other depends (in some way or other) on there being Dasein, then the first hand's gesture, as it were, in the direction of realism appears to be rescinded by the second hand's gesture. Hence the feeling that the second gesture does not so much complement the first as cancel it out.

The two-handedness on display in this passage naturally invites comparison to that greatest of all two-handed philosophers, Kant, whose *empirical realism* is to be accommodated within an overarching *transcendental idealism*. Why the latter does not simply cancel out the former is a vexing question when it comes to Kant;[1] reading Heidegger in a similar manner, as Blattner (1999a) does in his reading of Heidegger as a *temporal idealist*, is apt to provoke similar feelings of frustration.[2] That is, the idealist aspect of the view on offer clearly seems to have the upper hand, so qualifying the realist aspect as to threaten rescinding it altogether. I will not in this chapter consider further such Kantian two-handedness. Instead, I want to focus on readings that try instead to give some form of realism the last word. I will argue that their shortcomings do not thereby lend a hand to idealist readings of Heidegger. Instead, they point the way toward an altogether different kind of two-handed position, where what each hand offers, as it were, cannot be considered apart from the other. As I will suggest, such a view lies *beyond* both realism and idealism, which is precisely the kind of view that Heidegger claims to be offering.

---

[1] See chapter IV of Stroud (1984) for an account of the difficulties Kant's transcendental-empirical distinction faces when it comes to providing an adequate response to skepticism.
[2] I discuss Blattner's reading at length in Cerbone (1996) and Cerbone (2007).

3.2 From Ontic to Minimal Realism

Taylor Carman, who ascribes to Heidegger what he dubs *ontic realism*, according to which "occurrent entities exist and have a determinate structure in the absence of any and all views, period" (Carman 2003, 167), is well aware of the tension Heidegger's second, other-handed claim about being and Dasein creates. He acknowledges that "without Dasein there would 'be' no *being*," but insists that "occurrent entities would still be, nonetheless" (Carman 2003, 202). Such insistence sounds more than a little forced, given the proximity of *be* to *being*. What, we might wonder, could it possibly mean for something to *be* without thereby having some form or mode of *being*. Carman (2003) claims that the absence of Dasein "would not mean that entities are not, only that there would be nothing intelligible to be understood by Dasein concerning what it means for entities to be" (203). So no Dasein, no being in the sense that there is no being that actually understands what beings are. But if entities *are*, there is still something *to be understood* – things that are intellig*ible* – only there is nothing around to take up the task, as it were. This in turn suggests that since there would be *ways* for them to be understood, they have their ways of being as well, and if they have *ways of being*, then being does *not* depend on Dasein after all.

Rather than reconciling Heidegger's two claims so that the two hands can join together peaceably, Carman's primary approach is to preserve what the first hand offers at all costs, which means not really taking the second claim to say what it appears to say. This is especially evident in his final remarks on the matter in the chapter on realism in *Heidegger's Analytic*. There, Carman offers a disambiguating maneuver, using (what else?) two hands:

> The ambiguity lies not in Heidegger's position, then, but in the peculiar proposition, *Entities can be without being*. On the one hand, the proposition can be understood in such a way as to be straightforwardly contradictory, analogous with, *He can walk without walking*. On the other hand, it can mean something perfectly coherent and consistent with both ontic realism and common sense, namely, that there would still be entities even in the absence of the entity that has an understanding of what it means to be, that is, for whom alone it is meaningful or significant in some way *that* entities are, and moreover that they are *what* they are. Again, in order for occurrent entities *to be*, it is not necessary for it to *mean* anything, or for it to be intelligible, *that* anything is. (Carman 2003, 203)

Notice that Carman allows that one way of understanding "the peculiar proposition" to which Heidegger appears committed is *straightforwardly contradictory*. In order to preserve ontic realism *and* "common sense," what that hand offers must be vigorously slapped away. The slap made by the other hand is meant to remove the sting of straightforward contradiction, replacing it with an understanding of Heidegger's "peculiar proposition" that is "perfectly coherent." Carman's preferred rendering of this proposition maintains (perfect?) coherence only by means of a fundamental *equivocation*. What I mean here is that the appearance of contradiction is removed only by construing the meaning of "be" in the first part of the sentence ("Entities can be . . .") as disconnected from the meaning of "being" in the second part (". . . without being"). Such an equivocation within one sentence ought to give us pause: what is the meaning of "be" in the phrase "entities can be" that does not in some way spill over into what the meaning of "being" is? Why isn't it an instance of a contradiction along the lines of "He can walk without walking"?

While my remarks here are critical of Carman, I should acknowledge that he can easily marshal textual support for his disambiguating maneuver. In his *Basic Problems* lectures, Heidegger allows that "nature can also be when no Dasein exists" (*BP* 170), which suggests that there is a sense of "to be" that is detachable from Dasein. What belongs to Dasein is *world*, and "it is not necessary, however, that nature be uncovered, that it should occur within the world of a Dasein" (*BP* 174). What Heidegger refers to as "intraworldliness" is not a "determination" of the being of nature, but only a "*possible* determination," and so "being within the world does not belong to the *being* of nature" (*BP* 169). Heidegger's emphasis here is, however, just as puzzling as Carman's attempt at disambiguation, since we are left wondering just what this sense of "being" is that is detachable from the sense of "being" that there "is," as *Being and Time* would have it, "only as long as Dasein *is*." Consideration of one further passage from *Basic Problems* suggests a way forward. Again remarking on the interplay between intraworldliness and nature, Heidegger writes:

> An example of an intraworldly entity is nature. It is indifferent in this connection how far nature is or is not scientifically uncovered, indifferent whether we think this being in a theoretical, physico-chemical way or think of it in the sense in which we speak of "nature out there," hill, woods, meadow, brook, the field of wheat, the call of the birds. *This being is intraworldly.* But for all that intraworldliness does not belong to nature's being. Rather, in commerce with this being, nature in the broadest sense, we understand that this being *is* as something extant, as a being that we come up against, to which we are delivered over, which on its own part already always is. It is, even if we do not uncover it, without our

encountering it within our world. Being within the world *devolves upon* this being, nature, solely when it is *uncovered* as a being. (*BP* 168–169; whole sentence emphasis is mine)

Consider the emphasized sentence that appears roughly midway through this passage. My suggestion is that what Heidegger writes here can be enlisted to explain the kind of equivocation Carman relies upon to rescue Heidegger from straightforward contradiction. Two more hands are needed, as it were, to spell out what Heidegger is after here: on the one hand, there is being as being-intraworldly and, on the other, the plain being of nature. While we "come up against" nature in this plain sense, whatever determinations we make regarding nature, whether scientific or more casual and everyday, are intraworldly determinations that only *devolve* upon nature. What devolves upon nature depends on Dasein – these determinations belong to our ways of making sense of nature – but nature itself can be without any such determinations. Apart from those worldly determinations, nature is only as something we come up against in some bare sense. This idea of a *bare sense* of nature has seemed to some a way to cash out the idea that Heidegger is to be read as a realist. But just what kind of realism a "bare sense of nature" allows bears examination in light of what some see in *Being and Time* as contributing to the sense that Heidegger is in the end some kind of idealist.

For many readers of Heidegger, that any kind of determination – any way of *understanding* entities – depends upon Dasein is what generates a threat of idealism. As Piotr Hoffman sees it, Heidegger appears vulnerable to what he deems the "menace of idealism" because he seems to be committed to the idea that "entities are rendered intelligible, both in their essence and in their existence, only on the basis of Dasein's understanding of their being" (Hoffman 2000, 403). From this, it follows that "any ascription, to entities, of an existence truly independent of Dasein must be deemed unintelligible and contradictory" (Hoffman 2000, 403). What Hoffman refers to here as *rendering intelligible* accords with what Heidegger says in *Basic Problems* about intraworldly determinations of nature: as bound up with *world*, which in turn is bound up with Dasein, such "ascriptions" of existence cannot – on pain of contradiction – be "truly independent of Dasein." For Hoffman, rescuing Heidegger from the "menace" of idealism requires a mode of access to what there is that runs independently of the understanding of being. Hoffman finds what is needed for this rescue operation in Heidegger's account of *moods*, "for the mood brings Dasein before the 'that–it–is' of its 'there,' which, as such, stares it in the face with the inexorability of an enigma" (*BT* 175/136). Within the phenomenon of moods is a mode of access to reality that is unmediated by the understanding of being. Moods afford access to a reality that is "truly independent," in the sense of not enlisting in any way the concepts and categories of the understanding. As Hoffman puts it:

> The threat of idealism can be removed, because knowledge of being is not our only access to what there is; our knowledge of the overwhelming is just as important and, at least as far as the issue of idealism is concerned, it is precisely our knowledge of the overwhelming which carries the day in favor of realism, both on the metaphysical and on the plain, everyday level. (Hoffman 2000, 410)

Carman (2003) also touches on this aspect of Heidegger, noting our sense of "occurrent reality [as] radically, stubbornly, awesomely independent of us and our abilities, our hopes, our fears, indeed the very conditions of our interpretations of things at large" (195). While we can "understand entities only from our own existential situation," this does not, for Carman (2003, 198), rule out "the possibility of anxiously apprehending the real as 'devoid of meaning,' as 'the unintelligible pure and simple'; indeed, such an apprehension is part of our understanding of being."[3] While Carman cites these moody, anxious revelations of what is in the course of his exposition of ontic realism, he does not, to my mind, fully integrate these different dimensions of Heidegger's views. Carman's ontic realism centrally involves a commitment to the idea that what is "out there" has "a determinate structure in the absence of any and all views, period." Having "a determinate structure" would appear to be bound up with what Heidegger in *Basic Problems* counts as intraworldly being, which means that ontic realism goes well beyond a bare sense of "the unintelligible pure and simple" in ways that one would be hard-pressed to deny enlist the understanding of being. Bare moods won't deliver the goods, so to speak.

Hoffman's ideas, however, find a far more elaborate articulation in Jeff Kochan's work on Heidegger and the sociology of scientific knowledge.[4] On Kochan's reading, the sociology of scientific knowledge harbors a residual commitment to external world skepticism. Since, on these sorts of accounts, all knowledge is socially constituted – all knowledge is a

---

[3] Notice that Carman's final "indeed . . ." does not sit well with Hoffman's desire to make out a mode of access to a "truly independent" reality that bypasses the understanding altogether. As I note below, *being unintelligible* is still a form of *understanding*.

[4] See Kochan (2017). I discuss Kochan's work in greater detail, including his reading of Heidegger as a "minimal realist" in Cerbone (2019).

"product" of socially mediated and socially negotiated processes and relations – any such knowledge never truly breaks free – or breaks out – of the social sphere. To be sure, this form of skepticism is a far cry from the standard-issue Cartesian skepticism, where the issue is one of there being *anything* external to the mind and its stock of "internal" representations. Any sociological account is at least committed to the reality of the *social world*, a world of scientific investigators (those deemed *scientists* by the prevailing norms of a community), laboratories, instruments, conferences, journals, grant-conferring institutions, and so on. In order for a sociological account of knowledge to make any sense at all, it must be robustly realistic about the social world. Insofar as the sociologist of knowledge is an external world skeptic, *external* means something like external to – or lying beyond – the social world. Why think there is *anything* "outside" or "independent" of the world as articulated by the kinds of social processes and relations studied by the sociologist of knowledge?

The brand of external world skepticism Kochan detects within the sociology of scientific knowledge converges with the kind of idealism whose threat Hoffman wishes to avert: for both, the key idea to be countered is that there is nothing beyond – nothing truly independent of – the way things are rendered intelligible by the understanding of being. Whatever we can make sense of as existing is *mediated* by the sense-making capacities constitutive of the understanding of being; as mediated, such things are for all their seeming reality (they are, after all, not the "ideas" of early modern philosophy) nonetheless *dependent* on those capacities. To put it very crudely, whatever is *understood* as real ultimately has the status of *hammers*. Hammers are real – they are "to be met with in space," to use Moore's phrase in his famously two-handed proof of an external world – but they are not "truly independent" of Dasein. There is a further point of convergence between Hoffman and Kochan in terms of the resources they find in Heidegger to overcome both the kind of external world skepticism lurking in the sociology of scientific knowledge and the "menace" of idealism that some readers of Heidegger detect in *Being and Time*. While Kochan charts a more elaborate course involving the detachment of *that*-being from *what*-being (yet more two-handedness!), both he and Hoffman appeal to the more moody dimensions of Heidegger's account as a way to attest to a fully independent reality. Kochan focuses more specifically on the mood of anxiety rather than moods in general as Hoffman does, but the upshot is more or less the same: the moody revelation of an "overwhelming" reality unmediated by the concepts and categories of the understanding. As Hoffman puts it, realism "carries the day" in a twofold sense: there is a reality that is truly independent of anything pertaining to Dasein's (our) forms of understanding *and* we have *access* to it *as* so independent. Both of these are relevant here, as the former alone would be compatible with Kantian idealism: things–in–themselves are fully independent of anything pertaining to the categories of the understanding, but just for that reason, we lack any access to them. Kochan refers to this kind of realism as *minimal* realism: what moods, viz. anxiety, reveal is not properly a *what* at all, but only a bare *that–it–is* of reality (what we might dub simply THE REAL).[5] Any articulation of THE REAL in terms of what-being immediately and thereby enlists the understanding of being; for the sociologist of knowledge, what is thereby enlisted is socially mediated through and through, and so is no longer, in Hoffman's terms, "truly independent" of the understanding of being.

If idealism – or, on Kochan's variant, external world skepticism – is indeed a "threat" and a "menace," one might well wonder how much in the way of reassurance the kind of *minimal* realism both Kochan and Hoffman offer really provides. That a bare sense of an independent reality is attested to in moods – most notably the mood of anxiety – does nothing by itself to reassure us that we are getting it right about such an independent reality once the concepts and categories of the understanding of being are enlisted. Compare, for example (a central example, as it happens, for Kochan's overarching project in the philosophy of science), minimal realism and scientific realism. While there are numerous versions of the latter, with subtle differences among them, a core commitment of any scientific realism is that what scientific theories refer to – when those theories are true – exists independently of those theories, but in more or less the manner those theories depict them as existing. Science is in the business of *getting it right*, according to the scientific realist, where "getting it right" is not just about what scientists agree upon, the social forces at work in the formulation and testing of theories, or anything like that. As Kochan acknowledges, scientific realism is a far stronger view than minimal realism, as the terminology would suggest. Given that kind of differential, minimal realism provides nothing by way of support or

---

[5] I should note here that although Heidegger does in some places use the distinction between that-being and what-being, the distinction never appears explicitly in the discussions of reality and the real. When Heidegger says that being rather than entities depends on Dasein, he says only *being* without any further qualification or restrictions. McDaniel (2015) ignores this in his ingenious but exegetically untenable take on Heidegger's two-handed passage.

motivation for scientific realism, or really any other realism about anything conceptually articulated in any manner whatsoever. Any kind of articulation or determination goes beyond plain or brute that-being into the domain of what-being, which means going beyond the bounds of minimal realism. In Hoffman's terms, this means going beyond the enigmatic revelation associated with moods to the workings of the understanding, which brings us right back to the problem that motivated Hoffman's quest: we are back to rendering entities intelligible on the basis of Dasein's understanding of being. All of this means that when it comes to anything worthy of designation as a *what*, idealism as Hoffman understands it can just as well "carry the day," as idealism about *all that* is fully compatible with the kind of minimal realism he and Kochan extract from Heidegger's account of moods. That there is a bare that–it–is attested to in moods provides no kind of reassurance about whether anything we *understand* as existing is "truly independent" of the ways in which we understand them. If that is what is at issue in any concerns about the threat of idealism, minimal realism does nothing to assuage those concerns.

Here's another way to put the problem. Consider the activity – central, no doubt, to scientific practice – of adjudicating among competing hypotheses. As the history and philosophy of science can attest, such adjudication is no simple matter. In some cases, there may be something resembling a "decisive experiment," but overall, there is a wide array of factors in determining which of two rivals is preferred: predictive and explanatory power, tractability of calculations, connections to other hypotheses and theories, and even simplicity and elegance play a role (and yes, there is no doubt that non-scientific factors like funding, power, and prestige are at work, as the sociologist of science will be quick to point out). I am not for a moment going to pretend to have an account of how such adjudication can or should work. I ask for consideration only to make one point: however it is in any given case that the adjudication among competing hypotheses works, whatever it is that the minimal realist is committed to plays absolutely zero role. Scientists may look for data that tip the scales toward one or the other hypothesis, design experiments that create some daylight between the two, and so on, but nowhere in those procedures will any bare that–it–is of THE REAL come into play. But if any such bare that–it–is plays no role whatsoever in scientific practice, then (again) it is not anything the scientific realist and anti-realist are disagreeing about. And if it is not anything they are disagreeing about, then it is a realism *so* minimal as to not matter at all, and certainly not if one feels in any way threatened by the menace of idealism.

3.3 The "Threat" of Idealism Reconsidered

Let us consider again this "threat" of idealism. The term comes from Hoffman, who begins his discussion by citing Alphonse de Waehlens' mid twentieth-century commentary on Heidegger, noting how it strikes a "rather pessimistic note." The occasion for this air of pessimism is de Waehlens' conclusion that "Heidegger is in no position to escape the *threat of idealism*" (Hoffman 2000, 403). On the same page, Hoffman again refers to the "threat of idealism," this time more fully in his own voice, while later in the essay, he twice refers to the "menace of idealism." Just what *is* the "threat" of idealism? What kind of "menace" does it pose? I should note here that Hoffman's use of such terms is not inflected with any kind of irony. There is no sly wink or hint of playfulness: for Hoffman, idealism really is a kind of menace and Heidegger's philosophy would be all the less attractive if it were vulnerable to the threat or, even worse, actively fostered such a menace in its workings. That Hoffman's use lacks irony is particularly striking in light of Heidegger's own remarks on idealism, particularly in *The Basic Problems of Phenomenology*. There, noting how the fact that the notion of *world* might be understood as containing a "subjective" element seems to mark a perilous descent into idealism, he writes that "we have to ask what this idealism – which today is feared almost like the foul fiend incarnate – really is searching for" (*BP* 167). Hoffman's approach to Heidegger is itself predicated on such fear, which Heidegger himself seems to regard with a rather bemused disdain. We should for that reason subject these cries of alarm to more critical scrutiny. (The question of what Heidegger takes idealism really to be "searching for" will be considered in due course.)

As noted above, Hoffman in the opening paragraph frames the problem of idealism in the following terms:

> Entities are rendered intelligible, both in their essence and in their existence, only on the basis of Dasein's understanding of their being. Consequently, any ascription, to entities, of an existence truly independent of Dasein must be deemed unintelligible and contradictory. (Hoffman 2000, 403)

According to this passage, what generates a threat of idealism is Heidegger's apparent commitment to the idea that we are *only* able to do something (render entities intelligible) on the basis of something else (Dasein's understanding of being). If, the worry goes, entities can only be rendered intelligible on that basis, then the threat of idealism arises.

The nature of the problem here strikes me as elusive, if not downright baffling: *rendering intelligible* would by all accounts appear to be an exercise of the understanding; in Heidegger's terms, such an activity enlists the understanding of being. After all, as Heidegger says early on in *Being and Time*, being is "that which determines entities as entities, that *on the basis of which entities are already understood*" (*BT* 25–26/6, my emphasis). So, when it comes to rendering entities intelligible on the basis of Dasein's understanding of being, we might well ask, "As opposed to what?" What, that is, might it look like to render entities intelligible *without* in any way enlisting our understanding of being? This would seem to be – to use a turn of phrase enlisted by Frege to similar ends – an attempt to "wash the fur without wetting it" (Frege 1980, 36). Trying to do otherwise would be like trying to *say* what entities are without using *language* (any language, and not just this or that language (such as English, German, and so on)).[6] Even the moody disclosures Hoffman and Kochan appeal to do not elude the understanding of being entirely: if THE REAL is disclosed *as being unintelligible*, that is still a way of understanding it, namely, as *being* just that.

Suppose we ask: "What is an electron?" While the question admits of more and less elaborate answers, with varying degrees of technical sophistication and rigor, *any* answer to the question marshals our understanding of the physical world and in that way enlists our understanding of *physics*. That is, answering this question draws upon our understanding of such notions as *atomic* and *sub-atomic*, *negative* and *positive charge*, *mass* and *energy* (and their interconnection), and so on. And any such answer – if it is to be a good answer – ought to be informed by our understanding of such things as how electrons are detected, how scientists model them, how they figure in our current theories of the atom and sub-atomic phenomena, what issues and controversies there are surrounding electrons, and so on. If someone were to say, "Yes, I know scientists have various theories, models, and experimental techniques, replete with claims, hypotheses, conjectures, and disagreements, but what *is* an electron apart from *all that*?" it is not clear what kind of answer she is seeking. To try to say what an electron is *without* drawing upon all of those aspects of scientific theory and practice would appear to be a kind of fool's errand, as scientific theory

---

[6] See Gordon (2018) for a discussion of Adorno's critique of Heidegger as a "crypto-idealist." The charge turns on Heidegger's alleged inability to countenance an "'irreducible reality' that 'breaks in' on the arrogance of an idealist consciousness" (Gordon 2018, 48). Both Hoffman and Kochan would deny the charge. For my part, I am as suspicious of the demand to acknowledge such an "irreducible reality" – an "excess" that is somehow "beyond language" – as I am of attempts to meet it.

and practice is just the thing – and, really, the only thing – to draw upon in trying to say what electrons are.[7] So far, then, it is not clear just what kind of "threat" or "menace" is at issue, as there appears to be no alternative enterprise – some other *way* of rendering entities intelligible – that the menace of idealism in any way threatens to block.

For Hoffman, however, the threat is obvious, as signaled by the "consequently" that introduces the second sentence in the passage above. Tethering the activity of rendering entities intelligible to Dasein's understanding of being makes the "ascription" of an existence "truly independent of Dasein" "unintelligible" and even "contradictory." My sense is that the adverb qualifying "independent" is carrying a great deal of the load here. After all, one of the ways that Dasein (we) makes sense of entities – one way that our understanding of being serves as the "basis" for rendering entities intelligible – is *as* independent of Dasein.[8] One of Heidegger's fundamental distinctions in *Being and Time* concerns two modes of understanding – two ways of understanding the being of entities other than Dasein – the ready-to-hand and the present-at-hand. The former of these involves understanding entities in terms of their practical availability, most basically as *something-for-something*. As such, what it is to *be* a ready-to-hand entity is constituted by its being caught up in a web of "referential relations" that refer ultimately to Dasein's projects and forms of self-understanding. Making sense of entities as ready-to-hand thus does not make sense of them as "truly independent" of Dasein: absent that web of referential relations, there would not be anything ready-to-hand. On an orthodox Heideggerian account, electrons are not ready-to-hand entities; rather, they belong among those entities Heidegger categorizes as present-at-hand, entities understood in ways that do not refer to ways they might be put to use.[9] Although electrons can certainly be used *for* various things, what it is to be an electron is not bound up with those various uses. Our understanding of electrons pictures them as naturally occurring entities that can be just what they are without in any way being put to use within Dasein-ish activities. Electrons are independent of those activities in a way

---

[7] See Schear (2015), which addresses Moore's (2014) attribution of an "untenable idealism" to Heidegger.
[8] Regarding independence, Heidegger says in *Being and Time*: "When Dasein does not exist, 'independence' 'is' not either, nor 'is' the 'in-itself'" (*BT* 255/212).
[9] By *orthodox* I mean readings that leave the distinction between the ready-to-hand and the present-at-hand firmly in place, in contrast to *corrective* readings, such as Rouse (1990), that seek to effect a merger between the two.

that an entity like a hammer (*qua* hammer)[10] is not: to be a hammer is to be used for hammering, so no hammering, no hammers full stop. There is no analog for electrons, no electron-ing that tethers electrons to Dasein's practices and modes of self-understanding. Hence the contrast between saying that we *discovered* electrons but *invented, constructed,* or just *made* hammers.

But what about those theories, models, and experimental techniques that we draw upon in answering the question, "What is an electron?" Aren't electrons "tethered" to all that? This notion of being tethered might be unpacked in the following manner: even a cursory glance at the history of science attests to the idea that scientists at some point along the way *posited* electrons as elements of their ongoing theorizing. Positing electrons was motivated in all sorts of ways that would take more than a cursory glance to articulate. The basic idea of an electron is a *negatively charged subatomic particle*, but that idea has been refined and revised in all manner of ways since first being introduced.[11] Even while still maintaining only a cursory glance, we can note that *negative charge* is likewise something posited as part of the ongoing exploration of nature (and that *nature* – or *Nature* – is what is being investigated is something posited too). Calling electrons *posits* conveys a sense of electrons being *artifacts* of the theories within which they are posited: no positing, no talking or conceptualizing about anything in terms of electrons, and so (therefore?) no electrons as "truly independent," to use Hoffman's phrase. From the standpoint of our understanding of being, entities are apt to appear to be posits made in the course of *our* ongoing sense-making; as posits, entities are thereby *dependent* on our so positing. The menace of idealism thereby threatens.

3.4 Posits and Perspectives

It would be wise at this juncture to consider Quine on the matter of *posits*:

> To call a posit a posit is not to patronize it. A posit can be unavoidable except at the cost of other no less artificial expedients. Everything to which we concede existence is a posit from the standpoint of a description of the

---

[10] I add this qualification to indicate that while *being a hammer* is Dasein-dependent, what the hammer is *made of* – wood, steel, and ultimately things like electrons – need not be. Hence the sense of a kind of resilience or independence: if all of us were to disappear tomorrow, there would still be "hammer-things" lying around, only they would no longer be *for* anything. See Cerbone (1999) for a discussion on the relation between items of equipment and their material composition.

[11] Whether it is right to refer to electrons as *particles* at all has been a matter of considerable debate ever since the famous two-slit experiment.

> theory–building process, and simultaneously real from the standpoint of the theory that is being built. Nor let us look down on the standpoint of the theory as make–believe, for we can never do better than occupy the standpoint of some theory or other, the best we can muster at the time. (Quine 1960, 22)

While there is for Quine a standpoint or perspective from which any and all entities can be regarded as "posits," the availability of that perspective does not in any way impugn the standpoint of what he refers to here as simply *theory*, according to which electrons are among those things that populate reality. The idea that the latter standpoint is only "make-believe" is encouraged by what Quine considers to be an improper understanding of the relation between the two perspectives, wherein the standpoint of "theory-building" *looks down* on the standpoint of theory. According to that (improper) understanding, one perspective is privileged in relation to the other; this sense of privilege is what gives rise to the idea that the theories whose construction is being pondered consist of an elaborate array of *fictions (i.e., posits in a "patronizing" sense)*. The privileged perspective is the perspective of what Quine refers to as *first philosophy*, a foundational set of principles that are accessed and articulated in ways not involving any posits. Quine, of course, emphatically rejects just this sense of privilege. What motivates that rejection – and what puts the two perspectives in proper perspective – is the recognition of the *interdependence* between the two perspectives (what Quine in some places refers to as the "mutual containment" of the two points of view).[12] Quine's insight here is that the perspective of theory-building – the perspective wherein the idea of entities as posits gets a footing – is not detached from the theories whose construction is at issue. On the contrary, making sense of the theory-building process uses – indeed must use – the resources of that very theory. So when Quine says:

> No inquiry being possible without some conceptual scheme, we may as well retain and use the best one we know – right down to the latest detail of quantum mechanics, if we know it and it matters. (Quine 1960, 4)

That includes any kind of inquiry into the process of theory-building. Quine's naturalized epistemology accords to the epistemological enterprise only a kind of relative privilege, wherein the idea of posits gets any kind of grip, rather than the absolute sense accorded to first philosophy, wherein the idea of posits has final authority.

---

[12] See Quine (1969).

Heidegger's Evenhanded Approach to Realism and Idealism 63

Quine's naturalism rejects any kind of transcendental perspective that affords traction to the kind of idealism that worries Hoffman: any such idealism would give to the notion of posits the last word, which has the net effect of making how we conceive reality nothing more than that – our conception – that does not somehow "reach" all the way to reality in and of itself. Quine's rejection of what I've been calling a privileged perspective might be usefully contrasted for our purposes with Heidegger's near-contemporary, Eugen Fink, whose extension of Husserl's phenomenology in the *Sixth Cartesian Meditation* offers a kind of *ne plus ultra* privileged perspective.[13] The "phenomenology of phenomenology" Fink (1995) articulates in this lengthy and difficult work offers an "idea of phenomenological science" that "altogether *transcends* all known notions of science or any other that are ever possible in the natural attitude" (133). The transcendence Fink refers to here is affected via the *phenomenological reduction*, which marks a decisive break from the worldly, natural attitude and so occasions the entrance into the phenomenological domain of transcendental subjectivity:

> By performing the reduction we altogether *transcend* the universal situation in which all worldly knowing as a whole has its *home and origin, captivation* in the natural attitude, we realize a comprehending grasp, a cognizing, a knowing, and a science of a quite new kind, of a new, hitherto unimaginable radicality. (Fink 1995, 139)

So for Fink (1995), phenomenology promises the possibility of a radically new – "hitherto unimaginable" – perspective that stands apart and above the natural attitude, including the natural sciences. While Fink (1995) is quick to reassure us that "transcendental clarification of the world in no way cancels and discredits mundane cognitions and sciences" (140), the perspective opened by transcendental phenomenology nonetheless qualifies such "mundane cognitions" as only *relative*, as can be seen in this particularly dramatic passage:

> The *world* as the total unity of the really existent, boundlessly open in space and time, with the whole immensity of nature filling it, with all the planets, Milky Way, and solar systems, with the multiplicity of existents such as stones, plants, animals, and humans, as soil and living space for human cultures, for their rise and fall in the turn of history, as locale for final ethical and religious decisions, the world in this manifoldness of its existence – in a word, *being – is only a moment of the Absolute*. The awful tremor everyone experiences who actually passes through the phenomenological reduction

---

[13] I have discussed Fink's views in detail elsewhere. See Cerbone (2015), (2016), and (2017).

> has its basis in the dismaying recognition that the inconceivably great, boundless, vast world has the *sense of a constitutive result*, that therefore in the *universe of constitution* it represents only a *relative "totality."* (Fink 1995, 143–144)

What Fink envisions here is a perspective that stands apart from the kind of "mundane theorizing" that concerns Quine and makes sense of whatever such mundane theories are on about in a manner that displays their status as posits relative to "transcendental subjectivity." This is what makes transcendental phenomenology a form of transcendental idealism, whose "basic central thought" is that *"the existent is in principle constituted –* in the life processes of transcendental subjectivity" (Fink 1995, 158). Hoffman's "menace" is here welcomed with open arms, at least at the transcendental level, as the very idea of an entity that is "truly independent" of transcendental subjectivity is rejected out of hand.

I cited previously Quine's framing remarks from the opening of *Word and Object* that sketch out his naturalistic take on the notion of posits and positing. Quine's attitude toward Fink's "radicality" might be gauged by considering the closing section of *Word and Object*, wherein he sets forth the notion of *semantic ascent*. Talk of "ascent" suggests the occupation of a kind of higher, loftier position – a standpoint concerned only with *meanings* rather than worldly objects – but for Quine that sense of loftiness is only apparent. Semantic ascent is only a device or tool – a kind of toggle-switch – for facilitating clearer communication in certain contexts: talk of what a *word means* rather than what *something is* can sometimes be convenient, especially when interlocutors are leery of appearing overcommitted to whatever is at issue (in the course of his discussion, Quine cites such "things" as points, numbers, and propositions). Semantic ascent thus provides a kind of neutral ground in particular cases: "The strategy of semantic ascent is that it carries the discussion into a domain where both parties are better agreed on the objects (viz. words) and on the main terms comparing them" (Quine 1960, 272). But there is nothing magical about this "domain," as "the philosopher's task differs" only "in detail" (Quine 1960, 273) from the task of the scientist at large. In contrast to Fink, Quine (1960) declares that for the philosopher "there is no cosmic exile,"[14] as the philosopher "cannot study and revise the fundamental conceptual scheme of science and common sense without having some conceptual

---

[14] I leave aside the question of whether Quine remains true to his prohibition on "cosmic exile." See Stroud (2000a) and Cerbone (2016) for a more critical perspective.

scheme, whether the same or another no less in need of philosophical scrutiny, in which to work" (273–274). The philosopher therefore "can scrutinize and improve the system from within," rather than survey it from some exalted perspective. Fink's "awful tremor" is here met with something more like a shrug.

3.5 Heidegger in Perspective: Sympathy for the "Foul Fiend Incarnate"

At the close of the introductory sections of *Being and Time*, Heidegger lists as included within the "task" of the forthcoming existential analytic "a *desideratum* which philosophy has long found disturbing but has continually refused to achieve: *to work out a 'natural conception of the world'*" (*BT* 76/52). He concludes the paragraph by noting that "if the 'world' itself is something constitutive of Dasein, one must have an insight into Dasein's basic structures in order to treat the world-phenomenon conceptually" (*BT* 77/52). If *world* is "constitutive" of Dasein, then in reviewing the discussion of the previous section, we should see more daylight, so to speak, between Heidegger and Fink than between Heidegger and Quine. This is so despite Heidegger and Fink's historical and philosophical proximity as practitioners of Freiburg-era phenomenology. When Heidegger appends to the assertion that "the question of whether there is a world at all and whether its being can be proved, makes no sense if it is raised by *Dasein* as being–in–the–world," the almost mocking "and who else would raise it?" (*BT* 246–247/202), Fink's post-reduction "phenomenological onlooker" might be seen sheepishly (or perhaps defiantly) raising a hand. Fink's conception of phenomenology envisions a kind of extra-mundane perspective – a form of cosmic exile – that both Quine and Heidegger reject in their own respective ways. While Heidegger cannot be comfortably accommodated within the ranks of scientific naturalists, my sense is that his attitude toward the "threat" of idealism is akin to Quine's insofar as the route to idealism is supposed to be through an appeal to positing. Heidegger's attitude is thus neither one of capitulation, as Hoffman worries, nor a triumphant embrace, as would be the case were his conception of phenomenology closer to Fink's. But his attitude toward the supposed threat is also not the kind of armed response that Hoffman desires. Such a militant response presupposes that there is indeed a threat that needs to be countered. Recall that when Heidegger in the *Basic Problems* lectures refers to idealism as something "which today is feared almost like the foul fiend incarnate," he is not reporting his own feelings of fright. This is especially evident if we take in more of what Heidegger says leading up to his invocation of "the foul fiend":

> [W]e must say that even if the definition of the world as being subjective led to idealism, that would not yet have decided and proved that this interpretation is untenable. For to this day I am unaware of any infallible decision according to which idealism is false, just as little as I am aware of one that makes realism true. We may not make into the criterion of truth what is the fashion and bias of the time, a solution belonging to some faction or other. (*BP* 167)

We can see here a resistance on Heidegger's part to declaring either a winner or a loser in the realism–idealism divide, to side with "some faction or other" in keeping with "the fashion and bias of the time."

In keeping with this resistance to "fashion and bias," Heidegger does share with Fink a flair for the *radical* (although "radical" is a term famously associated with Quine as well), a subversion of standard categories and oppositions:

> Only with the aid of a radical interpretation of the subject can an ungenuine subjectivism be avoided and equally a blind realism, which would like to be more realistic than things themselves are because it misconstrues the phenomenon of the world. (*BP* 175)

While the focus of this discussion has been on the apparent threat of idealism, it is worth asking here what Heidegger means by "a blind realism."

One form of blindness might be the sort of moody, minimal realism favored by Hoffman and Kochan, where the *blindness* is the lack of any kind of delineation or articulation of THE REAL. There is only a kind of bare affective assault that resists any form of conceptualization. While Hoffman and Kochan appeal to a small handful of passages from the discussions of mood and anxiety in *Being and Time*, what Heidegger says within the discussion of reality and the real in chapter 6 of Division One of *Being and Time* runs counter to the idea that he countenances any brute revelation of what there is. The passage I have in mind concerns the phenomenon of *resistance* rather than moods, but it is not clear to me why Heidegger's claim would not generalize in a manner that impugns Hoffman and Kochan's strategy:

> Nor is resistance experienced in a drive or will which 'emerges' in its own right. These both turn out to be modifications of care. Only entities with this kind of being can come up against something resistant as something within the world. So if 'reality' gets defined as 'the character of resisting,'

we must notice two things: first, that this is only *one* character of reality among others; second, that the character of resisting presupposes necessarily a world which has already been disclosed. (*BT* 254/211)

But there is perhaps another way to understand what Heidegger might mean by *blind realism*. Consider again the question of what an electron is and the way answering that question enlists our best theories concerning what electrons are. That answering the question takes this form signals the inevitability of what Quine refers to as "working from within."[15] The blind realist is someone who fixates on the "within" in Quine's formulation, seeing in that preposition a kind of *confinement*: the enlistment of those theories somehow detracts from the "independence" of electrons. But to fixate in this way is to be blind to the *working* bit of Quine's formulation, that is, to the *work* required to bring entities such as electrons into view. "To be more realistic than things themselves are" is to imagine that the world could somehow stamp our intellects directly – that the world somehow shouts ELECTRONS!!! at us – so that we can in that way be impressed by their existence. But even if it is true that my retinas are bombarded continuously with photons, it is only via physical theory that this fact can be appreciated. So when Heidegger writes that "we have to ask what this idealism – which today is feared almost like the foul fiend incarnate – really is searching for" (*BP* 167), we might see that as a reminder of the way the *mutual* containment characteristic of Quine's naturalized epistemology precludes both "ungenuine subjectivism" and "a blind realism."

While I have been trying when it comes to the divide between Quine and Fink to bring Heidegger closer to Quine's side, there is a significant issue that needs to be addressed. I have suggested that Heidegger's appeal to *world* as "constitutive" of Dasein precludes the kind of extra-mundane perspective to which Fink aspires. But what Heidegger means by *world* is not what Quine means. After all, Quine (1954) famously begins his essay, "The Scope and Language of Science," with the declaration, "I am a physical object sitting in a physical world" (228), and this is a far cry from what Heidegger has in mind in his explication of Dasein as being–in–the–world. The latter world is the practically articulated world of everyday life, replete with a kind of significance that outstrips the entities, processes, and relations countenanced by physics. Given this distinction between the everyday world and the physical world, then there is more than one way

---

[15] See Quine (1955) for further discussion of the idea of "working from within."

to rule out an extra-mundane perspective: even if it is the case, as I think it clearly is for Heidegger, that Dasein's sense-making activities cannot be understood apart from the world in which those activities occur (there is mutual containment in that sense), it does not follow that this idea extends to Quine's notion of the physical world. After all, Kochan's motivation for minimal realism was precisely that one could apparently be a kind of realist about the social world while a skeptic or anti-realist about any kind of world beyond that. And this idea appears to get traction from Heidegger's talk of "intraworldliness" devolving on "nature."

I would suggest here that this talk of "devolving" needs to be handled with care. While Heidegger does distinguish between the human or social world – the world of Dasein – and the natural world or simply *nature*, I do not think that we can see these as radically independent of each other, even on Heidegger's view. That intraworldliness devolves on nature is one way to look at things – in keeping with Quine's idea of a perspective that sees entities as posits – but the world's being beholden to the natural world as its site and foundation is another, equally legitimate way of looking at things as well. We understand the social world in terms of a "referential totality" of equipment, roles, institutions, and so forth, but a great deal of that points toward a world that science targets: much of what is understood as equipment, for example, is made of naturally occurring materials that have their own natures and properties irrespective of how we choose to use them. Understanding those natures and properties plays a role in choosing certain materials for certain kinds of equipment, so there is an interplay between the two forms of understanding. More generally, it is not clear how sense can be made of the social world without already invoking a broader conception of the natural world, even while recognizing that it is only via the goings-on of the social world that anything like the natural world comes into view.[16]

3.6 Joining Hands

Throughout our discussion, two-handedness has been cast as a problem to be overcome insofar as one hand seems to offer a form of realism while the other offers a menacing or threatening idealism. Hence many readers'

---

[16] To read Heidegger this way means resisting what Brandom (1997) refers to as "layer cake" models of the relation between the ready-to-hand and the present-at-hand. Brandom's argument provides one way of resisting an understanding of the distinction between the different senses of world that Heidegger delineates which allows the understanding of one (the everyday world) to be entirely sealed off from the other (the natural world).

attempts — whether in the direction of realism or idealism — to depict a one-handed Heidegger (and if not one-handed, at least a Heidegger that gives to one side the upper hand). By now it should be clear that what Heidegger is after is something other than this sort of push and pull, this one hand giving and the other taking away, so that we have to try to determine who the winner really is in this ontological thumb-war. As we have seen, Heidegger is not interested in declaring a winner in the realism–idealism debate, since hewing to either side involves problems and presuppositions his existential analytic seeks to overcome. We should thus take Heidegger at his word when, in *The History of the Concept of Time* lectures, he both outright rejects realism and idealism while still offering a conciliatory gesture in each direction:

> When we have seen that the elucidation of the reality of the real is based upon seeing Dasein itself in its basic constitution, then we also have the basic requirement for all attempts to decide between *realism* and *idealism*. In elucidating these positions it is not so much a matter of clearing them up or of finding one or the other to be the solution, but of seeing that both can exist only on the basis of a neglect: they presuppose a concept of 'subject' and 'object' without clarifying these basic concepts with respect to basic composition of Dasein itself. But every serious idealism is in the right to the extent that it sees that being, reality, actuality can be clarified only when being, the real, is present and encountered. Whereas every realism is right to the extent that it attempts to retain Dasein's natural consciousness of the extantness of the world. (*HCT* 222–223)

The important point here is that the both–and gesture in the latter part of this passage is preceded by a far more emphatic neither–nor. For readers hoping to find vindication for an "–ism" – a (suitably qualified) version of realism or idealism – Heidegger's remarks here (and in *Being and Time*)[17] will no doubt be frustrating and more than a little disappointing; for readers who instead have a nagging suspicion that there is something amiss in the back–and–forth of realism and idealism, release from the idea that there is a debate here to be settled will count as a positive enough result. Whatever each hand offers should thus not be viewed as the beginnings of a revamped realism or idealism, but only handfuls of wisdom – both *realistic* and *idealistic* – that can be preserved from a perspective that rejects

---

[17] The cited passage from *The History of the Concept of Time* clearly foreshadows Heidegger's remarks in *Being and Time* that register his "doxographic" agreement with realism, while noting the greater depth of insight contained in idealism. See *BT* 251/207.

and surpasses both. What to call the evenhanded view this perspective affords is not entirely clear, but it is one in which the unitary character of the phenomenon of *being–in–the–world* can be seen without the distorting effects of prior philosophy. Call it an evenhanded view, although it may be better understood as simply hands-free.[18]

---

[18] Thanks to Filippo Casati for discussing an early draft of this chapter. I would also like to thank the editors of this collection for their many helpful comments and corrections.

CHAPTER 4

Discourse as Communicative Expression
Taylor Carman

Language is a prominent theme in Heidegger's later work, but it plays a very minor role in *Being and Time*. He devotes about eight pages in §33 to "assertion" (*Aussage*), but of the three aspects (or "senses," he says) of the phenomenon he enumerates, only one (predication) appears to be essentially linguistic. The other two, "pointing out" (*Aufzeigung*) and communication, don't seem to depend on anything like words or sentences, since, after all, gestures and facial expressions are often sufficient to indicate or convey something to someone. Moreover, Heidegger analyzes assertion at this point in the text not to broach the subject of language, but to draw attention to the way in which the propositional structure of judgment manifests itself concretely, namely in the practice of assertion-making. His point is that the propositional content of thought, which can be expressed and communicated in assertions, is derivative of a prepredicative kind of understanding and interpretation. What is really at issue in §33 is thus not language, but the priority of skillful practical intelligence to the subject-predicate structure of cognition.

Language (*Sprache*), Heidegger then goes on to say, "*now first* becomes the theme" in §34 – but only obliquely, for here again the topic is not language as such, but "discourse" (*Rede*), or *talk* in a more general sense than mere verbal utterance. How general? General enough, I shall argue, to include all distinctively human forms of *expressive-communicative* practice or comportment. There are nonlinguistic kinds of expression and communication, but without expression and communication, there could be no language.[1] This is why Heidegger says (emphatically), "*The existential-ontological foundation of language is discourse*" (*BT* 203/160). But while discourse both underlies and goes beyond language, it cannot be so general and diffuse as to be indistinguishable from two other equally basic

---

[1] At least not as we ordinarily experience it, which is what is relevant to a phenomenology of language, as opposed to an empirical theory of innate grammar *à la* Chomsky.

structures of being-in-the-world, namely understanding (roughly, intelligence) and disposedness (roughly, mood): "*Discourse is existentially equiprimordial with disposedness* (Befindlichkeit) *and understanding* (Verstehen)" (*BT* 203/161); "discourse is constitutive of Dasein's existence" (*BT* 204/161). What exactly *is* discourse?

4.1 The Articulation of Intelligibility

Like much of Heidegger's vocabulary in *Being and Time*, the term serves an idiosyncratic technical purpose even though it is an ordinary word. The verb *reden* normally just means to talk, that is, saying something or having a conversation, while the noun *Rede* refers to the kind of talk one "gives" (*eine Rede halten*), for example, a lecture or address one delivers at a conference (*BT* 204/161). That makes discourse sound very much like *speech*, namely the active, performative character of language use. Cristina Lafont (2000, 73) is not alone in supposing that *Rede* must be essentially verbal: discourse, she maintains, manifests itself "*only in language.*"[2]

But that is not what Heidegger says. What he says is that the overt or "spoken expression" (*Hinausgesprochenheit*) of discourse is language, and that "*[t]he existential-ontological foundation of language is discourse*" (*BT* 204/161; emphasis in original). Assuming that nothing is the "existential-ontological foundation" of itself, it seems safe to conclude that *Rede* is not just another word for language. Perhaps what Heidegger meant is that speech or speaking (what Saussure called *parole*) is the foundation of language as a system of signs (what Saussure called *langue*). But discourse does not consist solely in utterance, since Heidegger also says, "*Hearing and remaining silent* (Schweigen) are possibilities belonging to discursive speech (*redendes Sprechen*)" (*BT* 204/161). So, even if discourse is "speech," it is so in a very broad sense, which includes not only listening and understanding, but also refraining from speaking.

Sacha Golob takes a slightly different approach, acknowledging the distinction Heidegger draws between discourse and language while also trying to identify what ties them together. Discourse need not take the form of a proposition, Golob (2014, 10) argues, but its content must be

---

[2] Lafont's interpretation rests on a misreading of Heidegger's remark that "being-a-sign-for can itself be formalized into a *universal kind of relation*, so that the sign-structure itself provides an ontological clue for 'characterizing' all entities in general" (*BT* 107–108/77). Heidegger was criticizing that formalization or generalization of the sign-structure, not endorsing it.

conceptual – that is, it must be the kind of content that *can* in principle be expressed in declarative sentences. On this reading, discourse appears to be (something like) our conceptual grasp of the world (and ourselves), which then grounds the propositionality of cognitive judgments and linguistic assertions. So, Golob (2014, 106) concludes, "there is a genuine continuity between discourse and language because both are conceptual."[3]

That is a rather tenuous link, however, especially considering that Golob sees conceptual content everywhere – not just in discourse, but in the entire structure of understanding and intelligibility in *Being and Time*. Moreover, the generality of Golob's conceptualism has the dubious consequence of saddling Heidegger with a classical conception of language as the expression of *thought* – which for most of the philosophical tradition (rightly or wrongly) was not restricted to the subject-predicate form propositions, but contained everything we would now call "conceptual," including theoretical insight and intellectual intuition. Golob's identification of discourse with the articulation of conceptual content thus at once overstates and understates the breadth and variety of phenomena Heidegger has in view, which, as we shall see, include not only noncognitive expression and the expression of mood, but also the posture or "attitude" of remaining silent, that is, refraining from expressing anything.[4]

What does it mean to remain silent? It could simply mean performing a speech act by *not* speaking or gesturing overtly, for example, abstaining in a vote by not raising one's hand. But it could also mean refusing to enter into discussion or conversation at all, that is, remaining communicatively opaque by neither saying nor even implying, hinting, or suggesting anything. Remaining silent, that is, could be a kind of expressive-communicative behavior that is precisely *not* the expression or communication *of* anything in particular that one *could* say by saying something.

---

[3] Crowell (2013a, 232ff, 234) argues similarly that discourse involves a "conceptuality" that implies "an explicit orientation toward the universal (measure as norm)." As far as I know, Heidegger nowhere suggests that discourse entails universally valid norms of any kind. Nor do I think that anything he says about discourse implies that it has "conceptual content" in any technical sense of that phrase. In its ordinary use, the word "concept" is too vague to hang a philosophical argument on.

[4] The conceptualism that Golob ascribes to Heidegger is difficult to assess, in part due to the obscurity of the concept of a concept, but also owing to Golob's inconsistent application of it. He concedes that moods are not themselves concepts (Golob 2014, 71 n1, 207), but also insists that "Heideggerian states such as anxiety and death remain conceptual," since he regards them "as 'standard' parts of Dasein's functioning" (Golob 2014, 150). Standard parts or not, it is hard to imagine Heidegger agreeing that the significance of such things as mood and mortality is fully expressible in declarative sentences.

Generously affording someone space by not pulling them into conversation, cultivating silence in order to contemplate a landscape or work of art, shutting down communication by giving someone "the silent treatment" – these are instances of discourse that cannot necessarily be made explicit in speech acts, for they constitute a fundamentally different kind of expression and communication. If Heidegger had something like these latter examples in mind, then no identification of discourse with either language or thought will be plausible, for what we are now considering is a kind of expressive-communicative comportment that stands in contrast to *all* verbal behavior, and indeed objective cognition of any kind, including listening and as it were "saying" something simply by omitting a word or a gesture.[5]

That such a broad – nonlinguistic, noncognitive – form of expression and communication is what Heidegger had in mind becomes clearer when he says in Division Two that the "call" (*Ruf*) of conscience, which is an "appeal" (*Anruf*) or "summoning" (*Aufruf*) of Dasein back to itself – back to its finite, concrete particularity – "is a mode of *discourse*" (*BT* 269/314). It is hard to construe that moment of existential self-awareness as literally a kind of "language" or "speech" without draining those words of all meaning. A gnawing feeling of shame or a sudden pang of conscience is not itself a linguistic event, even if it turns out that, for whatever reason, only creatures with language can have that kind of feeling.

It is important, however, not to let the pendulum swing too far in the other direction. Some scholars in recent decades have suggested not only that discourse is not language, but that it has nothing in particular to do with either expression or communication at all. Following John Haugland's suggestion, for example, Hubert Dreyfus (1991, 215ff) translates *Rede* as "telling," which echoes the notion of *saying* but also includes, he says, "being able to tell the time, or tell the difference between kinds of nails." To tell, according to Haugeland (1982, 17), is just to "respond differentially." So, "without expression, I can tell your pawn from my rook, that the rook is threatened, and what to do about it" (Haugeland 1989, 35 n28). Likewise, Dreyfus (1991, 215) says, "A surgeon does not have words for all the ways he cuts, or a chess master for all the patterns he can tell apart and the types of move he makes in response." Similarly,

---

[5] It is worth remembering that *schweigen* is the last word in the famous concluding sentence of Wittgenstein's *Tractatus Logico-Philosophicus*. Wittgenstein would certainly deny that remaining silent (in his sense) is just one more way of saying something with determinate semantic content. The reticence of philosophical insight, as he conceived it, is precisely *not* anything that can be captured in a proposition.

although he concedes that Heidegger's account of discourse "is shot through with linguistic suggestions," William Blattner (1999a, 72) maintains that even just walking down the sidewalk is discursive, in Heidegger's sense of the word. Blattner (1999a) calls discourse "*communicatively* differentiatory comportment" (75, my emphasis), but he can do so only by robbing the word "communicate" of its ordinary sense: "Every act of walking on a sidewalk tends publicly to communicate, that is, make known, that sidewalks are to be walked upon" (Blattner 1999a, 73).[6] Mark Wrathall (2011, 107), too, construes *Rede* – which he prefers to translate as "conversation," or better yet "conversance" – as "living with, having intercourse with, or being skillfully engaged with a person or thing," quite apart from literally expressing or communicating anything. Being "conversant," for him, just means "knowing how to deal with something or someone" (Wrathall 2011, 108). In the same spirit, Golob (2014, 82) argues that discourse is just the "capacity which allows for the 'articulation of intelligibility,' i.e. for the rendering of entities meaningful by locating them within a relational context," which, again, has nothing specifically to do with language, other than that Golob supposes its content must be conceptual.

Haugeland, Dreyfus, Blattner, Wrathall, and Golob base their interpretations, which differ in detail but are alike in denying any essential connection to communication and expression, on Heidegger's definition of discourse as a kind of *articulation*: "Discourse is the articulation (*Artikulation*) of intelligibility" (*BT* 203–204/161); "Discoursing is the 'signifying' articulation (*Gliedern*) of the intelligibility of being-in-the-world" (*BT* 204/161).[7] Notice that in these two sentences Heidegger uses two different German words: *Artikulation*, which usually means something like verbal expression, and *Gliedern*, which means articulating in the sense of structuring or differentiating. The practical significance of our everyday

---

[6] Likewise, an author "writes with the computer, thus, as it were, stating publicly that computers are to be written with" (Blattner 1999a, 73). That "as it were" is doing a lot of work. In his later treatment of discourse, Blattner connects it more closely to expression and communication, as I do in this essay, and as I did in my own earlier account (Carman 2003, ch. 5), though his inclusion of "gardening" as an example (Blattner 2006, 101) makes me wonder how close it remains to any ordinary notion of expressing or communicating something. One *can* express and communicate something by gardening, but one need not be doing so. Maybe I grow tomatoes just to have them for eating.
[7] The word "signifying" (*bedeutend*) here is a technical term that does not mean semantic sense or reference, but rather the practical *significance* or intelligibility relations among tools, projects, purposes, and the ultimate "for-the-sake-of" (*Worumwillen*) or *point* of what we do (*BT* 120/87). The "signifying" goes backwards, or trickles down as it were, from the for-the-sake-of through the long-range purposes and proximal projects, finally to the equipment. So, for example, as Heidegger uses the word, being a poet "signifies" writing, which in turn "signifies" pen and paper.

environment is structurally articulated (*gegliedert*), Heidegger says elsewhere, but more in the way a skeleton or a clock is articulated, namely by having parts or joints, than in the way a thought or a feeling is articulated in words. On this reading, then, to say that discourse "articulates (*gliedert*) intelligibility" (*BT* 316/271) is to say that it is our structured response to the practical significance of our everyday environment, in virtue of which we can, as Dreyfus says, "tell" time and "tell" hammers from nails.

But it is no accident that Heidegger uses the word *Artikulation*, and Blattner and others are right to acknowledge that language is at least central to his account, even if does not exhaust the subject. Setting aside for the moment what particular phenomenon Heidegger has in mind, there is a simple but powerful *methodological* argument against the approach taken by Haugeland, Dreyfus, Blattner, and Wrathall – namely, that Heidegger *already* provides an elaborate account of things like telling time, telling pawns from rooks, and "being skillfully engaged with" and "knowing how to deal with" things *before* he introduces the concept of discourse in §34. If "discourse" turns out to be just another word for practical intelligence, it is hard to see how the concept adds anything to what Heidegger previously said about worldliness (*Weltlichkeit*) and understanding (*Verstehen*) in chapter 4 (especially §18) and chapter 5 (especially §§31–32). If, as one might reasonably expect, the concept of discourse is supposed to add something new, then we must take more seriously its apparent affiliation with language, speech, and verbal behavior. The best way to get the phenomenon into sharper focus, then, is to see more clearly how the notion is related to – and how it differs from – understanding and interpretation (*Auslegung*).[8]

4.2 What is Said and What is Talked About

"Understanding" means *intelligence,* for Heidegger above all *practical* intelligence. Ironically, though his definition of the term was groundbreaking, it managed to be so precisely by remaining true to ordinary usage and common sense, far more so than its predecessors in the history of philosophy, which usually drew sharp, invidious distinctions between theoretical understanding on the one hand and practical judgment, skillfulness,

---

[8] For a more detailed presentation of my account of interpretation as what I call "demonstrative practice" (showing how) and of discourse as communicative expression (saying something about something to someone), see chapter 5 of my book *Heidegger's Analytic* (Carman 2003).

competence, and perceptual acuity on the other. In ordinary language, Heidegger says, "we sometimes use the expression 'to understand something' in the sense of 'managing (*vorstehen*) an affair,' 'being up to it,' 'being able to [do something]'" (*BT* 183/143). Likewise, the technical meaning of the term for Heidegger's purposes "harkens back to common linguistic usage when we say: someone can manage (*vorstehen*) an affair, i.e. he has an understanding of it (*versteht sich darauf*)" (*BP* 391–392, 276).

Interpretation is a closely related but distinct notion. Simply put, interpretation is understanding made "explicit" (*ausdrücklich*): it "has the structure of *something as something* ... The 'as' makes up the structure of the explicitness of something understood; it constitutes interpretation" (*BT* 189/149). Whereas for much of the philosophical tradition (and still for nearly all of contemporary psychology) understanding presupposes interpretation, for Heidegger it is the reverse: interpretation presupposes understanding; understanding is a primitive phenomenon, and interpretation is possible only on the basis of an understanding that is already at work. But what does "explicit" mean in these formulations?

Here again scholars disagree. Dreyfus (1991, 4–5) tends to equate explicitness with consciousness and mental representation, which puts it a long way, conceptually speaking, from primordial understanding in the sense of skillfully knowing our way around. Blattner (2006, 96) rightly denies that it is essentially tied to consciousness, but he agrees with Dreyfus that "by 'interpretation' Heidegger means roughly what Kant means by 'cognition,' [and] what Searle means by 'representation'" – namely, that it "can be captured in propositional form, because it is conceptually articulated." In support of this reading, Blattner quotes a passage in which Heidegger says that "[t]he 'as' of interpretation can be expressed in propositions"; that is, precisely "*because* cognition is a form of interpretation, its content can be expressed in propositions" (2006, 97, 94; emphasis added).[9] Blattner observes that his reading "dovetails nicely" with

---

[9] I think this is a misreading. Two sentences prior to the passage Blattner quotes, Heidegger specifies that the case of interpretation he is describing is the perception of something "occurrent" (*vorhanden*) (*BT* 89/61–62), which is to say, abstracted from our practical use of it as something "ready-to-hand" (*zuhanden*). He then adds, "What is perceived and made determinate can be expressed in propositions and can be retained and preserved as what has thus been asserted" (*BT* 89/62). I read this as saying only that anything perceptible *as occurrent*, not anything interpretable *in any way*, can be expressed in propositions. After all, "assertion" *means*, in part, predication (*BT* 196/154), which just is propositional structure, and not all interpretation is assertoric: "The primordial 'as' of an interpretation ... we call the existential-*hermeneutic* 'as,' in distinction from the *apophantic* 'as' of the assertion" (*BT* 201/158). Discerning Heidegger's exact meaning in passages like this can be difficult, though, and Blattner's reading is plausible, both here and at greater length in his paper, "Is Heidegger a Representationalist?" (Blattner 1999b).

the fact that "explicit" (*ausdrücklich*) in German, like "express" in English, is cognate with "expression" (*Ausdruck*), which at least alludes to language.

But again, not all expression is linguistic expression, and not all linguistic expression is assertoric, nor even implicitly propositional: consider expressive utterances like "wow" and "oops."[10] I think we should take Heidegger literally and regard interpretation precisely as what is "explicit" in the sense of *expressed*, or at least *expressible*, but not just linguistically or propositionally. On this approach, the concept of interpretation is not so wide as to be empty, since there are things we can understand but not express, from matters as lofty and elusive as love, death, or the meaning of life to things as subtle and fine-grained as the cognitive and motor skills of artists, athletes, and experts of all kinds. In any case, the realm of the expressible is larger than the realm of words. We express a wide range of nonverbal moods and understandings in our bodily comportment, in our facial expressions and unreflective gestures, not to mention in dance, music, and the visual arts. To "interpret" in Heidegger's sense of the word, then, means *to make explicit*, which in turn means simply to express (including the parasitic case of expressing something only to oneself). Sometimes we express what we understand and how we feel by uttering words, but just as often we do so by smiling, frowning, sighing, sulking, slouching, laughing, pointing, dancing, singing, or drawing a picture.[11]

This concept of interpretation is broad, then, but not so all-encompassing as to be vacuous, and I believe it provides the key to

---

[10] Granted, sometimes such words function as abbreviations for full assertions and so can be said to convey propositionally structured semantic content (see Kaplan 2004). But they often resist determinate propositional explication owing the uniqueness and complexity of the situations in which we utter them.

[11] Steven Crowell is right to say that my account of interpretation as demonstrative expression, which includes not just speech, even broadly construed, but also "bodily postures and facial expressions" (Carman 2003, 211; cf. note 8), puts Heidegger in close company with Merleau-Ponty (Crowell 2013a, 232). He is wrong, however, to object that including such things in Heidegger's account of discourse blurs the line between human comportment and mere animal behavior. It is, on the contrary, Crowell's (2013a, 233) assertion that animals "engage in practices, make things, gesture to each other, twitter noisily, exchange information, and so on" that muddies the water. We do not call animal behaviors "practices" precisely because they do not have the articulable normative structure that our practices do. And the phrase "gesture to each other" confuses mere signaling with *ostension*, that is, demonstratively indicating something to someone, usually by means of gesture and eye contact, which is a uniquely human ability. Dogs look where we point (thanks to thousands of years of adapting to our behavior), but they do not point things out to us. Our nearest biological relatives, chimpanzees, do neither. As for "bodily postures and facial expressions," those words can refer to things other animals do, but I have in mind things like slouching in defiance of authority, scowling with disapproval, and faking a smile to avoid a conversation. Such bodily instances of communicative expression involve no articulation of conceptual content, yet they are distinctively human.

to forget or evade that primitive fact about ourselves when we lose ourselves in publicness and conformity to custom and convention, but often enough our own concrete particularity as individuals, like a leash, pulls us back to ourselves, and that moment of recognition is what Heidegger calls the summoning of conscience: the self, he says, "gets brought to itself by the call" (*BT* 317/273).

Admittedly, the call of conscience has a somewhat attenuated communicative dimension, as it is merely myself calling myself back to my guilt. But there is nothing inherently paradoxical in that. After all, talking to oneself, whether silently or aloud, is perfectly normal (up to a point). It is even more evident that the experience Heidegger is describing exhibits the distinction between content and object: in being pulled back to my particularity, I feel myself addressed by *something said about* my being, namely, that I am *this* person and no other, that is, that I cannot evade my being who I am. What, Heidegger asks, is being talked about (*das Beredete*) or called upon (*Angerufene*) in conscience? "Obviously Dasein itself," he says (*BT* 317/272). And what does it say of me? *That* I am, more particularly, that I am *this* one. In conscience, "the '*that*' itself is disclosed to Dasein" (*BT* 321/276). Crucially, however, the proposition *that I am* or *that I am this one* is not strictly speaking the content of the call, for Heidegger insists that conscience calls to us precisely by *not* speaking, *not* saying anything: "*Conscience talks* (redet) *solely and constantly in the mode of remaining silent* (Schweigen)" (*BT* 318/273). Conscience speaks not by saying anything, let alone uttering words, but always only in an uncanny silence or reticence (*Verschwiegenheit*) (*BT* 322/277). Indeed, the caller is not even exactly *me* in any ordinary ontic sense, namely the person answering to a proper name or a description: "The caller in its *who* is determinable in a 'worldly' way by *nothing*. It is Dasein in its uncanniness- ... the naked 'that' in the nothing of the world" (*BT* 321/276–277) . The "discourse" of conscience, then, is my being called back *to* a recognition of the facticity of my existence, *by* that facticity itself.

Notwithstanding this seemingly private, or at least solitary, discursive relation one has to oneself, it is clear that the phenomenon Heidegger has in view is predominantly collective, public, and social in nature. His way of putting this is to say that it is closely tied to our "being-with" others (*Mitsein*). Discourse is not identical with being-with any more than it is identical with understanding or interpretation, and again the way to appreciate this is to see that discourse is precisely the way all the other existential structures of Dasein's existence are *augmented* in communicative expression. Conveniently, the German word for communication

(*Mitteilung*) means literally *sharing with* (*teilen* meaning both to divide and to share, which is echoed in our word "impart"). "Being-with," Heidegger therefore says, "is *shared* [or *imparted*] 'expressly' [*ausdrücklich*] in discourse; that is, it *is* already, but is uncommunicated as something not taken up and appropriated" (*BT* 205/162). Discourse, that is, opens up our shared being-in-the-world with one another in its specifically *expressive-communicative* dimension.

What else is entailed by this? Maybe not much. Some have tried to see it, together with Heidegger's account of guilt or "answerability," as hinting at a robust normative or ethical principle of some kind. But I think we should be careful to avoid projecting such constructions onto the frankly austere phenomenology that Heidegger actually advances. Steven Crowell, for example, reads the words "taken up and appropriated" as suggesting a quasi-Kantian principle of universal ethical validity. To take up and appropriate our being-with in discourse, he writes, "means to relate to measure (the Good) as *normative* – that is, as rule-like, potentially holding for everyone, as *universal*" (Crowell 2013a, 234). Furthermore, the discourse of conscience – which, recall, for Heidegger just means being called back to your concrete particularity as an individual – according to Crowell (2013a, 234), "articulates the possibility of first-person responsibility and, as a summons, calls 'I myself' into an *explicit* appropriation of my being-with in the form of owing reasons to others."

But Heidegger says nothing about "the Good" *qua* measure, universally valid normative rules, or "owing reasons" (of any kind) – or anything else for that matter – to others. A less tendentious, less moralizing reading of the text, I believe, reveals nothing more (or less) in Heidegger's phenomenology of the call of conscience than what we find in the scene in *The Trial* in which the "powerful, well-trained voice" of the priest cries out in the otherwise empty cathedral, "Joseph K.!" (Kafka 1998, 211). The only "content" of the call is K.'s name, which is not even a full name, but a common given name followed by an initial, a mere placeholder. It identifies him only to pick him out and command his attention, reminding him of his being *this one*, "delivered over" (*überantwortet*), as Heidegger likes to say (*BT* 173/134), to the world and to others – a man accused of nothing in particular and answerable to no worldly authority. Like Kafka's fiction, Heidegger's phenomenology is a rich (yet austere) landscape depiction of human existence. It is not discourse ethics.

In sum, discourse is neither language nor the articulation of conceptual thought, which gets expressed in language, but neither is it simply the intelligibility of the world disclosed to our practical understanding. It is instead the expressive-communicative dimension of our being-in-the-world, which encompasses not just speech acts, but all modes of comportment that (in the widest sense) "say" or impart something to someone, including bodily posture and facial expression, as well as the existential drama of our being "called" back to our own concrete particularity as individuals, answerable to others, in a world we are condemned to share with them.

CHAPTER 5

On Curiosity as Epistemic Vice

Irene McMullin

What does Heidegger mean by "curiosity" and why does he characterize it as a kind of epistemic vice, when most contemporary accounts view it as a virtue? *Being and Time* disparagingly notes that curiosity "concerns itself with a kind of knowing, but just in order to have known" (*BT* 217/172); the curious person busies herself with "entertaining 'incidentals'" (*BT* 358/310). Building on previous work – wherein I argue that virtues are best understood as tendencies to cope well with existential obstacles to flourishing (McMullin 2019) – I show that curiosity as Heidegger frames it is an epistemically vicious misunderstanding of self and world arising in large part from our tendencies toward impatience, arrogance, and fear. Because Heidegger's account of curiosity in *Being and Time* is not well-developed, we will look at nearby texts to get a better understanding of this sometimes-overlooked concept in Heidegger's corpus.

5.1 Curiosity and the Love of Seeing

The epistemic virtues are typically understood as character traits – ways of seeing, feeling, and doing – that are constitutive of flourishing insofar as they enable us to be good knowers. For example, adjudicating well between competing testimonies, recognizing good evidence, and being honest in one's claims to knowledge, are all epistemic virtues. By most contemporary accounts, curiosity is one such epistemic virtue, defined by open-minded inquisitiveness and resistance to complacency. It thereby enables us to acquire knowledge reliably and responsibly.[1]

---

[1] The main camps in these debates are virtue reliabilists (who assess the virtuousness of knowers in terms of how reliably their cognitive faculties or dispositions result in true beliefs) and virtue responsibilists (who link the epistemic virtues to traditional moral virtues by emphasizing the degree to which agents are responsible for developing the skills necessary for being good knowers). I will not discuss this distinction here, but my approach is broadly responsibilist. See Ross (2020),

In contrast, Heidegger's account of curiosity seems entirely negative. He characterizes it as a paradigmatically inauthentic stance in which we cultivate distraction via anonymous and captivating possibilities that have little bearing on one's life. We find comparable criticisms of curiosity in figures like Plutarch and Seneca – with the former viewing it as "a desire to learn the troubles of others" (Plutarch 1939, 475/515D) and the latter rejecting it as a kind of arid knowledge-mongering detached from meaning (Walsh 1988, 84). Condemnation of curiosity finds further support in St. Augustine and St. Thomas Aquinas,[2] who both hold that in curiosity the desire to know – which Aristotle characterizes as a fundamental feature of being human – is perverted into a craving for gossip and distracting spectacle. Hobbes (2008, 37), too, argues that curiosity is "a Lust of the mind" that gravitates toward the greedy consumption of controversy, although he also compares it favorably to other basic desires.[3]

Heidegger's discussion follows these thinkers in characterizing curiosity as a perversion of the natural desire to know. And like Augustine's (2008, 211–212, Book X) characterization of curiosity as a lust to see, Heidegger frames it in terms of a natural tendency toward visual consumption (*BT* 214/170).[4] Although he goes on to speak of curiosity as a perceptual mode in general, he nevertheless invokes Aristotle's famous opening of the *Metaphysics* such that the visual is emphasized – translating πάντες ἄνθρωποι τοῦ εἰδέναι ὀρέγονται φύσει not in the standard way as "All men by nature desire to know" (Aristotle 2001, 980a1 A.I.I.), but rather as "The care for seeing is essential to man's being" (*BT* 215/171), a translation that attempts to "undo the exclusively cognitivist connotation of the more standard translation" (McCall 2011, 181). What is essential to human being is a normatively governed caring that expresses itself in a circumspective attunement to the world – "seeing" – that only occasionally results in the cognitive grasping typically associated with knowledge. Hence what "all men desire by nature," Heidegger argues, is skillful, perceptive engagement with the world – not concepts, but *understanding*, with "understanding" taken in its existential sense as an ability to act into and master the possibilities through which Dasein can be who it is.

Wright (2017), and Greco and Reibsamen (2017). For examinations of curiosity in these terms, see Alfano (2013), Baehr (2011), and Zagzebski (1996).

[2] Aquinas distinguishes between virtuous *studiositas* and vicious *curiositas*: with the latter defined as "the vice of inordinate seeking after knowledge" (Hibbs 1999, 51).

[3] See Engel (2018) for an overview of curiosity's evolution from vice to virtue.

[4] See McNeill (1999) for a book-length treatment of curiosity, theory, and the role of vision in Heidegger's thought. I am indebted to McNeill's careful scholarship on these topics.

In contrast with seeing that is oriented by or in the service of genuine practical understanding, Heidegger characterizes curiosity as seeking "*only* to see" (*BT* 216/172) or "*only* to see and to have seen" (*BT* 397/346). In curiosity, "Dasein lets itself be carried along solely by the looks of the world ... it concerns itself with becoming rid of itself as Being-in-the-world" (*BT* 216/172). Curiosity is perception mobilized to help Dasein forget its own being by focusing instead on that which is "far" and "alien" (*BT* 216/172), that which calls for only superficial engagement: "The principal quality of the curious is reflected in the fact that whatever they are curious about ultimately and even from the outset means absolutely nothing to them. All curiosity thrives on this essential indifference" (*N II* 81). Similar themes are found in everyday usage: Something is *a* "curiosity" if it is the object of an interest untethered to the specificity or import of one's projects; idle curiosity is a mere playing at knowledge-pursuit that lacks grounding in one's life commitments. Hence, Heidegger notes that curiosity "accepts as valid only what is interesting [*Interessante*]. And interesting is the sort of thing that can freely be regarded as indifferent the next moment, and be displaced by something else, which then concerns us just as little as what went before" (*WCT* 5).

The disengagement that curiosity fosters may help explain the emphasis on sight – the perceptual capacity that is most conducive to forgetting one's entanglement with the thing seen. Sight brings distant things near but without touching the seer; it locates things against a horizon in terms of which they can be comprehended from a distance; it enables a forgetting of the self and its limits, facilitating a sense of mastery from afar.[5] In contrast, the sense of touch makes real one's entanglement with the world in a way that is foreign to the spectator position at work in vision (see Husserl 1989).

Accounts that characterize curiosity as a virtue, however, view this decoupling of curiosity from one's practical concerns as largely being what *makes* it a virtue; it is admirable insofar as the agent can pursue and appreciate knowledge for its own sake, not simply as a tool for achieving utilitarian ends. On this view, it is precisely this distance from the specificity of the knower that enables the careful theoretical work necessary for, say, scientific knowledge.

Heidegger recognizes the degree to which certain kinds of knowledge – including theoretical knowledge – depend on interruptions to everyday practical coping (*BT* 216/172), but he distinguishes between the

---

[5] Levinas (1995, 94, 128) critiques Husserlian phenomenology for the same problematic orientation.

problematic anonymity and lack of practical connection operative in curiosity from the interruption to everyday instrumental praxis that can give rise to the questioning and openness to possibility operative in both true scientific inquiry and authentic modes of being.

The capacity for this latter kind of interruption is a function of Dasein's condition of ontological freedom – a condition that becomes known to us in fundamental attunements like anxiety and boredom. Problematic modes of interest-seeking and entertainment-production – curiosity's *modus operandi* – are largely ways to avoid these revelatory moods.

5.2 Boredom and Anxiety

Heidegger famously notes that Dasein is constantly bored – boredom "attunes our Dasein through and through" (*FCM* 166) – although we don't always recognize it. Ontological boredom reveals Dasein to be free from the determination that comes with animal being, demonstrating the indifference that underwrites our free capacity to act into different possibilities of being. There is no fundamental instinct, cause, or destiny governing who we must be; each of us is "held out into the nothing" (*PM* 91) and must take a stand despite this lack of ultimate ground. In *Being and Time*, it is anxiety that plays this revelatory role, stripping the world of the normative grip through which it manifests its meaning. Both boredom and anxiety confront Dasein with the groundless contingency or freedom from determinacy that helps make it what it is: a condition that can be resolutely taken up in authenticity or actively denied in curiosity, idle chatter, and ambiguity (*BT* 211–225/167–180).

Curiosity's favored objects – distracting spectacle and salacious gossip – are well-suited to "fill up" the nothing that defines us, concealing, thereby, the responsibility posed by our freedom:

> [W]e can ask whether our contemporary everyday traits, our being human, is not such that in everything – in all its doing and acting and being blinded by this – it acts counter to the possibility of that profound boredom arising. We can only ask whether contemporary man narrows down that *expanse of his concealed and most profound need* to those needs against which he immediately finds some self-protection, so as to satisfy and appease himself in this. (*FCM* 166)[6]

---

[6] Translation altered slightly.

Curiosity directs our sight to only those needs that can be easily appeased, blinding us to the more profound needs operative in the injunction to self-becoming. Gossip and idle chatter point attention outward and thereby distract us from our failure to take up our own role as "the custodian of the inner greatness of Dasein and its necessities" (*FCM* 163).

Further, the objects of curiosity are often manifestations of the weakness and finitude of others – grotesque bodies, ridiculous scandals, failings of all kinds.[7] Focusing on the spectacle presented by other people's failings distracts us from our own finitude, providing us with a sense of our own power by witnessing the powerlessness of others. Hence, we can recognize the morally worrying implication of Dasein's drive toward distraction: treating the lives of others as objects for consumption and judgment. As Plutarch notes:

> [T]here are some who cannot bear to face their own lives, regarding these as a most unlovely spectacle, or to reflect and revolve upon themselves, like a light, the power of reason, but their souls, being full of all manner of vices, shuddering and frightened at what is within, leap outwards and prowl about other people's concerns and there batten and make fat their own malice. (Plutarch 1939, 479/516)

In contrast to contemporary tendencies to separate off the epistemic from the moral virtues, we see here the moral implications of certain forms of knowledge-seeking, which both rely on and enable damaging relationships to others and to self.[8] The orientation to the superficially satisfying or interesting event prevents Dasein from answering the profound need of facing up to its ontological condition as entrusted with its own life in conditions of finitude and answerability to others.

5.3 Craving the New

The German word for curiosity – *Neugier* – means desire or craving for the *new*, a fact that highlights another core feature of curiosity. It is not solely an appetite for distracting and salacious worldly spectacle, but also a restless clamor to experience something *new*. Hence, Plutarch (1939, 487/517–518) notes that "curiosity apparently takes no pleasure in stale calamities [e.g., from history], but wants them hot and fresh; enjoys the

---

[7] Augustine's (2008, 211, book X) discussion of the concupiscence of the eyes highlights the fact that we are often drawn to horrible yet fascinating things, like the "mangled corpse." See also *PRL* §§13–14.

[8] On whether moral and intellectual virtues are distinct, see Baehr (2011, 206–222).

spectacle of novel tragedies." This feature of curiosity, Heidegger argues, displays how it is a distortion of the temporal foundation of Dasein's way of being.

Curiosity's distortion of the futural and "projective" dimension is evident in that it constantly "leaps away" toward the new, projecting endlessly into an untrammeled future. Curiosity is "so little devoted to the 'thing' it is curious about, that when it obtains sight of anything, it already looks away to what is coming next" (*BT* 398/347). The aim of curiosity, Heidegger argues, is not to dwell with something in order to gain understanding, but rather to undergo "a constant change of presence ... the non-tarrying of curiosity is basically concerned with not having to get involved and with merely being entertained by the world" (*HCT* 277). Curiosity is a constant movement of replacing the current object of interest with the next novelty, with a preference for objects and events that can easily fit within the distraction-dismissal movement of endless novelty consumption.

Basic Problems of Phenomenology gives us one of Heidegger's most detailed accounts of this kind of pathological relationship to time, whereby the future is represented as something on hand, ready for consumption. Time is treated as *extant* (*BP* 274); each now is experienced as a succession of use objects *within* time (*BP* 272). The result being that future possibilities are not experienced *as* possibilities – namely, as identity-defining risks and opportunities about which one must deliberate and choose – but are instead treated as quasi-actual objects for indifferent observation. Curiosity is aimed at eradicating or concealing possibility qua possibility. If I "merely reflect on some empty possibility into which I could enter and, as it were, just gab about it, then this possibility is not there, precisely as possibility; instead for me it is, as we might say, actual" (*BP* 277; see also *BT* 396–400/346–349). These "possibilities" carry none of the risk or uncertainty of the genuinely experienced future, the domain of indeterminacy and freedom (Cf. *BP* 277, *FCM* 363–366, and *BT* §31). They are instead consumables determined in advance as such no matter how "hot and fresh" the particular content. The aim is "killing" time, as the bored say. Hence the frenzied movement of constant actualization that feigns futurity but eradicates its essential qualities of risk, contingency, and possibility – the fact that the existential question "who am I?" is always at stake in one's choices. Living one's futurity in this impoverished way means that it does not draw one forward in the genuine work of creating oneself via the patient cultivation of one's abilities to be, but rather restlessly leaps outward toward an anonymous banquet of ready-to-hand options available for voyeuristic enjoyment. Their actualization is guaranteed in advance because they are grasped as in some sense *already* realized – on hand waiting to be seen and enjoyed by any anonymous spectator who happens to come along. The epistemic upshot of this restless experience-consumption is, "contrary to many analytic accounts of curiosity as essential for truth-acquisition," loss of "the ability to commit to a line of inquiry long enough to reach the truth" (Dancy 1995, 197–198).

Hence, Heidegger notes that this inauthentic mode of temporalizing involves Dasein living "at a faster rate" in contrast to the "essentially slower time" of reticence (*BT* 218/174). For curiosity, each now is no different than the next because "[m]atters like significance and datability remain a closed book for this way of understanding" (*BP* 272). In *Being and Time*, Heidegger had already made clear that the four features that characterize Dasein's originary temporality are spannedness (or duration), datability, publicity, and significance (*BT* 469/416). These four features manifest the *ecstatic* nature of originary temporality: the "being-outside-self" (*BP* 267) constitutive of Dasein's being in the world.[9] In the case of datability, its "relational structure" (*BP* 262) indexes Dasein's being to some meaningful worldly event or thing. This anchoring of Dasein's originary temporality in worldly things can occur through the individual projects of Dasein's unique for-the-sake-of, or through the intersubjectively shared "reckoning with time" that Heidegger analyzes under the heading of "publicity." Together these features help constitute the fourth structural feature of temporality: significance, which is equivalent to the normative structures of appropriateness that constitute the worldliness of the world (*BT* 467/414).

Curiosity distorts Dasein's embeddedness in the world via its temporal self-indexing to existentially meaningful things and projects: it "discloses everything and anything, yet in such a way that Being-in is everywhere and nowhere" (*BT* 221/177). It is a worldless consumption of the *process* of experiencing, the content of which is ultimately meaningless insofar as it bears no essential relationship to the significance of the world. *Towards the Definition of Philosophy* contrasts the experiential structures of processes vs. events: In the former, lived experience "pass[es] in front of me like a thing," whereas the latter "is an experience proper to me" wherein I am fully at stake in it (*TDP* 63). Curiosity relates to the world qua process – encountering it as a mere spectacle passing in front of Dasein and not engaging it as the domain of significance in terms of which it struggles to be who it is. But without the significance and datability that account for

---

[9] For a fuller discussion of Dasein's temporal structure, see McMullin (2013).

the variability of duration that characterizes authentic praxis, time becomes a standing now of pure presence that can be passively experienced instead of actively lived. The possibility of resolutely taking up one's unique situation is covered over in an eternal now of absolute and endless visibility in which Dasein moves restlessly from one meaningless experience to the next, each viewed from a safe distance. "Starting from this view, [Dasein] arrives at the opinion that time is infinite, endless, whereas by its very nature temporality is finite" (*BP* 272). This belief in the infinity and endlessness of time, Heidegger notes, "can enter the Dasein's mind only because temporality itself, intrinsically, forgets its own essential finitude" (*BP* 273). In curiosity, Dasein attempts to forget itself and occupy a kind of temporal infinity.

The aim of curiosity, then, is to go through the temporal motions of being Dasein by bringing worldly experiences to presence, but in a purely passive expectation of "what is just coming on" (*BP* 287) and not for the sake of enacting who one is trying to be in the world. Hence, McNeill (1999, 173) notes that this is a kind of "fleeing of time from itself in which it nevertheless remains itself as a specific possibility of presence." Curious Dasein "kills time" by rushing from one anonymous interchangeable moment to the next, creating the illusion of projecting into the future but with none of the risk.

5.4 The Past

Curiosity's distortion of the possibility-nature of the future is coupled with a distortion of Dasein's essential relationship to the past such that it "has forgotten what has gone before" (*BT* 398–399/347; *BP* 287). *Phenomenology of Intuition and Expression* points out that one can "find the genuine only provided that the old is also there, [and] for a certain stretch of the way goes along behind it" (*PIE* 21). But it is characteristic of factical life that "the old" has a tendency toward a "fading of meaningfulness" wherein "relations wear themselves out and where merely the content that is itself no longer primordially had 'is of interest'" (*PIE* 26). This foreshadows *Being and Time*'s account of curiosity, whereby interest in content divested of primordiality takes the form of unthinking acceptance and "being-busy-with" something in its availability:

> From this disintegrating and depraving fading, factical life experience is endangered in its primordiality and therefore mixed with faded content, relation, and enactment. Therein is based the peculiar mixed character of

factical life, from out of which a number of phenomena ... like boredom, emptiness, fleetingnesss, speed, restlessness, insecurity of life become understandable. (*PIE* 141)

Although he characterizes curiosity as an orientation to the constantly "new," Heidegger also insists that "[t]he genuine is always new" (*PIE* 21). How should we understand the "newness" operative in authentic temporality – which genuinely "goes along with" its past – as different than curiosity's constant craving for novelty? In the case of the former, the "new" cannot mean "a first-time appearing and occurring in an individual stream of consciousness" (*PIE* 64). Whereas curiosity accepts only first-time occurrences – "hot and fresh" events – as fulfilling the craving for novelty, the newness characteristic of the genuine arises out of and retains an essential connection to that which has already been.

In *Phenomenology of Intuition and Expression*, Heidegger examines six different meanings of history, or ways in which Dasein lives its relationship to pastness. He considers a (hypothetical) tribe that has no history, not because events haven't transpired for its members, but because they have no *tradition*: "they do not 'feel' as the later ones of earlier ones. The past for them is not a character in which they factically live and which somehow permeates the content of their life experience; they do not cultivate the past" (*PIE* 35). As a result, "They live each day as it comes, according to what the day may bring. They also have no future, no tasks" (*PIE* 35).

Here we see a cultural model of curiosity's distorted relationship to the past, whereby there is no cultivation of or dwelling with the past and consequently no genuine future. Rather, each day is consumed in isolation from the sweep of care-driven self-becoming; each new thing is a novelty or "curiosity" disconnected from the past and hence delineating no essential tasks in the project of being who one is. In curiosity, as for the ahistorical tribe, "what we are – and what we have been is always contained in this – lies in some way behind us, *forgotten*" (*BP* 289). And indeed, the fact of this forgetting is itself forgotten (*BP* 290).

In contrast, to genuinely "have" one's past requires a relationship of preserving of that which has been in one's becoming or self-achievement; preserving is not a mere "attitudinal complex" that is "externally attached to Dasein" (*PIE* 40). Rather, preserving "belongs to the innermost Dasein itself" embodied in "the rhythm of one's own Dasein" (*PIE* 40): a rhythm of "constantly having anew" one's own having been (*PIE* 40). Hence, "having the past" is not merely following on from what has come before, but is a way of understanding one's present and future tasks as arising from and ongoingly indebted to one's having been.[10] A genuine grasping of the past thereby establishes the *rhythm* of being who one is – a deeply temporal notion echoing on an individual level the cultural structure of tradition as a renewed but repeating pattern or style of being: a way of "repeat[ing] the being we have been" in order to be who we are (*BP* 290).[11]

This structure of repetition – returning to the possibilities one has chosen in order to make them new and thereby enable them to ongoingly shape the future – enables Dasein to "*run out in front of itself*" (*BP* 287). Here we see why Dasein's authentic way of being should be understood in terms of resolute *commitment*: namely, a stance in which the past is brought into the future by way of an ongoing renewal of self-understanding that shapes the present (Cf. Burch (2020), Crowell (2013) and (2022), and Haugeland (2000)). Dasein's authentic relationship to the past is a renewal or cultivation – a re-possibilizing – of the constituent elements of who it is. This involves aiming "at the past as what was earlier" but "as the yet still vital part of one's own self-proper [*Selbsteigentlichkeit*] [authentic] tendencies at the time" (*PIE* 45). In such a relationship to the past, Heidegger argues, "I seize my own past so that it again and again is had for the first time" such that "I myself am always affected anew by myself and 'am' in renewed enactment" (*PIE* 64). Hence the past "does not wear itself out but becomes with itself always more surprising" (*PIE* 64). As a result, there is in this relationship to the past "*the rejection of every trace of finality*" (*PIE* 65): a position in direct contrast to the relationship to the past operative in curiosity, whereby each new spectacle or novelty is abandoned for the next, is stale the moment it arrives: each "surprise" more predictable and shallow than the last.

These disordered modes of living one's temporality are ways that Dasein fails to cope with its own ontological structure as transcendence and finitude, ways it turns away from the fact that it is at stake in the possibility-nature of the future and answerable to the constraint-nature of the past. Curiosity seeks to elude both aspects of our temporal unfolding by constraining it to the constant now of meaningless infinite novelty. Indeed, Heidegger notes that "Even if one has seen everything, this is precisely when curiosity *fabricates* something new" (*BT* 399/348). In curiosity, Dasein creates for itself the illusion of infinity, an eternal

---

[10] Interesting questions arise here regarding the relationship to habit – a key concept for virtue ethics – which Heidegger insists is "blocked" by this constant renewal of the past (*PIE* 65). The role of "epistemic playfulness" in this process of renewal is also of import here (Roberts and Wood2007, 161).

[11] Gadamer's work on tradition in *Truth and Method* is relevant here.

noon-day now that never shades off into the challenging darkness of the given past or the risky future.

5.5 The Production Model

This idea of *fabricating* novelty is important for understanding how curiosity mobilizes the ancient Greek production model of reality, whereby the material reality of a thing is understood to be secondary to its look [*eidos*] insofar as the craftsman uses the latter to guide the shaping or forming work necessary to bring the former into being. *Eidos* is the "anticipated look" (*BP* 107) that is "sighted beforehand" (*BP* 106), with the material form realized by way of comportments of shaping, forming, and making – which Heidegger specifies via the general concept of producing (*Herstellen*) (*BP* 108). On this ontological model, concrete, contingent matter is secondary to form because the latter guides the productive activity that brings something into being as what it is.

Under Plato's watch, *eidos* was increasingly understood as a non-sensible exemplar – not merely a thing's (anticipated) look but its truest (and separate) form. The material thing came to be viewed as a pale imperfect copy of a reality located elsewhere.[12] The basic ontology of the production model remained, however: that one "sees" the *eidos*/Form and this seeing orients the praxis through which reality is produced as meaningful.

Of course, a key feature of reality is that it is "met with directly in intuition and perception as something already finished" (*BP* 112); in other words, it is primarily experienced as *not* being the result of production but as independent or "already finished" – a feature of the encounter that helps establish its status as real. But Heidegger insists that the productive mode of engagement always intends the product to be released from any relation to the producer. The independence of the produced thing from the producer is itself built into the production model's understanding of being:

> [T]he productive activity ... absolves what is to be produced from relation to the producer. Not *contrary* to its intention but in *conformity* with it, it releases from this relation the being that is to be produced and that which has been produced. Productive comportment's understanding of the being

---

[12] McNeill (1999, 245) points out that the desire to see can acquire the pejorative connotation that it does "only when a veritable gap opens between the sensible and the nonsensible, only when truth is no longer a truth belonging to and inherent in the sensible world."

toward which it is behaving takes this being beforehand as one that is to be released for its own self so as to stand independently on its own account. (*BP* 113)

Hence, a key feature of the production ontology that Heidegger traces back to the Greeks is understanding reality as *extantness*; readiness to hand; availability (*BP* 108–109) – with Dasein's role as producer increasingly hidden.[13]

Modern appropriations of this model more firmly established the separation of producer from produced, allowing the "character of setting-free" (*BP* 118) or "release" (*BP* 70) characteristic of production to come more explicitly to the fore; "every reference to the subject is pushed into the background" (*BP* 118). But Heidegger insists that the modern equation of actuality with perceivedness still operates within the horizon of a production ontology insofar as this "*intuitive finding present* . . . is only a modification of seeing in the sense of circumspection, of productive behaviour" (*BP* 109–110). In other words, Dasein's productive work increasingly comes to be modeled on the idea of "finding" as opposed to creating, further obscuring Dasein's creative role in the meaningful appearing of reality:

> [T]he extant is conceived of ontologically not so much by referring to the disposability for use or by reverting to the productive and in general the practical mode of activity as, rather, by reverting to our *finding present* [finding there before us, *Vorfinden*] what is thus disposable, [nevertheless] this comportment, too, the finding present of the produced and present-at-hand, belongs to producing itself. (*BP* 109)

Such perceptual "finding present" presupposes – but does not acknowledge – the enabling look (or understanding of being, as he later comes to understand it) whereby the thing is available for use. But the (unacknowledged) role that the look/*eidos* plays in the modern perceptual model of reality undermines the distance between producer and produced that is the primary characteristic of that view. It shapes and enables the "finding present" – the productive activity of perception – through which reality shows up as extant, a fact that is increasingly concealed in the attempt to push the producing subject further into the background. This attempt comes to fruition in the modern theoretical sciences and their desire to know for the sake of knowing – the tendency "just to perceive" (*BT* 216/172) – that characterizes them. Heidegger's later

---

[13] For a helpful discussion of the Greek production model of reality and its role in Heidegger's thought, see Haugeland (2007, 170–172).

work on technology shows how modern science produces its own objects of knowledge through mechanisms of enframing/measurement – and then pretends to itself that it didn't. This enables a spectator stance toward the world – think of the pure "observation" mode treasured by modern science – with little awareness of the concealed productive activity that makes possible any meaningful appearing within that space of spectatorship.

A core epistemological commitment of the production ontology is important here. Namely, the idea that the maker is viewed as having a unique kind of epistemic access to the thing: "a genuine cognitive grasp of a being in its being is available only to that being's creator" (*BP* 150). It is the *producer* who knows a thing insofar as she brings it into being – by making it (ancient model) or by "finding it present" (modern model) in conformity with its pre-existing essential look (*eidos/Form*): "The anticipation of the prototypical pattern which takes place in production is the true knowledge of what the product is. It is for this reason that only the producer of something, its originator, perceives a being in the light of what it is" (*BP* 151).

Much more could be said about the way that technology helps itself to the epistemic authority guaranteed to "producers" while pretending to itself that it merely "finds present" what was always already there. In doing so, it ignores the productive enframing that enables this "finding" to occur. In other words, it ignores the fact that Dasein's technological way of being – which enables things to be encountered as "found" – is itself an activity of "representing-producing [*vorstellend-herstellenden*] humanity" (*OBT* 82–83). Hence, Dasein's modern productive activity specifies in advance how things can show up as real while pretending that it does no such thing, a delusion that inhibits a renewal of the original Greek understanding of production as a creative partnership between Dasein and the coming into meaningful being of the world.[14]

A comparable structure operates on an individual level in curiosity. In curiosity, one "finds" the world interesting and distracting, a finding that obscures a prior self-production as the locus of an infinite anonymous now in which we have no ultimate stake and for which we need take no responsibility. In curiosity, Dasein "finds" the world as an object of entertainment and distraction, a finding predicated on first producing itself as a kind of experience-machine and then pretending to itself that

---

[14] See Crowell (2020, 41) for an examination of the passive/active structure at work here: "Now, a disclosing that does not 'make' but 'lets lie' or 'appear,' and a 'keeping disclosed' that is no passive acceptance but a 'concern,' have the structure of something *at issue*, meaning (*Sinn*)."

it hasn't done so. Dasein thereby eradicates genuine possibility as a practical imperative to which it is answerable in conditions of contingency and risk. The world becomes mere spectacle and Dasein a voyeur, enjoying the security of a total epistemic authority predicated on being the "fabricator" of the novelties by which it is distracted. The aim of curiosity is to produce a discrete consumable timeless present of pure experience events or pure knowledge bits, torn free of the repetition and renewal work necessary for genuine situation-responsive praxis. By existing in the mode of curiosity, Dasein (almost) succeeds in being little more than a location of passive consumption that can nevertheless claim for itself a certain kind of total knowing and thereby cover over the uncertainty intrinsic to being tasked with self-becoming in conditions of thrownness.

Heidegger contrasts the production of reality at work in curiosity with the kind of creation characteristic of phronesis. According to the former, the end product is always seen in advance and conceptualized as complete. Not so with the creative self-making at work in phronesis, which is governed throughout by the risk and contingency of a genuinely open future and a beholdenness to the constantly changing world. Truly practical wisdom acknowledges that Dasein is inherently incomplete and underway, at stake in what it does, and answerable to the contingent circumstances.

In *Phenomenological Interpretations of Aristotle*, Heidegger points out how Aristotle contrasts this capacity to "be otherwise" with a "higher" or "better" way of being: contemplative *sophia*'s state of *being finished*. But Aristotle's conception of the highest realization of human life – the stillness of pure contemplative apprehending – is modeled on the norm of perfection innate to the ontology of products: completion.

> That which is in being moved, together with the possible features of its structural meaning, is regarded in advance in terms of the exemplary kind of movement belonging to *producing*. Being means *being finished* [Fertigsein], that way of being in which movement has attained its *end*. The being of life is seen as intrinsically unfolding movement, and it exists in such movement when human life has come to its end with regard to its ownmost possibility of movement, that of pure apprehending. Such movement lies within the *hexis* of *sophia*. (*PIA* 37–38)

But Heidegger insists that Dasein is irrevocably "That which is in being moved" that which is "intrinsically unfolding movement"; thus, we cannot understand Dasein using a model that frames its highest realization as a cessation of the very thing that makes it what it is. To be changing and incomplete is what it is to be Dasein. Thus fetishizing the actual – whether in curiosity or in "sophia" – is fundamentally at odds with the kind of open-ended movement of becoming that defines Dasein's being qua possibility. Because the production model attempts to fix Dasein's end in advance and then produce it, that model is at odds with phronesis, which demands open responsivity to the moment and the changing immediate circumstances.[15] The fact that "*phronesis* is oriented toward something always yet to come" – that is, it embodies a condition of radical and irrevocable incompleteness – only justifies subordinating it to *sophia* if we (mistakenly) assume in advance that the production model – and its commitment to completion as the measure of reality – is the appropriate way to understand Dasein (McNeill 1999, 126–130).

In curiosity, then, Dasein aims to produce itself not by way of "taking action and carrying something through" (*BT* 218/174) – a self-creation rooted in the ontology of radical uncertainty, answerability, and risk at work in phronetic authenticity[16] – but rather by working hard to "find" itself as the kind of thing for whom such genuine action is not necessary.

5.6 Curiosity and Virtue

How does this view of curiosity as a vice square with more recent accounts of its virtuousness? Recall that the virtues are skillful responses to existential obstacles to flourishing. In what follows, I briefly discuss three such skillful responses and show how they help distinguish virtuous forms of "care for seeing" from more worrying forms.

Patience

Patience is best understood as a response to the challenge posed by our temporal finitude, which manifests for Dasein as both temporal scarcity and temporal dispersal – the fact that the project of self-becoming is dispersed in time such that it necessarily resists completion and

---

[15] See McManus (2020), for a discussion of how *phronesis* relates to the question of what it is best to do in the "here and now," not with general questions about the good (134). See also Zoller (2020, 5) and Brogan (1990, 126–130). Thanassas (2012, 50) criticizes Heidegger's treatment of phronesis as separable from moral/evaluative content; in such an interpretation all that is left is self-elucidation.

[16] Simply equating "authenticity" with "flourishing" is problematic; but for the purposes of this chapter, I will assume that authenticity is a necessary but not sufficient condition for flourishing, and hence that overcoming existential obstacles to authenticity can be understood as conducive to or partially constitutive of flourishing. For a concept of flourishing informed by existential themes such as authenticity, see McMullin (2019).

determinacy (McMullin 2019, ch. 7). Curiosity seeks to deny or conceal both of these aspects of Dasein's temporal being. In its fixation on the endless consumption of constant novelty, curious Dasein ignores its own temporal boundedness: the fact of being anchored in a now that arises from a distinct past and unfolds into a future answerable to that past. Similarly, Dasein's dispersal in time – its necessary incompleteness and openness to possibility – is denied in curiosity's attempt to understand being as extant and hence already in some sense actual, an interpretation predicated on a self-conception that covers over the risk and openness to possibility that define Dasein's temporal way of being. Curiosity does not view Dasein as unfolding into self-becoming but as a largely static site for the predictable display of novelties determined in advance as incapable of challenging this understanding of the self. Like impatience, then, vicious curiosity involves a failure to appreciate or cope with how we're thrown into time: into a past to which we are condemned to respond, into a future that is fundamentally open. Instead, it denies our temporal predicament by attempting to live in an eternal yet homogeneous process of making actual/now/present, creating and then consuming a quasi-actual future that is circumscribed in advance by the mandate of the "interesting" or "useful." Vicious curiosity "cares for seeing" simply as an enjoyable but rootless process.

Patient or virtuous curiosity, on the other hand, demands that we recognize and accept the kind of temporality characteristic of our way of being. Virtuously curious Dasein is not fixated on fabricating an endless stream of interesting spectacles but is focused on the existentially significant projects of understanding as they are beholden to the constraints of finitude. The role of patience in genuinely virtuous curiosity plays out in concrete terms as an ability to make epistemic commitments, to be persistent in the pursuit of worthwhile knowledge. If curiosity contributes to achieving or maintaining epistemic goods, as contemporary accounts of curiosity argue, then it must be capable of taking a form that is not intrinsically distractible and impatient, but rather is capable of committing to the gradual unfolding of understanding that characterizes most genuine intellectual inquiry.[17] Hence, Ross (2020, 110) notes that virtuous curiosity avoids "dilettantism or flaccidity."

---

[17] Recall Dancy's (1995, 197–198) worry about distraction.

Humility

As we have seen, Heidegger argues that we have a deep-seated tendency to deny an intellectual limitation that we all have: namely, the tendency to misunderstand our own being and the role that we play in the possibility of knowledge. Hence, virtuous curiosity depends in part on honest inquiry into – and acceptance of – the kinds of beings we really are.[18] A key aspect of this is accepting that we are at the mercy of the world, called upon to react to and wonder at it instead of controlling it or translating it into consumable form. This requirement has resonances with the definition of intellectual humility that Whitcomb et al. (2017, 11) provide: namely, that it involves "owning one's intellectual limitations."[19]

Whitcomb et al. (2017), like Heidegger, insist that facing up to what we really are – taking responsibility for our limitations – does not involve a fixation on the self, but rather enables us to fully engage with the world on its own terms.[20] Intellectually humble curiosity – what the late Heidegger might call *thinking* – thereby enables a responsive partnership in the unfolding of meaning.

Chappell (2012, 184) makes the case that this kind of relationship to the world falls outside the usual attempts to categorize knowledge as either propositional, ability, or experiential in kind, finding further support for the call to epistemic responsivity and humility in Murdoch (2014, 87): "I am confronted by an authoritative structure which commands my respect. My work is a progressive revelation of something which exists independently of me." Part of this work of progressive revelation is an abdication of the dream of completion; what we have instead is a "humble and unending pilgrimage" (Chappell 2012, 187). Hence, intellectual humility and patience are deeply linked (McMullin, forthcoming). Like Heidegger, then, these accounts hold that exemplary forms of inquiry demand humility in answering the claims of a world that exceeds our capacity to encompass it: a humility demonstrated in forms of curiosity that foreswear narratives of dominance and own up to our epistemic limitations. As Heidegger puts it: A being

> does not acquire being in that man first looks upon it in the sense of representation that has the character of subjective perception. Rather, man

---

[18] See Miščević (2020) on the need for "self-inquisitiveness."   [19] See also Inan (2017).
[20] "[W]hen limitation-owning is an intellectual virtue, it is motivated by the love of epistemic goods, which will largely focus an intellectually humble person on things outside of herself, as she navigates the world and attempts to increase her understanding of it" (Whitcomb et al. 2017, 20).

is the one who is looked upon by beings, the one who is gathered by self-opening beings into presencing with them. To be looked at by beings, to be included and maintained and so supported by their openness, to be driven about by their conflict and marked by their dividedness, that is the essence of humanity in the great age of [pre-Platonic] Greece. In order to fulfill his essence, therefore, man has to gather (λέγειν) and save (σώζειν), catch up and preserve, the self-opening in its openness; and he must remain exposed to all of its divisive confusion. Greek humanity is the receiver [*Vernehmer*] of beings, which is the reason that, in the age of the Greeks, the world can never become picture. (*OBT* 68–69)[21]

Here we see Heidegger endorsing a humility that eschews the arrogance at work in vicious forms of curiosity, whereby Dasein attempts to control reality and the possible future by establishing the parameters of anything appearing in advance. In short, virtuous curiosity involves an intellectual flexibility, openness, and responsivity that rejects attempts to instrumentalize our innate desire to understand the world.[22] The connection between humility and wonder (*thaumazein*) – the paradigmatic motivation of philosophical curiosity – is clear: "[W]onder does not see its objects possessively: they remain 'other' and un-mastered" (Hepburn 1980, 4). The owning of limitations at work in intellectually virtuous curiosity involves owning the deepest limitation of all: the fact that we are at the mercy of a world that radically transcends us and our capacity to know or control it – a stance that manifests as wondering curiosity and the admirable forms of inquiry to which it can give rise.

Courage

Whereas humility involves recognizing and accepting our limits, courage helps us cope with the fear involved in doing so. We have seen that genuinely facing the infinite world and the unknown future means abdicating delusions of control, closure, completion – and living in the face of the radical indeterminacy and risk that is our birthright. In contrast, the

---

[21] See Crowell (2020) for a detailed analysis of Heidegger's intellectual journey toward the conclusion that thinking is the unity of *noein* and *legein* whereby we are oriented toward measure, and that this is a relationship to finitude that "yields 'the phenomena of phenomenology,' the world of meaning, *on hos alethes*, being in the sense of truth" (44).

[22] This is in many ways the point of Heidegger's infamous Rector's address, in which he calls for a return to the essence of the university as a place of questioning that opens us to pure possibility, not of questioning that is chained to instrumentalist political imperatives (*SA*). Ross (2020) and Miščević (2020) similarly characterize curiosity as virtuous if it's rooted in a non-instrumental appreciation of epistemic goods.

tendency to look away from our own finitude is, for Heidegger, ultimately grounded in fear of the painful consequences of being answerable for an existence that is not fully within one's power. And the stance in which we overcome the temptation to give in to this fear – via distraction or delusions of (temporal, epistemic) infinitude – is well understood as a form of courage. Whereas vicious forms of curiosity mobilize our love of knowledge (our natural desire to "see") to create spectacles and distractions that conceal those limitations from us – offering a false "guarantee to Dasein that all the possibilities of its being will be secure, genuine, and full" (*BT* 222/177) – virtuous forms face and overcome our fear, enabling us to know not only ourselves, but the world and the others who share it. Courage arises in conditions where one's identity is on the line; it involves pursuing some good in the face of risks to one's well-being (McMullin 2019, ch. 9). *Intellectual* courage involves pursuing specifically cognitive goods such as truth, knowledge, and understanding in the face of such risks (Roberts and Wood 2007, 234). Hence, a curiosity informed by intellectual courage eschews those forms of knowledge-pursuit that are complicit in Dasein's (self-)misunderstanding, regardless of the pain involved in genuinely taking responsibility for and answering to the world.

5.7 Conclusion

It is part of human nature to desire to know – a desire that finds expression in our curiosity. True knowing demands that we overcome the obstacles that our impatience, our arrogance, and our fear pose us. Hence, virtuous forms of curiosity involve an understanding of the world and our place in it that unfolds in its own time and on its own terms, uncontaminated by the fear and irresponsibility that always tempt us to look away toward the easy distraction, to dim down the field of possibilities and claim for ourselves a certainty and safety at odds with the world and our place in it. Those willing to seek understanding in the face of their own restless pride and fear – and thereby maintain the questioning openness to possibility at work in both genuine scientific inquiry and authentic modes of being – demonstrate a love of knowledge that rightly earns the title "virtue."

CHAPTER 6

Rethinking Being and Time *as a Resource for Feminist Philosophy*

Charlotte Knowles

To say that the feminist reception of Heidegger's thought has been lukewarm would be an understatement. Even the introduction to the volume of essays *Feminist Interpretations of Martin Heidegger* opens with the lines: '[o]ne might wonder how Heidegger could be useful to feminist theory, given that he was not primarily a political thinker. Nor was he *explicitly* concerned with social ontology, contemporary issues of sexual identity, moral epistemology, or social ethics' (Huntington 2001, 1). Among his more sympathetic commentators, one still has to go to great lengths to explain why a feminist appropriation of Heidegger is not only useful but also feasible. In many ways, these reactions are understandable. There appear to be multiple barriers. Firstly, Heidegger says very little about questions of gender and sexuality.[1] Although as Derrida (1983, 67) observes, this silence is *itself* worthy of investigation. Secondly, as Bartky (1970, 369) asserted in the 1970s, Heidegger's thought is 'far too vacuous and abstract to serve the needs of any radical world-renewing project'. However, one cannot straightforwardly argue that his concerns are irrelevant to feminist philosophy, given that Heidegger's work touches on freedom, the complexity of the social world, technology, nature, and art – all themes over which much feminist ink has been spilt. A third and more significant factor may be his texts themselves. Dense, complex, and employing a distinctive vocabulary, these works can, at first blush, appear impenetrable and even incomprehensible to the untrained or unwilling reader.[2] Taken together, Heidegger's lack of attention to issues of gender and sexuality, his initially obscure and ambiguous writing style, the regular denouncements of his work from within and outside of feminist philosophy, and his much-discussed affiliation with the Nazi

---

[1] *The Metaphysical Foundations of Logic* is a notable exception.
[2] See Carnap's (1932) infamous dismissal of Heidegger's work.

Party,[3] have until recently rendered him and his work a largely 'no go' area for feminist scholars.

Where feminist engagement does exist, it tends to critique his philosophy, levelling some of the charges made above (Chanter 2001; Caputo 2001; Nagel 2001); or if a more extended, positive 'appropriation' of his ideas is undertaken, it usually concerns his later work, focusing on the themes of language, nature, and art (Graybeal 1990; Bigwood 1993). Nevertheless, there is a small body of literature that looks not to critique Heidegger from a feminist viewpoint, but to explore what a Heideggerean perspective can contribute to feminist theory. Within this domain, one finds works which analyse Heidegger's influence on key feminist scholars, most notably Hannah Arendt and Simone de Beauvoir (Bernasconi 2002; Gothlin 2003; Bauer 2006; Knowles 2019; Garcia 2021), and work that openly makes the case for Heidegger's early philosophy as a resource for feminists, through analyses of the potential of concepts such as Dasein, *das Man*, (in)authenticity, and Being-with, to enhance feminist projects (Holland 2001; Leland 2001; Bauer 2006; Guenther 2008; Freeman 2011; Knowles 2022). It is within this latter camp that this chapter aims to contribute, defending the idea that *Being and Time* is a fruitful and underused resource for feminist philosophy, and that the structural analysis of Dasein Heidegger offers in *Being and Time* is ripe for feminist appropriation. The condition of such an appropriation, however, is to take seriously the criticisms feminists have levelled at his work and show how they can be addressed.

Accordingly, this chapter is structured around three interrelated feminist objections to Heidegger's thought. Firstly, that the analytic of Dasein is the analysis of an exemplary masculine subject; secondly, that Heidegger neutralises gender at an ontological level; and thirdly, that authentic modes of existence involve separating oneself from the social world. I treat each of these objections in turn. I begin in Section 6.1 by arguing that the analytic of Dasein should not be seen as the elaboration of an implicitly masculine exemplar, but rather that it is the articulation of a structural essence and, approached in these terms, we can see how feminist philosophers can and *have* put this structural essence to work. In Section 6.2, I argue that far from erasing the issue of gender at an ontological level, Heidegger's

---

[3] As O'Brien (2010) argues, Heidegger's involvement with the Nazi Party and its relation to his own philosophy is a complex issue. It therefore cannot be dealt with quickly or easily. Whilst I am mindful of the issue when exploring the feminist possibilities of Heidegger's thought, I do not explicitly address it in this chapter.

Rethinking Being and Time 105

understanding of Dasein's neutrality speaks to an anti-essentialist critique of binary gender that has much in common with contemporary feminist work on the multiplicity and fluidity of gender. In Section 6.3, I offer an interpretation of authenticity as a form of genuine self-understanding. I argue that, grasped as such, authenticity can be understood to have much in common with Bartky's (1990) notion of developing a 'feminist consciousness', and can be read as a means by which to critique and transform role-based relations and 'inauthentic' understandings prescribed by *das Man*. By demonstrating how these three common objections can be addressed, I aim to show that far from being inimical to feminist theorising, *Being and Time* is a fruitful resource.

6.1 Feminists Critique Heidegger: Dasein as Implicitly Male

Being and Time is structured around an analysis of Dasein, Heidegger's term for the human being and the human way of Being. The text 'lay[s] bare' the 'fundamental structures' of Dasein's existence so as to clarify the structural features that constitute our distinctive human mode of existence (*BT* 65/40). Among these fundamental structures are Being-in-the-World, articulated in terms of 'disclosedness' and the tripartite relation between mood, understanding, and discourse; Being-with-Others, an understanding of human agents not as isolated beings, but as fundamentally bound up with others at an existential level; and 'mineness', the idea that Dasein is always 'mine to be in one way or another', namely, in the modes of authenticity or inauthenticity (*BT* 68/42). Heidegger's analytic thus seeks to lay bare the distinctive and fundamental features of human existence *as such*, sketching a picture of human existence that is designed to apply universally.

This kind of universal project is one of which feminist philosophers have often been suspicious. Drawing on the work of Luce Irigaray, Chanter (1995, 140) puts the point thus: 'philosophy took itself to be neither male nor female. It assumed the neutrality of its discourse precisely because there was never any reason to suspect that its discourse could be other than it was'. The primary feminist critique levelled at the analytic of Dasein in *Being and Time* stems from this worry. As Chanter (2001, 74) puts it, 'Heidegger's ontology has pretentions to a neutrality and universality that I do not believe it can sustain'. She continues,

> Heidegger['s] methodology rules out in advance any serious consideration of significant differences between individuals (whether those differences are

> specified in terms of gender, race, class, ethnicity, sexuality, or some other culturally loaded difference). This characteristic of his methodology leads him to posit, almost by default, a culturally specific version of Dasein that he takes to be exemplary, but whose exemplarity is never made available for critical interrogation. (Chanter 2001, 74)

According to Chanter, Heidegger's attempt to sketch a universal human subject obscures not only sexual difference, but human difference as such. Given that feminist philosophies are united in their aim to end gender hierarchy, making gender difference as well as considerations of race, class, and sexuality unthinkable within his ontology, does indeed seem like a significant barrier to any appropriation of Heidegger's philosophy for feminist ends. In Chanter's eyes, Heidegger does not furnish us with the outlines of a universal human subject, but a culturally specific, white, middle-class, *masculine* subject. We find a similar objection levelled at the project of classical phenomenology and its methodologies by Sandra Bartky:

> I found the project of classical phenomenology, namely, the analysis of the *a priori* and necessary structures of any possible consciousness, quite useless for my purposes. It was not any possible consciousness I was after, certainly not the 'structures' in consciousness of a subject so 'pure' as to be elevated above the 'mere' determinants of gender and history. (Bartky 1990, 1–2)

Bartky's comments echo some of Chanter's concerns regarding the universal analysis of human existence offered by classical phenomenologists, and the way such a project may obscure the investigation of a specifically feminine subject. But Bartky's critique of this classical project also contains a first response to Chanter's objection.

6.1.1 Universal Exemplars vs Universal Structures

Where Chanter sees Heidegger as offering an 'exemplar' of the ideal human subject, Bartky understands classical phenomenologists, like Heidegger, to be sketching the 'necessary structures' of any possible subject. To offer an exemplar is to undertake a detailed analysis of one particular subject and hold it up as the subject *par excellence*, showing how it embodies the essence of what it is to be a subject. By contrast, to sketch the necessary structures of any possible subject is to attempt to think across various subjects, to dig down beyond the particularities, and to identify the underlying structures that shape and determine the human way of Being as such. If one offers an exemplar, those of us who do not fit the model are seen to be deficient in some way, or otherwise we must suppress those elements of ourselves that do not cohere with the exemplar in order to be understood as legitimate subjects (Caldwell 2002, 20–21). However, if one seeks the necessary structures of any human subject, finding subjects who do not embody the structures that have been identified as universal, should not involve seeing such *subjects* as deficient, rather a deficiency is revealed in what has been positioned as universal.[4] As I see it, Heidegger's ontology seeks to offer not an exemplary human subject, against which all other subjects should be measured. Rather, what he provides is a structural essence of human existence that can be instantiated in various different ways.[5]

This project is attested to by the centrality of the ontic/ontological distinction in *Being and Time*. Heidegger understands himself to be undertaking an ontological analysis of Dasein, or, as he also terms it, an '*existential analytic of Dasein*' (*BT* 34/13), 'existential' being the term for an ontological analysis when it pertains to Dasein's existence. The existential analysis of Dasein seeks to get clarity about the deep, universal structures of Dasein's existence. These are features that are common to all Dasein as a way of Being, regardless of the specific ontical or '*existentiell*' content of the existence of any particular Dasein. Ontical facts may affect the particular way Dasein encounters the world, but they nevertheless rely upon and reflect the fundamental ontological structures of Dasein's existence, which make these ways of Being-in and encountering the world possible. Dasein is not primarily an entity. Although we can talk ontically about Dasein in the way this mode of existence is instantiated in different human beings, 'the ontological analytic of this entity always requires that existentiality be considered beforehand' (*BT* 33/13). Which is to say, Heidegger is aiming to offer something more fundamental than an exemplar of Dasein. He wants to uncover Dasein as a way of Being *as such*. Indeed, he is critical of investigations that focus specifically on exemplars, because they often conceal what is more fundamental.[6] If we read the project of classical phenomenology – and Heidegger's project in particular – as something

---

[4] Or at least a much stronger argument will be needed for why these subjects count as deficient, rather than threatening the project itself.
[5] I am indebted to Fernandez (2022) for explicitly articulating this distinction between two approaches to phenomenology: the distinction between focusing on exemplars vs what he calls a 'schematic' or what I call a structural approach.
[6] See Heidegger's discussion of epistemology, which focuses on knowing as an exemplary mode of Being-in-the-world (*BT* 86–90/59–62). Focusing on 'knowing' as our primary relation to the world conceals the more fundamental way we are *in* and related to the world, which makes such an epistemic relation to the world possible.

that seeks to articulate a *structural essence* of human existence, one that can be instantiated in various different ways (albeit ways he does not discuss), rather than offering an *exemplary* model of the human agent, some of Chanter's concerns fall away.

Both Chanter and Bartky object that Heidegger ignores the concrete realities of our particular existence, but if we understand Heidegger's project as seeking to offer a structural analysis of Dasein's Being, we can see why such an objection is misplaced. Although Heidegger offers an analysis of the human agent as Dasein, he does so in order to reach his ultimate aim: an understanding of the meaning of Being (and not just the Being of us as human agents). The analytic of Dasein's 'limits are thus determined. It cannot attempt to provide a complete ontology of Dasein' (*BT* 38/17) because 'the analytic of Dasein remains wholly oriented towards the guiding task of working out the question of Being' (*BT* 38/17). The elision of concrete differences is thus not an oversight but a deliberate strategy.

However, one could still protest that in order to understand human existence, we need to attend to differences such as race, gender, class, and so on, that are so central to our lives. Does Heidegger's ontology rule out any consideration of difference? I think not. Although Heidegger is very clear that he does not want to provide an 'anthropology' (*BT* 37/16, 38/17, 71ff/45ff), which would involve attending to and elaborating concrete features at the level of 'ontic' analysis – that is at the level of 'beings' – he does not see his project as incompatible with such an analysis. As he puts it,

> The existential analytic of Dasein comes before any psychology or anthropology, and certainly before any biology. *While these too are ways in which Dasein can be investigated*, we can define the theme of our analytic with greater precision if we distinguish it from these. (*BT* 71/45; my emphasis)

We can understand the ontology of *Being and Time* as providing a *framework* with which any ontic study of Dasein can take place.[7] Which is to say, Heidegger's project of fundamental ontology illuminates the structural features of human existence that must be in place such that we can be-in the world in the way that we are. This is a project that is undertaken without providing the analysis of any particular subject. Dasein is not an exemplar, Dasein is only an articulation of the

---

[7] An explicit example of this use of Heidegger's ontology can be found in the work of Køster and Fernandez (2021), which draws on Heidegger to outline a program for phenomenologically guided qualitative research.

fundamental structures of human existence: temporality, intentionality, Being-in-the-world, and so on. It is in this sense that Heidegger's project can be understood as offering what I refer to above as a 'structural essence' of Dasein.

6.1.2 Dasein's Structural Essence and Feminist Analyses

A structural essence can be filled out in many different ways. It does not tell us what Dasein is *like*, or what Dasein *is*, as something fixed and static. This is where some of the complexity lies in interpreting what kind of picture of human existence Heidegger is offering. In *Being and Time*, Heidegger seems to be both resisting essentialist metaphysics at the same time as offering something akin to an essence of Dasein – the fundamental features or structures that make Dasein distinctive as a way of Being. The analysis Heidegger offers in *Being and Time* is not simply an alternative, for example, to Aristotle's definition of man as a rational animal (*BT* 47/25). Such a definitional project remains confined within a substance ontology, bound by inappropriate conceptions of Dasein as a thing in which certain properties inhere (*BT* 32/11–12, 73). Dasein is not fundamentally a thing or a subject with certain properties that make it what it is. Rather, 'Dasein *is* its possibility' (*BT* 68/42). Dasein has no fixed essence, 'the essence of Dasein lies in its existence' (*BT* 67/42). As Dahlstrom (2013, 65) argues, Heidegger is sceptical of any traditional notion of essence as '*essentia*'. In a traditional sense, then, Heidegger offers an anti-essentialist picture of the human agent. However, there are nevertheless certain 'structural' features that must be in place such that Dasein can *be* its possibility.

Now one might still object that these structures themselves are marked by male bias and are culturally and situationally specific, but this seems like a much harder task. Indeed, many of the structures Heidegger identifies seem to have much in common with the socio-relational picture of the self offered by feminist philosophers and theorists of relational autonomy. The existentially co-constitutive relation between Dasein and world (*BT* 445/396; *HCT* 202), the relational nature of Dasein's existence articulated in Being-with-Others (*BT* 162/124–125), and the fundamentally social nature of Dasein's existence expressed in the idea that *das Man* is an 'essential *existentiale*' (*BT* 168/130) can be read as not only compatible with feminist understandings of the self, but as useful and complementary resources for furthering such a socio-relational picture (Freeman 2011).

If we understand Heidegger's philosophical project as offering only a structural essence, we can see more clearly how feminist philosophers can and *have* put his insights to work. Although Bartky argues at the outset of *Femininity and Domination* that she found the project of classical phenomenology 'quite useless' for her purposes, later in the text she demonstrates precisely how classical phenomenological work – such as Heidegger's – can be employed for feminist ends. In the chapter 'Shame and Gender', Bartky draws directly on Heidegger's understanding of mood as an *existentiale* of Dasein. For Heidegger, moods are not fleeting emotions or subjective psychological states. They are what attune us to the world and enable us to be in relation to it (*BT* 176/137). Moods are necessary for our Being-in-the-world, they are a pervasive aspect of our existence, 'we are never free of moods' (*BT* 175/136), and they play a key role in disclosing our situation and the specific way we are 'in' the world (*BT* 174–175/135–136). In this respect, moods and Dasein's fundamental attunement to the world can be understood as a central aspect of Dasein's structural essence.

In 'Shame and Gender', Bartky takes these understandings of the structural and foundational nature of moods for human existence and demonstrates how these insights can be used to illuminate the concrete situation of her female students who, she argues, are attuned to themselves and their situation through a mood of shame.[8] This gendered shame, Bartky (1990, 85) argues, is 'a profound mode of disclosure both of self and situation', affecting how the students understand themselves, their educational situation, and their relation to their peers. She describes how shame affects their embodiment and their comportment in the classroom (Bartky 1990, 88–90), and demonstrates how the Heideggerean concept of mood does better than the understanding of moods we find in moral psychology or works of political philosophy for illuminating what it is to be a woman in the world (Bartky 1990, 85). As she puts it, 'the shame of some of these women was not a discrete occurrence, but a perpetual attunement, the pervasive affective taste of a life' (Bartky 1990, 96).

Far from obscuring the specificities of our concrete existences, Bartky's (1990, 92) text demonstrates how, approaching *Being and Time* as offering a structural essence of human existence – even if such an understanding is only implicit in her analysis – enables the analytic of Dasein to be put to work to illuminate the concrete situations of women and other minoritised

---

[8] I focus here on Bartky's text as just one example of the uses feminist philosophers have made of the structural essence of Dasein. For other examples, see Beauvoir ([1949]2011) on '*mit sein*', as well as my own work which draws on Heidegger's ontology to illuminate how women can be complicit in their own unfreedom (Knowles 2019, 2021a, and 2022), and how 'disclosedness' can be employed to illuminate what it is to give testimony on gendered violence (Knowles 2021b).

groups. Rather than 'rul[ing] out in advance any serious consideration of significant differences between individuals' as Chanter claims, we can observe these differences in the varying ways the fundamental structures of Dasein's existence are instantiated by different individuals and groups. If, for example, we recognise the fundamental role of moods in human existence, we can then proceed to investigate which moods more commonly characterise certain groups (Bartky 1990, 84); how this affects the ways of Being-in-the-world of such groups, directing self-understandings and relations to others (Sedgwick 2003, 37); and how and why the mood of shame often attaches to minoritised groups (Ahmed 2004, 106). Although Heidegger does not offer this particularist analysis himself, his work is not incompatible with such projects. His analytic includes the tools and terminology to make such distinctions in the way he encourages us to think about different modes of existence (*BT* 68/42–43). That is, the different ways in which the fundamental ontological structures of our existence can be instantiated in various ways at the ontic, concrete level of analysis.

6.2 Approaching Gender Through a Heideggerean Lens: Dasein's Neutrality

So far, I have focused my arguments primarily on establishing that there is nothing that immediately rules out Heidegger's ontology for appropriation by feminist scholars. I have also highlighted that some of his insights into the fundamental structures that enable us to exist as the beings that we are, can and *have* been employed to understand women's situation. But one might still wonder whether there is anything distinctive in Heidegger's ontology that means it is not only compatible with feminist projects but actively useful for them. This is the question to which I now turn.

A key concern of feminist philosophy is how to do justice to the idea that gender is central to our sense of ourselves, to social life, and our ways of Being-in-the-world, without slipping into gender essentialism: the idea that maintaining this claim commits us to identifying a certain property, trait, or characteristic that all women share and that grounds our membership in a particular gendered group.[9] Efforts to identify such a property have historically been critiqued by feminist scholars both on the basis that such arguments have traditionally been used to exclude women from certain fields by identifying a supposedly fundamental trait that renders

---

[9] For a recent attempt to resolve this issue, see Witt (2011).

women unsuitable for certain tasks, domains, and ways of thinking (Lloyd 1993), as well as being challenged on the basis of intersectional concerns, and the argument that there is no one unifying property, trait, or characteristic that all women share, given the various ways women are positioned in relation to other identity categories such as race, sexuality, disability, and class (hooks 1984; Stone 2004).

We have already seen that Heidegger's ontology in *Being and Time* will also be critical of this kind of essentialist project. As Aho (2009, 55) puts it, 'because Heidegger's ontology undermines traditional substance ontology, it is critical towards the essentialist category "sex"'. To endorse a Heideggerean ontology is to reject biological gender essentialism because 'for Heidegger, human beings should not be interpreted fundamentally in terms of the fixed objective "presence" of body parts' (Aho 2009, 55). Heidegger makes it clear that the 'neutrality' of the term 'Dasein' is not coincidental, but is 'essential, because the interpretation of this being must be carried out prior to every factual concretion' (*MFL* 136). Every claim Heidegger makes about Dasein is meant to be a claim that pertains to all people, regardless of factical matters such as gender, race, class, sexuality, nationality, etc. Heidegger further clarifies Dasein's neutrality in relation to gender and sexual difference by arguing that 'the term "man" was not used for that being which is the theme of the analysis. Instead, the neutral term Dasein was chosen ... [t]his neutrality also indicates that Dasein is neither of the two sexes' (*MFL* 136). In many ways, this conscious neutrality is laudable and sits in stark contrast to the work of other classical scholars such as Rousseau, Kant, and Hegel who explicitly comment on the differences between the sexes and offer a picture of the female subject as not fully human, in the way she exists primarily as the complement to man (Lloyd 1993).

However, appeals to neutrality (re)introduce the worries we have seen articulated by Chanter and Bartky. We may be concerned that the assertion of neutrality at an ontological level goes too far in ruling out considerations of gender and sex *per se*, thus trivialising the effects they have on the way human agents are in, and opened onto, the world. Rosalyn Diprose, for example, argues that to retreat into neutrality is to do a disservice to women, as it obscures their difference and attempts to subsume them under a male norm (Diprose 1994, 71). She argues that positing neutrality in discussions of gender ignores the oppression suffered by women in a society founded upon gender hierarchy (Diprose 1994, 65). Moreover, she suggests that such a move does women a further injustice by suggesting they must deny the harm done to them and embrace a system of neutrality

(Diprose 1994, 71). Although neutralising sex and gender at an ontological level might guard against problematic forms of gender essentialism, one might worry that such a move trivialises these issues and fails to appreciate the importance of gender for our existence. In our brief discussion of Bartky's work, we have already seen one example of how the ontological structures of Dasein can be examined in their concrete, ontic instantiations in order to illuminate the everyday situation of women. But does the ontological neutrality of Dasein ultimately jeopardise this project?

6.2.1 Gender Neutrality, but Not As We Know It

Although Diprose's comments may bear weight with regard to accounts which attempt to replace considerations of difference with a 'faulty neutrality' (Scott 1988, 39), I argue that Heidegger's understanding of neutrality in fact aids the feminist project by providing a basis on which to critique binary notions of gender, whilst doing justice to the idea that gender is a central aspect of our existence.

In his essay '*Geschlecht*', Derrida argues that Heidegger neutralises gender as a duality, but not the possibility of gender as an ontological constituent of Dasein. Heidegger himself explicitly states that neutrality 'is neither of the two sexes. But [that] here sexlessness is not the indifference of an empty void' (*MFL* 136). Derrida takes this to mean that neutrality is not to be interpreted in terms of sexlessness at all. Owing to Heidegger's characterisation of neutrality as a 'primordial positivity and potency' (*MFL* 137), neutrality can instead be understood as a 'pre-differential, rather than a pre-dual, sexuality' (Derrida 1983, 72). Following Heidegger's lead, Derrida argues that the gender neutrality of Dasein should be understood in terms of dispersion,[10] dissemination, and multiplication rather than as a 'unitary, homogenous, or undifferentiated' whole which is then divided into the two sexed instantiations of Dasein one finds in the world (Derrida 1983, 72). This understanding of gender has much in common with post-structuralist accounts found in the work of thinkers like Judith Butler who emphasise the 'fluid possibilities of such [gender] categories once they are no longer linked causally or expressively to the presumed fixity of sex' (Butler 1999, 128). Similarly, Derrida (1983)

---

[10] Derrida (1983, 71) claims that dispersion is not only the clarification of an inauthentic way of Being but is 'marked *twice*, as a general structure of Dasein and as a mode of inauthenticity'. *Zerstreuung* as a general structure of Dasein's Being is said to be an 'originary dispersion', which grounds Dasein's ability to concern itself with a multiplicity of objects (Derrida 1983, 65–66).

takes the 'positivity' Heidegger associates with neutrality to mean that it is 'sexual division itself which leads to negativity' (72). He concludes that Heidegger's ontology neutralises 'less sexuality itself than the "generic" mark of sexual difference, belonging to one of *two* sexes' (Derrida 1983, 82). Interpreted in this way, we can see that Heidegger's neutrality doesn't erase considerations of gender as a fundamental aspect of our existence, rather what it neutralises is thinking of gender or sexual difference in binary terms.

Far from being an obstacle to a feminist appropriation of Heidegger's work, the neutrality of Dasein's Being can function as an enabling factor for feminist critique. As hooks (1984, 29) argues, 'either/or dualistic thinking ... is the central ideological component of all systems of domination in Western society'. If Dasein is fundamentally neutral at an ontological level, in the way described above, then we can both recognise the importance of gender to our existence, while being critical of binary and essentialist ideologies and the social forms they generate. Any ontic social organisation, such as patriarchy, that relies on fixed, binary, oppositional understandings of sex and gender can be critiqued on the basis that such understandings and social arrangements fail to reflect Dasein's ontological neutrality. Which is to say, Dasein's ontological neutrality understood in terms of possibility, dispersion, and multiplicity, represents an alternative source of intelligibility regarding how we are gendered, to the binary understandings proliferated at the ontic level in the social world of *das Man*.

Of course, Heidegger does not make these arguments himself, but his ontology lends itself to these conclusions in the way he speaks of our inauthentic existence in *das Man* 'obscur[ing]' and 'cover[ing] up' more genuine understandings of ourselves and the world (*BT* 165/127). Applying these insights in relation to gender means that we can highlight the way the public understandings of gender found in *das Man* often 'level down' and 'cover up' (*BT* 165/127) more primordial understandings of our gender neutrality, which are not characterised by an 'empty void', but by multiplicity and possibility. *Das Man* is 'insensitive to every difference of level and of genuineness' (*BT* 165/127), and so replaces more nuanced, complex understandings of our gendered Being with simplistic binary understandings of gender, which 'get passed off as something familiar and accessible to everyone' (*BT* 165/127). Developing the ontic implications of Heidegger's ontological analysis in this way means calling into question binary understandings of gender and claims that women are *essentially* more predisposed to certain tasks, ways of thinking, or Being-in-the-world. Rather than obscuring the plight of women, then, the ontological neutrality of Dasein provides an impetus to critique and transform women's concrete situation so that it more accurately reflects what we are at an ontological level, and so that we can all live more authentically as Dasein.

6.3 Authenticity and Self-Understanding: A Project of Social Critique

Heidegger's conception of authenticity is often critiqued on similar grounds to those noted above: that it is the articulation of a male norm, an agent set up in a 'masculinist, agonistic game where a solitary (heroic) player makes his decisive move in silence in order to exist authentically' (Nagel 2001, 296). Such analyses have led feminist commentators to argue that authenticity is too individualistic, reflecting masculine norms of independence and autonomy at the expense of taking seriously the relations we have with other people (Chanter 2001; Nagel 2001). As I have argued elsewhere (Knowles 2017), this asocial understanding of authenticity cannot be accurate given that Being-with and *das Man* are both fundamental *existentiales*. To read authenticity through the lens of an individualistic existentialism and an idea of radical freedom is, as Guignon (1993, 268) notes, a mistake. However, the motivations for this kind of analysis are understandable given the way Heidegger describes Dasein's Being in the social world in terms of a situation where a 'dictatorship of *das Man* is unfolded' (*BT* 164/126) and Dasein stands 'in subjection to Others' (*BT* 164/126). From these statements, it is clear to see why one might think authenticity involves escaping such a social situation and striking out on one's own.

However, although authenticity may involve 'clearing away [the] concealments and obscurities' that plague us in inauthentic modes of existence, a better way of making sense of both the fundamentally social nature of our existence (*BT* 167/129) and the possibility of authentic modes of Being, I argue, is to interpret authenticity as a mode of Being in which we understand ourselves more clearly as Dasein.[11] This interpretation fits better with the logic of Heidegger's ontology and enables us to see more clearly the feminist potential in this concept. On this reading, becoming authentic does not mean acceding to an individualistic male

---

[11] This interpretation finds support in passages such as 'the meaning of Dasein's Being is not something that is other than and "outside of" itself, but is the self-understanding Dasein itself' (*BT* 372/325).

norm, or separating oneself from others and the social world. Nor does it mean ignoring or obscuring difference. Rather, it entails better understanding ourselves, the social world, and the barriers that exist for living out an ontological understanding of ourselves as free possibility (*BT* 232/286), by taking up and working out our Being as an 'issue' for us (*BT* 32/12), rather than turning away from this.

6.3.1 *Authentic and Inauthentic Modes of Being*

Although it is not the case that inauthentic Dasein is somehow not yet Dasein, or that one only becomes Dasein when one is authentic, it is the case that authentic Dasein manifests its Being as Dasein in a more explicit way than inauthentic Dasein. This is because authentic Dasein grasps itself more explicitly as Dasein.[12] This does not mean that authenticity is simply a matter of 'knowing' my Being has a certain structure. Rather, it is a matter of manifesting an understanding of my Being in my way of Being. Authenticity is the extent to which I have become 'transparent' to myself. 'Transparency', Heidegger argues, is 'the sight which is related primarily and on the whole to existence' (*BT* 186/146). That is, it is a way of understanding ourselves that gets to the heart of what we fundamentally are. Or, in the words of Beatrice Han-Pile, 'transparency is Dasein's pre-reflective grasp of its own ontological make-up' (Han-Pile 2013, 303). In authentic modes of Being, Dasein is more transparent to itself and manifests this in its way of Being, whereas in inauthentic modes of Being, Dasein's understanding of itself is opaque (*BT* 187/146–147).

Understood in this way, to be authentic means to understand oneself in terms of the structural essence outlined above: Being-in-the-world, temporality, intentionality, being in a mood, Being-with-Others, and so on. But grasping ourselves as Dasein in these terms also means grasping that we cannot speak of our essence in any more substantial terms than these because, as we have seen, 'the essence of Dasein lies in its existence' (*BT* 67/42). There is no pre-ordained way Dasein should be, no specific possibility upon which Dasein should embark simply in virtue of being Dasein. Rather, Dasein is essentially a 'not-yet', it is characterised by possibility and could always be other than it currently is (*BT* 185–186/145–146). Taken in a feminist context, we can see how this notion of authenticity builds on what was said at the end of Section 6.2. Authenticity, as an alternative and more

---

[12] Heidegger argues that inauthentic Dasein misunderstands its own nature, 'existing primarily in forgetfulness of its own self' (*BP* 170).

genuine understanding of ourselves, can act as a basis for critiquing the limited and limiting self-understandings prescribed to women by the *das Man* of everyday patriarchal social contexts.[13]

As I have argued elsewhere (Knowles 2017), the everyday world of *das Man* Heidegger describes in *Being and Time* is not inherently inauthentic, although Heidegger elaborates it in its inauthentic form. It is not that sociality *as such* is constitutive of inauthentic ways of Being, but rather that certain forms of social life can lead to inauthenticity because of the way they 'disburden' Dasein of the responsibility of understanding itself and its world (*BT* 165/128). In such modes, Dasein primarily grasps itself and its world in terms of 'public' understandings by which 'everything gets obscured, and what has thus been covered up gets passed off as something familiar and accessible to everyone' (*BT* 165/127). Such inauthentic modes of Being-in and understanding the world are characterised by an attunement in which Dasein becomes 'stubborn [*Versteifung*] about the existence one has achieved' (*BT* 308/264, translation modified). This stubbornness, as Blattner (2013, 326) argues, leads to a misinterpretation, namely, 'taking the possibilities that the public insists upon as being somehow unchallengeable'. Accordingly, in inauthentic modes of Being, Dasein's more primordial and authentic understanding of itself in terms of possibility and a 'not-yet' is covered up.

Whereas to understand oneself authentically is to understand oneself in terms of 'possibilities as possibilities' (*BT* 185/145), to grasp oneself inauthentically is to grasp oneself in terms of the fixity of the public, levelled down, socially available self-understandings and social roles made available by *das Man* (*BT* 165/127–128). As Schmid (2017, 264) argues, to understand oneself primarily in terms of social roles involves 'a basic self-misapprehension, or self-misunderstanding', as 'being oneself [i.e. being authentic] and playing a social role are in a fundamental tension with each other'. Whereas social roles provide us with fixed conventions, rules, and norms, which can direct one's behaviour and tell us who we are and how we should live, to grasp oneself authentically as Dasein is to recognise that there are 'no norms binding on Dasein qua Dasein'

---

[13] Authenticity can function in this way because it is a possibility we always carry with us. More authentic understandings of ourselves are 'uncovered' rather than created (*BT* 167/129). In contrast to some dominant interpretations, I do not see authentic and inauthentic modes of existence as mutually exclusive. Rather, I follow Lewis (2005, 15) in understanding Dasein as existing on a spectrum, 'stretched between' the poles of inauthenticity and authenticity, and thus always characterised by both, albeit in varying degrees. For more on this point, see Knowles (2017).

(Golob 2014, 239), and thus that there is nothing that can ultimately determine who we are and how we should live our lives.

This analysis does not entail that becoming authentic means jettisoning all role-based self-understandings, but it does involve recognising their contingency and that they cannot be totalising with regard to our existence.[14] Such an insight enables us to recognise that there is always a distance between who we are and the social roles we perform. As Lear (2011, 50) puts it, 'we do not fit without remainder into socially available practical identities', a fact which can help make sense of the discomfort we can feel with regard to gender- and social role-based understandings that are supposed to say something about who we fundamentally are, but that seem to be at odds with our sense of ourselves. For example, in her book *Gender Outlaw,* Kate Bornstein writes: 'I didn't feel like I was the gender I'd been assigned. I felt there was something wrong with me, something sick and twisted inside me, something very very bad about me' (Bornstein 1994, 12). One way of explaining this feeling in Heideggerian terms is to note the tension between authentic self-understandings, which manifest in terms of possibility and a lack of fixity, and the static categorisations made available for self-understanding in our social contexts. One could argue that what Bornstein is articulating here in Heideggerian terms is a confrontation with the anxiety one feels when one encounters the 'break down' and insufficiency of publicly available social understandings for capturing who we are (*BT* 232/187–188). Moreover, the Heideggerian explanation situates the deficiency not in Bornstein herself, but in the socially available self-understandings for capturing who and how she is. This distinction between authentic and inauthentic self-understanding can thus not only serve a descriptive and explanatory function but also a therapeutic one.

6.3.2 *The Feminist Credentials of Authentic Self-Understandings*

The idea that who and what we fundamentally are is possibility, is an insight Heidegger shares with feminist philosophers. In *The Second Sex,* Beauvoir argues for the importance of centring possibility in understandings of woman:

> Woman is not a fixed reality but a becoming; she has to be compared with man in her becoming; that is, her possibilities have to be defined: what

---

[14] Mulhall ([1996] 2005, 73) makes a similar point: '[a]uthenticity is a matter of the way in which one relates to one's roles, not a rejection of any and all roles'.

skews the issues so much is that she is being reduced to what she was, to what she is today. (Beauvoir[1949] 2011, 45–46)

For Heidegger, as for Beauvoir, the human agent is not a being, but a *becoming* (*BT* 287/243), defined by possibility and a 'not-yet'. To understand oneself fundamentally in terms of possibility means being future-directed, recognising that things do not have to be as they currently are, which is a foundational tenet of any feminist philosophy that seeks women's liberation and an end to gender hierarchy.[15]

But the significance of possibility in relation to our self-understanding is not simply the recognition that things could be different, it also articulates a particular way of Being-in and relating to the world, that I argue is productive for feminist projects. In Heidegger's ontology, understanding is fundamentally bound up with existence. Understanding refers not only to something in my mind, but also to some practical way of Being-in-the-world: understanding is, Heidegger argues, 'a competence ... over Being as existing' (*BT* 183/143). This means that the way I understand myself affects the way I exist (*BT* 283/239), and the way I exist affects the way I understand myself (*BT* 385/336). Given this characterisation of understanding, becoming authentic and understanding oneself authentically cannot be something that happens in isolation from the world. Whereas Heidegger is often read as indicating that, in authentic modes of existence, we *extricate* ourselves from the social world, I argue that a change in my understanding is better understood as a change in the way I am in, and relate to, the world, and specifically the social world. Indeed, Heidegger argues that *'Authentic Being-one's-Self* does not rest upon an exceptional condition of the subject, a condition that has been detached from *das Man*; it is rather an existentiell modification of das Man – of das Man as an essential existentiale' (*BT* 168/130). Rather than an individualistic project of social escape, I argue that authenticity is more productively understood in line with the critical, but engaged relation to the world Bartky (1990, 11–22) describes in terms of developing a 'feminist consciousness'.

Like the move to more authentic modes of Being, developing a feminist consciousness involves not just a change in ways of *thinking*, but a change in ways of Being-in-the-world: 'the feminist changes her *behaviour*. She makes new friends; she responds differently to people and events ... [sometimes she alters] her whole style of life' (Bartky 1990, 11), and it is

---

[15] For Bartky (1990, 14), understanding that one's situation is not natural, inevitable, or inescapable, and instead grasping the possibility that it can be other than it is, is central to having a feminist consciousness.

a change precipitated by a new understanding of the social world. Specifically, 'social reality is revealed as *deceptive*' (Bartky 1990, 17). Similarly, as we have seen, authentic modes of existence involve 'clearing away concealments and obscurities [and] breaking up ... disguises' (*BT* 167/129), but this does not involve transcending the social world, it involves relating to it in a new way. Just as Bartky's feminist is 'no more aware of different things than other people; they are aware of the same things differently' (Bartky 1990, 14), in authentic modes of Being Dasein continues to appreciate *das Man*'s *existentiale* role in making possible shared intelligibility, but without regarding *das Man* as the ultimate source of intelligibility (Knowles 2017). We thus develop a new relation to the social world in which we rid ourselves of the stubborn, unquestioning, and distorting relation to public understandings that served to conceal rather than promote the understandings of ourselves in terms of possibility, and we ready ourselves for taking responsibility for who we are and how we live our lives.[16]

6.3.3 *Authenticity and Social Transformation*

Both authenticity and the development of a feminist consciousness involve coming to see new possibilities for inhabiting and relating to one's social context. For Bartky (1990, 21) this is an explicitly social process, involving feelings of 'solidarity' with others and the recognition of 'possibilities for liberating collective action'. As I shall argue, authenticity can also be understood in this way: as a mode of Being in which we not only endeavour to make changes for *ourselves*, but also help to bring about changes that enable us *all* to live more authentically as Dasein.

To discover myself as Dasein in authentic modes of Being is not only to make a discovery about my own existence, but about human existence *as such*. Authentic modes of existence not only direct Dasein towards its ownmost potentiality-for-Being, but 'makes Dasein, as Being-with, have some understanding of the potentiality-for-Being of Others' (*BT* 309/264). To discover oneself as Dasein is thus also to discover the other as Dasein and relate to them in a new way. This is indicated in Heidegger's discussion of solicitude and its different modes. In inauthentic modes, our care, like our inauthentic self-understanding, is directed only to what the other does – the roles they perform or the projects they are engaged in (*BT* 158/121–122). By contrast, in authentic modes, we are concerned with

---

[16] For more on this point, see Knowles (2021a).

'the existence of the Other' (*BT* 159/122), that is, the other as Dasein. Such a relation is described as 'liberat[ing]' because it does not dominate the other by defining them in terms of a fixed project or role (*BT* 159/122). Rather, it is a mode in which we relate to the other authentically, as someone with an existence – like ours – that is unfixed, undecided, and characterised by possibility. Whereas in inauthentic modes of Being-with, Dasein 'leaps in and dominates' the other, in authentic modes, Dasein 'leaps forth and liberates', 'free[ing] the Other in his freedom for himself' (*BT* 159/122).

As we have seen, for Heidegger, understanding cannot be separated from ways of Being-in-the-world, and thus, if Dasein understands the other *as Dasein* and hence as essentially free and undetermined, Dasein will not be able to engage in relations with others that do not reflect such an understanding of the other's existential freedom.[17] In authentic modes of Being, when Dasein has understood both itself and the other as Dasein, Dasein will be motivated (even if only implicitly) to seek out ways of Being-in-the-world and Being-with others that reflect the ontological possibility and freedom of Dasein, and work collectively to challenge those social forms that contradict, undermine, or cover up more authentic understandings of our fundamental existence.[18]

However, this is not to say that coming to recognise the social distortions and unjust concealments of contemporary social life automatically means being able to transform them. '[T]he possible does not exceed the real' (Beauvoir [1949] 2011, 270).[19] Whereas some situations may be too restrictive to allow women to manifest their authentic self-understanding in their way of Being, other situations may be fundamentally incompatible with realising oneself in authentic modes. Nevertheless, on my interpretation, we can see how the possibility of authenticity can be seen to arise as a result of our social and material conditions, rather than in abstraction from them. As Holland (2001, 37) argues, 'precisely the fact that women's [social] scripts are banal and ultimately unrewarding can sometimes create a revealing distance between an individual woman's consciousness and the larger social world in which she is immersed'. This implies that in some

---

[17] Dasein can still slip back into inauthentic modes of understanding and Being-with others, but when Dasein understands the other authentically as Dasein it will relate to (Be-with) the other authentically as Dasein.
[18] Leland (2001, 123–124) offers a similar picture of authenticity.
[19] Heidegger makes a similar point in his discussion of 'pseudo-understanding' and the idea that for genuine understanding there must be a certain 'match up' between the (self)understandings we project and the possibilities we have in the world (*HCT* 260).

cases it may be easier for women and minoritised groups to come to understand themselves more authentically than it is for men or those who occupy more privileged social positions. If women are more likely to feel dissatisfied with, and restricted by, their social roles, they may be more likely to be assailed by the anxious mood that can be engendered as the result of such dissatisfaction and that can, in turn – if self and social conditions allow[20] – engender more authentic ways of understanding and Being oneself (*BT* 230–234). Authenticity can thus be seen as inherently social because it is a possibility that arises out of our social and material conditions, and because it is one that involves engaging with and transforming these conditions so that we can all live more authentically as Dasein. Interpreted in this way, rather than the journey to authenticity being a 'masculinist game', it can be understood as something more accurately capturing what it is to develop a feminist consciousness. By highlighting these parallels, we can see how authenticity can be linked to 'struggles over social meanings' more broadly 'and as taking shape as part of a political practice' (Leland 2001, 124). Becoming authentic thus becomes a process of social critique, a way of Being-in and relating to the world that can precipitate social change.

6.4 Conclusion

In this chapter, I have endeavoured to refute three objections which are commonly identified as barriers to feminist appropriations of Heidegger's ontology in *Being and Time*. I have argued that rather than presenting an implicitly masculine exemplar of human existence that obscures difference and positions women's existence as 'deviant', Heidegger should be understood as offering a structural essence of human existence that can usefully be employed to illuminate women's ways of Being-in-the-world. I have suggested that the ontological neutrality of Dasein is not a way of making gender irrelevant at a fundamental level, but of challenging binary notions of sex and gender and offering a basis for developing a more fluid and multiplicitous understanding of these concepts. Finally, I have argued that authenticity is not an individualistic project that involves separating oneself from the social world, but rather that it can be understood as the basis for a liberatory understanding of the self in terms of possibility, which can in turn be used to critique the contingency of existing, oppressive social orders without ignoring the social and material challenges this involves.

[20] For more on this point, see Knowles (2019, 2021a, and 2022).

In offering this analysis I hope to have furthered the case that *Being and Time* can be understood as a productive resource for feminists, and to have indicated some of the directions in which in-roads may be made. In particular, we have seen the important role mood or affect plays within Heidegger's philosophy and how, by making connections with the work of thinkers like Bartky and Bornstein, we can draw out some of the political implications of this analysis. A focus on Heideggerean notions of affect through a social and political lens presents itself as a particularly fruitful avenue for future research, given the emerging body of literature on 'affective injustice'. Affective injustice names the 'injustice faced by someone specifically in their capacity as an affective being' (Archer and Mills 2019, 76), but the field is still relatively young and many key questions currently remain open: how should we evaluate people's affective lives? What is it for someone's affective life to go well or badly? And thus, how should we more precisely define affective injustice? (Gallegos 2021, 186). Given Heidegger's concern with mood as a key aspect of disclosedness, determining how we are opened on to or closed off from the world (*BT* 177/137–138), his philosophy is well placed to address many of these questions. Moreover, owing to the existential connection Heidegger identifies between affect and understanding (*BT* 182/142–143), a Heideggerean lens has the potential to fruitfully illuminate the relation between affective injustice and the more studied 'epistemic injustice' – how an agent can be harmed specifically in their role as a knower (Fricker 2007) – in a way that can enhance our understanding of both concepts. For example, a Heideggerean perspective could draw our attention to the role of affect in 'hermeneutical injustice', a central form of epistemic injustice in which an agent is deprived of the (epistemic) resources to make sense of their situation and communicate this to others (Fricker 2007, 158). As Heidegger argues, mood can close off our situation 'more stubbornly than any "not-perceiving"' (*BT* 175/136). His work thus draws our attention to the role that moods and our affective states can play in depriving us of certain understandings. By developing this line of thought, we may gain a deeper insight into the way affective injustice can function as a form of hermeneutical injustice, and how the social production of certain moods and affects can prevent agents from effectively understanding and being able to testify about their situation.[21] In pursuing the

---

[21] For more on this point see Knowles (2021b).

political potential of Heidegger's philosophy in ways such as these, we can thus not only see how notions like authenticity and anxiety can help illuminate a situation of social critique, but also how Heidegger's philosophy in *Being and Time* can be mobilised to enhance our understanding of some of the central issues of oppression and injustice with which contemporary feminist, social, and political philosophers are presently concerned.

CHAPTER 7

Authenticity, Truth, and Cultural Transformation
Aaron James Wendland

In Division Two of *Being and Time*, Heidegger tells us that we lead an authentic life when we take responsibility for our existence by making a series of identity-defining choices. According to the standard reading, Heidegger's account of authenticity amounts to an existentialist theory of human freedom.[1] Against this existentialist interpretation, John Haugeland reads Heidegger's account of authenticity as a key feature of Heidegger's fundamental ontology: that is, Heidegger's attempt to determine the meaning of being via an analysis of human beings or "Dasein." Haugeland's (2013, 202) argument is based on the idea that the self-understanding achieved when we adopt a particular way of life or "potentiality-for-being" involves understanding what it means for entities *to be* within that way of life or potentiality. Specifically, Haugeland (2013, 203) claims that taking responsibility for our existence entails getting the *being* of entities right. So again, Haugeland sees Heidegger's so-called existentialist account of human freedom as part of Heidegger's attempt to come to terms with the meaning of being through a study of human beings.

Haugeland's ontological reading of authenticity is based on the link he sees between three types of truth: ontic, ontological, and existential. Ontic truth refers to our comportment toward facts about entities. Ontological truth relates to the way facts about entities are presented to us via a disclosure of being, where "disclosure of being" means the practices, theories, ways of life, or potentialities via which the world is intelligible at a particular point in history. Finally, existential truth involves taking

---

[1] For a Nietzsche-inspired existentialist reading of authenticity, see Wolin (1990, 6–65). For a reading of authenticity as an attempt to secularize Kierkegaard's existentialist account of religious experience, see Dreyfus and Rubin's appendix to Dreyfus' *Being-in-the-World* (Dreyfus 1991, 283–340). For a textbook existentialist interpretation of authenticity, see Guignon and Pereboom's *Existentialism: Basic Writings* (Guignon and Pereboom 2001, 203–210).

responsibility for our existence by questioning and testing our practices, theories, ways of life, or potentialities against the facts. As Haugeland sees it, taking responsibility for our existence requires us to test our comportments against the factual truth about entities (ontic truth) that are presented to us through a particular way of life. If, however, we are unable to clear up any factual mistakes about entities that we happen to find, then we have to question and test the very way of life through which facts about entities are presented (ontological truth). And the fact that we can question and test our way of life is based on our ability to choose and adopt alternative ways of life (existential truth). This means taking responsibility for our existence entails the possibility of giving up our current way of life when it fails to meet the truth test, and on Haugeland's reading, cultural transformation and the movement of human history are based on the truth-seeking of authenticity.

Given the unorthodoxy of Haugeland's interpretation of authenticity, I begin this chapter with a detailed sketch of his position. Although I agree with Haugeland's general claim that Heidegger's existentialism is a key feature of Heidegger's fundamental ontology, I go on to argue that the details of Haugeland's interpretation are inconsistent. My objection is that if, as Haugeland maintains, entities are only intelligible through a particular disclosure of being, then it is incoherent for Haugeland to claim that those same entities can serve as an intelligible, disclosure-independent standard against which that disclosure can be truth-tested. And if no sense can be made of testing a disclosure against disclosure-independent entities, then no sense can be made of Haugeland's claim that authenticity entails testing and transforming a disclosure of being against disclosure-independent entities. To substantiate this objection, I analyze the case Haugeland makes for his position via an analogy with Kuhn. Specifically, I indicate Haugeland's commitment to intelligible, disclosure-independent entities in his account of paradigm shifts, but then I turn to Heidegger and Kuhn to show why Haugeland's commitment to intelligible, disclosure-independent entities is inconsistent with their views. Finally, I offer an alternative to Haugeland's truth-based account of authenticity and cultural transformation through a methodological interpretation of authenticity that is built on an ends-based ontological reading of Heidegger and Kuhn. Here I argue that taking responsibility for our existence explicitly exhibits the temporal horizon that is fundamental for all our purposive activities and the intelligible disclosure of entities, generally.

7.1 Haugeland's Truth-Based Account of Authenticity

In *Dasein Disclosed*, Haugeland reads Heidegger's so-called "existential concepts" – authenticity, anxiety, guilt, death, conscience, and resoluteness – as crucial features in Heidegger's attempt to come to terms with the meaning of being. Haugeland writes:

> *Everything* in *Being and Time* has to do with the question of being – and, with it, truth. The existential concepts are introduced for this reason and this reason only. Our task as readers is to understand how. (Haugeland 2013, 209)

The connection Haugeland (2013, 203, 199) sees between existentialism and the meaning of being can be traced back to the fact that our self-understanding incorporates an understanding of the being of entities and aspects of our world – "in knowing how to be me," as he puts it, "I must know how to deal with the entities amidst which I work and live" – so our self-understanding entails "getting the entities *themselves* right." This, for Haugeland, implies that when we take responsibility for our existence by choosing a particular way of life we take responsibility for the truth of entities as well. The basis for Haugeland's account is found in two passages where Heidegger connects authenticity to the most primordial phenomenon of truth. "*Authentic* disclosedness," Heidegger asserts,

> shows the phenomenon of the most primordial truth in the mode of authenticity. The most primordial, and indeed the most authentic, disclosedness in which Dasein, as a potentiality-for-being, can be, is the *truth of existence*. This becomes existentially and ontologically definite only in connection with the analysis of Dasein's authenticity. (*BT* 264/221)

And after examining human beings in their average everydayness in Division One of *Being and Time*, Heidegger begins Division Two by saying:

> *Our existential analysis of Dasein up till now cannot lay claim to primordiality.* Its for-having never included more than the *inauthentic* being of Dasein, and of Dasein as *less* than a *whole*. If the interpretation of Dasein's being is to become primordial as a foundation for working out the basic questions of ontology, then it must first have brought to light existentially the being of Dasein in its possibilities of *authenticity* and *totality*. (*BT* 276/233)

Identifying authenticity with the most primordial phenomenon of truth, for Haugeland, means that when we take responsibility for our existence, we not only take responsibility for the truth of our comportment toward entities, but also take responsibility for the truth of the practices, theories, ways of life, or disclosures of being through which we have access to entities. "Ontological truth," Haugeland (2013, 218) claims, "is beholden to *entities* – the very same entities as ontical truth is beholden to." And when confronted with "a failure of ontological truth," Haugeland (2013, 218) says, "the only responsible response (eventually) is to take it all back." Finally, Haugeland (2013, 188) argues that our ability to question, test, and take a disclosure of being back is based on our finitude, and this suggests that resolute being-towards-death is "the fulcrum of [Heidegger's] entire ontology."

Haugeland begins his reading of Division Two by defining several of Heidegger's key terms and illustrating how they relate to their traditional predecessors. "It is *definitive* of Dasein," Haugeland (2013, 190) writes, "that it is the entity that understands being, hence can comport itself towards entities *as entities*." *Entities* is Heidegger's term of art for "*everything* that there *is* – no more, no less" (Haugeland 2013, 189). And Haugeland is quick to point out that the class of entities is not reducible to "present-at-hand" or "Kantian" objects that can be known via theoretical judgments, such as the physical objects studied by physics, but also includes "ready-to-hand" entities, like tools and other kinds of equipment, and "existing" entities, such as Dasein. This means that all objects are entities, but not all entities are objects, so Haugeland (2013, 189) treats Heideggerian entities as a generalization of Kant's notion of objects. Similarly, Haugeland reads Heidegger's conception of *comportment* as a generalization of Kantian knowledge and then a further generalization of Husserl's idea of intentionality insofar as *comportment toward entities* includes not only knowledge of objects (Kant) and other cognitive attitudes like perception (Husserl), but also non-cognitive engagements with the world such as our skillful use of equipment and our fluid interactions with other human beings. Yet, on Heidegger's account, we are only able to comport ourselves toward physical objects, equipment, and other human beings *as* the entities that they are if we understand the *being* of those entities. "The *being* of entities," Haugeland (2013, 191) writes, "is that in terms of which they are *intelligible as entities*," and he goes on to say, "the qualifier 'as entities' (as I am using it) is short for this: with regard to the fact *that* they are (at all) and with regard to *what* they are." As an example of the way being makes entities intelligible, Haugeland (2013, 192) appeals to the way physical theories make physical entities accessible. "The *being* of the physical – the essence and actuality of physical entities – is spelled out by the laws of physics," and therefore, "*disclosure* of the being of the physical is the condition of possibility of comportment toward physical entities *as* physical entities." *Disclosedness* is Heidegger's word for the fact that we understand the being of entities, and Haugeland sees it as a successor of Kant's transcendental apperception. Apperception, for Kant, "is consciousness of an object that is, or at least could be, conscious of itself as conscious of that object," and according to Kant, "the fact that it could be conscious of itself in being conscious of an object is a prerequisite to the possibility of its being conscious of the object *as an object* at all" (Haugeland 2013, 190). This, Haugland (2013, 190) says, "is why apperception is *transcendental*," and he claims that disclosedness is *transcendental* for a structurally similar reason: that is, any disclosing of entities *as* entities "is *at once* a disclosing of Dasein itself *and* a disclosing of the being of entities." To show how our self-disclosure is simultaneously a disclosure of the being of entities and thus a condition through which we are able to comport ourselves to entities *as* entities, Haugeland shows how discovering the truth about the entities toward which we comport ourselves is grounded in the disclosure of being we achieve through our authentic, resolute being-towards-death.

Haugeland illustrates the extent to which factual truth is rooted in our authentic existence in three steps. First, he shows why discovering the truth about entities presupposes a disclosure of their being. Discovery is Heidegger's word for our *ontic* comportments toward entities *as* entities, and such comportments are ontic precisely because they have to do with *facts* (or ontic truth) about entities. Disclosure, as noted above, is *ontological* because it deals with the *being* of entities (or ontological truth) that enables facts about them to appear. And again, the initial step in Haugeland's account is to show how disclosing being makes discovering the truth about entities possible, but in doing so he also shows how our comportments toward entities are beholden to facts about the entities that they discover. Step two shows how our disclosure of being (and the entities discovered therein) is inseparable from our self-disclosure, and therefore also indicates how our self-disclosure both enables our discovery of facts and binds us to truths about them. Finally, Haugeland illustrates how our self-disclosure, and thus the disclosure of being and thereby our discovery of facts, is grounded in and achieved when we own up to our finitude and take responsibility for our existence (existential truth).

Haugeland begins his account of the derivation of discovery (the ontic or factual truth of entities) from disclosure (the ontological truth of being) by indicating that each has three aspects: understanding (*Verstehen*), telling (*Rede*), and findingness (*Befindlichkeit*). Understanding is *competence* or *know-how* whereby understanding a hammer is to know how to hammer with it. Telling is the *articulation of intelligibility*, and it involves expressing the distinctions that make up one's environment. So, Haugeland (2013, 195) says, "when hammering, I can *tell* whether I am swinging hard enough, whether the nail is going in straight, or whether the board is splitting; and these distinctions *articulate* what, in knowing how to hammer, I understand." Lastly, findingness refers to the fact that we are "always responsive to what *matters* in our current, concrete situation" (Haugeland 2013, 196) and in the case of hammering, it involves being responsive to the strength of the hammer, the fit of the boards, the angle of the nail, and so on. Although the aforementioned definitions of understanding, telling, and findingness are neutral between ontic discovery and ontological disclosure, each of the examples is ontic: that is, they indicate how we competently use, distinguish between, and respond to entities as they are *in fact*. In contrast, ontological understanding, telling, and findingness grasp entities in terms of a distinction between what is *possible* and what is *impossible* for them. As Haugeland (2013, 197) puts it, "projecting entities onto their possibilities is the same thing as projecting them onto their being." Insofar as physical entities are concerned, specifying what is possible and impossible for such entities is what the laws of physics do, and understanding physical entities in terms of these laws means nothing more than projecting them onto their possibilities. As for tools, what is possible for them is how they *can* be used and how they *ought* to function in such use. Thus, a hammer *can* be used to pull a nail and it *ought* not to break in the process, but propping open a door with a hammer is ruled out for a hammer *as* a hammer, and so is a hammer that breaks when pulling said nail. The ability to project a hammer onto its possibilities is an example of ontological understanding, making all the determinate distinctions between what is possible and impossible for a hammer is an example of ontological telling, and the fact that making the distinction between the possible and the impossible *matters* for our use of a hammer is an example of ontological findingness. The fact that distinguishing between what is possible and impossible is important for our comportment toward entities means that discovering the factual or ontic truth about entities is both a possibility and an implicit goal of our comportments. And this, in turn, implies that our comportments are *beholden to* the entities to which they are directed. As Haugeland (2013, 201) puts it: "Beholdenness belongs to the essential aim of any comportment toward an entity *as* an entity – namely, that it gets the entity itself 'right.'" In sum, disclosing what is possible and impossible for an entity is necessary if we are to discover the factual truth about that entity, and this, for example, is why the "disclosure of the *being* of the physical is the condition of possibility of comportment toward physical entities *as* physical entities" (Haugeland 2013, 192).

After indicating how discovering facts about entities presupposes the disclosure of their being, step two in the grounding of ontic truth in our authentic existence shows that our disclosure of being is inseparable from our self-disclosure, and therefore illustrates how our self-disclosure enables our discovery of entities and binds us to facts about them. As noted above, Heidegger characterizes us as beings whose identity can be changed by adopting alternative ways of life or "potentialities-for-being" (*BT* 182–188/143–148). It also implies that concrete self-disclosure is a case of coming to terms with the social role one currently holds. If, for example, I am a teacher, then I must come to terms with the materials I teach, the times at which I am teaching, and to whom I am obliged to teach. And by coming to terms with such things "we understand *ourselves* as entities and as the entities that we are – that is, as *who* we are" (Haugeland 2013, 202). Of course, I could not be a teacher without comporting myself toward the materials I teach, the students I supervise, and so on, and this means that my self-understanding presupposes that I understand the being of the entities with which I engage. If, as Haugeland says,

> my self-understanding depends on my understanding of the being of other entities, then I must also *be able* to project those entities onto their possibilities. *This* ability, therefore, belongs essentially to my ability-to-be *me*. My ability to project those entities onto their possibilities is not merely another possibility onto which I project myself, but rather is *part of* my ability to project myself onto my own possibility at all. In other words, my *self*-understanding literally *incorporates* an understanding of the being of other entities. (Haugeland 2013, 203)

While self-understanding incorporates an understanding of the being of other entities, it also involves an imperative to be true to one's way of life and thereby discover the truth about the entities with which one deals. For instance, being a teacher requires that I do what I am supposed to do as a teacher (master the material, give lectures, grade papers, and the like), but in order to do that I must get the entities I deal with *as a teacher* right. This, for Haugeland (2013, 204), means self-disclosure amounts to taking responsibility for our existence as well as ontic truth. And the fact that taking responsibility for our existence discloses being and thus discovers entities means that self-disclosure is a condition via which the truth about entities is attained. It also indicates a potential link between authenticity and Heidegger's fundamental ontology, and spelling this out takes us to the final stage of Haugeland's grounding of ontic truth in the "existentialist" elements of Heidegger's thought.

On Haugeland's (2013, 205–206) account, taking responsibility for our existence means that we own it, and he chooses to translate Heidegger's words for authenticity and inauthenticity, *Eigentlichkeit* and *Uneigentlichkeit*, as ownedness and unownedness. The distinction Haugeland sees between ownedness and unownedness is one of disclosedness: Unowned disclosedness is *public* whereas owned disclosedness is *resolute*. Public disclosedness refers to the disclosure of being that is commonly accepted in a given sociohistorical context. As an example, Haugeland cites the fact that physicists learn the theories that disclose the being of physical entities as part of their education and broader cultural heritage, and such a disclosure is "unowned" precisely because we generally fail to take responsibility for or question the assumptions that disclose physical facts and allow physicists to do the work that they do. In contrast, resolute disclosedness, as an "owned" disclosure of being, involves taking responsibility for the disclosure of being one inherits by calling it into question. As Haugeland (2013, 215) puts it: "Taking responsibility for something is not only taking it as something that matters, but also *not* taking it for granted." This means that when we take responsibility for our existence we not only take responsibility for getting the entities one deals with right (ontic truth) but also for the disclosure of being (ontological truth) that enables those entities to appear in the first place. Taking responsibility for a disclosure of being means holding oneself open for the possibility of taking back a disclosure when it fails to disclose entities and aspects of the world *as* the entities and aspects that they are. Haugeland writes:

> Ontological truth is beholden to *entities*—the very same entities that ontical truth is beholden to, and via the very same means of discovery. The difference lies in the character of the potential failure and the required response. A failure of ontical truth is a mis-discovery of an entity, such as a factual mistake. With more or less work, it can be identified and life goes on. A failure of ontological truth is a systematic breakdown that undermines everything – which just means a breakdown that *cannot* be "fixed up with a bit of work." So the only responsible response is to take it all back; which means that life, *that* life, does *not* "go on." But this response too is a response to discovered entities, and only to them – a refusal to accept what we might paradoxically call "*real*" impossibilities among them. Intransigent impossibilities can *only* show up among entities as ostensibly discovered. To be sure, they may turn out in the end not to have been discovered entities after all; but that eventuality *presupposes* ostensible discoveries of entities. (Haugeland 2013, 218)

Authenticity, Truth, and Cultural Transformation

While Haugeland (2013, 215–216) does not offer a concrete instance of "taking it all back," his reading of Heidegger draws on Kuhn and the shift from a Newtonian to an Einsteinian conception of the universe is a standard example of what Haugeland has in mind. Haugeland's emphasis on "taking it all back" also suggests that the truth-testing of authenticity is the basis for cultural transformation and the movement of human history, but Haugeland's (2013, 219) main point is this: If disclosures of being (or ontological truths) are arbitrary and neither beholden to entities nor binding on us, then factual (or ontic) truth would not really be any kind of *truth* at all. And it is precisely our resolute being-towards-death, in which we take responsibility for our existence by owning up to our finitude (existential truth), that enables us to question and test a given disclosure of being (or ontological truth).

Death, as the mark of our mortality, indicates the limits of our understanding and highlights the fact that we are able to "take it all back." Haugeland articulates the bounds of our understanding through an appeal to Kant's distinction between divine knowledge and human understanding:

> Infinite (divine) knowledge is perfect-in-itself in that it is not in any way *limited* by what it knows. Infinite just means unlimited: unbounded and unbound. Such knowledge is therefore originary or creative; that is how the relationship to what it knows is non-arbitrary (in effect, what is known is bounded and bound by the knowing of it). (Haugeland 2013, 219)

In contrast:

> Finite human knowledge ... is *not* perfect-in-itself. Since it is not originary, it can only be knowledge insofar as it is bounded and bound by what it knows. But that means that whatever it knows must stand over against it as an *object*. So, finite knowledge can *only* (at best) be *objective* – it falls short of being creative. (Haugeland 2013, 219)

Since our understanding is imperfect and bound by the entities it understands, it is subject to revision and open to being replaced. And while the *possibility* of revising or replacing a particular disclosure of being is based on the finite nature of our knowledge, our *ability* to make any such change is also based on our finitude or what Heidegger calls the "'not yet' which belongs to Dasein as its possible death" (*BT* 287/243). And again, if we own up to our death by orienting our life toward it, that is, if we own up to the fact that we are always in a position to choose a different way of life so long as we live, then we are in a position to take responsibility for ourselves, the disclosure of being in which we dwell, and the truth about entities discovered therein. As Haugeland (2013, 218) puts it, "disclosure itself is *beholden* for its 'success' to entities as discovered," and "that beholden disclosure is *binding* on Dasein in that its very life depends on it." As authentic, Haugeland (2013, 218–219) continues, "resolute Dasein *takes over* that beholden bindingness – binds *itself* – in existential responsibility." And the fact that we can take responsibility for a disclosure of being by taking responsibility for ourselves means that "resolute being-toward-death is the condition of the possibility of *ontological truth*" (Haugeland 2013, 219).

In short, authenticity is a condition of possibility for ontological truth to the extent that taking responsibility for our finite existence, and thus owning up to the finite nature of our understanding as well as our ability to take that understanding back, allows and in fact requires us to question and test the truth of our practices, theories, ways of life, or potentialities. In the case of physics, being authentic amounts to questioning, testing, and coming to terms with the laws that specify *that* and *what* physical entities *are*. And since coming to terms with the laws of physics is a condition through which we discover physical facts, being authentic is not only a condition of possibility for attaining the truth about physical *being* but a condition of possibility for reaching the truth about physical *entities* as well. This, on Haugeland's (2013, 188) account, means that resolute being-towards-death is "the fulcrum of [Heidegger's] entire ontology," and for Haugeland it explains why Heidegger thinks the most primordial phenomenon of truth is achieved in the mode of authenticity. "In our ontological clarification of the proposition that 'Dasein is in the truth,'" Heidegger writes, "we have called attention to the primordial disclosedness of this entity as the *truth of existence*; and for a delimitation of its character," Heidegger goes on to say, "we have referred to the analysis of Dasein's authenticity" (*BT* 343/297).

7.2 Objecting to Haugeland's Truth-Based Account of Authenticity

For all the subtlety and innovation in Haugeland's reading of authenticity, I think it fails as a faithful and philosophically sound interpretation of *Being and Time*. My objection here is that if, as Haugeland maintains, entities are only intelligible through a particular disclosure of being, then it is incoherent for Haugeland to claim that those same entities can serve as an intelligible, disclosure-independent standard against which that disclosure can be truth-tested. And if no sense can be made of testing a disclosure of being against disclosure-independent entities, then no sense can be made of Haugeland's claim that authenticity entails testing and transforming a disclosure against disclosure-independent entities. To substantiate this objection, I examine the case Haugeland makes for his reading via an analogy with Kuhn. Specifically, I indicate Haugeland's commitment to intelligible, disclosure-independent entities in his account of paradigm shifts. But then I go on to show that this commitment is inconsistent with a position held by both Heidegger and Kuhn that Haugeland otherwise endorses, namely, that the intelligibility of entities presupposes a particular disclosure of being or paradigm.

As mentioned above, Haugeland's ontological reading of authenticity is based on the link he sees between three types of truth: ontic, ontological, and existential. Again, ontic truth refers to our comportment to facts about entities. Ontological truth relates to the way facts about entities are presented to us via a particular disclosure of being. And existential truth involves taking responsibility for our existence by questioning and then testing a disclosure of being against the facts. Our ability to test disclosures of being against the facts is, for Haugeland (2013, 218), the foundation of his truth-based ontological reading of authenticity, "for it means that ontological truth, though historical, is not arbitrary" but "beholden to *entities*." And since questioning and testing a disclosure of being against the facts is *both* the crux of Haugeland's interpretation of authenticity *and* the basis of my objection to it, it is crucial to examine the case Haugeland makes for his reading through an analogy to Kuhn's description of scientific discoveries in *The Structure of Scientific Revolutions*.

Haugeland begins his analogy between Heidegger and Kuhn with an account of the "fallenness" of our inauthentic or unowned existence. Falling, for Heidegger, refers to the fact that we are engaged in one activity or another, and it is an essential aspect of our existence insofar as the activities we engage in shape our identity and disclose entities within our world (*BT* 420/369). Heidegger, however, also says that when Dasein falls into a given activity "it gets *entangled* in its own concern" (*BT* 222–223/178). And when caught up in its current concerns Dasein "drifts along toward an alienation in which its ownmost potentiality-for-being is hidden from it" (*BT* 222–223/178). Our ownmost potentiality-for-being is to be that being whose identity is open to change, and this means falling into our everyday activities and getting caught up in our current concerns alienate us from the fact that our existence is ours to choose. And if we fail to take responsibility for our existence by making identity-defining choices, then we lead an inauthentic life. As Haugeland (2013, 207) puts it, "*falling* is the basic characteristic of Dasein that, in each case, it inevitably tends toward unownedness."

After noting our tendency to lose ourselves in our daily activities, Haugeland equates fallenness with the progress of what Kuhn (1996, 35–39) calls "normal science," and for Kuhn, normal science progresses when scientists solve puzzles presented to them through a specific paradigm. "Paradigm" is Kuhn's (1996, 10) word for "accepted examples of actual scientific practice – examples which include law, theory, application, and instrumentation together – [that] provide models from which spring particular coherent traditions of scientific research." As an example of a paradigm, Kuhn (1996, 40–41) cites Newton's Laws and states that the Newtonian paradigm "told scientists what sorts of entities the universe did and did not contain" as well as "what many of their research problems should be" so that for eighteenth and nineteenth century science "quantity-of-matter was a fundamental ontological category for physical scientists, and the forces that act between bits of matter were a dominant topic of research." Since paradigms tell scientists *that* and *what* entities *are* (and thereby set their research agenda), Haugeland identifies Kuhn's "paradigms" with Heidegger's "disclosures of being." It is, however, important for Haugeland's analogy that it is "no part of the aim of normal science to call forth new sorts of phenomena" (Kuhn 1996, 24). Instead, Kuhn (1996, 24) says, "normal-scientific research is directed to the articulation of those phenomena and theories that the paradigm already supplies." And Kuhn (1996, 24) goes so far as to claim that the practice of normal science "resists" and is "often intolerant" of any attempt to challenge the paradigm upon which its research is based. This resistance is crucial for the progress of normal science. "If scientists were not *tenacious* in their efforts to solve even highly recalcitrant puzzles," Haugeland (2013, 207) writes, "then hard but solvable puzzles would seldom get solved. Yet it is precisely these solutions that are often the most valuable achievements of science." At the same time, this dogged or fallen commitment to a paradigm means that practitioners engaged in normal science fail to take responsibility for their existence by questioning and testing their given disclosure of being. And it is only by examining Haugeland's analogy between Kuhnian paradigm shifts and authenticity that we come to see what Haugeland means when he says authenticity entails questioning and then testing a disclosure of being against facts about entities.

Paradigm shifts are the defining feature of "revolutionary science," and for Kuhn (1996, 52–53), they start "with the awareness of anomaly, that is, with the recognition that nature has somehow violated the paradigm-induced expectations that govern normal science." Paradigm shifts continue "with a more or less extended exploration of the area of anomaly" (Kuhn 1996, 52–53). Finally, paradigm shifts come to an end "only when the paradigm theory has been adjusted so that the anomalous has become the expected" (Kuhn 1996, 52–53). As an example, Kuhn again turns to Newton:

> Newton's new theory of light and color originated in the discovery that none of the existing pre-paradigm theories would account for the length of the spectrum, and the wave theory that replaced Newton's was announced in the midst of growing concern about anomalies in the relation of diffraction and polarization effects to Newton's theory. (Kuhn 1996, 67)

Here it seems that *facts* about the "length of the spectrum" and "the relation of diffraction and polarization" induced the shift from one paradigm to another. Indeed, Kuhn (1996, 169) tells us "nature itself must first undermine professional security by making prior achievements seem problematic." Haugeland, however, is quick to point out that fact-based paradigm shifts presuppose the importance of getting entities right for our way of life as well as the contingency and questionability of paradigms generally. So, Haugeland develops the connection he sees between paradigm shifts and authenticity through a discussion of the relevant truth-testing and responsibility that scientists ought to undertake when faced with an anomaly.

Remember that Haugeland's (2013, 203) ontological account of authenticity rests on the relatively straightforward notion that "in knowing how to be me I must know how to deal with the entities amidst which I work and live." This, for Haugeland, means that one of the most important features of our activities is that they get entities themselves right. "Beholdenness," as Haugeland (2013, 201) puts it, "belongs to the essential aim of any comportment toward an entity *as* an entity – namely, that it gets the entity itself 'right.'" And he elaborates on this idea by saying: "[W]hat *matters* is that the entities, as ontically discovered, be in fact *possible* – that is, *not im*possible – according to the understanding of their being" (Haugeland 2013, 198). For the sake of his analogy, Haugeland identifies Kuhn's nature- or fact-induced anomalies with what he calls "discovered impossibilities." And as Haugeland (2013, 200) sees it, the discoveries of a given scientist "can impugn the discoveries of others if their respective discoverings of entities as entities are mutually *incompatible*," whereby "discoverings of entities are incompatible just in case the entities themselves, as (ostensibly) discovered, would be *impossible*." For example:

> If you discover that something is a hammer but shatters against a nail, or that something is an electric current but generates no magnetic field. Since that would be impossible, *something* is wrong. (Haugeland 2013, 200)

When anomalies or impossibilities are discovered, Haugeland (2013, 200) says responsible scientists "double-check and re-examine [their] means of discovery" and then "seek confirmation from other people" until "it becomes clear *which* of [their] earlier *apparent* discoveries was wrong." Such procedures "make feasible a non-arbitrary distinction between (mere) *appearance* and *reality*," but Haugeland acknowledges that

> there is and can be no antecedent *guarantee* that all that double-checking and whatnot, no matter how assiduous, will actually succeed. That is, no matter how hard the relevant individual and community try, they may not find a way to reconcile their apparent discoveries with what they know to be possible. What then? (Haugeland 2013, 214–215)

Haugeland answers:

> A discovered impossibility rests on two factors: what is in fact discovered [ontical truth] and what is ruled out by the projection onto possibilities [ontological truth]. The careful and persistent double-checking has eliminated the discoveries as the culprit. That leaves the possibilities – in other words, the *being* of the entities discovered. (Haugeland 2013, 216)

Haugeland then articulates the appropriate response to discovered impossibilities at both the ontic and ontological levels:

> A failure of ontical truth is a misdiscovery of an entity, such as a factual mistake. With more or less work, it can be identified and corrected; and life goes on. A failure of ontological truth is a systematic breakdown that undermines everything – which just means a breakdown that *cannot* be "fixed up with a bit of work." So the only responsible response is to take it all back; which means that life, *that* life, does *not* "go on." (Haugeland 2013, 218)

Both responses, however, are responses to entities, or what Haugeland (2013, 218) calls "a refusal to accept what we might paradoxically call '*real*' impossibilities among them." So again, "ontological truth is beholden to *entities* – the very same entities that ontical truth is beholden to, and via the very same means of discovery" (Haugeland 2013, 218). This implies that something like an appearance-reality distinction exists at the ontological level insofar as entities can serve as an intelligible, disclosure-independent standard against which disclosures can be truth-tested or transformed. This, for Haugeland, is "an important result," for

> if the possibilities themselves (the disclosed being of the entities) were to remain arbitrary, and therefore neither beholden [to entities] nor binding [on us], then the achievement of the first two stages [of grounding ontical truth] would be hollow at best – even ontical truth would not be a sort of *truth* after all. (Haugeland 2013, 219)

Of course, our ability to question and then test a disclosure of being against entities presupposes the contingency and questionability of both our paradigmatic understanding and the way of life that is coextensive with it. This contingency and questionability is a function of our finitude. And it means that authenticity is a condition of possibility for ontological truth to the extent that taking responsibility for our finite understanding and existence allows us to question and test our paradigms and ways of life against the facts. In Haugeland's words:

> Heidegger's (and Kuhn's) "historicism" about being does not imply relativism. Discovery of entities does indeed presuppose – hence is "relative" to – Dasein's disclosure of their being (or "paradigm"), which is historical. But whether a way of life with its ontical comportments works or not is not up to Dasein, either individually or historically. So that disclosure itself, in turn, is *beholden* for its "success" to those very entities as discovered – entities that are independent of it in the concrete and inescapable sense that they are out of control. And that beholden disclosure is *binding* on Dasein in that its very life depends on it. Authentic Dasein *takes over* that beholden bindingness – binds *itself* – in existential responsibility. Therefore, resolute being toward death is the condition of the possibility of *ontological truth*. (Haugeland 2013, 218–219)

In the end, Haugeland leaves us with a picture of authenticity-induced but fact-based paradigm shifts in which we take responsibility for our existence by ensuring that we get the entities we deal with right. This process begins by ensuring that our comportments toward entities that are discovered through a particular paradigm are in fact true. As a responsible physicist, we need to make sure that our descriptions of gold are correct. And if our predictions about the behavior of gold do not turn out as expected, then we must check and see if we have made a mistake in our initial depiction. This provocation to look and see is a response to an anomaly or discovered impossibility amongst a set of entities (ostensibly) discovered through a specific paradigm. If, however, we are unable to resolve the apparent anomaly by fact-checking those (ostensibly) discovered entities, then we turn to questioning and testing the paradigm that makes certain facts about entities available to us. This is also a response to an anomaly or discovered impossibility amongst a set of entities (ostensibly) discovered through a particular paradigm. But we can no longer reliably test our comportments against facts about entities (ostensibly) discovered through that paradigm. Instead, we are required to test that paradigm against the entities themselves. As an authentic physicist, this means the law, theory, application, and instrumentation that collectively guide our otherwise coherent activity must be truth-tested against gold itself. And our current paradigm should be taken back if it fails to disclose gold as the entity that it is. Again, our ability to question, test, and take a given paradigm back is based on the fact that we as finite human beings are able to choose our identity by adopting alternative ways of life or potentialities. And since Haugeland thinks taking responsibility for our existence by making identity-defining choices entails getting entities right, he thinks authenticity entails questioning and testing paradigms against entities as they are in themselves.

Haugeland's emphasis on the importance of our comportments getting entities right, his claim that ontological truth would be arbitrary if disclosures of being were not beholden to entities themselves, and his appeal to physical facts, independent entities, and a distinction between appearance and reality in his analogy between Heidegger and Kuhn indicate his commitment to something like metaphysical or robust realism. Metaphysical realism, as Putnam (1988, 107) puts it, is made up of "a bundle of intimately associated philosophical ideas," including:

> The world consists of some fixed totality of mind-independent objects. There is exactly one true and complete description of "the way the world is." [And] truth involves some sort of correspondence relation between words or thought-signs and external things and sets of things. (Putnam 1981, 49)

And of robust realism, Michael Devitt writes:

> An object has objective existence, in some sense, if it exists and has its nature whatever we believe, think, or can discover: it is independent of the cognitive activities of the mind ... It is not *constituted* by our knowledge, by our epistemic values, by our capacity to refer to it, by our imposition of concepts, theories, or languages ... For the realist, the world exists *independently of the mental*. (Devitt 1997, 15–16)

Haugeland (2013, 58) also explicitly says entities "precede and are independent of whatever claims may be put forward about them." And he asserts that to understand an entity as real is to understand it "as an independent *thing* that bears properties in the traditional sense" whereby "the mark of reality in that sense is *independence*: a thing is *at all* and also is *what* it is *all by itself*" (Haugeland 2013, 57). When it comes to truth, Haugeland claims:

> Entities are such that they determine what is and is not true – that is, what is true *of them*. The determinacy of entities is that there are truths about them – truths that are determined by them. (Haugeland 2013, 58)

And he sums up his reading of *Being and Time* by stating that the "essential aim" of Heidegger's text is to show how

> understandings of being are beholden to *entities*: the very same entities to which ontical claims are beholden. Exhibiting that ontological beholdenness will complete the explication of the truth character of being. (Haugeland 2013, 59)

While Haugeland does not speak in terms of "mind-independence" or "correspondence," here we see that robust realism is an integral part of Haugeland's truth-based ontological interpretation of authenticity insofar as truth-testing a disclosure of being presupposes the intelligibility of disclosure-independent entities against which that disclosure can be held to account. Put otherwise, the possibility of questioning and then truth-testing a particular disclosure of being against entities themselves suggests that we can somehow discover *that* and *what* entities *are* independent of that disclosure of being. But both the general intelligibility of disclosure-independent entities and our alleged discovery of them in specific cases seem inconsistent with Haugeland's endorsement of the Kuhnian and Heideggerian notion that discovering *that* and *what* entities *are* presupposes a particular disclosure of being or paradigm. And to tease out this inconsistency, it is worth examining Kuhn's and Heidegger's stance on metaphysical realism as well as their reason for rejecting that view.[2]

Although Haugeland appeals to Kuhn to help make his case that disclosures of being can be tested against entities themselves, Kuhn (1996, 77) is clearly skeptical of this idea: "No process yet disclosed by the historical study of scientific development at all resembles the methodological stereotype of falsification by direct comparison with

---

[2] Haugeland takes the easy way out in his analogy between Heidegger and Kuhn: He appeals to natural science where we intuitively believe in paradigm-independent entities, yet he has little to say about other domains, like art and politics, where we tend to think that entities are paradigm-dependent. But since I argue that paradigm-independence is incoherent even in the natural sciences, I will not pursue this matter further.

nature." Instead, Kuhn (1996, 77) says, "the decision to reject one paradigm is always simultaneously the decision to accept another, and the judgment leading to decision involves the comparison of both paradigms with nature *and* with each other." Kuhn's invocation of "nature" in this quote suggests that he shares some sympathy with Haugeland's robust realism, but much of the rest of Kuhn's text calls that position into question. After examining the record of past scientific research, Kuhn remarks:

> The historian of science may be tempted to exclaim that when paradigms change, the world itself changes with them. Led by a new paradigm, scientists adopt new instruments and look in new places. Even more important, during revolutions scientists see new and different things when looking through familiar instruments in places they have looked before. It is rather as if the professional community had been suddenly transported to another planet where familiar objects are seen in a different light and are joined by unfamiliar ones as well. Of course, nothing of quite that sort does occur: there is no geographical transplantation; outside the laboratory everyday affairs usually continue as before. Nevertheless, paradigm changes do cause scientists to see the world of their research-engagement differently. Insofar as their only recourse to that world is through what they see and what they do, we may want to say that after a revolution scientists are responding to a different world. (Kuhn 1996, 111)

Of competing paradigms, Kuhn writes:

> When paradigms enter, as they must, into a debate about paradigm choice, their role is necessarily circular. Each group uses its own paradigm to argue in that paradigms defense ... As in political revolutions, so in paradigm choice – there is no standard higher than the assent of the relevant community. (Kuhn 1996, 94)

And in a postscript responding to the so-called relativistic tendencies of his initial text, Kuhn asserts:

> There is, I think, no theory-independent way to reconstruct phrases like "really there"; the notion of a match between the ontology of a theory and its "real" counterpart in nature now seem to me illusive in principle. (Kuhn 1996, 206)

To see why the idea of matching a theory with its "real" counterpart in nature is illusive in principle, let us return to Haugeland's example of physical being. If, as Haugeland (2013, 192) says, "disclosure of the being of the physical is the condition of the possibility of comportment toward physical entities *as* physical entities," then we cannot comport ourselves toward physical entities *as* physical entities without disclosing their being. And, if we cannot comport ourselves to physical entities apart from a disclosure of their being, then physical entities cannot function as a disclosure-independent standard against which a disclosure of being can be truth-tested or transformed. It is for precisely this reason that Kuhn (1996, 170) ends *The Structure of Scientific Revolutions* by saying "we may have to relinquish the notion, explicit or implicit, that changes of paradigm carry scientists and those who learn from them closer to the truth."

Heidegger, for his part, occasionally refers to "nature" and the "real" in *Being and Time*, but he rejects the metaphysical or robust realism of intelligible, disclosure-independent entities that Haugeland assumes in his attempt to ground ontological truth in the truth of our existence. Two passages in *Being and Time* are often cited in support of Heidegger's "realism." The first reads: "Being (not entities) is dependent upon the understanding of being; that is to say, reality (not the real) is dependent upon care" (*BT* 255/212).

And the second appears in a discussion about truth and Newton's Laws:

> Before Newton's laws were discovered, they were not "true"; it does not follow that they were false, or even that they would become false if ontically no discoveredness were any longer possible ... To say that before Newton his laws were neither true nor false cannot signify that before him there were no such entities as have been uncovered and pointed out by those laws. Through Newton the laws became true and with them entities became accessible in themselves to Dasein. Once entities have been uncovered they show themselves precisely as entities which beforehand they already were. (*BT* 269/226–227)

Each quote makes a distinction between being and entities that resembles the distinction Haugeland makes between historically contingent paradigms and entities as they are in themselves such that the *disclosure* of entities is dependent on a historically contingent paradigm, but the actual *facts* about said entities are not. However, attention to the text surrounding the aforementioned passages suggests that no intelligible engagement with or comportment toward entities is possible outside a particular paradigm or disclosure of being. Of Newton's Laws, Heidegger says,

> these are true only as long as Dasein *is*. Before there was any Dasein, there was no truth; nor will there be any after Dasein is no more. For in such a case truth as disclosedness, uncovering, and uncoveredness, *cannot* be. (*BT* 269/226)

And in the case of entities as they are in themselves, Heidegger writes:

> When Dasein does not exist, "independence" "is" not either, nor "is" the "in-itself." In such a case this sort of thing can be neither understood nor not understood. In such a case even entities within-the-world can neither be discovered nor lie hidden. *In such a case* it cannot be said that entities are, nor can it be said that they are not. But *now*, as long as there is an understanding of being and therefore an understanding of the presence-at-hand, it can indeed be said that *in this case* entities will still continue to be. (*BT* 255/212)

Figuring out how to read these quotes in light of the previous two has led to an extended debate in the secondary literature. Taylor Carman thinks that Heidegger is committed to a version of "ontic realism" in which a subset of entities *exists* independent of us, but their *being* – as that which determines *that* and *what* those entities *are* – is unintelligible. As Carman (2003, 202) puts it: "Without Dasein there would 'be' no *being*, which is to say there would be no understanding of being, so that *that* and *what* entities are would add up to nothing intelligible. But present-at-hand entities would still be, nonetheless."

Against Carman, Lee Braver offers an "anti-realist" reading of Heidegger in which "ontic realism is really best understood as a description of how present-at-hand objects present themselves to average everyday Dasein" such that

> part of the way objects appear to us is as not dependent on appearing to us. That does not mean that they really *are* independent of their manifestation, just that they manifest themselves that way; paradoxically, they depend on Dasein to manifest themselves as *in*dependent of all manifestation. (Braver 2007, 192–193)

While there are passages in *Being and Time* that support Carman's "ontic realist" reading and others that support Braver's "anti-realist" interpretation, the most important point for present purposes is that on both readings nothing intelligible can be said, known, or understood about entities apart from a particular paradigm or disclosure of being. "In no case," Heidegger says, "is Dasein untouched and unseduced by the way in which things have been interpreted, set before the open country of a 'world-in-itself' so that it just beholds what it encounters" (*BT* 213/169–170). And in a later lecture series, Heidegger explicitly denies any attempt to ground a disclosure of being in anything, let alone test a disclosure of being for truth against disclosure-independent entities:

> Being "is" in essence: ground/reason. Thus, being can never first have a ground/reason that would supposedly ground it. Accordingly, ground/reason

is missing from being. Ground/reason remains at a remove from being. Being "is" the abyss in the sense of such a remaining apart of ground/reason from being. To the extent that being as such grounds, it remains groundless. (*PR* 51)

This, in Haugeland's idiom, means that ontological truth is *not* beholden to entities. And Heidegger emphasizes the groundlessness of being for the same reason Kuhn rejects the notion of matching the ontology of a theory with its "real" counterpart in nature: that is, if, for example, gold is only intelligibly presented to us through a particular paradigm, then "gold itself" could not function as an intelligible, paradigm-independent standard to which we could comport ourselves and against which we could test and transform the paradigm that makes it available. As Heidegger puts it in his lectures leading up to *Being and Time*:

> It is phenomenologically absurd to speak of the phenomenon as if it were something behind which there would be something else of which it would be a phenomenon in the sense of the appearance that represents and expresses this something else. A phenomenon is nothing behind which there would be something else. More accurately stated, one cannot ask for something behind the phenomenon at all, since what the phenomenon gives is precisely that something in itself. (*HCT* 86)

In sum, if, as Heidegger, Kuhn, and Haugeland claim, entities are only intelligible via a disclosure of being, then it is incoherent for Haugeland to say that entities can serve as an intelligible, disclosure-independent standard against which a disclosure can be truth-tested. And if no sense can be made of testing a disclosure of being against disclosure-independent entities, then no sense can be made of Haugeland's claim that authenticity entails taking responsibility for our existence by testing and transforming a disclosure against disclosure-independent entities.

7.3 An Ends-Based Account of Authenticity

Although I have argued that the details of Haugeland's ontological interpretation of authenticity are inconsistent, I agree with Haugeland's general claim that Heidegger's existentialism is a key feature of Heidegger's fundamental ontology. So, in the rest of this chapter, I offer an alternative to Haugeland's truth-based take on authenticity and cultural transformation via an ends-based reading of Heidegger and Kuhn. First, I take a closer look at the relation Heidegger sees between disclosures of being and potentialities, and in doing so illustrate the extent to which the intelligibility of entities is relative to the ends pursued by a particular historical community. Second, I analyze the *methodological* import of authenticity for Heidegger's fundamental ontology. Specifically, and unlike Haugeland (2013, 188) who argues that taking responsibility for our finite existence allows us to question and test all disclosures of being against disclosure-independent entities and thus sees resolute being-towards-death as "the fulcrum of [Heidegger's] *entire* ontology," I claim that Heidegger's analysis of our authentic existence *explicitly exhibits* the temporal horizon that is *fundamental* for all our purposive activities and the intelligible disclosure of entities, generally. Finally, and in support of my position, I return to Kuhn to show that paradigm shifts are not a function of sciences' steady movement closer to the truth but are instead motivated by the ends members of a specific scientific community pursue.

As we have seen, Heidegger's aim in *Being and Time* is to "work out the question of the meaning of *being*" (*BT* 22/4). And in order to ask about and offer an interpretation of being, Heidegger provides a detailed analysis of the being that both questions and understands being: the human being. As Heidegger puts it: "Dasein is ontically distinguished by the fact that, in its very being, that being is an *issue* for it," and he goes on to say that an "understanding of being is itself a definite characteristic of Dasein's being," such that "with and through Dasein's being this understanding of being is disclosed to it" (*BT* 32/12). Briefly, the methodological idea is that by analyzing a being that questions and understands being we learn what it means to ask about and understand being *simpliciter*.

Our basic understanding of being is embedded in our particular way of life or potentiality-for-being, and in Division One of *Being and Time* Heidegger illustrates the extent to which the *being* or *intelligibility* of entities is disclosed via our way of life or potentiality. Specifically, Heidegger offers a detailed and technical account of the "worldliness" of our average, everyday life in order to show that the ends of our activities determine *that* and *what* entities *are* within that life. Worldliness refers to several contextual aspects of our existence that characterize our intelligible interactions with entities, and Heidegger teases out these aspects through an analysis of a specific but ordinary "work-world" in which *that* and *what* a hammer *is* is determined by the activity of carpentry and our general need for a home. First, Heidegger shows us that a hammer is a hammer only in relation to nails, skill saws, tape measures, tool belts, and all other items in a "totality of equipment" that are part of a carpenter's work-world. Second, a hammer is what it is by referring to the raw materials "upon which" it works, say, wood or steel, and the end product "towards which" it is used, such as the frame of a house. Finally, a hammer is a hammer insofar as it points to a "public world" from whence it was manufactured and to which the products of its use will be sent. Taken together, the "totality of equipment," "upon which," "towards which," and "public world" are contextual aspects of our existence that characterize our intelligible interaction with any entity whatsoever, but Heidegger introduces three more features – "involvement," "for-the-sake-of-which," and "significance" – to indicate the teleological aspects of our existence that determine *that* and *what* entities *are* within a worldly context. For example, a hammer is involved in the activity of building a house insofar as it is held in the hand of a carpenter and used to hit nails into a piece of wood for the purpose of building a wall. But building a wall is not the end of the involvement chain:

> With hammering there is an involvement in making something fast; with making something fast, there is an involvement in protection against bad weather; and this protection "is" for the sake of providing shelter for Dasein – that is to say, for the sake of a possibility of Dasein's being. (*BT* 116/84)

Here Heidegger shows us that the final for-the-sake-of-which in involved activity refers to our potentialities-for-being. In the case of carpentry, it relates to *being* a carpenter and *being* sheltered in stormy weather. Yet to engage in the activity of carpentry at all, we must understand that being a carpenter and being sheltered are live and worthwhile possibilities for us. Heidegger calls this understanding significance. And in his technical terminology, the worldliness that defines our existence can be described as a totality of significant involvements that are directed toward various potentialities-for-being and that determine *that* and *what* entities *are* through those potentialities. In short, being, as "that which determines entities as entities" or "that on the basis of which entities are already understood" (*BT* 25–26/6), is relative to the ends of our various activities.

In a perspicuous discussion of the relation between worldliness, truth, and our potentialities-for-being, Mark Wrathall offers a good example of Heidegger's ends-based ontology. Specifically, Wrathall (2011, 29) examines the conflict between two definitions of gold: the medieval "gold is the noblest of the metals," and the modern "gold is an element with the atomic number 79." According to Wrathall (2011, 31–32):

> The fight between the medieval and modern conceptions of gold is based ultimately in different ways of picking out salient entities in the world ...

> One way of being disposed might lead us to find the true being of a thing in the extent to which it approaches God by being like Him. Another way of being disposed might lead us to find the true being of a thing in its ability to be turned into a resource, flexibly and efficiently on call for use. When someone disposed to the world in the first way uncovers a lump of gold, and subsequently defines gold as such and such a *kind* of thing, what she takes to be an essential property will be driven by her background sense of what is most essential in everything is its nearness to God. When someone disposed to the world in the second way uncovers it, she will take the essential properties to be whatever it is about it that allows us to break it down into a resource, and flexibly switch it around and order it, since our background sense for technological efficiency shapes our experience of everything. (Wrathall 2011, 31–32)

Like Kuhn's claim about competing paradigms, Wrathall (2011, 29) says "neither camp could ever persuade the other that their essential definition was correct, because, on the basis of their respective definitions, each would reject exactly those particular substances that the other took as decisive evidence in favor of his or her definition." Heidegger echoes this sentiment when he writes:

> Every time we attempt to prove an essential determination through single or even all actual and possible facts there results the remarkable state of affairs that we have already presupposed the legitimacy of the essential determination, indeed must presuppose it, just in order to grasp and produce the facts that are supposed to serves as proof. (*GA* 45, 79)

Again, we are reminded that entities are only intelligible as the entities that they are through a specific paradigm or disclosure of being. And as Wrathall's example indicates, *that* and *what* "gold" *is* depends on whether worshiping God or attaining technological efficiency is the goal of our particular way of life or potentiality.

While potentialities-for-being refer to the various goal-directed activities that help define our identity and determine the way entities are disclosed to us, Heidegger's stress on the worldly aspects of our existence shows that our particular potentiality-for-being is part of a broader context comprised of other people who make our specific way of life possible. My ability to take up carpentry, for example, depends on others supplying me with the materials and tools that I need to build a house. It also requires a consumer to purchase the house I produce. And this network of suppliers, producers, and consumers presupposes a host of other people engaged in a variety of tasks, from financer to truck driver, for its successful operation. The fact that our specific way of life is always part of a context of collective activity illustrates the extent to which the intelligible disclosure of entities achieved in a particular potentiality-for-being presupposes a collective disclosure of being through which entities are equally intelligible to everyone. Heidegger's word for this collective intelligibility is "publicness," and it underwrites the efficient functioning of our activities by ensuring that each individual interacts with entities in a similar fashion. Publicness, as Heidegger puts it, "controls every way in which the world and Dasein get interpreted" (*BT* 165/127, 212/168), and it does so by establishing a set of standards that regulate our mutually intelligible interactions with entities. "We have the *same thing* in view," Heidegger asserts, "because it is in *the same averageness* that we have a *common* understanding [of the world]" (*BT* 165/127, 212/168). Heidegger dubs this common understanding the "destiny of a historical people," and "it is not something that puts itself together out of individual fates," but instead Heidegger says "our fates have already been guided in advance, in our being-with-one-another in the same world and in our resolution for definite possibilities" (*BT* 436/384). Here again we see that the public nature of intelligibility suggests that our specific potentialities-for-being are always part of a collective disclosure of being, and this means that *that* and *what* entities *are* is relative to the ends pursued by a particular historical community.

Although the public nature of intelligibility underwrites the efficient functioning of our activities, the norms that regulate our mutually intelligible interaction with entities also foster our tendency to lead an inauthentic life. Specifically, the conformity required for the seamless operation of our everyday activities makes it easy for us to lose ourselves in our publicly supported potentiality. Heidegger's technical term for the public norms that organize our everyday existence is "*das Man.*" *Das Man* is often translated as "the they." It is meant to illustrate the extent to which "we take pleasure and enjoy ourselves the way *they* take pleasure; we read, see and judge about literature and art as *they* see and judge;" and so on (*BT* 164/127). And *das Man* enables our inauthentic existence insofar as the public acceptance of our chosen way of life lulls us into an unquestioned complacency with that way of life. As Heidegger writes:

> Dasein's projection of itself understandingly is in each case already alongside a world that has been discovered. From this world it takes its possibilities, and it does so first in accordance with the way things have been interpreted by the "they." This interpretation has already restricted the possible options of choice to what lies within the range of the familiar, the attainable, the respectable – that which is fitting and proper. This leveling off of Dasein's possibilities to what is proximally at its everyday

disposal also results in a dimming down of the possible as such. The average everydayness of concern becomes blind to its possibilities, and tranquilizes itself with that which is merely "actual." (*BT* 239/194)

The fact that we are blind to alternative possibilities in our average everyday existence does, however, cast doubt on Heidegger's method for coming to terms with the meaning of being in Division One of *Being and Time*. Concretely, Heidegger's analysis of humans who are lost in their everyday activities is incomplete insofar as it examined us when we are actually alienated from the "truth of our existence": that is, that we are beings that are always in a position to take responsibility for our being by making a series of identity-defining choices. So, if Heidegger is to come to terms with the meaning of being through an analysis of human beings, he needs to analyze human beings in their "true" or "authentic" existence. As he puts it:

> *Our existential analysis of Dasein up till now cannot lay claim to primordiality*. Its for-having never included more than the *inauthentic* being of Dasein, and of Dasein as *less* than a *whole*. If the interpretation of Dasein's being is to become primordial as a foundation for working out the basic questions of ontology, then it must first have brought to light existentially the being of Dasein in its possibilities of *authenticity* and *totality*. (*BT* 276/233)

This means that Heidegger's account of authenticity is not, as Haugeland (2013, 188) would have it, "the fulcrum of [Heidegger's] entire ontology," but is instead the *method* that allows Heidegger to determine what the fulcrum of ontology is. And to spell out the methodological connection between authenticity and fundamental ontology, we need to reinterpret the way our finitude enables us to take responsibility for our existence and then explain how existing authentically *explicitly exhibits* the temporal horizon that is the *basis* of our purposive activities and the intelligible disclosure of entities.

In Division Two of *Being and Time*, Heidegger calls attention to our finitude through a discussion of two interrelated phenomena: guilt and death. Guilt, for Heidegger, means that "Dasein is something that has been thrown; it has been brought to its 'there', but not of its own accord" (*BT* 329/283–284). We are, in other words, always acting in a world that we did not create but to which we are indebted for our basic understanding of entities and our various potentialities-for-being. And while we are necessarily conditioned by the culture we inherit, the thrown aspect of our existence also speaks to the contingency of our situation as well as our ability to question its significance: that is, our innate ability to adopt

Authenticity, Truth, and Cultural Transformation 151

alternative potentialities implies that our identity is not reducible to our current way of life, and so we always maintain a certain critical distance from our inherited potentiality. Once we have recognized the contingency of our current situation and questioned its significance, we can take responsibility for our existence by choosing from a range of identity-defining potentialities that are available in our cultural inheritance. For instance, my education may have prepared me for a life as a professional carpenter, but I have the ability to be a mechanic, a teacher, an engineer, and a host of other things. So, I am always able to take responsibility for my existence by making a choice between carpentry and another profession. The fact that our identity is *indebted* to a contingent cultural inheritance that we can nevertheless take *responsibility* for via our choices is why Heidegger speaks of our *guilt*. Yet taking responsibility for our existence via our choices not only presupposes a contingent cultural inheritance, it also requires an indeterminate future into which we project our chosen potentiality. Heidegger calls this indeterminate future the "'not yet' which belongs to Dasein as its possible death" (*BT* 287/243), and death refers to the fact that we are always able to choose an alternative way of life so long as we are alive. "*Death is*, as *Dasein's* end, in the being of this entity *towards* its end," and in being-towards-death, Heidegger says, "Dasein *hands* itself *down* to itself in a possibility which it has *inherited* and yet has *chosen*" (*BT* 259/303, 384/435). Taken together, guilt and death express the historical contingency and future indeterminacy that typify our finite existence. And we humans exist authentically when we take responsibility for our identity by decisively projecting a historically given potentiality into an indeterminate future.

When we take responsibility for our existence by explicitly projecting a *historically* given potentiality into an indeterminate *future* we confront the temporal horizon that is the basis of *all* our activities, but that we otherwise overlook when we are caught up in our *current* concerns. The temporality that characterizes our various activities consists of three ecstatic aspects – past, present, and future – that open up a worldly context and thereby enable our intelligible interaction with entities. Heidegger calls these aspects "ecstatic" to distinguish them from linear time and capture the fact that in our existential experience the past and future "stand out" and "play off" of each other to make entities intelligible in the present (*BT* 377/329). To continue with the carpentry example, my *previous* education in carpentry allows me to identify and use hammers in a skillful way. But the fact that a hammer *currently* shows up as an intelligible entity within my world requires that I actually take up carpentry and work *toward* the various ends of that activity. Again, the contingency of my previous education and the indeterminacy of my future action allow me to question and take responsibility for my identity by making a choice between carpentry and other potentialities. But in our average everyday life, Heidegger says, we are so *fascinated* with our current activities that we lose sight of the historical contingency and future indeterminacy that characterize our existence (*BT* 222/176). Thus, it is only through an analysis of our authentic existence that we come to terms with the temporal horizon that is the basis of our purposive activities and the intelligible disclosure of entities. In Heidegger's methodological idiom: "If the interpretation of Dasein's being is to become primordial as a foundation for working out the basic questions of ontology, then it must first have brought to light existentially the being of Dasein in its possibilities of *authenticity* and *totality*" (*BT* 276/233). And after a complete account of our authentic existence has been articulated we can see why Heidegger identified "*time* as the possible horizon for any understanding whatsoever of being" (*BT* 19/1).

While Heidegger's methodologically driven analysis of our authentic existence illustrates the extent to which the ends of our temporally based activities determine *that* and *what* entities *are* at a certain point in history, his account of historical contingency and future indeterminacy combined with his ends-based ontology allow us to explain the movement of history without an appeal to intelligible, disclosure-independent entities. Specifically, Heidegger's analysis of our ability to take responsibility for our existence by questioning our cultural inheritance and projecting a specific potentiality-for-being into an indeterminate future indicates that changes in our average everyday existence are relative to the goals we choose to pursue. These changes may involve altering our current way of life in light of the ends we are striving toward, but they may also involve shifting the goals we pursue entirely. With that said, and in support of my ends-based reading of authenticity over Haugeland's truth-based account, I re-examine the transition from normal to revolutionary science in Kuhn's take on paradigm shifts. In doing so, I show that cultural transformation is not a function of science's steady movement closer to the truth, but is instead based on the goals a specific community pursues.

As a puzzle-solving activity, Kuhn (1996, 52) says normal science "is a highly cumulative enterprise, eminently successful in its aim, the steady extension of the scope and precision of scientific knowledge." Yet "normal science does not aim at novelties of fact or theory and, when successful, finds none" (Kuhn 1996, 52). This is because there are "rules that limit both the nature of acceptable solutions and the steps by which they are to be obtained," such that established paradigms provide "a criterion for choosing problems that, while the paradigm is taken for granted, can be assumed to have solutions" (Kuhn 1996, 38, 37). For Kuhn (1996, 24), this means "normal-scientific research is directed to the articulation of those phenomena and theories that a paradigm already supplies." And he concludes: "One of the reasons why normal science seems to progress so rapidly is that its practitioners concentrate on problems that only their own lack of ingenuity should keep them from solving" (Kuhn 1996, 37).

Although normal science does not aim to discover novelties of fact or theory, Kuhn (1996, 52) acknowledges that "new and unsuspecting phenomena are repeatedly uncovered by scientific research, and radical new theories have again and again been invented by scientists." This implies that "research under a paradigm must be a particularly effective way of inducing paradigm change" (Kuhn 1996, 52). And normal science induces such change when anomalies "produced inadvertently by a game played under one set of rules" require "the elaboration of another set [of rules] for their assimilation" (Kuhn 1996, 52). Anomalies, Kuhn (1996, 68, 153) writes, "are generated by the persistent failure of the puzzles of normal science to come out as they should," and he goes on to say, "the single most prevalent claim advanced by the proponents of a new paradigm is that they can solve the problems that have led the old one into crisis." However, new paradigms that claim to solve old problems are often incommensurable with the previous paradigm. As Kuhn (1996, 150, 94, 151) puts it: "the proponents of competing paradigms practice their trades in different worlds" such that a new paradigm "cannot be made logically or even probabilistically compelling for those who refuse to step into the circle"; therefore, "the transfer of allegiance from paradigm to paradigm is a conversion experience that cannot be forced." This means scientific revolutions are not "reducible to a reinterpretation of individual and stable data," but are instead "a special sort of change involving a certain sort of reconstruction of group commitments" (Kuhn 1996, 121, 180–181). And Kuhn sums up the process of a paradigm shift as follows:

> Paradigm-testing occurs only after persistent failure to solve a noteworthy puzzle has given rise to crisis. And even then it occurs only after the sense of the crisis has evoked an alternative candidate for paradigm. In the sciences

the testing situation never consists, as puzzle-solving does, simply in the comparison of a single paradigm with nature. Instead, testing occurs as part of the competition between two rival paradigms for the allegiance of the scientific community. (Kuhn 1996, 145)

Kuhn (1996, 23) spells this out through a detailed analysis of the Copernican, Newtonian, chemical, and Einsteinian revolutions, but the main point of each example is this: "Paradigms gain their status because they are more successful than their competitors in solving a few problems that the group of practitioners has come to recognize as acute."

Kuhn's stress on anomalies, puzzles, unsolved problems, and the goal-directed nature of normal science suggests that paradigm shifts are not fact-induced movements that bring us closer to some paradigm-independent truth but are rather motivated by a given paradigm's inability to help a specific human community achieve a particular end. This process begins in a way that is like Haugeland's description of paradigm shifts: it is a response to an anomaly that is presented to us through a particular paradigm. Yet anomalies are not reducible to discovered impossibilities or inconsistent appearances amongst a certain set of entities disclosed via a specific paradigm. Instead, anomalies are gaps in our current understanding: they are unsolved puzzles or possibilities that are concealed in light of the way the world is currently revealed. Why, for example, couldn't we account for the length of the color spectrum with pre-Newtonian theories? Or why couldn't we explain the relation of diffraction and polarization in terms provided by Newton's own theory? Heidegger's word for an unsolved puzzle or a concealed possibility is "mystery" (*BW* 130–135). And if we as scientists are unable to solve a problem with the tools provided by our current paradigm, then we begin questioning the status of the paradigm that presents us with the mystery. This questioning is not a case of comparing the suspect paradigm with paradigm-independent entities, but rather a matter of measuring it against the claim of a new paradigm to solve the same problem. And as we have seen, a paradigm shift occurs if a particular group of scientists come to see that a new paradigm is better at helping them achieve their research aims. "In paradigm choice," Kuhn (1996, 94) says, "there is no standard higher than the assent of the relevant community."

Kuhn's analysis of paradigm shifts in various scientific domains looks at the way normal science is altered relative to a specific end that a community of scientists is trying to reach. Yet cultural transformation and the movement of human history also involve altering the ends we pursue completely. And we can see this by examining the analogy Kuhn makes between political and scientific revolutions. Kuhn writes:

> Political revolutions are inaugurated by a growing sense, often restricted to a segment of the political community, that existing institutions have ceased adequately to meet the problems posed by an environment that they have in part created. In much the same way, scientific revolutions are inaugurated by a growing sense, again often restricted to a narrow subdivision of the scientific community, that an existing paradigm has ceased to function adequately in the exploration of an aspect of nature to which that paradigm itself had previously led the way. In both political and scientific development the sense of malfunction that can lead to crisis is a prerequisite for paradigm changes. (Kuhn 1996, 92)

Simplifying profoundly for the sake of brevity, the shift from monarchy to republicanism during the French Revolution can be read as entirely changing the goal of government *from* maintaining a hierarchical order rooted in the idea of divine right *to* promoting and protecting the liberty and equality that all citizens are entitled to because of their basic dignity. In Kuhn's words:

> Political revolutions aim to change political institutions in ways that those institutions themselves prohibit. Their success therefore necessitates the partial relinquishment of one set of institutions in favor of another, and in the interim, society is not fully governed by institutions at all. (Kuhn 1996, 93)

He then completes the analogy by asserting: "Like the choice between competing political institutions, that between competing paradigms often proves to be a choice between incompatible modes of community life" (Kuhn 1996, 94). So, in the sciences and other areas human activity changes to our normal or everyday way of doing things may involve altering our current way of life in light of the ends we are striving toward or simply shifting the goals we pursue completely.

In the end, Kuhn provides us with an account of cultural transformation that applies to all areas of human activity whereby members of a specific community attempt to solve the problems that they face by the usual means until they arrive at an unsolvable anomaly and thus are required to amend their way of life or alter their goals entirely. Of course, our ability to amend our way of life or alter our goals completely is based on the historical contingency and future indeterminacy that characterize our finite existence. And after indicating the inconsistency in Haugeland's appeal to disclosure-independent entities and offering an alternative to his truth-based account of authenticity, we are now in a position to see that both the meaning of being and the movement of human history are determined by the ends pursued in particular historical communities.

7.4 Conclusion

In Division Two of *Being and Time* Heidegger tells us we lead an authentic life when we take responsibility for our existence by making a series of identity-defining choices. Heidegger's account of authenticity has often been read as an existentialist theory of human freedom that stands apart from Heidegger's groundbreaking inquiry into the ontological basis of our everyday existence in Division One of his *magnum opus*. Against this existentialist reading, John Haugeland interprets Heidegger's account of authenticity as a key feature of Heidegger's fundamental ontology: that is, Heidegger's attempt to determine the meaning of being through an analysis of human beings. Haugeland's argument is based on the idea that taking responsibility for our existence entails getting the *being* of entities *right*. Specifically, Haugeland says that our ability to choose allows us to question and test the disclosure of being through which we understand entities against the entities themselves. As he puts it: "Ontological truth is beholden to *entities* – the very same entities that ontical truth is beholden to, and via the very same means of discovery" (Haugeland 2013, 218). Haugeland (2013, 59) then says, "exhibiting that ontological beholdenness completes the explication of the truth character of being." So he concludes that our ability to choose is "the fulcrum of [Heidegger's] entire ontology" (Haugeland 2013, 188). Finally, Haugeland claims that taking responsibility for our existence entails giving up a disclosure when it fails to meet the truth test, and this means cultural transformation is based on the truth-seeking of authenticity.

I agree with Haugeland's general claim that Heidegger's existentialism is a key feature of his ontology, but I think the details of Haugeland's truth-based ontological account of authenticity are inconsistent. My objection is that if, as Haugeland maintains, entities are only intelligible through a particular disclosure of being, then it is incoherent for Haugeland to claim that those same entities can serve as an intelligible, disclosure-independent standard against which that disclosure can be truth-tested. And if no sense can be made of testing a disclosure against disclosure-independent entities, then no sense can be made of Haugeland's claim that authenticity entails taking responsibility for our existence by testing or transforming a disclosure of being against disclosure-independent entities. To substantiate this objection, I examined the case Haugeland made for his position via an analogy with Kuhn. Specifically, I indicated Haugeland's commitment to intelligible, disclosure-independent entities in his account of paradigm shifts. But then I went on to show that this commitment is inconsistent with a position held by both Heidegger and Kuhn that Haugeland otherwise endorses, i.e., that the intelligibility of entities presupposes a particular disclosure of being or paradigm.

After calling Haugeland's position into question, I offered an alternative to his truth-based interpretation of authenticity and cultural transformation via an ends-based reading of Heidegger and Kuhn. I began by taking a closer look at the relation Heidegger sees between disclosures of being and potentialities, and in doing so I illustrated the extent to which the intelligibility of entities is relative to the ends pursued by a particular historical community. I then analyzed the *methodological* import of authenticity for Heidegger's fundamental ontology. Specifically, and unlike Haugeland (2013, 188) who argued that taking responsibility for our finite existence allows us to test disclosures of being against disclosure-independent entities and thus sees authenticity as "the fulcrum of [Heidegger's] entire ontology," I claimed that Heidegger's analysis of our authentic existence *explicitly exhibits* the temporal horizon that is *fundamental* for all our purposive activities and the intelligible disclosure of entities, generally. Finally, in support of my position, I returned to Kuhn to show that paradigm shifts are not a function of sciences' steady movement closer to the truth but are instead motivated by the ends members of a specific community pursue.

CHAPTER 8

What Does Authenticity Do in Being and Time?

Sacha Golob

Authenticity (*Eigentlichkeit*) plays a foundational role in early Heidegger. To 'work out the question of Being adequately', Heidegger states, 'we must make an entity – the inquirer – transparent in his own Being' (*BT* 27/7; similarly, *BP* 103). Authenticity is central to such transparency: if our understanding of Dasein is to serve as 'a foundation for the basic question of ontology, then it must first have been brought to light . . . in its possibilities of authenticity and totality' (*BT* 276/233). Authenticity, in other words, underpins the ontological project. The aim of this chapter is to better understand what authenticity is and why it matters so much to Heidegger.

Before getting underway, note one restriction in scope. I will not address the idealism which may seem implicit in the claim that the existential analytic is the best way to grapple with ontology (*BT* 27/7, 424/372).[1] Instead, I want to focus on authenticity itself. What is the nature of this state? How does Heidegger's use of the term link to broader ideas of 'being true to oneself'? or 'expressing oneself'? And why should it be so significant for his work?

Most recent literature on Heideggerian authenticity frames the issue in terms of reasons. We can distinguish two dominant positions. On one approach, let's call it the 'Transcendental Reading'; authenticity explains our ability to *recognise* reasons – our capacity, as it is often put, to act 'in the light of' norms, rather than 'merely in accordance with them'. I will consider work by Crowell and Kukla in particular. On another approach, let's call it the 'Unity Reading'; authenticity allows us to identify a *particular group* of reasons to which the inauthentic are blind – these reasons play a distinctive role in our lives, unifying our commitments. I focus on analyses by Guignon and McManus. I believe that both

---

[1] I discuss this in Golob (2014, ch. 4). I argue that Heidegger is ultimately a realist.

approaches contain important insights. But I also think neither captures the core of Heidegger's view. I thus present a third option, call it the 'Structural Reading', on which authenticity consists in an at least inchoate awareness of certain *structural* facts about normative space. The Structural Reading, I argue, allows us to make perfect sense of authenticity's relationship to philosophy: Heidegger's preference for it is not a matter of 'moralizing critique' but a condition for ontological investigation (*BT* 211/167).

We can alternately frame the issue in terms of the self. There is a classic ambiguity in non-Heideggerian 'authenticity talk'. For some, an authentic life is one expressive of my own very particular individuality, my unique character traits. For others, it is one expressive of deep truths about all human selves. You can see the distinction in early Sartre, for example, where a truly authentic life consists in recognising that neither I nor anyone else is defined by unique character traits, at least in anything like the usual sense. It is clear that Heidegger's concern is with the broader notion: even when the focus is on 'mineness', it is on 'the essence of mineness and selfhood as such' [*das Wesen von Meinheit und Selbstheit überhaupt*] (*MFL* 242). Framed in these terms, the three approaches again offer different results. Roughly, the Transcendental Reading equates authenticity with the very conditions on selfhood, whilst the Unity and Structural Readings identify it with particular forms of selfhood, particular achievements.

The structure of this chapter is simple. I will take the Transcendental, Unity, and Structural Readings in turn. I argue that the last provides the most plausible analysis of Heidegger.

8.1 Transcendental Readings

Kant's *Groundwork* draws a famous contrast between two types of being:

> Everything in nature works in accordance with laws. Only a rational being has the capacity to act *in accordance with the representation* of laws, that is, in accordance with principles. (Kant [1784] 1902, 412; original emphasis)

Kant ([1783] 1902, 34) equates acting on principles with acting on the basis of 'a connection that is expressed by ought'. The claim is this: to explain the behaviour of rational beings we must refer not just to the laws of nature, but to what those beings *take to be* laws, that is, to what they take to be required or forbidden or permissible. This explains why the laws of logic, unlike the laws of physics, sometimes fail to determine my behaviour: I ought to avoid inferential errors, but unlike gravity, the efficacy of logical laws is 'mediated by our attitude' towards them (Brandom 1994, 31).

Compare the case of a dog. For Kant, Fido's behaviour is governed by a lawlike pattern of associative input-output correlations (Kant 1900, 52). But the efficacy of biological laws in determining this action is entirely independent of Fido's own (non-existent) attitude to such laws. In contrast, to explain why someone acted morally or failed to do so, I need to reference both the law *and* their attitude to it (Kant [1785] 1902, 412). Even if that attitude is one of ignorance or indifference, it needs to be cited if we are to explain why, unlike biological laws, it failed to have an effect.

Kantians standardly express this point as follows: Fido acts merely *in accordance* with a law, whereas rational agents act *in the light of them*. Kant himself aligns this distinction with moral responsibility and with a highly theorised notion of first-person awareness: he is explicit that animals lack such 'I' states, which are thus sharply distinguished from a merely egocentric spatial awareness (Kant [1798] 1907, 127).

I introduce this background because, stripped of Kant's assumption that all norms are laws, it plays a vital role in shaping contemporary readings of *Being and Time*. This is because Dasein's world is essentially normative: to see something 'as' a hammer as opposed to 'as' a sculpture is, amongst other things, to see it as appropriate for certain tasks. Indeed, for Heidegger, 'the "as" is the basic structure whereby we understand and have access to anything' (*LQT* 153).

> The 'as', and the relation that sustains it and forms it, makes possible a perspective upon something like Being. (*FCM* 484)

Similarly, to see that there are things 'one just doesn't talk about' is to refer to a norm, that there are certain things that *ought not* be addressed. The Heideggerian world is thus suffused with an awareness of norms. As he puts it, in a deliberately Kantian idiom, for Dasein 'entities are manifest in their binding character [*Verbindlichkeit*]' (*FCM* 492): that is, as located within a web of obligations, prohibitions, and requirements.

Crowell, perhaps the most influential current commentator on Heidegger, reads *Being and Time* as an analysis of the structure and conditions of such normative awareness. In Kant's language, it illuminates the conditions that allow us 'to think and act not merely in accord with norms, but *in light* of them' (Crowell 2001, 170; original emphasis).

What Does Authenticity Do in Being and Time? 161

Elsewhere he talks of Dasein's distinctive 'responsiveness to the normative *as* normative' (Crowell 2013d, 24; original emphasis).[2]

The Transcendental Reading works by linking these ideas to authenticity. The place to start is by distinguishing three similar sounding claims.

(1) Only if we are authentic can we identify the transcendental condition for Dasein's acting in the light of norms rather than merely in accordance with them.
(2) The possibility of being authentic is a transcendental condition for Dasein's acting in the light of norms rather than merely in accordance with them.
(3) Being authentic is a transcendental condition for Dasein's acting in the light of norms rather than merely in accordance with them.

Let's take these in turn.

(1) is an epistemic claim. It chimes with the suggestion, in my opening paragraph, that authenticity is key to a transparent understanding of Dasein. Heidegger makes similar remarks about other states closely linked to authenticity: for example, 'resoluteness' 'brings us before the primordial truth of existence' (*BT* 355/307). Also note that (1) is perfectly compatible with both authentic and inauthentic agents acting in the light of norms, just as both moral and immoral agents act on maxims for Kant. The point would be that Division Two identifies transcendental conditions on my sensitivity to the normative, conditions of possibility which are assumed, but not described, in Division One.[3] For these reasons, I will proceed for the moment as if (1) is unobjectionable.

What about (2)? There are passages where Crowell, for example, does endorse it. Consider this:

> When I give reasons and communicate as the one-self, this is a trace of my subjectivity, possible only for a creature that can be responsible, can answer the call of conscience. (Crowell 2001, 450)

Only a creature that *could* answer the call of conscience, which I take to at least overlap with authenticity, could also give reasons: in other words, the

---

[2] I discuss such 'responsiveness' in Golob (2020).
[3] A comparison might help: on a widespread reading of Kant, the Transcendental Analytic sets out various arguments which are in fact already assumed, but cannot yet be made explicit, in the Transcendental Aesthetic. In that sense, an account consisting solely of the Aesthetic would be 'unintelligible'.

capacities are co-extensive and all Dasein necessarily possess both. This seems to me unproblematic as well.

This brings me to the stronger (3): it is this which is the heart of the Transcendental Reading. Here again is Crowell:

> The agent functions within the nexus of practices in much the way that she functions within the constraints of nature: she acts in accordance with norms but not in the light of them; hence such behaviour is largely predictable from a third-person point of view. This is the picture of the functioning of norms within social practices which we get from Division One of *Being and Time*, where it is difficult to distinguish human from animal teleological action ... there are reasons for what Larry Bird does on the court, just as there are reasons for what the wasp does, but neither does them *for* those reasons, in light of them. (Crowell 2013b, 207; original emphasis)

Similarly:

> There is, however, a further aspect to the project whereby Dasein enters into the space of reasons ... Heidegger terms such a project 'resoluteness' (*Entschlossenheit*) ... To be resolved is to take responsibility for the standards inherent in the practices in which I am engaged; only so is it possible for there to *be* practices rather than mere occurrences. (Crowell 2013b, 210; original emphasis)

The former passage implies that an agent 'within the nexus of practices' is not acting in the light of norms, any more than the wasp is. The latter passage similarly implies that only with resolution do we enter normative space. These seem endorsements of (3).

Crowell's view is a highly complex one, and at times, he distances himself from such claims. For example, he argues against Korsgaard precisely on the grounds that she is forced to analyse mindless coping in non-normative, animalistic terms (Crowell 2013c, 257). Perhaps this shows that I am giving those remarks too much weight?

I think, however, that there is a genuine and important tension in Crowell's position, driven by some deep-seated philosophical issues. As Blattner notes, Crowell often ties authenticity to the first-person perspective. Crowell writes: 'It becomes evident from [Heidegger's] description of the one-self that it understands (is aware of) itself wholly in third-person terms' (Crowell 2001, 173–174).

I agree with Blattner (2015, 121) that this is implausible: when Tom starts talking, whether that act is described from his own first-person perspective or his listener's third-person viewpoint, is simply orthogonal

What Does Authenticity Do in Being and Time? 163

to the question of whether Tom's self-understanding is deformed by conformism or the other problems Heidegger associates with inauthenticity. Idle talk, to take a classic marker of inauthenticity for Heidegger, is supposedly a widespread social phenomenon: viewing oneself in the third-person, at least for any length of time, is much more unusual. The two cannot be equated. But Crowell's move is explained once we see the role of (3). (3) uses authenticity to define what *brings* an act within the space of reasons as opposed to being merely a natural occurrence. Given the very widespread Kantian assumption that normativity is tied to the first-person perspective, echoed in Heidegger's analysis of 'mineness' (*BT* 67/42), a commitment to (3) will immediately imply that inauthentic agents must operate in third-personal form. Hence Crowell:

> Heidegger's account of the one-self, then, describes my practical identity as a specific form of anonymity: engaged in the world, I am aware of myself only as 'another' or as 'anyone' – that is, in third-person terms. (Crowell 2001, 437)

So, whilst Crowell's attitude to (3) is complex, it does have a systematic role in his position: it explains, amongst other things, his claims regarding the inauthentic and the third person that Blattner criticised.

In other cases of (3), matters are more straightforward. Consider Blattner's incisive summary of Kukla's (2002, 4–5) attempt to link Heideggerian anxiety and Hegel's Antigone.

> [Kukla] argues that an agent who is responsive to norms must always already have been alienated from the norms by way of what she calls 'moments of authenticity'. (Blattner 2015, 129)

In my terms, this is (3): no authenticity, no normativity.

The basic problem with (3) is that it represents a confusion of levels: it treats a rare achievement, authenticity, as a condition on some very basic aspects of human intentionality. The issue with the first-person is symptomatic of the same error. Fleshing this out, those who either endorse or flirt with (3) are committed to either:

(3a) The behaviour of inauthentic Dasein is not analysable as acting in the light of norms.

or

(3b) There are no truly inauthentic Dasein: any putative case is or was authentic.

Note that (3b) is not the claim that all Dasein have experienced anxiety. Kukla's (2002, 4–5) story, for example, requires that we react to anxiety in a certain way, namely by recognising the possibility of challenging norms; it is not enough that an agent merely experiences anxiety and immediately chokes it down and carries on exactly as before.[4] Once this is appreciated, (3b) is manifestly too strong as a reading of Heidegger. It misrepresents his pessimism about mass culture and contemporary society: it also conflicts with texts such as *BT* (190/234) which emphasises the 'rare' nature of 'real anxiety' and the 'even rarer' cases of a proper understanding of it.

What about (3a)? Well, this also fails textually. Heidegger gives relatively little concrete detail about the life of the inauthentic but one of the most striking facts he does offer is how *normatively sophisticated* they are. For example, both *HCT* and the 1931 *Schwarze Hefte* use the same example of agents dominated by *Gerede*: in each case, they are engaged in sophisticated, and yet in an important sense sophistical, academic work. For example, Heidegger views scholarly exegesis of *Sein und Zeit*'s links to Kierkegaard as a derailment device by which academics serve to distract themselves and the public from the book's real import (*GA* 94: 74; see also 39). Similarly, *HCT* (376) presents academic conferences as devices for 'covering up' ideas through parroting them out. If we turn to *BT* itself, we find similar results: inauthentic agents, dominated by idle talk, are masters at derailing conversations, with a set of rote talking points already 'stowed away' for whenever discussion of death, for example, gets a little real (*BT* 297/254). The behaviour of these agents is surely both inauthentic and an instance of acting in the light of norms, of putting forward arguments, defending principles, raising counter-examples, albeit distracting and irrelevant ones – behaviour that is completely different from that of non-human animals, for example.

Note that appealing to 'mindless' or 'automatic' coping, for example via Crowell's allusion to Larry Bird, doesn't help: the sophistical academics are as at home in logical space as Bird is on the court, debating with complete fluidity and immediacy – yet they are engaged in a very direct and complex fashion with norms, principles, and counter-examples.

Pulling these points together, (3) is a mistake. Authenticity for Heidegger is a rare and highly valued state; by extension, it is not well read as a transcendental condition on comparatively basic human achievements such as acting in the light of norms. The Transcendental Reading

---

[4] For extremely helpful discussion, see Blattner (2015, 126–129).

either collapses into (1) and (2), claims which are better absorbed by other approaches as we will see, or reveals itself as (3) – in which case it should be rejected.

8.2 Unity Readings

I now turn to what I called 'Unity Readings'. Here authenticity consists not in the foundational ability to respond to reasons *per se*, but in a grip on a *specific class* of reasons – reasons which in an important sense unify our commitments. In the literature, this approach takes two forms: I deal briefly with the older version, illustrated by Guignon, before turning to McManus' more recent work to see the view in its most sophisticated form.[5]

Guignon defined authenticity in terms of the imposition of a 'coherent, cumulative narrative' across our commitments.

> In contrast to the dispersal and endless 'making-present' of everydayness, such a life is authentically futural to the extent that it clear-sightedly faces up to the inevitable truth of its own finitude and lives each moment as an integral component of the overall story it is shaping in its actions. (Guignon 2000, 89)

A few years later, he writes:

> Martin Heidegger's conception of authentic resoluteness gives us a picture of life as an unfolding story aimed at a fulfilment of a specific sort. Such resoluteness provides a focus and continuity to a life that can help an individual find meaning and order during times of personal difficulties. (Guignon 2013, 204)

The authentic life is thus marked by unity, unity with important similarities to that of a story.

One immediate problem is that such stability seems insufficient for 'authenticity' either as Heidegger understands it or in a looser sense. I can live a life marked by 'continuity and constancy' in the service of a wildly delusional self-narrative. It is hard to see how that could contribute to the self-transparency Heidegger prizes. Conversely, Guignon obscures the links between inauthenticity and rigidity. The authentic for Heidegger are marked by flexibility and a responsiveness to the individual contours of

---

[5] McManus (2019) himself distinguishes his approach from Guignon's which he refers to as a 'standpoint account'. But for me, the two share an underlying identification of authenticity with an awareness of a particular class of reasons, that is, those that unify our commitments, even if they differ over the nature of that unity.

the situation, in contrast to the predictability of inauthentic behaviour (*BT* 355/307). Agents who seek above all to maintain narrative consistency must force the world into a set mould rather than genuinely responding to it on its own terms. As Fisher (2010, 262) suggests in an acute discussion of Mallick's *The Thin Red Line*, the authentic person 'does not appropriate the situation to his life by projecting a life-gestalt in order to make sense of it. On the contrary, he allows his life to be appropriated for the sake of the situation'. Guignon was aware of such concerns, but he took them to be problems with Heidegger's position, evidence of 'something deeply dissatisfying about the final picture that emerges in *Being and Time*' (Guignon 2000, 91). Perhaps though there are better exegetical options?

This brings me to McManus' more sophisticated version of the Unity approach. The idea is that authentic agents achieve a distinctive unity which 'pulls together in an overall judgment of her situation all the demands that it makes upon her' (McManus 2019, 1195). Unlike Guignon's, McManus' authentic agent thus finds unity in a close engagement *with* the world, rather than a narrative that might diverge from it.

At the heart of McManus' account is the 'all things considered judgment model' or ATCJM.

> The ATCJM understands Heidegger's 'openness to the concrete situation' as a responsiveness not just to the particular aspect of my situation that would strike a holder of office *a*, the pursuer of goal *b*, the adherent of norm *c* or project *d*, but instead a responsiveness to all of those aspects at once and to the need to adjudicate between them. I am capable of such responsiveness – and indeed it is demanded of me if am not to be 'closed' to the normative multi-dimensionality of my life – precisely because I may *be* not only the holder of office *a*, but also the pursuer of *b*, as well as the adherent of *c* and of *d*. Through all-things-considered judgment, I make of my situation a whole and I act as a whole. (McManus 2019, 1191)

In an earlier paper, he expresses this in terms of 'full stop' judgments:

> The authentic possess an answer to the question, 'What should be done?' ... What does this situation call for? – not 'from some particular kind of person, with some particular interest, role or responsibility' – but 'What does it call for full-stop?' (McManus 2018, 195)

Inauthenticity is simply the mirror image of this, characterised by 'qualified' or 'Q' judgments (McManus 2019, 1194). These have two distinctive features. First, they are 'departmental': they state what one ought to do *qua* holder of some particular role or seeker of some particular goal. For example, 'as a lawyer, one ought to do x here' (McManus 2018, 195).

Second, they evade 'answerability'. If Tom tells us that 'as a lawyer, one ought to do x, as a friend y', he remains silent on the most fundamental question of what *he* thinks I should ultimately do. Here is McManus:

> When do I speak for a matter with my person? More idiomatically perhaps, when do I speak for myself? ... We *do* feel that we can intelligibly say to someone 'Yes, I know that you think that as a holder of office *x* you should do *y*, but what do you yourself think ought to be done all things considered?' (McManus 2019, 1194, 1200)

Inauthentic agents thereby fail to genuinely express themselves.

One immediate concern might be over the specificity of McManus' definition: Heidegger's account of inauthenticity is often taken as a broad exercise in *Kulturkritik*. Consider a student body or a residents' association enthusiastically caught up in some new social movement. Even if one agrees with the political goals, the discourse will have many of the features Heidegger aligns with inauthenticity: strong group pressure; predictable, rehearsed patterns of argument whereby 'everyone is acquainted with what is up for discussion ... and everyone discusses it, but everyone also knows already how to talk about' it; a preference for speech that allows the group to self-position as 'doing the right thing', with real action relegated to second place ('talking about things gets passed off as what is really happening, while taking action gets stamped as something merely subsequent and unimportant', *BT* 218/174); a continual escalation of what counts as 'the very newest thing' and what is already unacceptably retrograde (*BT* 218/174); and etc. Such people are plausibly behaving inauthentically in a Heideggerian sense – but they are very unlikely to make hedged judgments in the way McManus suggests. On the contrary, they tend to be enthusiastic purveyors of 'full stop' verdicts.

To properly assess the proposal, however, we need to tease apart various strands. For example, is what matters that the agent pulls together the various demands *as she sees them* or the various demands as they *in fact* are? McManus (2019, 1194) defines a Q judgment as 'one that does not take into account – is not true to, one might say – some of what I think or value', strongly suggesting the former. To press these questions, let's consider McManus' own example:

> For example, rather than listen to my wife's worries or help my son resolve an argument with his friend, I sit down to mark essays on the grounds – when challenged – that 'I've got to do my job!' But I do not see or present myself as a locus of decision here: 'I've got to do my job!' and, of course, I do have to do my job. On a superficial level, I am beyond reproach: I am

acting in line with a norm that is generally accepted in my society, by my family and by myself. But in fact I am seeking here to be 'relieve[d]' – 'disburdened' – 'of [my] choice, [my] formation of judgments, and [my] estimation of values' (*HCT* 247) by – so to speak – dispersing the decision that my action expresses across my mere Q judgment – 'In order to do my job, I need to do my marking.' – and the background general acceptance that one indeed ought to do one's job. (McManus 2019, 1197)

There are several dimensions here and varying them independently will dramatically vary the case.

Suppose first I minimise family obligations because, having weighed all factors, I sincerely and correctly believe that my job must take priority – of course, marking is unlikely to be an emergency but there are obviously plenty of careers that will generate such emergencies (it would be criminal for the fire chief to settle down for a family dinner as the town burns). Surely, this is unproblematic and not McManus' target. Next, suppose, having weighed all factors, I sincerely believe that my job must take priority, a belief that follows from a reasonable assessment of the information available to me – but which is in fact false. Perhaps, although the evidence was invisible to anyone but a professional therapist, my son's falling out was really a sign of deep depression. Depending on one's broader epistemology and ethics, I may or may not have fallen short in some way, but again it is hard to see this as inauthentic and thus hard to see as the case McManus has in mind.

Next, suppose I minimise family obligations because I want to avoid grappling with those normative demands. This seems a better bet and it fits with McManus' talk of 'seeking to' escape responsibilities. Note further this remains plausibly inauthentic and a 'Q judgment' even if, *were* all factors considered, it would emerge that my job should indeed have taken priority, that is, even if my verdict were, in some objective sense, the 'all things considered' right one. This is because my behaviour is still marred by a problematic escapism. This is a familiar TV trope: the fire chief who hides from personal problems by attending obsessively to what are nevertheless real emergencies. Pulling this together, I suggest that the McManus account identifies inauthenticity with a certain decision structure: a failure to weigh all factors of which the agent is aware out of a desire to escape responsibility.

We can express this in terms of an internal/external reason contrast. McManus' authenticity does not require us to identify the 'all things considered' external reasons: that would beg the question as to how such a class might be defined. Rather, it is the 'all things considered' internal reasons: when I am inauthentic I fail to 'take into account – [am] not true to, one might say – some of what I think or value' (McManus 2019, 1194). In failing to unify their judgments, the inauthentic are thus not true to themselves.

McManus' (forthcoming) account is an ingenious one and I cannot do full justice, in particular, to the links he posits to Heidegger's Aristotle. But we now have enough on the table to identify some problems with it.[6]

First, the view entails that individuals who are simply blind to a whole host of considerations will find it easier to be authentic. The convinced bigot laying down the law leaves no doubt as to what they think, offering plenty of 'full stop' verdicts. Yet it is hard to see them as any kind of model: they achieve unity precisely because their grasp of the factors to be unified is *impoverished*. One possible response would be that this person might be 'no model' in a moral or epistemic sense, but nevertheless be authentic: they can be 'true to themselves' in a pre-theoretic sense. There are two problems here, though. One, Heidegger aligns authenticity with a high degree of sensitivity to the situations we are facing (*PS* 163–164; *BP* 407–408), and one of the attractions of McManus' account, as noted in contrast with Guignon, is that it initially seemed to accommodate this. But the proposed reply allows for authenticity in cases even of utter insensitivity. Another, which I will develop below, is that it is hard to see why such authenticity would be so methodologically significant for Heidegger: after all, our authentic bigot might endorse principles utterly incompatible with Heidegger's project (for example, they might insist that racial categories should underpin the existential analytic).

Second, it relies on a precarious alignment of the 'all things' dimension of the judgment with the 'I' dimension: the Q judgment hedges that 'qua lawyer, one ought to do x' whereas the authentic judgment declares what 'I' think in giving an overall verdict. But consider a case in which I conclude 'As father, I must do y, as husband I must do z' – and yet where there is no 'all things considered verdict' that I can identify with, no overall solution I can regard as anything but a squalid compromise, inexpressive of who I am. In such a case, there is no reason to treat the ATC judgment as distinctively expressive of myself and thus no reason to see it as distinctively linked to authenticity.

Third, it is unclear why the remedies Heidegger offers would help if McManus' diagnosis were right. For example, McManus (2020, 140; emphasis added) reads anxiety as an experience in which the options facing

---

[6] I am indebted to Denis McManus for very generous discussion of the following objections.

me appear 'insignificant *in themselves*' since a full adjudication of their weight rests on the 'all things considered' judgment to come. But this is hard to square with the phenomenology Heidegger describes, which is of a global collapse of meaning, one in which 'the world has the character of completely lacking significance' (*BT* 231/186). If McManus' 'insignificance in themselves' were correct, the phenomenology should surely be of multiple values clamouring for attention, as when we feel the pull of incommensurable goals. Similarly, it is unclear why Heidegger would suggest that philosophy fosters authenticity: the 'task of philosophizing is to evoke the Dasein in man', to 'liberate' it from the layers of misconstrual and self-deception (*FCM* 258, 255).[7] This is partly because McManus' account is too focused on the speaker's motivations: if the task is to get me to face up to all my various responsibilities, family, job, friends, etc., I may need a pep talk but I am unlikely to need an understanding of the history of being or even an analysis of how we are all thrown into social roles. Why should that move me if the pleas of my own son have already failed?

Fourth, McManus' model does not explain Heidegger's suggestion, noted in the opening lines of this chapter, that authenticity is a uniquely enabling condition for philosophy. As he puts it in *BT*, it is authentic awareness which 'guarantees ... that we are coining the appropriate existential concepts' (*BT* 364/316). There are countless people who have successfully made 'all things considered' judgments, and yet believed the philosophical nonsense Heidegger sees as characteristic of modernity or of organised religion. For example, someone could be authentic on McManus' account and be an utterly convinced Cartesian: this is impossible to square with the idea that authenticity 'make[s] an entity – the inquirer – transparent in his own Being' (*BT* 27/7). Conversely, it is not unheard of for those who evade their personal responsibilities to have great intellectual insights: I need not belabour Heidegger's own case here. Of course, that does not exempt them from challenge but, as Heidegger stresses, his aim is 'purely ontological', not to offer a 'moralizing critique' (*BT* 211/168). Blanking your son, as in McManus' example, is unattractive, but there is no reason why it should connect to good or bad philosophy.

The underlying problem here is that McManus' notion of authenticity is too ontic: I am true to myself in the sense that I am taking into account

---

[7] Thus, philosophy is a 'questioning' which seeks to 'develop a readiness for the moment of vision', that is, for the 'liberation of the Dasein in man' (*FCM* 254–255).

all my own individual, ontic commitments: my family, my friends, my job. Those are the 'all things' which I must consider.

McManus' account is, however, an immensely rich one, particularly in its appeal to Heidegger's Aristotle, and there may be other lines on which it can develop: for example, in forthcoming work, he suggests that the unity characteristic of ATC judgments could map the unity of types of being that Heidegger aims to analyse (McManus, forthcoming, 34).[8] I cannot address this here, but we have at least some idea of the attractions and weaknesses of the ATC model and of Unity stories more broadly. The final task is to introduce the Structural approach.

8.3 Structural Readings

I will now introduce the third approach on which authenticity consists in an at least inchoate or pre-theoretic awareness of certain *structural* facts about the space of reasons. This is equivalent, as we will see, to the claim that authentic Dasein possesses at least an inchoate or pre-theoretic understanding of its own fundamental nature.

Let me start by connecting the first of these formulations, in terms of reasons, with the second, in terms of self-understanding. As in Section 8.1, Dasein's world is a web of obligations, prohibitions, and requirements, of behaviour, tools, and even assertions understood as appropriate or inappropriate. Heidegger's early work ultimately grounds such norms in Dasein's self-understanding: the pile of scripts precariously balanced on the office floor shows up for me 'as for marking' just as they may show up to the cleaners 'as for disposal'. As Crowell nicely observes:

> This holds of my affective intentional states as well, whose reason-responsiveness is tied to what I am currently trying to be. For instance, as I lecture I notice a student sleeping and I become angry. A sleeping student is not inherently a reason to get angry, but given my practical identity as a teacher it is an instance of what Heidegger might call 'obtrusiveness' and constitutes a (defeasible) reason for anger. (Crowell 2014, 255)

It is thus Dasein's self-understanding which anchors the normative web. Here is the claim in Heidegger's own terminology:

---

[8] My worry would be that the two unities are very different: ATC's primarily unify a range of competing goals within a broad 'ready-to-hand' horizon, whereas the unity of being concerns radical ontological diversity.

> Why is there anything such as a why and a because? Because Dasein exists ... The for-the-sake-of-which, as the primary character of world, i.e., of transcendence, is the primal phenomenon of ground as such. (*MFL* 276)

What is distinctive about authentic Dasein then? Authentic Dasein is marked by a particular self-understanding: it lives with a 'primordial' awareness of its own nature (*BT* 276/233). Since Dasein is a normative being, this awareness implies an awareness of certain general or structural facts about the space of reasons, facts which are picked out by Heidegger's existential analytic. The two formulations with which I began this section thus merge. Heidegger often captures this in perfectionist terms: authentic Dasein is one that lives in the light of, and thereby realises, its essence, 'becom[ing] "essentially" Dasein in that authentic existence' (*BT* 370/323), fulfilling the ancient injunction to 'become what you are' (*BT* 186/145, 312–313/267–268).

Before proceeding, let me stress that my proposal is independent of what exactly these structural facts are: full discussion would require detailed treatment of the throw, conscience, etc. But one can see the main idea with a simple example. Suppose we agree with Carman (2003, 307) that *Being and Time* shows that all value is 'worldly through and through, embedded in the contingencies of historical tradition and social life'. This implies, for example, that there are no transcendent moral laws in either a religious or a Kantian sense. On my reading, authentic Dasein would be aware of this and live its life in recognition of it. It is thereby defined by a certain 'intimacy' or 'transparency' with itself, stemming from a harmony between Dasein's self-conception and its reality (*HCT* 282; *BT* 27/7). *In short, authentic Dasein understands the normative landscape on which it operates, and thus the horizon against which particular choices appear.*

We can now understand the relationship between authenticity and philosophy. On the one hand, it makes perfect sense that it is 'authentic' pre-theoretic awareness which 'guarantees ... that we are coining the appropriate existential concepts' (*BT* 364/316).[9] This is because authenticity is an inchoate grip on Dasein's existential structure. On the other hand, we can see why philosophy fosters authenticity. Insofar as it unpacks the structure of normativity, it 'leads us to the brink of our possibilities', making the contours of our world clear (*FCM* 257). Of course, there is always a risk that the discipline will degenerate into 'free-floating speculation'. But at its best philosophy can:

---

[9] Theory must thus 'be attested in its existentiell possibility by Dasein itself' (*BT* 312/267).

[m]ake manifest the Dasein in contemporary man once more, so that he can in general perceive ... what is essential in Dasein. (*FCM* 257)

With my account in place, let me now highlight some key contrasts with those discussed above.

First, the transcendental reading. I hope it is now clear why I endorsed this in Section 8.1:

(1)   Only if we are authentic can we identify the transcendental condition for Dasein's acting in the light of norms rather than merely in accordance with them.

This epistemic claim reflects authenticity's methodological role: authentic self-understanding implies an awareness of the structures which ground our engagement with reasons. Crucially, that awareness need *not* be explicit or thematised. For example, Heidegger believed that early Christian communities 'lived temporality as such' (*PRL* 82). This was marked by Paul's rejection of an 'objective' model of time in favour of one in which talk about the future, say, is not about 'when' but about the 'how of self-comportment', that is, in which it is an inchoate way of delineating the distinctively teleological orientation that Heidegger analyses as 'originary temporality' (*BT* 373–374/326–327; *PRL* 106). The Pauline Christian thus possessed an authentic but inchoate understanding of the foundational structures that define Dasein's intentionality: the philosopher's task is to use phenomenology to articulate that understanding in systematic terms.

We can also see how my account avoids the problematic (3):

(3)   Being authentic is a transcendental condition for Dasein's acting in the light of norms rather than merely in accordance with them.

On my reading, all Dasein operate 'in the light of', rather than merely in accordance, with norms: recall the highly sophisticated, if sophistical, Kierkegaard scholars attacked by Heidegger. Since Heidegger, like Kant, equates normativity with 'mineness', it follows that such 'mineness' is a constitutive feature of all Dasein, be it authentic or inauthentic:

> That being which is an *issue* for [Dasein] in its very being is in each case mine ... As modes of being, authenticity and inauthenticity ... are both grounded in the fact that any Dasein whatsoever is characterised by mineness. (*BT* 68/42–43; original emphasis)[10]

---

[10] Heidegger follows almost exactly the orthodox Kantian line on which the boundary between normativity and non-normativity is co-extensive with the boundary between humans and non-human animals: the latter cannot see something 'as' a hammer and thus cannot see it as appropriate or inappropriate for certain tasks (*GA* 27: 192; *FCM* 397, 416, 450)

In the case of inauthentic agents, however, the 'I', the 'mineness' that characterises Dasein, is occluded or inoperative (*BT* 151/115–116). This is not because inauthentic Dasein ceases to act in the light of reasons, as on the Transcendental reading, but rather because its engagement with reasons is inadequate: inauthentic Dasein abnegates its own responsibility, whilst nevertheless remaining responsible precisely for that in a way that a dog, say, simply could not be (*BT* 164/127; *HCT* 340). This abnegation can take many forms, but it is rooted in an attempt to deny or silence or blot out the normative facts of which authentic Dasein is aware. This explains why inauthenticity is such a broad phenomenon for Heidegger: destabilised and threatened by guilt or anxiety, burying oneself in triviality is one option, a dogmatic adherence to theism another.

Second, consider Unity approaches such as Guignon's. As McManus (2019, 1182–1183) notes, one reason these may seem attractive is that Heidegger talks of *Das Man* as 'dispersed' [*zerstreut*] (*BT* 167/129) or 'fragmentary', Stambaugh's rendering of '*als unganzes*' (*BT* 276/233). This seems to locate authenticity in the context of post-MacIntyrean or post-Frankfurtian concerns about the need for commitments such as narratives in achieving unity and thereby genuine selfhood. But, as I argued in Section 8.2, narrativity is no guarantee against inauthenticity and we can now see that the very same primary texts in fact support the Structural approach better. To begin, we must not overread '*zerstreut*' which Heidegger often uses loosely for quite general facts about Dasein that are neutral between authenticity and inauthenticity (for example, *BT* 82/56). Next, note that the distinctive sense in which the inauthentic man is dispersed is that he loses himself in trivial matters, desperately seeking 'distraction' [*Zerstreuung*] in 'things of little significance' to the point that 'he does not genuinely see himself' (*BT* 441/389–390; *BT* 216/172; *PS* 51).[11] This fits perfectly with my model: the problem is not lack of unity, but *lack of depth*, superficiality. Inauthentic Dasein flees from the inchoate awareness of its own nature, encountered in states such as anxiety, desperately fixing its eyes on the busy work of everyday life instead. Similarly, the full text reference to inauthentic Dasein as '*als unganzes*' makes clear that what the inauthentic lack is precisely an adequate grip on their own nature:

> One thing has become unmistakable: our existential analysis of Dasein up till now cannot lay claim to primordiality. Its fore-having never included more than the inauthentic Being of Dasein and of Dasein as less than a

---

[11] Translation modified.

whole [*als unganzes*]. If the Interpretation of Dasein's Being is to become primordial, as a foundation for working out the basic question of ontology, then it must first have brought to light existentially the Being of Dasein in its possibilities of authenticity and totality. (*BT* 276/233)

Inauthentic Dasein is 'less than a whole' not because it lacks consistent principles or a narrative that govern its life – it may have plenty of those – but because it fails to acknowledge the full facts of its nature: in Heideggerian terms, the full span of originary temporality.

Third, consider McManus' more sophisticated version of the Unity reading. I allow the inauthentic to make a very wide range of errors: this matches the broad *Kulturkritik* style of Heidegger's presentation which I suggested McManus could not explain. What matters is simply that they lack and seek to dodge the awareness the authentic possess. This will sometimes manifest itself in elaborate system-building as a form of reassurance, sometimes in a clinging to inherited views, most often in a simple refusal to engage with anything beyond trivialities. It is also now clear why Heidegger insists that only the authentic can accurately philosophise, another point which made little sense on McManus' account.

> Only he can philosophise who is already resolved to grant free dignity to Dasein in its most radical and universal-essential possibilities. (*MFL* 22)

As Crowe (2006, 29) nicely puts it, 'authenticity ... is a concrete experience that provides ... a purchase on the phenomenon that is to be interpreted'.

Other problems for McManus also now ease. For example, I suggested that on his account Heidegger's focus on anxiety and the history of Being as remedies for inauthenticity made little sense: why should that bring me to attend to my family, as in his example, when I am deaf to their own pleas? But if the aim is to open the way for at least an inchoate grip on Dasein's structure, it makes much more sense: in deconstructing the canon, for example, Heidegger can break down long sedimented assumptions about agency. Yet we need to be careful with the word 'remedy' here. Heidegger's aim is not to supply internal reasons that might move the inauthentic to authenticity in the way much moral philosophy seeks to persuade the egoist on their own terms. Rather, Heidegger's goal is to create openings, for example by drawing attention to overlooked experiences such as anxiety or boredom, through which at least some agents can glimpse a more accurate self-understanding.

The account I have given is not the full story. Heidegger aligns multiple other states with the inauthentic/authentic divide and a complete analysis would need to account for those. One can see how that might be done. Conscience and anxiety, for example, are further ways in which the true structure of Dasein makes itself manifest, intruding into even everyday life, offering a chance to 'hear [our] own self' (*BT* 363/315). Similarly, resoluteness is fundamentally an acknowledgement of the structural normative facts I have stressed: for example, 'a self-projection upon one's ownmost being-guilty that is ready for anxiety' (*BT* 343/296–297). A full analysis would also need to discuss the links which Heidegger draws between authenticity and phronesis, to detail the structural normative facts which I have only gestured at here and to unpack the relationship between the inchoate awareness of them found in the authentic and the explicit articulation of them in Heidegger's text. I have attempted to do these things elsewhere (Golob 2014, ch. 6 and forthcoming).

I asked what authenticity 'does' in *Being and Time*. Phenomena such as guilt, the throw, and anxiety map the structure of the self, where this self is understood in normative terms. Authenticity is a distinctive form of self-knowledge, or 'transparency' in Heidegger's terms, regarding that normative structure. Given Heidegger's premise that to investigate being we must investigate Dasein, it follows that authenticity underpins the entire project. We can also see now how this dovetails with the other great phenomenological pillars of the text: Heidegger must explain in what sense the authentic can have an 'inchoate' or 'inexplicit' or 'pre-judgmental' grip on such knowledge and how the philosopher can translate that into systematic form without thereby distorting it.

CHAPTER 9

Why Ask Why? Retrieving Reason in Being and Time
Steven Crowell

In late writings, Heidegger is fond of quoting Angelus Silesius – "The rose knows no why / it blooms because it blooms" – as an emblem of existence untroubled by the principle of sufficient reason, and already in *Being and Time* he had replaced the traditional definition of human being, *animal rationale*, with "care" (*Sorge*). Dasein, the "entity which each of us is," is most broadly described as that entity "for which, in its being, that very being is essentially an *issue*" (*BT* 27/7, 117/84). This description epitomizes what matters in the replacement of reason by care: to *be*, in the case of Dasein, is to be concerned with what it *means* to be – not just now and then, but always, "essentially." In Heidegger's usage, care is not one affect or attitude among others but an ontological whole whose moments are the equally "primordial," only conceptually distinguishable, categories or "existentialia": *Befindlichkeit, Verstehen*, and *Rede* (*BT* 224/180).

In *Being and Time* Heidegger is at pains to show that, among the modes of *Rede* (discourse), *logos apophantikos* or "assertion" is not fundamental (*BT* 195–203/153–160). Thus, it might appear that Heidegger not only rejects the traditional definition of human being but also refuses reason any constitutive role in the ontological account that replaces it. This has led some commentators to hold that Heidegger's thinking is fundamentally irrational, with all that implies (skepticism, relativism, nihilism), while it has led others to see a liberation from the iron cage of reason, freeing the creative powers of ambiguously measured self-fashioning.[1] There is a grain of truth in both views, but I won't engage them here. Instead, I deny the premise: the care-structure does not render reason a contingent and ultimately dispensable option for Dasein; it resituates reason as reason-*giving*,

---

[1] The lineage of the former group includes Max Horkheimer, Jürgen Habermas, and Ernst Tugendhat, and more recently Richard Wolin, Tom Rockmore, and Johannes Fritsche. The latter group would include Jean-Paul Sartre, Paul Tillich, and more recently Reiner Schurmann, Charles Guignon, and Hubert Dreyfus. For an account of the ambiguities involved in this either/or, see Woessner (2011).

something *demanded* of us by our being as care. *Being and Time* thus offers what I will call a "normativity-first" account of reason in contrast to a "reasons-first" approach to normativity.[2] The latter – exemplified in what follows by Kant's transcendental philosophy – determines what norms are by the reasons we have for being bound by them, whereas a normativity-first account of reason determines what reasons are by (phenomenologically) grounding them as responses to a normative claim.[3]

Defense of this interpretation requires going beyond the text of *Being and Time* to what remains unsaid in it. Transgressing traditional exegetical norms in this way may seem "violent" in Heidegger's sense (*KPM* 141), but if it is violent, it is not unprincipled. The principle is the free employment of the method Heidegger himself adopts in *Being and Time*: phenomenology. To practice phenomenology freely is not to abandon the text; rather, it is to "retrieve" (*wieder-holen, KPM* 143) a set of issues that belong to the phenomena Heidegger examines in *Being and Time* but are only tangentially thematized by him. Heidegger adopts such an attitude toward Kant in his "destruction" of the history of ontology, which strives to uncover the "primordial experiences" that still speak in traditional ontological concepts and yield "positive possibilities" for further insight (*BT* 44/22). Thus, the retrieval we will practice on *Being and Time* is, as Heidegger says of his own approach, "aimed at 'today'" – motivated by a conviction (even if Heidegger might not share it) that the phenomenology of care has much to contribute to contemporary philosophical discussions.

The retrieval of reason in *Being and Time* requires consideration of two texts composed during the same period: *On the Essence of Ground* (1928) and *Kant and the Problem of Metaphysics* (1929). In the Preface to the first

---

[2] In *Der Satz vom Grund* (1957), where the line from Angelus Silesius is extensively discussed, Heidegger tacitly acknowledges, and rejects, this result of his transcendental project in *Being and Time*. I discuss this matter in Crowell(2020), arguing that Heidegger simply relocates the "demand" in question from the call of conscience to the call of *Beyng*. On conscience, see Section 9.4 below.

[3] This way of putting the point might make it sound self-contradictory, since "grounding" is often understood as a matter of providing a rational account of something. Recent analytical literature on metaphysical grounding has challenged this by conceiving grounding as a metaphysical *dependence* relation which might provide the material for an explanation but is not itself one. See, for instance, the contributions by Paul Audi, Kathryn Koslicki, and David Liggins in Correia and Schnieder (2012). We cannot explore those issues here, but Heidegger himself, in *Der Satz vom Grund*, distinguishes between reason's "why" and the different sort of ground he hears in the "because" (*PR* 36–38). See Crowell (2020, 39–40). As I will argue in Section 9.5 below, already in the period of *Being and Time*, Heidegger provides an analysis of ground (*Grund*) that is not equivalent to reason. Thus, in what follows I will use the term "ground" in a way that does not *require* that we think of all grounds as reasons, holding open the possibility that grounding reason in a normative claim – the normativity-first thesis – is not *eo ipso* contradictory.

edition of the latter, Heidegger notes that the book grew out of his 1927/28 lecture course, a "phenomenological interpretation" of Kant's *Critique of Pure Reason*, and "arose in connection" with his (aborted) work on Part Two of *Being and Time*. In that same Preface, he suggests that the reader consult *On the Essence of Ground* for "further clarification" of the "guiding manner of questioning" in *Being and Time* (*KPM* xix). Thus, the author seems to authorize a reading which emphasizes the continuity of these three texts, a reading that will permit us to recover elements of a phenomenology of reason that do not become thematic in Heidegger's *magnum opus*.[4]

Fortunately, a comprehensive interpretation of either supplemental text is not necessary for retrieving the place of reason in *Being and Time*. Though that book devotes no heading or subheading to the topic of reason, there is much discussion of knowledge and truth, which have tight connections with the traditional concepts of reason and rationality and provide touchstones for Heidegger's interpretation of Kant. Here too we must be selective, but some consideration of what Heidegger calls "ontological knowledge" will highlight what he takes to be the phenomenological yield of Kant's *Critique of Pure Reason*: a concept of "pure *sensible* reason" as the "ground" of metaphysics. Since Heidegger claims that Kant's project corresponds *in intention* to that of *Being and Time* (*KPM* 141–142), such clarification will suggest where we should look to retrieve reason in the Analytic of Dasein.

9.1 Reason and the Rejection of Neo-Kantian Approaches to Knowledge

Early on in *Being and Time*, and throughout, Heidegger identifies two elements of our knowledge of beings ("ontic knowledge"): *nous* and *logos*, *noein* and *legein*. Heidegger resists translating either term as "reason," but both enter into the concept as handed down. *Logos* is reason in the sense of giving an account of something (*logon didonai*) – in Aristotelian terms, an answer to the question "why" – and so involves saying, asserting, something about something. To adopt this sense of reason is to conceive truth as a property of judgments or propositions (*logos apophantikos*), organized into a logical system of grounds and consequents governed by the principle

---

[4] For an argument that the continuity is not quite as thoroughgoing as Heidegger hopes, with regard to the relation between phenomenological ontology and metaphysics, see Crowell (2000) and (2018).

of sufficient reason. "Theory of knowledge" is *Wissenschaftslehre*, a construction of those categories that make scientific knowledge possible as the ideally complete system of "already known knowledge" (*IPR* 42–47). This is essentially the position of Marburg Neo-Kantianism (e.g., Hermann Cohen, Paul Natorp, and, with important differences, Ernst Cassirer), and it provides the foil for Heidegger's phenomenological reading of Kant.[5]

Reason in the sense of *nous* – which Heidegger usually translates as *Vernehmen* (perception) or *Anschauung* (intuition) in *Being and Time* – is quite different; it is the immediate encounter with something, a kind of "truth" whose opposite is not falsity but unreceptivity: one either does or does not see. In Aristotle, such seeing is reserved for immediate sense qualities, but also for the ultimate principles, *archai*, or grounds of things: the categories (*BT* 57/33). In the latter sense, "noetic" reason is the source of ontological, rather than ontic, knowledge. Ontological knowledge is not concerned with the properties of beings and the relations between them but with being (*Sein*), that which *constitutes* beings *as* beings. The Neo-Kantian epistemological program eliminates this sense of reason ostensibly on the authority of Kant, for whom, they suppose, *nous* is the "intellectual intuition" ruled out by the first *Critique*, resulting in the need for an "objective deduction" of the categories.[6]

In contrast, *nous* is central to Husserl's *phenomenological* project, whose "principle of all principles" subordinates *logos* to *nous* in a decisive way: "Each intuition affording [something] in an originary way is a legitimate source of knowledge," and "no conceivable theory can make us stray" from this principle because any theory "can draw its truth only from originary givenness" (Husserl 2014, 43). Heidegger follows this phenomenological path in *Being and Time*: all talk, all assertion and judgment, is measured by "seeing," by "exhibiting it directly [*Aufweisung*] and demonstrating [*Ausweisung*] it directly" (*BT* 59/35). Despite his many criticisms of Husserl, Heidegger describes how reading Kant "against the background of Husserl's phenomenology" confirmed the "accuracy of the path" he was pursuing toward *Being and Time* (*PIK* 292), a path marked by the phenomenological subordination of *legein* to *noein*. Understanding this methodological commitment is decisive for any retrieval of reason in *Being and Time*.

---

[5] Space constraints preclude discussion of the 1929 "Davos dispute" between Heidegger and Cassirer, but see Friedman (2000), Gordon (2010), and Truwant (2022).

[6] The core of Heidegger's extensive argument that the "subjective deduction" should have sufficed for Kant's project can be found in *PIK* (223–226).

We may begin by recalling that Heidegger sees his own "fundamental ontology" prefigured in Kant's project of "laying the groundwork" for metaphysics in the sense of *metaphysica generalis* (*KPM* 141).[7] To lay the groundwork is not to engage in metaphysics directly, but to reflect on what makes it *possible* to do so; it is thus a "transcendental" project concerned "not so much with objects as with the kind of knowledge we have of objects, insofar as this is possible a priori" (*KPM* 10; Kant [1781/87] 1968, 59). While Kant does liken transcendental ground-laying to the "method of the natural scientists" – namely, their realization that "reason has insight only into what it produces itself according to its own design [*Entwurf*]" and so "constrains nature to answer its own questions" – his *aim*, says Heidegger, has "nothing to do with a theory of knowledge" (*KPM* 7, 11). Instead, that aim is to show how "comporting toward beings (ontic knowledge)" is made possible by "the preliminary *understanding* of the constitution of Being, ontological knowledge" (*KPM* 7).

For our purposes, two things distinguish this phenomenological approach from Neo-Kantianism. First, in contrast to the latter's appeal to the "fact of science," Heidegger insists that "nothing can be presupposed" in Kant's laying the groundwork for metaphysics (*KPM* 11). Second, if we nevertheless call the "preliminary understanding of the constitution of Being" toward which such *Grund-legung* aims "ontological knowledge," then what such knowledge has in view is the (phenomenological) "essence" of ontological *transcendence*. "Ontological transcendence" is Heidegger's term for Kantian synthesis, the critical examination of which is the main task of the 1929 *Kantbuch*, and its elucidation requires attending phenomenologically to the "preliminary understanding of Being," the *Entwurf*, which constitutes beings *as* beings (*KPM* 10).

We need not go into the details of Heidegger's exegesis of Kantian synthesis, however, because we are interested only in how ontological transcendence phenomenologically entails a retrieval of reason in *Being and Time*. In that regard, what matters is that, for Heidegger, Kant's critique of *pure* reason, with its attendant rejection of *metaphysica specialis*, does not leave us with a Neo-Kantian epistemology of science but points to a concept of "pure *sensible* reason" (*KPM* 121) – "human reason," *finite*

---

[7] At the end of *Kant and the Problem of Metaphysics* (*KPM* 172), Heidegger suggests that his reading calls for a new look at Kant's Transcendental Dialectic, which deals with *metaphysica specialis*. Does the phenomenological reading of Kant shed new light on the relation between reason and metaphysical "totalities" such as the cosmological, ontological, and psychological "Ideas"? Heidegger pursues this question in lecture courses from this period. For a variety of answers, see Tengelyi (2014), Schmidt (2016), and Crowell (2018).

reason – which embodies the relation between *noein* and *legein* occluded in logicism, Neo-Kantian or otherwise.

For Kant, *noein* and *legein* appear as the "two basic sources of the mind," sensibility and understanding: the *receptivity* of "intuition," through which alone something is given, and the *spontaneity* of "concepts," through which alone something can be thought. Kant conjectures that these sources may have a "common, but to us unknown, root" (Kant 1968, 61), a conjecture Heidegger develops into an interpretation of imagination, in its transcendental (temporal) aspect, as the unity of *noein* and *legein*. This should have yielded a concept of "pure *sensible* reason," but Kant "shrank back" from this insight and, in the second edition of the *Critique*, subordinated imagination to understanding so as to preserve the "purity" of reason (in the sense of *logos*) as a source of a priori knowledge (*KPM* 112, 119). Fearing that "the primacy of logic" in metaphysics might "fall" (*KPM* 117), Kant abandoned the phenomenology of ontological transcendence initiated in the first edition, thereby straying from the path that leads to pure sensible reason. In *Being and Time*, however, the phenomenology of comportment (*Verhalten*) shows us the way back to that path.

9.2 Ontological Transcendence and Care

On Heidegger's reading, Kant acknowledges the priority of *nous* over *logos* when he claims that "knowing is *primarily* intuiting," even while he recognizes that human intuiting is merely receptive and so demands that "understanding" (thinking, judging) "surpass intuition" in intuition's "finitude and neediness" (*KPM* 15). This surpassing, unnecessary for the divine *intuitus originarius*, is "taking the measure" of things given through intuition, which thereby become "accessible" in their being (*KPM* 17).

Empirical thought – science, among other forms of "ontic transcendence" or intentionality[8] – takes this measure according to a plan of its own, but the whole point of the *Critique* is to show that such "becoming accessible" has an *a priori* ground in "pure" intuition (time as self-affection) and "pure" understanding ("I think," apperception), which together make up "the totality of pure sensible reason" (*KPM* 170). Thus, all ontic transcendence, all intentional directedness toward beings,

---

[8] In *The Metaphysical Foundations of Logic* (1928), Heidegger explicitly identifies "ontic transcendence" with "intentionality" in the broad phenomenological sense: "Intentionality is indeed related to the beings themselves and, in this sense, is ontic transcending comportment" (*MFL* 134).

Why Ask Why? Retrieving Reason in Being and Time

presupposes *ontological* transcendence, a "projection" that takes the measure of their being *qua* being (*KPM* 163). Because Kant shrank back from his phenomenological insight into projection as the transcendental function of imagination, Heidegger devotes Part Four of *Kant and the Problem of Metaphysics* to sketching his own alternative: transcendence, the "subjectivity of the subject" (*KPM* 118), is care, the "understanding of being." Before doing so, however, he remarks on Kant's account of the *practical* self and its relation to *practical* reason, and what he says there proves decisive for the normativity-first retrieval of reason in *Being and Time*.[9]

If, in the first *Critique*, the self of "pure apperception" (self-consciousness) is "a *thought*, not an *intuition*" (Kant 1968, 168), things stand otherwise, according to Heidegger, in the *Critique of Practical Reason*. There, self-consciousness is not a formal condition but is experienced in the *feeling* of respect for the moral law. Moral feeling is the "feeling of my existence" as a practical being (*KPM* 112), and for Heidegger its analysis illuminates "the basic structure of the transcendence" of the practical self. How so?

As a feeling (*pathe,* hence "sensibility"), respect indicates "susceptibility" to the law, which means that respect is not a consequence of encountering the law but rather "the way in which the law first becomes *accessible* to us" (*KPM* 110–111). Understood phenomenologically, this means that I cannot grasp a law as a *law* (as opposed to a peculiar grammatical form, "deontological ought") without first being *receptive* to the normative as such – to the distinction, for example, between normative force and coercion. A law becomes accessible *as* a law only if I am able to feel myself bound by it. Such feeling is "respect" (*Achtung*). In "having a feeling for" the law, the "respecting I" becomes "manifest to itself" as an *acting* self: "reason, as *free*, gives to itself that for which the respect is respect." In thus subordinating myself to the law, I *project* ("elevate," says Heidegger, following Kant) "myself to myself as the free creature which *determines itself*" (*KPM* 111).

As Heidegger reads Kant, "respect is the manner of the self's *being-responsible*, ... authentic being-its-self," and this is the "essence of the acting being," that is, "of practical reason" (*KPM* 111). Phenomenologically, then, the exercise of practical reason – for instance, in deliberation – does not *define* being responsible but is *grounded* in the latter: an affective

---

[9] Further analysis of Kant's practical self and practical reason can be found in *Basic Problems of Phenomenology* (1927) (*BPP* 131–147). See also *Vom Wesen der Menschlichen Freiheit* (1930), where Heidegger argues for the derivative character of "law" (*GA* 27: 260–304).

responsiveness to a normative claim which, for Heidegger, need not take the form of law. As Heidegger puts it, neither the law (norm) nor the acting self can be "apprehended objectively"; they are manifest "in a more original, unobjective, and unthematic way as duty and action," the "unreflected, acting being of the self" (*KPM* 112). If we attend here to the unmistakable echoes of the phenomenology of care in *Being and Time* – let's say, to the latter's displacement of the "theoretical" attitude in favor of a phenomenology of Dasein's "absorbed coping"[10] – our question becomes: How much of this account of the acting self is actually found there? In particular, to what extent does practical *reason* show up in the Analytic of Dasein?

As in *Being and Time*, the starting point of Heidegger's retrieval of Kant's inquiry into the subjectivity of the subject involves directing phenomenological reflection away from the cognitive subject onto the subject as one who stands toward the world, and so also itself, as a *questioner* (*KPM* 150; *BT* 24–28/5–8). The question of how knowledge is *possible* bespeaks an ability, knowing, that is not sure of itself, a "reason" that is essentially *finite*. Indeed, for a being who questions, "in being-rational this finitude is itself at issue" (*KPM* 151–152). Here, the recursive "itself" introduces the basic feature of care into Heidegger's retrieval: any questioning is possible only on the basis of Dasein's "preconceptual understanding of being" – including its *own* being – which "for the most part" is "completely indeterminate" (*KPM* 159; *BT* 32–35/11–15).

In *Being and Time*, the entity that exists as care is *thrown-projection*: Dasein finds itself thrown into the midst of beings that are "manifest" in various meaningful ways thanks to its "projection" of their "being" (*KPM* 159, 165; *BT* 184–186/144–147). Care is thus the "structural unity" of the "transcendence of Dasein" (*KPM* 165; *BT* 226/181). But in contrast to Kant's project of rational grounding, Dasein's projection of the being of beings is never sure of itself. It cannot be firmly established by means of an "a priori construction" (or deduction) but involves a kind of "philosophical empiricism" in which ontological grounds are sought in response to a normative demand that precedes them.[11] This becomes phenomenologically evident in *anxiety* as the "basic disposition" which, Heidegger argues,

---

[10] This is the guiding thesis of Dreyfus(1991).
[11] The term "philosophical empiricism" appears in a note which is worth citing more fully: "But to disclose the *a priori* is not to make an '*a-prioristic*' construction. Edmund Husserl has not only enabled us to understand once more the meaning of any genuine philosophical empiricism; he has also given us the necessary tools" (*BT* 490, n. x/50; note 1). For Husserl, the normative demand that underlies the phenomenological project is the demand for "ultimate philosophical self-responsibility." Further discussion of this topic can be found in Crowell (2005).

"underlies all instances of finding oneself in the midst of beings" (*KPM* 167). If that is so, then care, unlike Kant's reason, is not a "harmless categorial structure" (*KPM* 167); it designates *Existenz* as a *task*, as *Zu-sein* (*BT* 67/42).

The project of *Grund-legung*, "philosophizing" as "the *explicit* transcendence of Dasein" (*KPM* 170), is one of these ways for Dasein to-be. Heidegger notes, without explanation, that carrying out such a project – namely, "the working-out of human finitude" as the condition of possibility for the "understanding of being" – requires "an existential interpretation of conscience, guilt, and death" (*KPM* 169). The missing explanation is found in *Being and Time*, where reflection on these phenomena, as I will argue in Section 9.4, yields the "pure *sensible* reason" phenomenologically adumbrated in Kant's project.

9.3 Comportment as Ontic Transcendence

Our reading of *Being and Time* must limit itself to issues that bear directly on the question of whether an essential role for reason can be phenomenologically attested within the care structure. We noted earlier that *Being and Time* subordinates *logos* (the "logic" of assertion) to *nous* (the "seeing" in which being is made available in its "difference" from beings), but this does not mean that *logos* as *logon didonai* (giving an account) plays no essential role in the ontology of Dasein. Rather, reason, as reason-giving, is grounded otherwise than in the tradition's conception of the human being as rational animal – namely, in the phenomenology of comportment (*Verhalten*; translated as "behavior" by Macquarrie and Robinson). Phenomenological elucidation of comportment, in turn, requires consideration of the relation between Division One and Division Two of *Being and Time*. Given the "circular" (hermeneutic) character of that text (*BT* 27/7, 358–364/310–317), the analyses of Dasein's "everydayness" in Division One everywhere *presuppose* the results of Division Two. This means that the derivative character of propositional truth, the truth of assertion, so heavily underscored in Division One (*BT* 256–269/212–227), may not be Heidegger's last word on reason as *logos*.

Division One introduces comportment in the context of a phenomenological examination of how things show up for us meaningfully – *as* what they are – in our practical dealings with them. Such dealings have their own kind of "sight," circumspection (*Umsicht*), thanks to which (e.g.,) the hammer I wield to drive a nail is there *as* a hammer, rather than as a thing with properties. Such sight does not require visually attending to the hammer; indeed, the hammer shows itself as it truly is when it "withdraws" into its use (*BT* 99/69). Nevertheless, circumspectively encountering the hammer *as* a hammer does require that it shows up within a *normatively* constituted "whole of relevance" (*Bewandtnisganzheit*) involving other things and the work being done, such that I can experience it as appropriate or inappropriate, suitable or unsuitable, in various ways (*BT* 115–117/ 83–86). *Being* a hammer – what it *means* to be one – is thus always already understood, more or less successfully, in such practical dealings. But to "understand," in this sense, is not simply to possess the *concept* "hammer." Mere possession of the concept, such that I might be able to reliably recognize hammers, does not allow me to grasp *this* hammer with the circumspective "sight" in which it shows itself as it is. Meaning, in this sense, is preconceptual; it is either seen or not seen (*nous*) and does not depend on my being able to give a true account (*logos*) of what it is to be a hammer. What, then, is the nature of the prior understanding of the "whole of relevance" that makes such sighting of meaning possible?

In *Being and Time,* the phenomenological analysis of comportment occupies the position that pure apperception or self-consciousness holds in Kant's project. In comportment, the self "sights" itself in a certain meaningful way – namely, as *trying* to *be* something. In the language of *Being and Time*, comportment is acting "for the sake of" (*Worumwillen*) some possibility of my own being (*BT* 116–117/84–85), where "possibility" is neither logical nor physical but ontological: *Seinkönnen,* ability-to-be (*BT* 183/143).[12] For instance, if I have the skills necessary to accomplish what carpenters are supposed to accomplish, then I am able-to-be one; that is, I can use the tools available in such a way that they can show themselves in the normative relations that determine their fittingness for the task. Lacking such skills, I cannot be sensitive to when things are going well or badly. In short, what a hammer *is* is unavailable to me. But even if I *have* such skills, they will avail me nothing unless I act for the *sake* of *being* a carpenter, "understand" myself *as* a carpenter. Such understanding is an instance of what Heidegger calls Dasein's "pre-ontological" understanding of being (*BT* 32/12), and since *all* understanding of being is tied to comportment, we need to look more closely at what is accomplished in Division One with regard to the sort of ontic transcendence or intentionality found in everyday comportments.

[12] *Worumwillen* is Heidegger's phenomenological translation of Aristotle's *hou heneka*, which he contrasts with *techne,* the *Um-zu,* whose "end" is fixed by the work to be done (*BT* 97/68). These matters have been widely discussed, but see Volpi (1989) for a reading of the whole of *Being and Time* along these lines, and Vigo (2010, 2016) for interpretations of the relevance of Heidegger's reading of Aristotle for contemporary issues in practical philosophy.

Comportment, acting for the sake of being something, takes many shapes: trades and professions, social roles (both explicitly codified, like being a senator, but also tacitly normed, like being a mentor, hipster, or celebrity), personal relations (parent, friend), and so on.[13] How these are understood will vary with time and place, and the norms pertaining to them will be familiar, publicly available, at such times and in such places. But neither knowing what a teacher or father is supposed to do around here, nor being institutionally authorized to do it, is enough to constitute one *as* a teacher or father. Dasein does not have its *practical* identity as a property; it "has" this identity only in trying to be it. And in such trying, what it *means* to be what I am trying to be is always at issue. Thus, we might say that in place of Kantian apperception – the "I think" which must be *able* to "accompany all my representations" (Kant 1968, 152) – Heideggerian self-consciousness is an "I project" that in fact *does* accompany my acting for the sake of being something, though mostly without becoming a theme in its own right. Such is the self-understanding involved in comporting myself for the sake of some practical identity – for instance, my understanding of what a teacher is (what it means to be a teacher) as I act for the sake of being one. Such projection is (ontic) transcendence, and it enables an encounter with beings not as "objects" (Kant), but as what they *are*.

As previously mentioned, such meaning (the "as") is initially understood in a public or "average" way, given the norms of the time and place. But in trying to be a teacher I can challenge those norms as inappropriate, as not fitting for what a teacher should be. It is in this sense that my self-understanding is always at issue in comportment, a practical matter whose success or failure is not measured by some temporally distant "end" but rather at every moment in which I am acting for the sake of being something. Thus, comportment requires that I *care* about living up to the norms of (say) teaching, even if, as Heidegger says, such norms, unlike technical norms, provide no recipes for what is required of me but are always at issue in my acting.

An aspect of the normativity-first character of Heidegger's phenomenological analysis shows itself here: I am *responsible* for the norms of

---

[13] For this reason, I have likened comportment to what Korsgaard calls "practical identity": a "description under which you value yourself, a description under which you find your life to be worth living and your actions to be worth undertaking" (Korsgaard 1996, 101; see Crowell 2007). While important differences obtain, they do not affect my argument here, so I will occasionally use the term "practical identity" as a shorthand for *Worumwillen*, that for the sake of which Dasein acts in doing what it does.

teaching – not in the sense that I invent them but in the sense that, in allowing them to exert normative force on my behavior, in "binding myself" to them, I am also committed to what they entail about the normative relations among *beings*, the paraphernalia of teaching here and now, the "whole of relevance" disclosed by the comportment of teaching. In short, my success in being a teacher cannot be measured if I am indifferent to how *things* should be in the matter of teaching.[14]

Before taking up the phenomenology of comportment as *ontological* transcendence, the central concern of Division Two of *Being and Time*, we need to pursue this last point a bit further. How does comportment enable the kind of "sight" (*Umsicht, nous*) that pervades our practical dealings with things? In Heidegger's terms, acting for the sake of being a teacher (caring about what teaching means) "discloses" the "world" of teaching, the totality of "significance" (*BT* 120/87) normatively adumbrated in what it means to be a teacher. Such world-disclosure allows a collection of mere things, as it were, to show up *as* useful or useless, serviceable or unserviceable, for the purposes of what teachers do with them. The point is not that I am originally confronted with a collection of mere things which I then "throw a 'signification' over" (*BT* 190/150); rather, the point is that ontic transcendence or practical identity is self-understanding in-the-*world*, and so also an understanding of the *being* of things that show up in the world, worldly things. Thus, the kind of *nous* that allows us to see (be sensible of) the hammer's normatively constituted availability (significance) is one in which I "sight" *myself*, understand myself, in terms of the norms pertaining to my current practical identity.

For Heidegger, such sight is not an infallible intuition; like everything else about Dasein, it is at issue in existing. But this finitude of self-understanding might seem incompatible with the idea that *nous* is an all-or-nothing affair, where one either sees or does not see. Addressing this worry requires examination of the phenomenological relation between noetic self-sighting and care, Dasein's being an issue for itself.

9.4 Comportment as Ontological Transcendence

That relation is clarified in Division Two, where the significance of Heidegger's brief allusion, in *Kant and the Problem of Metaphysics*, to the phenomena of anxiety, death, and conscience is fleshed out. For

---

[14] On *Bindung* (binding), see the analysis in Haugeland (2013). Heidegger's most extensive discussions of this notion are found in *MFL* (189–195) and *FCM* (339–343, 360–365).

Heidegger, these are not independent variables but belong to a *single* "distinctive way" in which Dasein is "disclosed to itself," a *verstehende Befindlichkeit* (*BT* 226/182) that has both existentiell and methodological import. Its existentiell import lies in being the ground of my ability to recognize – within *every* comportment, all ontic transcendence – a normative distinction between acting "resolutely" or "irresolutely," authentically or inauthentically (*BT* 343–346/296–300). Its methodological import within the transcendental project of *Grund-legung* lies in being the phenomenological attestation (*Bezeugung*) of ontological transcendence. The latter, following the parallel with Kant, is a "pure" or a priori ability-to-be that grounds "empirical" or ontic transcendence. Here too we will examine only those aspects of Heidegger's account that bear directly on the retrieval of reason in *Being and Time*.

The structure of ontological transcendence – the "unity" of facticity and existentiality – is phenomenologically attested in the *breakdown* of all our everyday comportments. If Dasein is thrown-projection, and if thrownness (*Geworfenheit*) – "finding oneself" in the midst of beings as a whole – is originally disclosed in "mood" or affect (*Befindlichkeit*), the affective character that belongs to breakdown is *Angst*. In *Angst*, "the 'world' can offer nothing more, and neither can the being-with of others" (*BT* 232/187); that is to say, nothing *matters* because everyday normative claims can get no affective grip on me. All ontic comportment requires that I care about what it means to be what I am trying to be – that is, it requires some level of commitment, *Bindung* – but *Angst* is that way of being disposed which affectively undermines any such commitment. And since the meaningful availability of beings depends on my trying to be something, *Angst* undermines the whole of relevance such that "the world has the character of completely lacking significance" (*BT* 231/186). Of course, *Angst* does not rob things of their *names*; I can still identify them conceptually and reason about them logically. But when I cannot project myself onto any ability-to-be, the noetic circumspection (*Umsicht*) in which the being of such things is sighted loses one of its necessary conditions: Dasein's ontic transcendence.

However, since projection of an ability-to-be (acting for the sake of being something) is essential to the ontological constitution of Dasein as thrown-project, it seems that *Angst* involves a paradox: if I cannot project myself onto any practical identity, *as what* do I understand myself in the breakdown of all my commitments? Heidegger answers this paradox with another: when all my abilities-to-be (teacher, father, citizen) are affectively disabled, I understand myself as dis-ability-to-be (*Nicht-mehr-dasein-können*; *BT* 294/250).

This would make no sense if Dasein were a thing with properties, but as a being whose being is always at issue, *Angst* introduces me to the finitude of the *practical* identities for the sake of which I act.

Thus the self-understanding, or projection, that belongs to breakdown is what Heidegger calls "death," distinguishing this from all forms of the ending of a life (*BT* 284/241). Death is a "way to be" for Dasein, one in which I understand myself as *solus ipse*, "I-myself," without further qualification (*BT* 233/188, 308/263).[15] All comportment, then, is "being-towards-death" – *finite* projection of what I am trying to be. This means that what is at issue in any comportment includes what it means to be *a self*, full stop. The methodological role of *Angst* lies in bringing Dasein to this noetic grasp of its own being: to be a self is to stand suspended between particular ontic commitments (abilities-to-be) and their possible collapse in such a way that I can either embrace the finitude of these commitments "transparently" (*Durchsicht*, noetic grasp of selfhood; *BT* 346/299) or "flee" that finitude by treating my possibilities as properties, thereby *occluding* what is phenomenologically attested in the breakdown of ontic comportments.

If, for now, this may suffice to suggest how "death" contributes to elucidating the structure of ontological transcendence, a question remains. On Heidegger's view, the "intelligibility" that is at issue (projected) in all comportment or ontic transcendence is "articulated" in "discourse" (*Rede*; *BT* 203–204/160–162).[16] If this is true for ontological transcendence as well, however, we seem to be faced with another paradox. Discursive articulation normally depends on the world opened up by one's commitment to a practical identity and is initially a function of the public character of such identities: "the they [*das Man*] itself articulates the referential context of significance" or world (*BT* 167/129). But if all such

---

[15] Here I draw on the accounts of existential death found in Blattner (1994b) and Haugeland (2000), though neither should be saddled with what I make of them.

[16] We cannot go into the complications to which the ontological notion of "discourse" gives rise. For one thing, such "articulation" does not necessarily involve "making an assertion that definitely characterizes" something (*BT* 189/149). For another, there is a certain ambiguity in the term "articulation," since Heidegger first introduces it in his analysis of "interpretation" as a kind of circumspective "taking-apart" (*aus-legen*) of the totality of significance projected in understanding. Interpretation yields the "hermeneutic as," the "something *as* something" (*BT* 189/149); so, in a certain sense, intelligibility is already articulated (*BT* 190/149) "before" discourse. However, Heidegger claims that discourse "underlies both interpretation and assertion. That which can be articulated in interpretation, and thus even more primordially in discourse, is what we have called 'meaning'" (*BT* 204/161). For my own attempt to sort out these ambiguities, see Crowell (2013a). In what follows, what is most important about discursive articulation is its *sensible* character – namely, that what the call of conscience "gives to understand" is something *heard*.

worlds have collapsed in *Angst*, it would appear that there is nothing to articulate. Heidegger addresses this paradox, as he did the previous one, by focusing on the phenomenon in question – the "call of conscience" – rather than on its supposed paradoxicality. Conscience articulates the self-understanding achieved in death as dis-ability to be (*BT* 322/277). As the mode of discourse that speaks in the experience of breakdown, the call must have "a character in every way the opposite" from that of engaged discursive practice; that is, it must give voice to how Dasein understands itself without the "mediation" of its practical identities (*BT* 316/271).

So the call of conscience "asserts nothing," provides "no information," but instead has the character of a "summons" (*Aufruf*; second-person address). Further, it is "silent" while losing nothing of its "perceptibility" (*Vernehmbarkeit*; noetic sensibility). Finally, what it communicates is "unequivocal," that is, beyond the reach of the pervasive "ambiguity" (*BT* 217–219/173–176) in everyday discourse between the way a practical identity is understood publicly and the meaning at issue in my trying to be it: "The call passes over *what* Dasein, proximally and for the most part, understands itself *as*" – its practical identities – and "what it counts for, can do, or concerns itself with in being with one another publicly," while nevertheless reaching the self "unequivocally and unmistakably" (*BT* 317–319/272–274).

Despite these negative characterizations, hearing the call does "give us 'something' to understand" (*BT* 314/269) about the self so reached: Dasein understands itself as "guilty" (*schuldig; BT* 326/281). What is this supposed to mean? Because the call addresses the self, the "I am," without reference to any practical identity, "being-guilty" cannot refer to anything I have *done* (*BT* 326/281). And in articulating the self as dis-ability to be, the call is *prior to* the "morally good and morally evil," making no reference to any "law or 'ought'" (BT 328/283). It "neither warns nor reproves" (*BT* 324/279) but articulates the meaning of ontological transcendence, the phenomenological ground of ontic comportments. It is thus a *logos* that is also *nous*, pure *sensible* reason.

In *Being and Time*, Heidegger's term for ontological transcendence is "responsibility" (*Verantwortlichkeit*), but we must attend closely to the second-person character of this term. Ontological transcendence is *answerability*, the ability to answer to the call which, as a summons, gives to understand what is at issue in being a self at all. For Heidegger, to be a self just *is* to be able to respond to the call, a response that is itself beholden to a measure (norm) at issue in it: "authenticity" (*Eigentlichkeit*; self-owning). *Any* comportment that issues from the call will involve the noetic sighting of selfhood as such, falling somewhere between the "transparent" (*durchsichtig*) or noetic attestation of my responsibility and the "listening away" from that responsibility, wherein I attempt to render myself unreceptive to the call.

The phenomenological basis for retrieving reason in *Being and Time* is found in this notion of responsibility as answerability, where reason is not a *constitutive* feature of care (an *existentiale*) but is no less necessary for that. If the possibility of breakdown shows that Dasein can *be* without being anything (any ontic comportment), it also shows that Dasein, a self, cannot be *anything* without being answerable for what it does and says. In the next section, I will support this claim by layering the account in *Being and Time* onto the phenomenological elucidation, in *On the Essence of Ground*, of ontological transcendence as a three-fold "grounding" phenomenon: *freedom* (BT 331/285) as "fundamental comportment."[17]

9.5 Retrieving Reason in *Being and Time*

Let us admit that, in Heidegger's discussion of the call of conscience, he makes no reference to reasons or reason-giving. Nevertheless, I can find no way to make sense of Heidegger's description of what "being-guilty," the content of the call, means if it is not the articulation of Dasein's responsibility *for reasons*, phenomenologically implied in care as ontological transcendence, thrown-projection.

Starting with thrownness, Heidegger emphasizes that Dasein always finds itself in the midst of beings over which it has no "power" (*BT* 330/284). I can manipulate beings in various ways, just as I can resist my inclinations, motivations, and other psychological givens, but I cannot change the starting points, as it were, of such manipulation and resistance. I am "delivered over" (*überantwortet*) to them – not as something that has nothing to do with me but as something I *am*: the "facticity" that belongs to the care-structure. Heidegger calls this the "thrown ground" (*Grund*) whose "weight" is disclosed "as a burden" – that is, as *mattering* – in "mood" (*BT* 330/284). In *On the Essence of Ground*, this is the *first* form

---

[17] In *On the Essence of Ground*, Heidegger suggests that ontological transcendence "occurs prior to all comportment" (*PM* 108). This is because he there limits the term "comportment" to ontic transcendence or practical identity. Yet in *Fundamental Concepts of Metaphysics* (1929–30), what Heidegger calls "fundamental comportment: being free in an originary sense" (*FCM* 343) mirrors the phenomenological analysis of the collapse of all comportment in *Being and Time*. I mention this only to forestall the objection that identifying transcendence with comportment attributes features to ontological transcendence that belong only to ontic transcendence.

that grounding takes: "taking up a basis" (*Boden-nehmen*). Dasein finds itself absorbed in beings as a whole, already "attuned" by them such that they affectively matter in one way or another (*PM* 127–128). In *Angst*, this attunement is such that beings *do not* matter at all, but this is still a way of taking up a basis within beings as a whole.

Thrownness, however, is what it is only together with Dasein's "project[ing] itself on possibilities into which it has been thrown" (*BT* 330/284), that is, taking up the various practical identities that are current in my time and place. In *On the Essence of Ground*, this is the *second* form that grounding takes: "grounding as establishing" (*Stiften*). The "projection of the 'for-the-sake-of'" is "freely letting the world prevail" (*PM* 127); that is, it discloses the world of a particular practical identity. In the context of *Being and Time*'s analysis of breakdown, however, the only "possibility" that remains is "death" – projection of the dis-ability to be any particular identity, the (noetic) grasp of the ability-to-be a *self* as such. As this is expressed in *On the Essence of Ground*, Dasein is disclosed "as a being-*entrusted* with having *to be*" (*PM* 126). Such self-understanding is a ground because it belongs to *all* comportment as the "freedom" thanks to which Dasein can "obligate" itself, "bind itself" to a practical identity (*PM* 126). In *Being and Time*'s analysis of conscience, Heidegger expresses this by saying that, even though the self can never get its thrownness into its power, "as existing" – that is, as projection – "it *must take over* being-a-ground" (*BT* 330/285). "To be its own thrown ground is that ability-to-be which is the *issue* for care," not just now and then but essentially. What does it mean, then, to "take over" being a ground? What does grounding as establishing mean?

If what is understood in the call of conscience, being-guilty, is that Dasein "must" take over being a ground, this is not simply a descriptive fact about Dasein. Rather, in breakdown, Dasein is positioned second-personally as the *addressee* of a summons or command: *you* must take over being a ground. Any response to this command, any taking over, will be a projection on possibilities, that is, the exercise of a particular, norm-sensitive, ability-to-be at which I can succeed or fail.[18] In this way, "Dasein makes possible for itself its factical existence" (*BT* 347/300).

---

[18] But what sort of response, or choice, is possible here? If, in anxiety, all ways to be appear equally uncompelling, it might seem that my choice must be entirely arbitrary, a "decisionistic" leap. Indeed, Heidegger asks, "On what basis is [Dasein] to resolve?" and answers, "Only the resolution can give the answer" (*BT* 345/298). We cannot treat this problem in detail here, but I believe we must acknowledge that, to the extent that anxiety continues to grip Dasein, no choice at all is possible. However, anxiety, like all moods, "assails us" (*BT* 176/136); that is, it comes and goes;

Obviously, this does not mean that Dasein creates its facticity. It means that in taking over being a *ground*, I "possibilize" the factic grounds that ground me as thrown. *Because* it is thrown, taking over being a ground is finite both in the sense that my facticity is *jeweilig*, a *particular* time and place where not every way to be is available, and in the sense that I can only project *one* possibility, act for the sake of *one* practical identity, and this choice is what lends the "binding character" to what is projected (*PM* 128–129).[19] The finitude of my choice in taking over *being* a ground "possibilizes" the givens of my natural, historical, cultural, social, and psychological condition – the circumstances (*Lage*) over which I have no power – into a normatively structured "situation" (*Situation; BT* 346/299) involving "grounds" for which I am *answerable*, "motivations" that take the form of *potentially* justifying (or normative) reasons for what I do and say. Thus, my being the addressee of the call to take over being a ground (grounding as establishing) entails a response that, as Heidegger puts it in *On the Essence of Ground*, "must *account for* itself." This is the *third* form of grounding: grounding as "legitimation" (*Recht-gebung; PM* 132), *logon didonai*.

This idea of legitimation provides the essential phenomenological link between reason-giving and the care-structure. As Heidegger describes it, legitimation is *Ausweis*, demonstration, pointing out, in which I propose (*anführen*) "a being that then makes itself known, for example, as 'cause' or as the 'motivational grounds' (motive) for an already manifest nexus of beings" (*PM* 130–131). Such account-giving can be done well or badly (*PM* 131), but it is not optional; rather, as taking over being a ground, ontological transcendence is *nothing but* being answerable for reasons. The finitude of care entails that no matter how I go on in comporting myself for the sake of being something, I will be exposed, *necessarily*, to the question, "Why *in this* way and not some other?" (*PM* 130). Because what it means to be whatever it is that I am trying to be (teacher, father, friend) is always at issue, my choice to go on in a certain way takes the form of an answer to the question of why I *should* go on in this way. And the general

---

and when anxiety has passed, the practical identities that previously made a claim on me become available again. It is at this point that talk of "choice" and "resolve" becomes relevant.

[19] The choice of one practical identity does not mean that other identities I care about disappear. Thus, all choice will involve establishing a kind of hierarchy of claims on me: If I act for the sake of being a parent (staying home with my sick child), I cannot simultaneously act for the sake of being a friend (going out with my pals for a beer). Baldly stated like this, it might seem that there is one "objectively" right thing to do, but on Heidegger's view, this is an illusion which arises from ignoring what he calls the "situation." For some suggestions on how to think about this hierarchization problem, see McManus (2019), McMullin (2019), and Crowell (2017).

form of the *answer* to such a question is that it is (or seems) *best* that I do so – namely, a *reason why*, "my" reason.

This interpretation is confirmed in *On the Essence of Ground* when Heidegger links "the transcendence of Dasein" to the *agathon* as *epekeina tes ousias* in Plato. It is "not by accident," he says, "that the *agathon* is indeterminate with respect to its content." Rather, what Plato situates in a *hyperouranios topos* is, phenomenologically considered, the ontological transcendence of Dasein, where what it means to go on in a certain way is always unsure of itself, at issue, finite (*KPM* 152). The "sovereignty over itself as *hou heneka* [for the sake of]" is not a property but a *hexis* toward "what is best," and this orientation is "the source of possibility as such" (*PM* 124). But since this sort of "freedom *is* only in the choice of *one* possibility" (*BT* 331/285), choosing to go on in a certain way closes off other ways of going on, such that my "legitimation" – the *Recht* of my reasons – itself remains at issue, *essentially* contestable. And because all comportment is worldly, and so involves being with others (*Mit-sein*), my being responsible for reasons is "equiprimordially" being *answerable* to others for those very reasons. Whether others are around or not, making something my reason is essentially reason-*giving*. There is no "timeless realm" (*huperouranious topos*) of reasons *prior* to the practice, demanded by the ontology of Dasein, of giving and asking for reasons. In this way, the three-fold character of grounding in *On the Essence of Ground* attests to the normativity-first character of Heidegger's account of reason.

Phenomenological examination of how Dasein understands itself when all its ontic comportments have collapsed – namely, its noetic grasp of what it is to be a self at all – shows that Dasein is "an entity whose being has to take over being-a-ground" (*BT* 331/285) in the three-fold sense presented in *On the Essence of Ground*. All ontic comportment depends ontologically on freedom as taking over being a ground, *fundamental* comportment. So understood, freedom is "pure *sensible* reason": My response to the summons constitutive of my being as care brings reason, as reason-giving, in its train. If this is so, then we should now be in a position to answer the question left open in our earlier look at Kant's account of the practical self and practical reason: How much of this is to be found in the Analytic of Dasein?

If for Kant, it is through the *feeling* of respect, our "susceptibility" to the law, that the law first becomes accessible to us, for Heidegger, it is through the affect of *Angst* that we are made aware of a normative demand or summons constitutive of our being as care. But for Heidegger, this demand does not stem from reason and so does not take the form of law. As a summons, it addresses me in the second-person accusative: "[Y]ou" must take over being a ground, act for the sake of what you take to be best (*agathon*) in what you are trying to be. Such acting is not subject to the test of a categorical imperative because, in "subordinating myself" to what I take to be best in my choice of what it *means* to be whatever I am trying to be, that meaning remains at issue for me. The "indeterminacy" of the *agathon* is thus *necessary*. Freedom, self-determination, is not self-legislation but projection (comportment) in which the acting self "gives to itself that for which the respect is respect," namely, that *meaning* for which it is responsible in going on in a certain way. For Heidegger, as for Kant, "the self's *being-responsible*" is "the essence of the acting being itself," and indeed it is "practical reason" (*KPM* 111). But for Heidegger, in contrast to Kant, practical reason is not limited to explicit deliberation, nor is it a "monological" assessment of the conformity of my "maxim" to the "form of law"; it is a dialogical practice of accounting for myself, being answerable to others in giving and asking for reasons. As Heidegger puts it, neither the "law" (the call that constitutes my responsibility for reasons) nor the acting self, is "apprehended objectively"; they show themselves only *in concreto*, in comportment as trying to be.

We might put it this way: The phenomenological elucidation of the acting self and practical reason found in *Being and Time* shows that care – letting things *matter* affectively in a certain way by binding myself to the normative demands of what I take to be the meaning of what I am trying to be – is not governed in advance by a rule but is the *condition* for any rule or law that can have normative force for me. Any such rule or law will be a function of how I, answerable to others, commit myself in response to the demand, inseparable from my being, that I assume responsibility for the normative force of what I take to be best in how I go on. To a rationalist who holds firm to a reasons-first account of normativity this might seem to leave action-guiding norms ungrounded, opening the door to decisionism and nihilism. But such a rationalist operates with a phenomenologically untenable concept of reason, one that presupposes the principle of *sufficient* reason, and so can safely be ignored.

Retrieving the place of reason in *Being and Time*, then, depends on adopting a normativity-first approach to reason. Norms do not become normative because we first have good reasons to adhere to them; there *are* no reasons until there is a being who "must" – is commanded or summoned to – take over *being* a ground, answer for a particular way of going on. Responsibility is not measured by being in accord with the law of reason; there can *be* a law of reason only because Dasein is a being whose life ("being") does not bottom out in a *Kampf ums Leben* but is always and already *normatively* at issue. Heidegger's phenomenological subordination of *logos* to *nous* does not exhaust itself in relegating the former to the "derivative" status of a propositional calculus; rather, it includes a retrieval of reason-giving, *logon didonai*, as a phenomenological implication of the care-structure. That such an implication was left unsaid in *Being and Time* is of no significance. Phenomenology is not a "philosophical 'system'" which springs forth "complete and full-panoplied from the head of some creative genius" (Husserl 1965, 75). It is a project of philosophical inquiry that always leaves much unsaid. But what is left unsaid can be said.

CHAPTER 10

Time's Origin

Daniel Dahlstrom

After indicating why Heidegger's fundamental ontology requires an analysis of the timeliness of human existence, this chapter reviews the analysis and its central thesis that this timeliness is the origin of other times (world-time and vulgar time). The chapter then identifies major criticisms of Heidegger's analysis of timeliness and historicity before detailing Ernst Tugendhat's criticism that Heidegger's argument for his central thesis is circular and cannot be sustained due to a reliance upon an allegedly derivative sense of time. The final part of the chapter offers a possible rejoinder to Tugendhat's influential criticism.[1]

10.1 Why Time?

What sets *Being and Time* apart as a philosophical work can be framed in the form of a supposition and an experiment. In the work, Heidegger supposes that being human is ontologically distinctive and he experiments with making the investigation of human existence fundamental for ontology. Fundamental ontology is accordingly designed to be different from previous metaphysical ventures that are all too often, as he later puts it, "meta-physics," where physical theory and considerations ultimately set the tone and call the shots. Since, however, we use the same terms to characterize human beings that we use to characterize other sorts of beings, merely elaborating the supposition of human ontological distinctiveness requires counterintuitive measures and some verbal gymnastics. Thus, for example, although there can be no mistake that human existence is the subject matter of the analyses in *BT*, Heidegger feels compelled to avoid the term "human being" in favor of "being-here" (*Da-sein*) and "existence" (*Existenz*) – terms that outside Heidegger's *Sprachspiel* apply to flora and fauna no less than to Dick and Jane. The rationale for talking about

---

[1] All translations from *Sein und Zeit* are my own.

human beings without explicitly saying so is ostensibly the need to steer clear of attempts to understand human beings as entities on hand within nature. Such studies (anthropological, biological, psychological) typically share ontological presuppositions with physicists and botanists, although the same can be said for many a historical investigation as well. This double talk is awkward but deliberate, besetting every major theme of *BT*.[2]

The analysis of existence (taking the term in Heidegger's restricted sense) is designated "existential analysis" and the existential analysis undertaken in *BT* is his first run at the sort of thinking that puts what it means for us to be here front and center. In this connection, he contrasts humanly being-here with being on hand (*Vorhandensein*) and being handy (*Zuhandensein*), two manners of being that are disclosed in our ways of being-here. Being handy, like the things that are handy (tools, equipment), is often overlooked, as is being-here, in favor of an age-old tradition of privileging being on hand as the sheer presence of things. To be on hand is to be present and, indeed, present to someone, in principle if not in fact, whether in the past, the present, or the future. Existentials are ways that we are here and disclose what it means for us and anything else to be; categories classify the manners of being of things that are on hand. Aristotle's list of categories includes πότε ("when"), a property of every being or substance (as οὐσια is typically translated) under the sun (as well as the movements of the spheres of all the other fixed stars).

In keeping with this effort to identify what is ontologically distinctive of human beings, Heidegger sets out to differentiate their timeliness (*Zeitlichkeit*) from the time of things on hand in nature. This concern with differentiating concepts of time goes back to his test lecture of 1915 where he distinguishes physical time from historical time. In physics, time is presupposed as a quantitatively determinable, independent variable in measurements of motion. Time and thereby motion are measurable because time is construed as flowing uniformly between points that differ only by virtue of following one another. This way of construing time, Heidegger adds (echoing Bergson), destroys the actual flow of time, converting the flow into a measurable surface (*Fläche*), "a homogeneous ordering of positions, a scale, a parameter" (*GA* 1: 424, 431). By contrast, "the times of history differ from one another qualitatively," lacking the homogeneity of the moments making up the serial time of physics" (*BT* 499v/418n1).

---

[2] On this practice and the essential ambiguity of philosophy, see *FCM* (11–23)/*GA* (29/30: 15–35).

But the problem of how time should be understood is not, Heidegger realizes, a problem for historians alone. In lectures on the phenomenology of the early Christian experience, he also emphasizes the necessity of setting aside the seemingly innocuous but ultimately falsifying, theoretical approach to time ("objective time') in favor of asking "how in factical experience we experience timeliness" and how "Christian religiosity lives its timeliness" (*GA* 60: 65, 104/*PRL* 44, 73). "Something like timeliness first arises" for the early Christians not through an expectation that takes us out of the present, but through the indeterminate certainty of the Lord's coming ("like a thief in the night") that demands full attention to the decisions demanded by the present moment (καιρός) (*GA* 60: 102ff/*PRL* 71ff).[3]

Having differentiated historical time and religious time from physical time in the ways indicated, Heidegger's 1924 lecture "What is Time?" shifts from the "time of nature" to "human being" (*das menschliche Sein*) to explicate time as such (*GA* 64: 112/*BH* 204). In this preview of the time analysis in *BT*, he characterizes authentic time as the time that consists, not in a series of now's, but in the anticipation of the most extreme possibility confronting me, my certain but indeterminate death. With unmistakable echoes of his interpretation of religious time, he insists that I can only relate to my death authentically as this certain but indefinite possibility, a possibility my own and no one else's, and that how I do so determines who I am. This most extreme possibility is "the authentic future that can never be present" and this future is "the basic phenomenon of time," as I come back to myself, abiding (*verweilen*) precisely in anticipation of that possibility (*BH* 206f, 209ff/*GA* 64: 116, 120ff).

Channeling his inner Bergson once again, he contrasts this time with the homogeneous time assimilated to space and compressed into a now (*Gegenwart*). Once time is defined as a measurable "clock time," arriving at its "original sense" is "hopeless," but this definition is commonplace precisely because we are mostly swept up in the everyday world, fleeing from our genuine future and taking time to be a measurable marker and property of things (*BH* 201f, 211/*GA* 64: 109f, 121f/). Yet time in the original sense, the time of being-here, is not a property of something like the spin of a wheel or the gallop of a horse. To the contrary, "being-here, conceived in its most extreme possibility of being, *is time itself*, not *in* time" (*BH* 209/*GA* 64: 119). Throughout the lecture, Heidegger repeats versions

---

[3] See also *GA* 60: 80ff, 102ff, 114ff/*PRL* 55ff, 71ff, 81ff; Pöggeler (1972, 165); McNeill (1999, 44ff, 116–117); Arrien (2013, 40ff); and Zagury-Orly (2015).

of this mantra equating being-here and time (again, echoing his interpretation of how early Christians "lived" their timeliness).

10.2 The Timeliness of Being-Here as the Original Time

In these pre-*BT* works, Heidegger thus analyzes the distinctiveness of historical time, religious time, and authentic time, differentiating each of them from physical or objective time. In *BT*, armed with these analyses, he argues (1) that timeliness provides the very sense of human existence, the constitutive and in that sense enabling condition of existing, and (2) that this timeliness is the original time, the foundation of other senses of time, including the serial time of things on hand in nature.[4] In §65 ("Timeliness as the ontological sense of care"), he begins his presentation of the first argument by glossing the meaning of "sense" in this context.

10.2.1 The Meaning of "Sense" and the Timely Sense of Being

Heidegger understands sense as the medium in which the intelligibility of something is maintained, the background against which we make our projections "on the basis of which something can be conceived as what it is in its possibility" (*BT* 371/324). Far from being "explicit and thematic," sense is like the air surrounding us, serving as a medium that permits light; it is like the transparency that, when projected, enables us to see an image, or even the surface (the screen) on which the image is projected.[5] We see through the air, we project the image through the transparency and onto a surface without focusing on any of these things – the air, the transparency, or the surface itself. Analysis of the experience thus demonstrates that, although tacit, each is inherently necessary to the experience, constitutive of it. When I drive home from work, there is a present focus (the road ahead) based upon a past that I retain (where the road leads) and a future that I project/expect (my destination) – even though, not least out of habit, I typically pay no attention to these temporal modalities. What is distinctive about the senses of these temporal

---

[4] Paralleling the differentiation of being-here, being handy, and being on hand, he distinguishes the original timeliness of being-here from "world-time" and "vulgar" time. Whereas world-time makes up our everyday worldly concerns and reckoning, vulgar time is its reduction to a serial conception of time, the "theoretical 'presentation' of a continuous flow of now's" (*BT* 460–461/408–409, 473–474/421–422).

[5] These metaphors correspond to different meanings of the prepositional phrase (*woraufhin*) used by Heidegger to characterize sense, where "sense" ≠ "meaning"; see Dahlstrom(2021).

modalities is that they are not independent of how I am here (focusing, retaining, expecting). Talk of "the experience of time" (Tugendhat 2001, 190) need not be off target here but only if the object of the experience is understood in this tacitly operative way and not as the direct object of an intentional experience, like a perception or memory.

With this characterization of sense in tow, Heidegger notes that the projection in question ("the primary projection") is precisely the projection and understanding of – at once (*gleichursprünglich*) – our own being (existence) and that of the innerworldly entities that we encounter (reality). Every experience of an entity is grounded in a "more or less transparent" projection of the entity's being and the sense "from which, as it were, the understanding of being is nourished" (*BT* 371f/324f). With the aim of thematizing, that is, bringing into the open (*freilegen*) the sense in question, Heidegger starts by reviewing authentic caring, that is, the resoluteness steeled by the anticipation of death, the possibility that is most one's own. The authentic timeliness of being-here consists in becoming – projecting as my future – what I already am (*gewesen*, mortal) and thus opening my eyes presently (*augenblicklich*) to my situation. I experience events in nature as having a before and after in time, but I cannot experience my death that way. But I can project it as the possibility that is most my own, precisely as the possibility that puts an end to all possibilities. Projecting this possibility (the existential conception of death) is my authentic future and, so construed, it is not to be confused with some later event that has not yet (*noch nicht*) occurred but will, at least for someone else. So, too, what I already authentically am is not to be confused with something over and done with (*nicht mehr*). Nor is the authentic present an isolated now, separate from an authentic future that consists in coming back to what we already are. In contrast to the past, present, and future of serial time and attempts to understand it as a moving now, Heidegger conceives the modes of timeliness as ecstatic, extending into the other two modes that form a distinctive horizon for the respective ecstasis in each case. The transcendence of the world is grounded in the unity of these horizons, enabling the encounter with innerworldly, spatial entities (*BT* 416–417/365–366, 471/419).

Whereas the timeliness just described is, strictly speaking, not shared (that future can only be respectively mine or yours), there is another sort of timeliness that looks away from this authentic future. Instead, it focuses on making things present with a view to a shared, expected future. This timeliness, although inauthentic (not indexically peculiar to you or me), is no less ecstatic and horizonal than the authentic timeliness of being-here.

Time's Origin

Nonetheless, Heidegger tends to speak of "original and authentic" timeliness, in part because the full meaning of this inauthentic timeliness supposes it – as do the other levels of time (cf. Heinz 2015, 183–184) .

10.2.2 Non-Original Times

Heidegger introduces the concluding chapter of *BT* by acknowledging the incompleteness of the analysis up to that point, incomplete because it does not explain the time "in which" entities are encountered or how we come to reckon with this time and orient ourselves to it. Nor does it explain the origin of serial time. He tackles these issues by explicating (1) how the time of our concerns (world-time) is distinctive yet derivative of the timeliness of being-here, (2) how the use of a clock supposes and tends to eclipse world-time, and (3) how serial time emerges from the use of clock time.[6]

10.2.2.1 World-Time (Weltzeit)

We speak of having time, taking time, and losing time. But where does the time come from? For Heidegger, part of the answer is to be found in the timeliness of pursuing our shared, everyday concerns. It is there, in our encounter with innerworldly things both handy and on hand, that we first experience time. In a shared world of concerns we conduct ourselves by determining times to do this or that for an extended period and marking them for one another accordingly.

Consider the following scenario: two sisters are vacationing on a lake, the younger sister for the first time, and the older sister tells her: "Sun-up is a good time to start fishing and, because the fish stop biting around midday, we'll stop then." "Sun-up" marks the start of a stretch of time that is meaningful, that is, appropriate and inappropriate times to do this or that within their world, a stretch that is identified by the terms "sun-up" and "then." This determination of a shared time to do something and its duration, along with the corresponding wording that makes it overt ("sun-up," "then"), is what Heidegger dubs "world-time." Its four features are its "datability" (broadly speaking, e.g., "sun-up," "then"), extendedness (from sun-up to midday), public character (use of temporal expressions), and, not least, worldliness (dawn, a good time to fish) (*BT* 467ff/414ff).

---

[6] "Serial time" and "vulgar time" are metonymies; both designate a succession of otherwise completely similar now's, applicable to everything on hand. Serial time is so dubbed since it is equivalent to McTaggart's A and/or B series. H's moniker "vulgar time" tips off his contention that it is not in fact universal, let alone original and authentic.

Through phenomenological analysis of the use of certain adverbs – "the most original citing of time" (*BT* 461/408) – Heidegger argues that world-time is made possible by making things present in view of certain things retained and expected. In this timely, everyday way of being-here, the ecstatic present (making present: *gegenwärtigen*) is paramount but only in its ecstatic-horizonal connection with the ecstatic past and the ecstatic future, that is, what is held onto (*behaltend*) and what is expected (*gewärtigend*), respectively (*BT* 405/354, 458/406). Thus, sticking to their plan midmorning and expecting the fish to be biting, our fisherwomen grab (make present) their poles, the bait, the boat, and so on. Sun-up is precisely the right time to fish and this purposive, expectant way of accordingly making things present signals the meaningfulness (*Bedeutsamkeit*), the worldliness of this timeliness. This meaningfulness is characteristic of world-time, a time not to be confused with any inner-worldly entity on hand.

> Insofar then as everyday concern understands itself on the basis of the "world" of its concern, it knows [*kennt*] the "time" that it takes, but *not as its* [*own*]; instead, in its concern, it *makes the most of* the time that "there is" [*es gibt*] with which *a group* [*man*] reckons. (*BT* 464/411)

In their absorption in the shared world of concerns, the sisters' time is identified with a more or less public (shared and discussed) time that is yielded (*es gibt*) by, among other things, their common reckoning. For this purpose, to mark time for this or that (*Zeit zu* . . .), the position of the sun is particularly useful. "The sun dates the time interpreted/laid out in the concern" (*BT* 465/412–413).

For similar reasons, the day becomes the most natural measure of time, and divisions in the day correspond to "the wandering sun." The regular recurrence of its passage allows us to reckon with the times of our worlds on a daily basis and, indeed, in a way not limited to individual concerns but accessible in "the nature surrounding us" (*Umweltnatur*) since we all find ourselves "under the same sky" (*BT* 466/412–413). In this sense, the sun's "movement" is a kind of "natural" clock (particularly for a "primitive" stage of human existence) that makes possible handier clocks (for a "more advanced" stage), but in each case as a handy means of measuring time.

Yet world-time is also typically a time when we are wrapped up in worldly concerns, a time when we forego our authentic future and the finitude of being-here. In this sense, world-time depends upon the timeliness of an inauthentic existence, an inauthentic timeliness.

Time's Origin   205

There are five salient points about world-time, as Heidegger conceives it.

(1) Although we count on and reckon with world-time in our encounter with innerworldly things, it is neither identifiable with any of those things nor a property, strictly speaking, of those things independent of that encounter.

(2) Although world-time informs every encounter with things within-the-world, it does so "unthematically and preconceptually" (*BT* 468/414–415). No concept of time is necessary to identify sun-up as the time to fish.

(3) What is decisive for reckoning with world-time is not the "quantification of time" but the "timeliness of being-here," reckoning with it (*BT* 465/412). That is to say, world-time is grounded in the timeliness of expectantly making things present (*im gewärtigenden Gegenwärtigen*), that is, the timing characteristic of everyday, worldly concerns. The meaningfulness of world-time, that is, its worldliness, is inseparable from the ways we determine (date) the time to do something and for how long, all the while articulating as much for ourselves and others.

(4) World-time is a time that is at once meaningful and datable, a shared time for this or that, lasting for a more or less extended period, and made public accordingly. What explains the interconnected character of these marks of world-time is precisely the ecstatic timeliness of being-here.

(5) Yet the meaningfulness of world-time is not that of an authentic timeliness, precisely because it is the timeliness of a manner of existing that ignores the authentic timeliness of a finite existence.

10.2.2.2   *The Use of a Clock*

Having made the case for world-time and its dependency upon inauthentic timeliness, Heidegger takes the next step toward explaining a streamed down version of time ("vulgar time" or "serial time") by first explaining how the use of clocks to measure time presents time as a manifold of now's that is simply on hand. When we read off time from a clock, what we are typically doing is saying "now" in the sense of "now it's time for that," "now there's only so much time left," "now we have to stop," and so on. In other words, we read time off the clock against the horizon of world-time. The full structural complement of world-time's four features is so self-evident that when we look at a clock to see what time it is now, we take no note of the fact that it is understood in terms of that unified structure. These different ways of saying "now" are ways of articulating a *presenting* that unfolds in unity with what is retained and expected, exemplifying again the originally ecstatic character of being-here's timeliness (*BT* 469/416). Yet this presenting of something on hand is distinguished by its character of *measuring*.

> The dating in the sense of *measuring* the time of concern lays it out or interprets it [*legt ... aus*] in view of something on hand that the view makes present [*gegenwärtigt*] and that becomes accessible as measure and measured only in a very distinctive process of making present [*ausgezeichnetem Gegenwärtigen*]. (*BT* 470/417)

Making present what is on hand in this distinctive manner (think of the minute hand of the clock and the space of each second as on hand measures of an interval) coincides with saying "now and now and now" such that the time becomes accessible to everyone.[7] This time, accessible in clocks, is "thus found in advance as an on hand manifold of now's" (a number of intervals represented as the equal lengths of spaces marking minutes on the clock's face). In the process, time-measurement becomes paramount, indeed, such that what is measured is forgotten in favor of the measure's number and extent (*BT* 470–471/417–418). The manifold of now's is bound to a place, a place that is constantly on hand (think of pocket watches before cell phones) and, as required by the adverb "now," accessible to everyone.[8] We become familiar with what we "commonly" call time through this time measurement by means of clocks and the pronounced way it is made public (*ausgeprägte Veröffentlichung*). We attribute to each thing "its time"; indeed, every innerworldly entity has its time because it is "in time" in this sense, that is, in a clocked worldtime. Innerworldly entities, whether handy or on hand, have the status of being within time (*Innerzeitigkeit*) by virtue of the fact that this status is constituted by world-time. Yet no such entity, regardless of whether it "really" occurs or "ideally" obtains, is itself *timely* (*zeitlich*) "in the strict sense" because that term and the phenomenon for which it stands are reserved for being-here (*BT* 472/420).

10.2.2.3 Vulgar Time and Serial Time (Der vulgäre Zeitbegriff, die Jetztfolge)

In everyday concerns, time is explicitly accessible through the use of a clock that consists, as noted above, in attending to – or, in Heidegger's terminology for timeliness in general, in "making present" to ourselves – the

---

[7] Here the difference between being on hand and handy seems to blur.
[8] In a likely reference to Bergson, Heidegger adds that the fact that the datable is bound to a place that is, as a measure, binding on everyone does not amount to a spatialization of time (*BT* 470/418).

moving hand of the clock and the uniform spaces marking seconds, minutes, etc., by counting them. Looking at the clock, I say "now" against the horizon of what was *earlier* and what is *not yet*, *retaining* the former and *expecting* the latter. In this respect, the counting that takes place in using a clock exemplifies the ecstatic-horizonal timeliness of being-here. Yet as the time clocked becomes a way of marking world-time, it significantly modifies the latter, so much so that we begin to see world-time as a succession of now's corresponding to the marked and counted spaces on hand – indeed, constantly and recurrently on hand – on the face of the clock. "We call the world-time 'seen' in such a manner in the use of a clock the *now-time*" (*BT* 474/421). The more absorbed we are in worldly concerns, the less we pay attention thematically to time and the more those concerns determine time, indeed, precisely as clocked now's: increments of former, present, and upcoming now's. For the vulgar understanding, time presents itself as a "successive series [*Folge*] of constantly 'on hand' now's, at once elapsing and oncoming" (*BT* 474/422).

Heidegger labels this understanding of time "vulgar," presumably because it lacks or, better, "covers up" (*verdeckt*) the timed (dated) meaningfulness of world-time (the time of concern) by reducing all times to the same level (*Nivellierung*), a sheer succession of now's, one no different from the other. Nor, he claims, is the eclipsing of world-time through this reduction contingent. The reduction is of a piece with understanding the being of things as being on hand, such that time itself (one now after another) is seen as something on hand along with them. This succession is also conceived as "unbroken and gapless," thereby forfeiting the tensed span of world-time (*BT* 475/423). So, too, it is "endless" in both directions, that of the now's no more and that of the now's to come. But this notion can only arise by supposing a free-floating run of now's, subsisting in itself and, indeed, such that the "full phenomenon of the now" with respect to its dating, meaning, tensed span, and placing has sunk to the level of "an unfamiliar fragment" (*BT* 476/424).

This leveling off of world-time and cover up of timeliness is grounded in being-here and thus, in a form of caring, specifically, the sort of caring that has lost itself in objects of concern (*das Besorgte*) and taken flight from itself, from death as its ownmost possibility. Looking away from its finitude is the mark of the inauthentic timeliness of everyday being-here that, having fallen prey to a crowd, necessarily overlooks "the authentic timeliness and with it timeliness altogether" (*BT* 477/424). This sheer succession of now's is not (pace Kant) a given; it owes its origin (*Herkunft*) to the "timeliness" of being-here in our everyday way of being with one another. Thus, the seeming endlessness of time that goes on and on is the time that belongs to everyone and no one, the publicly available time that never dies and that everyone can draw from (*BT* 477/425).

Nonetheless, Heidegger notes, vulgar time betrays some telling vestiges of world-time and even the original, authentic timeliness, and it does so in talk of "time's passing" and "time's direction." The primacy given to "time's passing" over "time's arising," inexplicable in terms of the succession of now's, can be explained as "the public reflection of the *finite futurity* of the timeliness of being-here" (*BT* 478/425). So, too, vulgar time can give no explanation for "the irreversibility of the succession of the flow of time" (*BT* 478/426).[9] But the explanation can be found, Heidegger submits, in the origin of vulgar time in the timeliness of being-here. "The impossibility of the reversal has its ground in the origin of the public time from a timeliness that, primarily futural, 'proceeds' ecstatically to its end, such, to be sure, that it already 'is' toward the end" (*BT* 478/426).

The serial conception of time – an "endless, irreversible succession of elapsing now's" – springs from the timeliness of being-here, wrapped up in its everyday concerns. Precisely for that reason, Heidegger insists, it has its "natural rightfulness" which it forfeits "only if it claims to be able to convey the 'true' concept of time and to outline the only possible horizon for the interpretation of time" (*BT* 478/426). Yet, precisely because timeliness allegedly can explain serial time and not vice-versa, Heidegger contends that we are justified in deeming the timeliness of being-here "the *original time*" (*BT* 479/426).

10.3 Criticisms of the Time-Analysis and Tugendhat's Objection

The analysis of timeliness in *BT*, together with the analysis of historicity, has long been the object of considerable criticism.[10] For an assortment of reasons, even defenders of Heidegger's existential analysis in Division One of *BT* often treat the temporal analysis in Division Two as dispensable. "With some right," Figal (1988, 273) observes, "Heidegger's foregoing of the publication of the third section of *BT* can be interpreted as a failure of

---

[9] These points are reminiscent of McTaggart's contention that the B series presupposes the A series, that without the latter, it collapses into the C-series.
[10] For excellent reviews of criticisms, see Fleischer (1991) and Heinz (2019) who include early criticisms by Grisebach (1928 and 1930) and Kraft (1932 and 1941) (see note 18 below).

his early philosophy of time."[11] Some critics (Fleischer 1991, 13–17; Schmitz 1996, 353; Tugendhat 2001, 191) question the need for the account of timeliness after the demonstration of care as the sense of being-here as a whole. Others (Kraft 1932, 90, 112; Schmitz 1996, 351; Marten 2017, 238; Heinz 2019, 269) protest a dearth of phenomenological evidence, replaced by a "fog of words" and "mythology of time." Others (Müller-Lauter 1960, 54ff; Pöggeler 1972, 178f; Fleischer 1991, 33–37, 41–46; Schmitz 1996, 351ff; Tugendhat 2001, 193) note inconsistencies in temporal ecstases' alleged alignment with basic existentials (three or four?). Still others object that Heidegger's analysis of timeliness forfeits time as we know it, while reifying time at the cost of human subjectivity, as Augustine's *distensio animi* and Kant's pure intuition of the transcendental ego give way to timeliness' self-timing.[12]

These criticisms are all substantive and any adequate examination of the trenchancy of Heidegger's analyses of timeliness and historicity must weigh them seriously. Although such an evaluation exceeds the constraints of the present essay's format, the second half of this essay nonetheless focuses on an objection made by Ernst Tugendhat that is no less substantive and, indeed, in a certain respect arguably even more fundamental than those mentioned. According to Tugendhat, Heidegger's argument that the timeliness of being-here is the original time appeals to a conception of serial time, thereby forfeiting any claim to its derivativeness from that timeliness.[13]

Tugendhat begins by objecting to a passage (§31) where, he contends, Heidegger describes the futural character of care ("being ahead of itself") in terms that apply to the (serial) time of something on hand. In the course of elaborating the projective character of existential understanding, Heidegger maintains that a potential-to-be (*Seinkönnen*) is inherent to being-here's facticity. To be sure, Heidegger advises, being-here in this respect is "more" than it "factually" is, "would one and could one register it as on hand." Nonetheless, after stressing that being-here is neither more nor less than it

---

[11] In Pöggeler's (1972, 154) view, a proper "phenomenology of time" can scarcely be found in Heidegger's work; on the perils of neglecting the second section of *BT*, see Schalow (2004).
[12] See Heinz (2019, 264, 266, 269): "Mit der Depotenzierung des Subjekts korreliert die Ermächtigung der Zeit." As for Heidegger's analysis of historicity, it has been criticized for leaving the relation between the primacy of the future and the weight of the past unresolved (Fleischer 1991, 46f), for being ahistorical (Pöggeler 1972, 87f) or historicist (Grisebach 1930, 228; Heinz 2019, 260), and for identifying selfhood with a people and its heritage in a normatively obtuse manner (Kraft 1932, 8; Adorno 1973, 331; Franzen 1975, 47–48 and 1976, 49; Pöggeler 1983, 180; Barash 2005, 175–184).
[13] Tugendhat's relevant 1992 and 2000 essays are found in Tugendhat (2001, 11–26, 185–198).

"factically" is, he declares that "what being-here in its potential-to-be is *not yet*, it *is* existentially" (*BT* 185f/145). The appeal to something "not yet" betrays, Tugendhat charges, a fatal appeal to serial time.

Yet this reading of the passage is highly questionable. Using terms applicable to what is on hand to describe this aspect of care (being-here) is, Heidegger notes, counterfactual (and his use of the subjunctive underscores as much). He is not conceding that he cannot describe that futural character on its own terms and, indeed, the fact that he does not do so at this juncture may have everything to do with the fact that at this point (§31) he has not yet introduced the analysis of timeliness (§65).[14]

Tugendhat can nonetheless press on and attempt to make his case on the basis of an analysis of the account of original timeliness in §65. That is precisely what he does, seizing upon Heidegger's characterization of the original future not as "a now that has *not yet* 'actually' come about but instead [as] the coming [*Kunft*] in which being-here comes to itself in the potential-to-be that is most its own" (*BT* 373/325). (Heidegger is clearly speaking of authentic timeliness here, as indicated by the reference to being-here's "ownmost potential," that is, death.) Tugendhat (2001, 191) rejects this talk of a *Kunft* (religious overtones or not) as trivial, given the fact that "if I am related to my impending [*bevorstehendes*] being, I am naturally 'not yet' this."[15] Indeed, we are hard pressed to interpret the notion of death coming to us as the potential-to-be most our own, without reference to the notion that for someone other than ourselves it will have a place in serial time, like any other event on hand in nature. Heidegger is right, Tugendhat allows, to contend that "coming to oneself" is not something happening in the future (*Zukünftiges*). But this contention hardly entails that "coming to oneself is thinkable, as Heidegger would have us see it, independent of an impending future." Only on the supposition that a "future in the usual sense" awaits him could someone, Tugendhat (2001, 19ff) continues, come to himself in the sense that matters to Heidegger. Because we can "define" what Heidegger dubs the "original future" (coming to oneself) "only by means of future in the usual

---

[14] Being-here can be understood in terms of what is on hand and within-time (*innerzeitig*), but this does not entail that being-here and its time can be described only and, indeed, primarily in those terms. Just as Heidegger contests that being on hand suffices as the description of the mode of being of every sort of entity, so, too, he contests that being within-time suffices as the meaning of the temporality of every sort of entity. In this connection, see Heidegger's acknowledgement that death in the broadest sense is a "phenomenon of life" and that without question "time goes on" after death (*BT* 246/290, 330/379).

[15] Heinz (2019, 269n50) aligns this criticism with that advanced by Kraft (1932, 90–95, 105–108, 112).

sense," Heidegger is badly mistaken to think that "the timeliness of being-here is more original than time in the normal sense" (Tugendhat 2001, 191f; Heinz 2019, 261n22).

On this reading, Heidegger's conception of an original future consists in nothing more than a confusion of a relation (comportment) to an event with the event itself. Although one may concede that talk of human possibilities ("I can") is not the same as contingent possibilities of things on hand in nature, death – like those contingencies – can come at any moment. "Anticipating death" is Heidegger's way of designating how we relate to this event and the synonymous phrase in his arsenal "being toward death" implies, Tugendhat submits, a difference between the relating (the existential possibility) and "a possible, on hand event." Heidegger's obsession with the difference between being-here and being on hand has led him to overlook the fact that talk of "being toward x" only makes sense if "being toward" and x – in this case, "a contingent event" – can be distinguished (Tugendhat 2001, 192f).

Tugendhat thus reads Heidegger as (a) having to suppose death as some future event on hand in nature (with talk of "end" as the giveaway) and (b) conflating possible relations to death (authentic or inauthentic) with death itself, so construed.[16] He regards this supposition and conflation as merely one instance of a familiar, flawed pattern of the existential analysis. The flaw is a reliance, fatal for the argument, upon a supposedly subordinate sense of being and derivative sense of time (being on hand and its serial-time character) to explicate being-here and its time. His criticism is patent: If Heidegger has to resort to the terminology of serial time to characterize the timeliness of being-here, he forfeits, on pain of circularity, any claim that the latter is more original. Thus, on the basis of the foregoing criticisms of the original future and being-toward-death, Tugendhat (2001, 193) concludes that "the so-called original time presupposes time in the usual sense and consciousness of it" and, hence, too, that the concluding chapter's project of deriving the latter from the allegedly original time cannot succeed.[17]

These criticisms clearly go to the heart of Heidegger's account of timeliness as the original time. To be sure, in his 2000 essay, Tugendhat helps himself to "the usual sense" of the future without providing an

---

[16] Tugendhat (2001, 192): "Aber gerade dieser Ausdruck, Sein zum Ende, impliziert doch, daß das Sein-zum unterschieden wird von dem, wozu es sich so verhält," whereby, he adds, death is an event, "ein mögliches vorhandenes Ereignis."
[17] Fleischer (1991, 63–66) also contests the trenchancy of the derivation of "vulgar time."

account of it, saving himself the considerable trouble of giving an account that comes to grip with enigmas and *aporiai* often associated with the concept of time. Does the "future in the usual sense" exist? If so, how? If not, how can it stand for a contingent event? In addition to "normal time," Tugendhat speaks of "time in the usual sense" or, as he prefers to label it, "natural" time. Tugendhat appeals in this context to McTaggart's contrast of a series of positions comprising past, present, and future (the so-called "A series") with a series comprising merely the before and after (the so-called "B series"). The general idea is that we can mark time or points in time as being past, present, and future (the A series) or as earlier and later than one another (the B series).[18] In his 1992 essay, Tugendhat (2001, 14–15) explains that he makes the "commonsense assumption" that the full phenomenon of our normal talk of time is constituted by the pair of concepts that McTaggart designates the A series and the B series.[19] This assumption seems cavalier to a fault, given that Tugendhat makes it without mention of McTaggart's argument that analysis of the two series entails "the unreality of time," hardly a commonsense idea. It is further notable that Tugendhat takes the B series as foremost (*vorgängig*) even as McTaggart argues that the B series must turn for the directionality of time to the A series, which, he also argues, is hopelessly incoherent. Thus, while considering both series essential to time, McTaggart (1908, 464) regards the distinctions of the A series as ultimate even as he contends that "the distinctions of past, present, and future cannot be true of reality."[20]

In this respect there is more than a little irony to Tugendhat's criticism.[21] While he helps himself to a conception of time that leads its author and not a few contemporaries to the conclusion that time is unreal,

---

[18] McTaggart (1908): "For the sake of brevity I shall speak of the series of positions running from the far past through the near past to the present, and then from the present to the near future and the far future, as the A series. The series of positions which runs from earlier to later I shall call the B series." For discussion of McTaggart's views and their critical appropriation by 20th century philosophers of time (D. C. Williams, Hugh Mellor), see Dahlstrom (1999).

[19] In the 1992 essay, he refers to the A series and B series but in the 2000 essay he glosses "time in the usual sense" as a "series of events determined by the relation 'later than,'" again presumably favoring the B series (Tugendhat 2001, 190).

[20] See, too: "Having, as it seems to me, succeeded in proving that there can be no time without an A series, it remains to prove that an A series cannot exist, and that therefor time cannot exist" (McTaggart 1908, 467), and: "Our conclusion, then, is that neither time as a whole, nor the A series and B series, really exist" (McTaggart 1908, 473).

[21] But perhaps it is not so ironic given the conclusions reached by Heinz and Fleischer in their respective studies of Heidegger's analysis of time. Heinz (2019, 266n37) speaks of a loss of time (*Entzeitlichung*) and Fleischer (1991, 63) speaks of Heidegger trying – albeit unsuccessfully – to drive a wedge between timeliness and serial time.

Heidegger's analysis at least manages to salvage a version of "time in the usual sense" by showing its lineage with time in an original sense.

But let us set this line of rebuttal aside for the moment and suppose that Tugendhat can make good on his commonsense assumptions about time's make-up (perhaps through recourse to language games, as he suggests). However the derivative sense of time is to be construed, does Heidegger's analysis presuppose it? Tugendhat is specific here. Tugendhat (2001) characterizes Heidegger's original timeliness as "comporting oneself to the future, the past, and the present," and he construes Heidegger's talk of coming-to-oneself as a matter of relating to my being insofar as it stands before me, since this means "that 'naturally' I am not yet this" (191). These formulations abet Tugendhat's (2001, 18, 20–21, 191ff) complaint in both essays that original time, on Heidegger's analysis, presupposes "normal time," that it has no structure independent of serial time, and, hence, that the purported derivation of the latter from the original time is circular, thereby falsifying the thesis of a time more original than "natural" time. Indeed, there is no need, he adds, to examine in detail Heidegger's "convoluted" (*gewundenen*) attempts in the concluding chapter of *BT* to derive serial time from the alleged original time "since one sees at once that they can only be circular" (Tugendhat 2001, 20).

10.4 A Possible Rejoinder to Tugendhat's Objection

Is Heidegger's argument in fact circular in a fallacious, self-defeating way, as Tugendhat contends? Tugendhat does not explain what he means by "circular" but presumably he would acknowledge that circular arguments are formally valid (*pq* implies *p*) and, hence, that the reason for their untoward character is a pragmatic or epistemological issue rather than a purely formal matter. A circular argument lacks persuasiveness because it fails to prove something that was not already known (Sanford 1972, 198).[22] In other words, because the conclusion is no different from a premise, a circular argument lacks the appropriate dialectical force of starting from premises already known or believed and proceeding to a conclusion not known or believed. We cannot believe and not believe the same thing and, hence, any argument framed in this manner is fallacious and incapable of advancing our knowledge.

---

[22] See also Smith (1987, 207–208): "Let us call an argument *circular* just in case it could not be known to be sound unless its conclusion were already known."

Tugendhat's charge is, as noted, that Heidegger's argument is circular in this offending sense because his use of "now" (and other temporal adverbs) in the characterization of original timeliness designates serial time. Hence, he insists, any derivation of serial time from that characterization can only be viciously circular.

But there are at least three problems with this charge. First, the temporal adverbs ("now," "not yet") used in the characterization of original timeliness do not necessarily signify serial time, if it is understood, as Tugendhat takes it, in the mold of McTaggart's series. Indeed, as noted above, Heidegger proposes that "now" and other temporal adverbs are, if anything, the initial expression of world-time, that is, a meaningful, distended time irreducible to a series of one-dimensional now's.

Second, if the use of those adverbs were a matter of serial time, the latter cannot be the time that is derived from original time. The putative circularity is absent. According to Tugendhat, serial time is supposed to be independent of the original time (the timeliness of being-here) and yet the whole point of chapter 6 is to demonstrate that there is no such time. In the chapter, Heidegger argues that original time is our only window into the significance of "vulgar time," the closest thing to what the proponents of serial time mistakenly take to be as original as the timeliness of being-here. Whereas circular arguments are said to be "valid but uninformative," betraying "the vice of dialectic inefficiency" (Sorensen 1991, 246), Heidegger's argument in fact delivers information that is not trivially present in the premises; we learn that the temporal adverbs employed in nondescript fashion to characterize original time do not designate a time independent of the timeliness of being-here.

Third, Tugendhat's talk of death as a possible event on hand in nature conveniently sidesteps the fact that the death in question is not shared and is only projected as a possibility by the one dying. We register a tree's death because we experience its lack of vital signs but we do not experience our death that way. So there is a problem with construing it simply as "a possible, on hand event," since it is never such for the person dying. Given the equivalence of being on hand and serial time, Tugendhat's criticism that Heidegger must have recourse to the latter amounts to the claim that death is in fact something on hand, that my relation to my impending (*bevorstehendes*) end is a relation to an event on hand in nature. Yet that is precisely what death cannot be *for me*, as Heidegger belabors to demonstrate. It remains the possibility that is most my own, the possibility of the end of possibilities. The end or closure of possibilities is not itself something on hand in time but is itself only a possibility projected in the course of existing authentically, and, as such, it is not an instance of a demise or perishing (*BT* 294–295/250–251).

Death is not a future present, at least not from an existential point of view. Inasmuch as being-here is defined as the potential to be (*Seinkönnen*) this or that, death is the preeminent possibility of the end of possibilities. Existentially understood as the indexical possibility that is mine or yours and not shared with anyone else, death does not occupy a place in the A series or B series and I have no experience of such a place. Just as, in coming to the potential-to-be that is most its own, being-here's future is not something not yet, so, too, being-here is existentially what it has been, not as something that is past (*vergangen*) and is no more, but as something that is in the very process of having been. Being-here is its having-been by "taking over" its thrownness and that includes, preeminently, its mortality. Only insofar as I am here as something having been (mortal), is it possible for me "futurally" to come to myself in a way that coincides with "coming *back*" to myself (*BT* 373/326).

But how do I know that I am going to die if not by experiencing others' deaths in serial time and concluding that the same fate awaits me, that I am no different from anything alive? This observation seems undeniable but it is hard to see how it can be used against Heidegger's understanding of authentic timeliness. My own death remains for me a possibility – the possibility of the end of all my possibilities – and this possibility is my lot, informing who I authentically already am; only in projecting it as such is it my authentic future, opening up my situation (my authentic present). That possibility and how it is projected (authentically or not, as exclusively mine or not) are inseparable. When Tugendhat glosses this original future as a matter of relating to some event in the future (*Zukünftiges*), he reduces what is mine or yours alone to a generic fact on hand in nature with no apparent connection to past or present.[23] Moreover, his insistence that we can be said to comport ourselves to something only if it is independent of the comportment is an unsupported supposition. Indeed, intentional phenomena would seem to present counterexamples (a dream is not independent of the dreamer; the color seen is not independent of seeing it; the purpose of *my* action is not independent of my act of envisioning, intending, and pursuing it). Nor would the fact that the timeliness of being-here is, phenomenologically speaking, the original time rule out that the times of things – from black holes and robins to operas and

---

[23] So, too, he can be said to reduce what is an indexical possibility (*mine* or *yours* alone) to a demonstrative possibility (*this* or *that* instance of the common fate of living things).

nations – are far more complex than the rather wooden, threefold differentiation of timeliness, world-time, and vulgar time would suggest.[24]

In sum, in his analysis of time, Heidegger is not guilty of the vicious circularity that Tugendhat claims besets and undermines the analysis. Indeed, Tugendhat's appeal to McTaggart betrays, by contrast, a highly truncated and barren understanding of time. In Heidegger's account, the richness and distinctiveness of both world-time and authentic timeliness are given their phenomenological due and, contrary to Tugendhat's contention, Heidegger has demonstrated the plausibility of regarding serial time as a derivative of world-time, which itself supposes the original and finite time of authentically being-here.

---

[24] Another possible rebuttal would be to argue that its circularity is benign in the sense that the various parts of the analysis are demonstrably coherent (implying each other). Such is the sort of circularity – the logical rigor – that Heidegger arguably upholds when he speaks of the inevitable circle of interpretation and the need to enter into it in the right way (*BT* 193f/152f). The appeal to this circle has affinities with what some thinkers (Dummett, Quine) deem the internal soundness and explanatory virtues of certain forms of circularity (Smith 1987, 213ff). Gesturing perhaps to circularity, Heidegger observes that in *ordo cognoscendi* the original time becomes fully visible once the "endless time" is set up and contrasted with it (*BT* 379/331); notable, too, in this connection is his use of *Erhellung* (*BT* 457/405).

CHAPTER 11

The Possibility of Death

Mark A. Wrathall

Heidegger's account of death plays a crucial role in the argument of *Being and Time*. There is, however, no broad consensus on how best to understand this account. There are several good reasons why it has proven so difficult to offer a convincing account of death in Heidegger.

First, Heidegger defines death (*Tod*) as the "possibility of the impossibility of existence," and he distinguishes death so-defined from related phenomena like demise (*Ableben*), perishing (*Verenden*), dying (*Sterben*), etc. Interpreters differ widely on how exactly to understand these distinctions, and some have despaired of differentiating between them in any meaningful way. Thus, the first hurdle to clear for any adequate account of Heideggerian death is explaining his definition of death and justifying the distinctions he draws between death and related phenomena – especially demise.

Second, Heidegger argues that relating to death in the right way transforms the character of our existence. Heidegger claims that in "running ahead to death," we are "absolutely individualized" (*BT* 311/266).[1] That means that when I relate to death authentically, I am liberated from responding to situations in the way that anybody else would. Instead, I disclose the situation of action in light of the individual that I am. Insofar as my relationship to death gives me individuality, it is a necessary (but perhaps not sufficient) condition of authentic existence – an existence in which I take responsibility for myself. "In running forward to its death," Heidegger explains, "Dasein can make itself responsible in an absolute sense" (*GA* 20: 440). Thus, the second hurdle that any adequate account of Heideggerian death needs to surmount consists in offering a coherent and plausible explanation of the existential force of death.

Finally, Heidegger also attributes to the analysis of death an important methodological role in his fundamental ontology. Death "delimits and

[1] All translations of *Sein und Zeit* are my own.

determines in each case the possible wholeness of Dasein" (*BT* 277/234). It is thus through an account of death that Heidegger secures his phenomenological analytic of the being of Dasein. And the account of death is a key element in Heidegger's argument for the idea that human existence is essentially temporally finite – that is, the idea that Dasein can only make sense of entities in terms of a finite temporality. Heidegger might even be committed to a stronger version of this thesis, according to which *only* temporally finite beings can make sense of the world. Death is central to constituting Dasein's temporal finitude: "the finitude of temporality" is "authentic being towards death" (*BT* 438/386). And so an account of death is foundational to Heidegger's ontology. Showing how Heidegger's account of death informs his ontology is thus a third hurdle that any adequate account of Heideggerian death needs to clear.

A complete account of Heideggerian death, then, would explain not just the distinctions Heidegger draws between death and demise, it would also account for the existential import and the methodological role played by death in Heidegger's ontology. But without a clear grasp of Heidegger's definition of death and the relationship between death and demise, we cannot hope to understand the significance of death in Heidegger's broader project. And so my primary focus here will be on the first hurdle – this is where most accounts of death in the secondary literature trip and fall. I will offer a critique of one popular interpretation of Heideggerian death, the "existential death interpretation," and I'll lay out an alternative approach that I think better tracks Heidegger's discussion in *Being and Time* (and related texts). At the end of the chapter, I will explore the implications of this account for understanding the connection between death and authenticity. I won't have anything directly to say about the third hurdle – about the implications of Heidegger's account of death for understanding his ontology – but I hope that the account of death that I develop here will lay the foundation for a future inquiry.

11.1 The Formal Structure of Heideggerian Death

Heidegger's distinctions between perishing, demise, and death are meant to capture the fact that different kinds of entities end in different ways. For those who know what to look for, the way an entity ends can illuminate the ontological structure of that entity.

Heidegger lists a number of different senses in which *nonliving entities* can stop (*aufhören*). For instance, an occurrent event like a rainstorm comes to an end when the rain "passes over into non-occurrentness."

Heidegger calls this "disappearing" (*Verschwinden*) (*BT* 289/244–245; for a more detailed taxonomy of the various ways in which nonliving entities end, see *BT* 289/244–245; Blattner 1999b, 64).

Living beings, by contrast, come to an end when some event or process occurs that renders their bodies incapable of continued organic functioning. Heidegger calls the ending of nonhuman living beings "perishing" (*Verenden*) (*BT* 284–285/240–241; see Blattner 1994b, 53).

But when it comes to *Dasein* – beings like us humans – Heidegger identifies two distinct kinds of end, which he names, respectively, demise (*Ableben*) and death (*Tod*).

Heidegger calls demise "an intermediate phenomenon" because it is defined in relation to perishing on the one side and death in Heidegger's specific sense on the other. Demise is meant to capture the kind of ending that follows from the fact that "even Dasein may be considered purely as life" (*BT* 290/246). Demise participates in the characteristics of perishing insofar as our demise is caused by a breakdown in the human organism. And yet, our "going-out-of-the-world in the sense of dying must be distinguished from the going-out-of-the-world of that which merely has life" (*BT* 284/240). Dasein is, after all, essentially determined by its existential openness to its world, and human life involves dimensions of consciousness and personhood that are not present in other living entities.[2] Thus, "Dasein never perishes," Heidegger explains, because its kind of ending is "codetermined by its primordial kind of being" (*BT* 291/247).

Consequently, the concept of a demise is not exhausted by an understanding of the cessation of organic function. Demise has a significance that can be cashed out variously in ethical, social, legal, anthropological, and psychological terms. It is Dasein qua a *person* that comes to an end in demise. Within everyday existence, *demise* is experienced as an event that "effects an alteration in the constellation of psychological, biographical, legal, social, historical, and ethnological meanings" (Wrathall and Murphy 2013, 23; see *BT* 291–292/247). A demise, one might say, is the event of the disappearance of a person capable of playing social and legal roles, of having experiences, or otherwise being involved in a world.

---

[2] This means that, even if we are considering human beings as biological entities, the cessation of human life arguably will have a different character than the cessation of life in a non-Daseinish lifeform. This is attested to by the ongoing debate over whether to define human death as "the *irreversible cessation of cardiopulmonary function*," or whether it ought to be approached as merely requiring the cessation of function of some part or whole of the brain (DeGrazia 2017).

What, then, is "death" in Heidegger's specific sense, and how does it differ from demise?

In defining "death," Heidegger engages in a terminological practice that he employs repeatedly in *Being and Time* (and which causes no end of confusion in the casual reader). Heidegger repurposes ordinary terms in such a way that they no longer refer to ordinary things and events; instead, they are redefined to name the ontological structures that constitute those ordinary entities. (Other examples of this practice in *Being and Time* are Heidegger's "ontologically broad" use of the words "truth," "guilt, " and "temporality," to name a few; see Wrathall (2011, 2–3).) The redefinition proceeds by, first, using the term with its ordinary meaning to formally indicate some phenomenon – in this case, Heidegger uses the word death to point to an event of the cessation of human life. The next step is to direct our attention away from the ordinary phenomenon and toward the ontological structures that guide us tacitly in our experience of that phenomenon. The final step is henceforth to use the ordinary term to refer to those ontological structures. "This structural definition of death," Heidegger explains "underlies each particular interpretation of death" (*GA* 80.1: 143). So to understand how Heidegger uses the word "death," we need to work out what he takes to be the definitive ontological structure that underlies human demise.

A demise is, in the Heideggerian turn of phrase, something ontic. It is a particular event or a process. "Demise," he explains, is "an event that occurs" (*BT* 297/253, 301/257; see also *BT* 296/252). Death by contrast is the framework that informs any particular understanding of demise. In particular, death is a peculiar type of *possibility* – namely, "*the possibility of the absolute impossibility of Dasein*" (*BT* 294/250, emphasis supplied; see also *BT* 377–378/329, 306–307/262, 353–354/306). We would thus expect that demise, as an ontic phenomenon, is a particular instantiation of death's modal structure. A demise thus can be understood as a "case of death" (*Todesfall*) (*BT* 296/253, 301/257).

Corresponding to the distinction Heidegger draws between death and demise is a parallel distinction between two different senses of "dying" (*Sterben*). The death-related concept of dying – *dying* in Heidegger's proper sense – is an existential stance of "being-towards-death" as a possibility. "Dying," he explains, "serves as a title for the way of being in which Dasein is towards its death" (*BT* 291/247). Dasein is always dying in this sense because it is "constantly coming to terms with its death" (*BT* 303/259) – even if it comes to terms by trying to avoid having to confront death as a possibility.

But, Heidegger notes, "'dying' may also be taken physiologically and biologically" (*BT* 284/241). This is the demise-related concept of *dying* (*Sterben*), and it understands "dying" as the process of physiological and biological decomposition that renders me unable to engage with the world – the process that takes me out of the world: "Does not dying mean going-out-of-the-world, and losing one's being-in-the-world?" (*BT* 281/238). Heidegger also designates this physiological or "medical concept" of dying an "*exitus*" (*BT* 284–285/241).

I've summarized in the following chart Heidegger's distinctions between perishing, demise, death, dying, and exitus.

Chart 1

Entity	Term for its end	Definition
Nonliving entity	Disappearing (*Verschwinden*)	passing over into non-occurrentness
Nonhuman living organism	Perishing (*Verenden*)	an event or process of physiological/biological change that results in the cessation of vital metabolic processes
Dasein	Demise (*Ableben*)	an event of the cessation of personal existence
	"Dying" ("*Sterben*") or *Exitus*	the process of physiological and biological decomposition as a result of which a human body irreversibly loses the capacity for the organic functioning necessary to sustain a human form of life
	Death (*Tod*)	the possibility of the impossibility of Dasein or existence
	Dying (*Sterben*)	actively being-towards death = constantly coming to terms with death in the way one lives

It is clear that Heidegger thinks of demise and death as distinct phenomena. But our description so far has been quite formal. Is it possible to give phenomenological content to the distinction between death and demise? Critics like Edwards insist that it is not possible:

> Heidegger's argument that we do not mean the same by "end" when we speak of the end of a human life, as we do when we speak of the end of the life of a plant or an animal or the end of an inanimate object, is totally

fallacious ... When a house has been wrecked or burned down its existence has come to an end. It has ceased to exist and ... exactly the same is true when a human being has died. (Edwards 1976, 182)

Philipse (1998, 354), explicitly drawing on Edwards' analysis, also dismisses Heidegger's attempt to make sense of these distinctions as "a mesmerizing play with words" that "does not contain significant philosophical insight." In his treatment of Heideggerian death, Philipse consequently never even so much as mentions the word "demise." For him, Heideggerian death is simply "the terminal phase of one's life" (Philipse 1998, 355). Even an interpreter as sophisticated, sympathetic, and nuanced as McManus argues that the "object of Being-toward-death is plain old death." According to McManus (2015, 268, 267), Heidegger introduces the death/demise distinction to track different kinds of attitudes toward death, not because death is something other than demise.

In a somewhat more interesting fashion, Sartre ([1943] 2018, 709) understands Heidegger as "hav[ing] constructed his entire theory of '*Sein-zum-Tode*' [being-towards-death] on a complete identification of death with finitude." But Sartre ([1943] 2018, 709) rejects this identification because "death [i.e., demise] is a contingent fact" while "finitude is an ontological structure." Not having recognized a death-demise distinction, Sartre is convinced that Heidegger has erroneously treated death as an ontic event while ignoring the ontological structure of finitude that gives the ontic event its significance. It seems not to have occurred to Sartre that Heidegger might be redefining "death" to name an ontological structure.

In recent years, however, commentators like Carol White, William Blattner, Iain Thomson, and John Haugeland have developed in impressive detail a general strategy for interpreting Heidegger's treatment of death that offers a plausible way of distinguishing death from demise. I'll dub their approach EDI (for "existential death interpretation") because it turns on arguing that Heideggerian death is not death in the ordinary sense, but death understood as the collapse of certain "existential" possibilities. Working through the virtues and flaws of the EDI approach will help illustrate what an adequate account of Heideggerian death demands.

11.2 The Existential Death Interpretation (or EDI)

In existing secondary literature, the "existential death interpretation" is perhaps the most fully developed approach to interpreting Heidegger's distinction between death and demise. According to EDI, a Heideggerian death is an event in which a particular, historically contingent understanding of being loses its viability. But this can happen without a demise; the intelligibility of my self-understanding can collapse without my individual life coming to an end. Indeed, a whole concrete world or set of social practices can break down without any particular human beings losing their lives. Thus, EDI offers a plausible way of distinguishing death from demise.

But is this Heidegger's distinction?

Before trying to answer this question, we should first consider the interpretation in more detail. I'll focus here primarily on Thomson's and Blattner's versions of EDI. EDI gets its name from the claim that the possibilities that become impossible in Heideggerian death are "existential 'possibilities,'" that is,

> the embodied life-projects that compose our particular ways of being (such as teacher and student, mother and father, son and daughter, man and woman, tall and short, fat and skinny, graceful and clumsy, brother and sister, skateboarder and bicyclist, friend and colleague, liberal and conservative, poet and revolutionary – and all the myriad other ways of being that Dasein takes up and lives in some particular, embodied way . . .). Such life-projects, taken together, help positively constitute our existences, allowing us to become intelligible to ourselves and to each other in worldly terms. Such existential possibilities are thus not merely the logically possible alternatives that can help us understand the structure of some conceptual space. Instead, existential possibilities are the embodied projects that we ordinarily project ourselves into (as I like to put it), and so understand ourselves in terms of, as we go about charting the course of our everyday lives. (Thomson 2021, 215)

Since Thomson defines a "possibility" as *a life project that I embody*, he reasons that an *im*possibility must be a life project that I can't embody. And from this, he concludes that when Heidegger speaks of death as the possibility of *im*possibility, he is referring to a condition in which a particular Dasein finds herself unable to continue acting in furtherance of some set of roles or projects that, up until that point, she had been pursuing.

Blattner (1994b, 63), in a similar fashion, distinguishes between a "thin sense" and a "thick sense" in which a Dasein exists. In the thin sense, a Dasein is a Dasein as long as its being is an issue for it. I exist in this thin sense when the question "Who am I?" is up to me to resolve. In the thick sense, a Dasein *is* when "it understands who it is by throwing itself into possible ways to be." Ordinarily, Dasein *is* in both the thin and the thick senses – that is, my being is at issue, even as I pursue one particular way to be. But, Blattner explains, Dasein can lose a thick sense of itself by losing the ability to throw itself into a particular identity and to engage in those "tasks" the pursuit of which constitutes inhabiting that identity. But if Dasein no longer *is* in the thick sense, it can nevertheless continue to be in the thin sense of continuing to "confront" the question "Who am I?" (Blattner 1994b, 58) Blattner thus defines *existential death* as the condition of being in the thin but not the thick sense. I am "existentially" dead when I confront the question of who I am without being able to answer it:

> existential death is the condition in which Dasein is not able to be or exist, in the [thick] sense that it cannot understand itself, press ahead into any possibilities of being. Existential death is a peculiar sort of living nullity, death in the midst of life, nothingness. What would it be like to suffer existential death? To be unable to understand oneself is not for one's life to cease to matter altogether ... The issue – Who am I? How shall I lead my life? – matters to me, but when existentially dead no possible *answer* matters. All answers to these questions are equally uninteresting. (Blattner 2005, 315)

Thomson echoes Blattner's analysis on this point:

> By repeatedly referring to death as "the possibility of an impossibility," then, Heidegger is deliberately designating a stark and desolate phenomenon in which we find ourselves (at least momentarily) unable to project ourselves into any of the existential projects that ordinarily bestow our lives with meaning. (Thomson 2021, 217)

EDI quite rightly highlights the fact that we ordinarily understand ourselves in terms of our existential projects and social roles. There is thus a certain plausibility when EDI argues that a breakdown in our ability to inhabit those roles amounts to an "existential death." If not a literal, it is at least a metaphorical kind of death when "the meanings that once structured one's life ... the possibilities that once beckoned, and the demands one once felt ... become inert" (Blattner 2006, 149). Thomson explains it in this way:

> To see what Heidegger means when he calls death "the possibility of the impossibility of existence in general," it helps to think, first, of someone whose fundamental life project was being a teacher (or a husband, son, communist, pet owner, or any other identity-defining self-understanding) but who then experiences the catastrophic collapse of this life project. What is crucial to recognize is that when such world collapse occurs, we do not instantly forfeit the skills, capacities, and inclinations that this identity previously organized. Instead, in such a situation, we tend to continue projecting ourselves upon an absent project (for a time at least – the time it takes to mourn that project or else replace it, redirecting or abandoning the forces it organized). After that world collapses, we tend to keep pressing blindly ahead (absent-mindedly filling the food bowl of a recently deceased pet, for example), even though the project that previously organized this

projection is no longer there for us to press ahead into (since, in this example, one no longer owns that pet). Thinking about such a paradoxical (but not uncommon) situation – in which we project ourselves toward a life project we can no longer project ourselves into – helps us grasp what Heidegger means when he calls death the possibility of an *impossibility*. (Thomson 2013, 269)

In the literature of EDI, one finds a variety of other examples meant to illustrate what an "existential death" would be like, including the collapse of alchemy as a practice in the face of the development of modern chemistry (Haugeland 2013b, 80), or the Crow Native American Indian tribe being moved onto a reservation (as described in Jonathan Lear's *Radical Hope*; see, e.g., Rouse 2013, xxi; n. 21).

There is some disagreement on how extensive the collapse of possibilities needs to be in order to count as an existential death. Blattner (2006, 148) seems to consider it to be an instance of death any time "a self-understanding stops functioning as a guiding principle in one's life." Death, he says, "is the inability to project oneself forth into *some way to be* Dasein" (Blattner 1994b, 63; emphasis supplied), and Blattner (2006, 149) writes of being "dead as . . . a student, when being a student no longer matters to one." Presumably one can be dead as a student while being "alive" as, say, a baseball player. Thomson (2021, 217) seems personally sympathetic to this view: "I do not think this process [death] is always best thought of as a *complete* collapse and transformation of the self." But, on Thomson's reading, Heidegger himself views death as a complete rather than a partial collapse:

> Heidegger thinks such a global collapse of our life-projects will follow from the collapse of our defining life-project (what *Being and Time* calls our "ultimate for-the-sake-of-which"), as this collapse of what we care most about . . . sets off a chain reaction that brings all our other life-projects cascading down in its wake. (Thomson 2021, 217)

Whether death is a partial or a complete collapse of life projects, advocates of EDI agree that it is possible to survive or "live through" your existential death because a Dasein can continue to *be* even when it no longer "exists" in this specific sense. Blattner, as we saw, thinks an existentially dead Dasein continues to exist as a Dasein in the thin sense. Thomson (2021, 218) argues that, through the experience of existential death, we discover an "ontological core of the self," "the utterly desolate core of the self that survives the shipwreck of all its worldly projects." It is this core that goes on existing during death, as it tries to project onto possibilities that have collapsed, and in the process allows the one who is dead to experience death.

EDI thus has the virtue of clearing the first hurdle. It identifies a phenomenon, distinct from the end of human existence in a demise, which could without too much semantic stress be referred to as "death." But is this Heidegger's way of distinguishing between death and demise? I think there are good reasons to doubt that it is.

11.3 Problems with EDI

If we focus just on Heidegger's explicit comments about death, without worrying about the functional roles that death is supposed to play in Heidegger's existential analytic, I would suggest that there are two and a half reasons that ought, at the very least, to raise significant concerns about the EDI conception of death as an interpretation of Heidegger.

Problem 1.   The Absoluteness of Heideggerian Death

We saw above that the key issue in understanding the Heideggerian conception of death involves making sense of the claim that death is "the possibility of the impossibility of Dasein." And we saw that EDI interprets this as a limited or circumscribed impossibility. When "existentially dead," I am still a Dasein – a Dasein who finds itself unable to pursue some set of my projects in the world. According to Blattner (2006, 162), Dasein loses only the possibility of pressing into "some aspect of [its] self-understanding," or into just those possibilities that define a particular life project or identity. But Dasein "lives" even while "dead" because, in all other respects, it remains a Dasein. Since it continues to exist in the "thin sense" of caring about its being, it retains the ability to start projecting onto other possibilities. Thus, even when in the throes of existential death, Dasein can "give up" its old self-understanding and "move on" by redefining itself in terms of other possibilities (Blattner 2006, 162). Thomson (2013, 271) agrees: In "existential death" "my projects collapse, and I no longer have a concrete self I can be, but I still *am* this inability-to-be." Dasein "lives *through*" death because it can come out the other side by "reconnect[ing] to the practical world" (Thomson 2013, 273).

But such a limited conception of death sits uneasily with the way Heidegger describes the phenomenon in *Being and Time*:

* "Death is the possibility of *the absolute impossibility of Dasein.*" (*BT* 294/250; emphasis supplied. See also *BT* 378/329)

* Death is "the possibility of *the impossibility of any existence at all.*" (*BT* 307/262; emphasis supplied)
* "Death ... is the possibility of *the impossibility of every way of comporting oneself towards anything,* of every way of existing." (*BT* 307/262; emphasis supplied)
* "We understood death as ... the possibility of the impossibility of existence – that is to say, as *the absolute nothingness of Dasein.*" (*BT* 354/306; emphasis supplied)

EDI reduces such language to hyperbole on Heidegger's part, since it insists that in death I remain a Dasein, that I continue to exist, that I still have available to me many alternative ways of existing, that I still comport myself toward the world (for instance, by continuing to fill the food bowl of my deceased cat, or by considering what possibilities to press into next). Existential death even allows that some things will continue to matter to me (recall Blattner's (2005, 315) claim that "the issue – Who am I? How shall I lead my life? – matters to me ... when existentially dead"). Surely, if there were an interpretation available that could do justice to the absoluteness of death, this would count in its favor.

Problem 2. The Category Mistake

Heidegger repeatedly insists that the ontological structure formally indicated by the word "death" is not an event or process:

> This interpretation, too, could suggest that death must be understood in the sense of some impending *event* occurring in the surrounding world. For example a thunderstorm, the remodeling of a house, the arrival of a friend ... Death as something impending *does not have this kind of being.* (*BT* 294/250; emphasis supplied. See also *BT* 297/253, 301/257; *GA* 20: 432; *GA* 80.1: 141–142; *GA* 64: 142; *GA* 64: 58; *GA* 62: 358)

Despite such emphatic claims – claims that EDI's advocates dutifully acknowledge in their discussions of death – EDI ends up treating death as something that *happens*. Thomson (2013, 281), for instance, says plainly that death "can actually happen to us." Blattner (1994b, 67; emphasis supplied) argues that "death is a limit-situation," and "this situation *occurs* when Dasein is beset by anxiety." To justify such a reading in the face of Heidegger's claim that death is not an *event*, that it does not *happen*, Blattner (1994b, 67) glosses Heidegger's claim as the claim that death "does not refer to an event that takes place at the end of every human being's life." But Heidegger's objection is not to the *timing* of the event, it is to the very idea that death is an event in the first place.

In defending the idea that death can be an event – a change we live through – advocates of EDI point to passages like the following:

> when Dasein dies – and even when it dies authentically – it does not have to do so with an experience of its factical demising, or in such an experience; (*BT* 291/247)

or this:

> Mortals die death in life. (*GA* 4: 165, 190)

At a casual glance, such passages might be read as saying: Death and demise are separate events, and thus one can undergo death without undergoing a demise. But the first passage is not even a passage about *death* (*Tod*); it is a passage about *dying* (*sterben*). Likewise, the second passage refers to "dying death." As noted in Section 11.1, Heidegger defines *dying* as *being-towards-death*, that is, as an orientation toward life that "constantly comes to terms with its death" (*BT* 303/259). Even inauthentic Dasein is constantly dying because one way of coming to terms with death is to distract oneself from the ever-present possibility of death. So "dying death" is a mildly redundant way of saying "coming to terms with death," and that is certainly something we do in life. In short, Heidegger does not in these passages or in any other claim that we pass through death.

There is one other key passage that Thomson relies on:

> Heidegger himself stresses the paradox that Dasein lives through its death when he writes, "Death is a way to be, which Dasein takes over as soon as it is." (Thomson 2013, 272; quoting *BT* 289/245)

But in fact, this passage makes no sense if death means a collapse of life projects. Our life projects do not collapse as soon as we come into being. Indeed, an "existential death" of the sort that EDI describes might *never* happen to a person. This passage, far from supporting EDI, gives us a good reason to look for a different sense in which death can be a way to be.

I take as a decisive refutation of EDI's notion that we can survive our death the following passage from *Being and Time*:

> death is . . . a possibility of *Dasein's* being. But it follows that effecting the actualizing of what is thus possible would have to mean "bringing about

one's demise." But if this were done, Dasein would deprive itself of the very ground for an existing being-towards-death.[3] (*BT* 305/261)

My death then is a possibility, any actualization of which results in my demise. Thus, death cannot be something that we live through. Just to be clear, the point is not that death only happens when demise happens; the point is rather that death does not *happen*. It cannot happen because possibilities as possibilities are not, on Heidegger's analysis, the kind of things that do happen. For Heidegger, then, death is a possibility (of the impossibility of Dasein); demise is an instantiation of that possibility, its realization or actualization (*Verwirklichung*).

Thus, it looks like EDI falls into a kind of category mistake, treating Heideggerian death as an *event* when Heidegger insists that death is not an event but a *possibility*. And Heidegger in fact precisely warns against falling into such error: "[D]eath is spoken of as a 'case' which is continually occurring" – that is, death is regarded as an event or a process. "Such talk," he continues, "presents death as something that is always already 'actual' and conceals its character as a possibility" (*BT* 297/253).

Problem 2½. The Missing Treatment of the End of Core Existence

I consider this half a problem because, unlike the other objections I've raised to EDI, this objection does not point to a direct inconsistency between EDI and Heidegger's pronouncements on death. It points rather to what would amount to a glaring omission from Heidegger's text, were EDI the correct way of interpreting Heideggerian death.

As we have seen, the intelligibility of EDI depends on appealing to some "core of the self" or some existence in a "thin sense" which endures through the collapse of existential roles or projects. "The existential crisis of death," Blattner (2013, 326) acknowledges, "is not a total collapse of self."

But, one might ask, what about the core self that survives existential death? Surely the core self can itself come to an end, extinguishing along with it any existence at all. One would think that the possibility of the impossibility of being a core self is at least as significant to understanding the character of human existence as is the possibility of the collapse of a particular self-understanding. Why, then, does Heidegger have nothing to

---

[3] This same point is made in other passages. See *GA* 20: 439, where Heidegger notes that "by suicide I surrender the possibility precisely as possibility; ... it becomes an actuality."

say about the death of the core self? I'd suggest that the likely answer is that he didn't think there was a "core self" that lives through death.

***

The discussion of EDI's failings is informative when it comes to making sense of Heidegger's distinction between demise and death. We can now appreciate that (a) when death is actualized, its actualization is unconditional – there is no sense in which Dasein continues to exist *qua* Dasein once death is actualized; and (b) this distinction turns on the difference between events on the one hand, and possibilities on the other.

In fact, I would argue that EDI's fundamental error is thinking that to "be" a possibility (or to "take over" the possibility *as* a possibility) necessarily requires being in a condition that *actualizes* the possibility. This is what drives Blattner (1994b, 57–58) to posit the distinction between being in a "thick" and a "thin" sense, so that I can be (in the thin sense) while actualizing death (i.e., losing my ability to be in the "thick" sense). Similarly, Thomson's (2013, 266) argument rests on the thought that I can only experience a possibility if I undergo its actualization: "[E]ven though we cannot 'experience' all experience having ended in demise, Heidegger remains convinced that there is an end proper to (or distinctive of) our being-here which we *can* experience" – namely, the collapse of an intelligible world.

On Heidegger's approach, however, this is to confuse the way we experience or inhabit possibilities with the way we experience or inhabit actualities. To experience an actuality, it must of course be actual. But to experience a possibility, by contrast, just is for the possibility to inform the significance of the present situations we encounter, whether it is actualized or not "A 'possibility' is experienced," Heidegger explains, when "significance has the content of a reference to something other ... To experience a possibility is to live in the open, to hold open, to open authentically" (*GA* 60: 248). Thus, we do not need to actualize a possibility to inhabit it; we are in the possibility whenever the possibility opens up the field of references that determine the sense and significance of things. To explain this thought, let's look more carefully at Heidegger's account of possibilities.

11.4 The Modal or "Dual-Aspect" Interpretation of Heideggerian Death

To understand Heidegger's account of death as a possibility, we need to pay attention to the distinction he draws between "that which is possible" (*das Mögliche*) and possibilities proper (*die Möglichkeit*). The expression "that which is possible" could encompass possible situations, possible entities, possible events, and possible actions. In what follows, I will refer principally to possible events and possible actions. This is because a demise – in this context, the principal example of something that is possible – is an event, and also because most of Heidegger's examples of "that which is possible" are actions or events.

Actions and events are closely related. An *event* is a *particular happening* which occurs in a specific space-time region of a world. As Heidegger understands *action*, it consists in "bringing about" or "accomplishing" (*Vollbringen*) an event.[4] So, while not all events are actions, all actions involve an event. Consequently, any action can be viewed either under an event description (when the focus is on what happened), or under an action description (when the focus is on the agent's bringing-about of what happened). For example, a particular happening is <Abby mixes yeast into warm water in her kitchen at noon on January 25th, 2023>. We can regard this as an event when we focus on the causes that brought about the mixing of yeast into warm water. We can regard this as an action when we focus on Abby's bringing it about that the yeast was mixed into the warm water.

A particular happening is a *possible* event if it is consistent with prior and subsequent actual states of the world: "the possible [event], arising out of the actual and directed toward the actual, is drawn expectantly into the actual" (*BT* 399/348). A possible event has specificity and determinacy; the only difference between a possible event and its actualization is the modality. For this reason, Heidegger often refers to a possible event or a possible action as a "possible actual" (*mögliches Wirkliche*; see, e.g., *BT* 306/262; *GA* 26: 124).

By contrast, a *possibility proper* (as distinct from a *possible actual*) is a *type* of action or event. We might call an event-type a second-order possibility, since it organizes particular happenings (first-order possibles) into a class. For example, <Abby mixing flour and yeast in her kitchen at noon today> is a particular happening. <Baking> is a possibility proper: It organizes a variety of particular happenings into a class of potential actualizations of the possibility <baking>. <Being a pastry chef> is a yet-higher-order possibility proper: It organizes the modal space within which action types make sense as particular ways of behaving in furtherance of a personal

---

[4] Heidegger insists that "bringing about" an event is to be distinguished from causing an effect, but he has little to say about how exactly he draws this distinction. See *GA* 9: 313; *GA* 31: 198.

identity or social role. The higher-order possibilities or action types that make up the range of the possibilities that define <being a pastry chef> include: <baking tortes>, <kneading dough>, <glazing cinnamon rolls>, <cleaning pans>, and so on.

To organize events "in terms of possibility" is to give them "a specific kind of significance" which determines our understanding of their place in our world (*GA* 58: 232). When "a 'possibility' is experienced, significance has the content of a reference to something else" (*GA* 60: 248). For instance, because Abby is committed to pursuing the possibility of being a pastry chef, the activity of baking tortes has a special weight for her: that activity refers to her identity as a pastry chef. In general, then, a possibility augments the meaning of events or actions by showing how they relate to other situations, actions, events, and possibilities.

When Heidegger talks about human possibility, he principally has in mind a possibility of engaging in a type of comportment: "'[P]ossibility' is a determination that fundamentally belongs to the modes of comportment" (*GA* 21: 228). So we could say that:

> A *Heideggerian Possibility* (in the proper sense) is a coherent modal space of action – a way of organizing and giving sense to some range of actual comportments by relating them to each other *qua* events of the same type.

Any one of a number of different particular happenings can actualize a possibility. Abby can actualize the possibility of being a pastry chef by, for instance, baking tortes on Wednedsay, glazing cinnamon rolls on Thursday, or cleaning the kitchen on Friday, and so on. This is, again, in contrast to particular events – there is only one event that is the actualization of a possible event. For instance, the possible action <Abby mixing flour and yeast in her kitchen at noon today> can only be actualized by Abby bringing about the mixing of flour and yeast in her kitchen at noon today. If a possible event is actualized, it is actualized in a single determinate happening, in a specific time, place, and manner. But no particular happening in which a possibility proper is actualized exhausts that possibility. As Heidegger explains in his 1925 lectures on *Logic*:

> whenever Dasein comports itself in a determinate type of comportment, this remains only one possible (*mögliche*) way of comporting, i.e., it can as a matter of principle be given up. Dasein can as a matter of principle enter upon a different way of comportment. Thus, possibility is a determination that belongs as a matter of principle to the ways of comporting, and in that case the possibility does not disappear when a determinate comportment is factically chosen and lived. (*GA* 21: 228)

This point is reiterated in *Being and Time*, where Heidegger explains that

> as factical Dasein, Dasein has in each case already diverted its ability-to-be into a possibility of understanding. (*BT* 186/146)

But, he notes,

> when one is diverted into [*Sichverlegen in*] one of these basic possibilities of understanding, the other is not discarded [*legt ... nicht ab*]. (*BT* /146)

This means that possibilities, unlike possible events, are not contained within the stream of events that make up any given world. While possibilities are actual*ized* by particular happenings, they are not properly speaking ever *actual* themselves. A *possibility* doesn't happen, but any of an indefinite number of happenings can be the actualization of a possibility. (In the vernacular of Worlds Theory, one might say that a Heideggerian possibility is a transworld object, the sort of thing that allows us to recognize relationships between entities – including relations to similar entities in different worlds. But a possibility cannot be actualized at *a* world because it is a function of the relations that obtain between possible worlds.)

Higher-order possibilities – remember, these are possibilities like the possibility of being a pastry chef or the possibility of being an authentic individual – do not need to be actualized to exist; rather they exist whenever they contribute to the overall sense of a world. We encounter them through the significance they give to our actions, whether they are actually being instantiated at any given moment or not. For instance, the meaning of Don Quixote's actions is fixed (in part) by the fact that he is trying but failing to actualize the possibility of being a knight errant. Or, to take a less fanciful example, we grasp the significance of the way Abby instantiates being a pastry chef precisely because we understand her actions in the context of other ways to actualize that possibility (as well as other identities she could have pursued but did not). Heideggerian possibilities, then, are ways of making sense of particular events, and they are capable of structuring our experience of the world even when we do not actualize those possibilities.

A set of Heideggerian possibilities make up what Heidegger calls "the horizon of choice" (*GA* 64: 54–55), "the scope of the achievable" (*GA* 26: 249), or the "region of projection" (*GA* 45: 200; *GA* 15: 334) – that is, the field of alternatives that fix the meaning of any given choice by holding it in relation to other similar, or contrasting, or alternative choices. Regions of projection are, for Heidegger, ontologically basic. Any given entity is what it is because of the profile it has when we "project it onto possibilities":

> In the projecting of the understanding, entities are disclosed in their possibility. The character of the possibility corresponds, on each occasion, with the kind of being of the entity which is understood. Innerworldly entities are as such projected upon the world – that is, upon a whole of significance, in whose reference relationships concern as being-in-the-world has been fixed. When entities within-the-world are discovered along with the being of Dasein – that is, when they have come to be understood – we say that they make sense. (*BT* 192/151)

A *possibility* is thus "higher than" an actual happening because it fixes the meaning of the happening.

As we noted above, Heidegger wants to emphasize that human beings are ontologically determined by their relationship to possibilities of this sort: "here is what is distinctive: this entity [i.e., Dasein] is *in its being* defined precisely as possible-being" (*GA* 18: 356). I understand this to be saying that to be a Dasein is itself to be a higher-order possibility – it is to organize a large set of possible particular events into a coherent order. Moreover, "Dasein, as a possible-being, is defined by its ability-to-choose" (*GA* 64: 53–54). It is definitive of any given Dasein, then, that things could have been different with it in the past, and yet could be different in the future, than they are now. EDI is right to emphasize the fact that any particular Dasein could have different "roles, identities, and commitments" (Thomson 2013, 269). But it also could do different things (vacation in Bali instead of Croatia); it could think different thoughts; it could develop different character traits; and so on. Heidegger calls the possibilities a Dasein has in virtue of being a Dasein its "possibilities-of-being" (*Seinsmöglichkeiten*).

One might sum up Heidegger's view in this way: To be is to inhabit a specific chunk of modal space. Insofar as I am a Dasein, I *have* possibilities even if I never enact them in particular happenings. Thus, I am who I am because of the specific configuration of possibilities I could pursue (whether I ever do pursue them or not). This specific pattern of the ways a particular Dasein *could* be is definitive of it as an individual because it orients that individual to his or her surrounding world: "being-there (*Da-sein*) ... is the possibility, the enabling (*Ermöglichung*), of an oriented being-here and being-there" (*GA* 27: 136). Or, as Heidegger explains in *Being and Time*, "Dasein is in every case what it can be, and how it is its possibility" (*BT* 173/134).

With this discussion of Heideggerian possibilities, we now have a perfectly straightforward way to understand the distinction between demise and death. *A demise is a particular happening. Death is a higher-order possibility.* This means that the difference between demise and death is like the difference between <Abby mixing dough in her kitchen now> and <Abby being a pastry chef>. The particular happening of a demise – for instance, Socrates drinking hemlock in a cell in Athens in 399 BC – actualizes or instantiates the possibility of death. But the particular happening in no wise can be considered identical to the possibility, because the possibility informs the significance of not just this possible demise, but also – or so Heidegger will argue – all other possibilities. As a higher-order possibility, death does not itself *happen* or *occur*, but it nonetheless *is*, precisely because it informs the significance of other possible events and particular happenings.

But what does it mean to say that death is the possibility of an absolute impossibility (namely, the impossibility of existence or of every way of comporting oneself)? Such an impossibility is the possibility that a particular Dasein is excluded from a given world at a given time. Death is the possibility that, at some point, a state of affairs will obtain such that I cannot inhabit the possibilities or the modal space that I now do. Now, what particular happening could instantiate or actualize such an absolute possibility? Obviously, it is demise. So death and demise are two aspects of a single whole phenomenon. Death is the possibility that informs the significance of demise. A demise is the particular happening that actualizes death.[5] When death is actualized through some Dasein *D*'s demise, this amounts to saying that given the prevailing condition of the world at time *t*, *D* cannot be at *t*: Death is "the possibility of the one who is dying going out of the world" (*GA* 20: 439). Death, then, is not the possibility of the collapse of some subset of my possibilities; it is rather the possibility that I be wholly excluded from the world:

> The possibility of death means that some day I will leave the world, that some day the world will no longer have anything to say, that everything I am attached to, everything with which I occupy myself, has nothing to say anymore, will no longer help. (*GA* 80.1: 144)

---

[5] Thomson's view converges on this point, insofar as Thomson recognizes a close connection between "death" and "demise." For one thing, "existential death underlies and conditions our experience of ordinary demise" (Thomson2021, 213). And while he thinks we can be dead without demising, our demises will necessarily result in "our intelligible worlds terminally collaps[ing]" – that is, existential death (Thomson2013, 264). Thus, for Thomson too, demise is an occasion of "existential death," even if he offers a different account of what death is.

As we will see, this means that death is the "ultimate" or "outermost" (*äußerste*) possibility, in the sense that it forms a background against which all other possibilities are arrayed. That is, death sets modal limits to every other possibility and thereby informs the significance of all my other possibilities.

We can thus see why it is a mistake to think, as EDI does, that death has to happen or be actualized in order to be experienced. As temporal beings who already inhabit the open horizon of the future, we are always already experiencing death:

> This possibility is a possibility of being in which I always already am. It is a singular (*ausgezeichnet*) possibility, *for I myself am this constant and ultimate possibility of myself,* namely, to be no more. Care, which is essentially care about the being of Dasein, is in its innermost nature nothing other than this being-ahead-of-itself in the ultimate possibility of its own ability-to-be. In this way, Dasein is essentially its death. With death, what is imminent is not something worldly, but Dasein itself. Dasein stands before itself, not in a possibility of being of its choosing but rather in its no-longer-existing ... Dasein qua being-possible is essentially already its death. (*GA* 20: 433; emphasis in the original)

Indeed, we not only experience the possibility of our own death, but the possibility of the non-existence of (most) other entities:

> entities are not able to shake off their openness to question: they, as what they are and how they are, could also *not* be. We in no way experience this possibility as something that we first think up; rather, the entities themselves express this possibility, express themselves as entities in this possibility. (*GA* 40: 32)

Experiencing the possible non-existence of something is thus a perfectly normal aspect of Dasein's ability to project onto possibilities.

For Heidegger, then, no special distinctions need to be drawn between "core" Dasein and full Dasein, or between being in a "thin" and a "thick" sense. This is because the important question is not how it is possible to experience the possibility of death – as a Dasein, we are always "experiencing" possibilities in the very act of understanding entities and ourselves.

With this, we are in a position to reconstruct Heidegger's solution to what I called the first hurdle. Death is distinct from demise because death is a possibility while demise is an event. Drawing the distinction in this way is not a mystification. It rather directs our attention to the question how death as a possibility informs the significance of our other possibilities. And it reminds us that this question is not at all answered by fixating on any particular event of demise. "To experience a possibility," Heidegger explains, is "to live in the open, to hold things open, to authentically open things up" (*GA* 60: 249). To further develop the account of death, we turn in the next section to a more detailed account of the way that experiencing death as a possibility opens up the modal structure of our being-in-the-world. This will put us in a position to address the second hurdle. In Section 11.6, we will ask: How does living in the openness of the possibility of death enable a transformation of our existence?

11.5 Death as the Outermost Possibility – The Possibility that Informs All Other Possibilities

Heidegger identifies two different ways to relate oneself to death as a possibility, which he designates respectively as *expecting* (*Erwarten*) and *running ahead* (*Vorlaufen*). We can think of expectation and running ahead as opposite ends of a spectrum which is made up of a continuum of states of more narrow or more expansive ways of understanding a possibility.

At one end of the spectrum – the *expectation* end – the agent is fully in the grip of present actuality and narrowly understands what is possible as that which is the natural consequence of an existing state of affairs. From Heidegger's perspective, to relate to the future in the mode of *expectation* is to cover over the possibility in its full breadth by fixating on a single possible event as *the* actualization of the possibility. Expectation can be, but need not be, a cognitive state. That is, expectation *can* take the form of *believing that* or *thinking that* a particular event will happen. But more typically our expectant grasp of possible events does not involve a "thematic" mental awareness of what is possible given the current state of the world. Rather, it consists in having our actions shaped by a sense for whether, when, and how some particular event will actually occur (or, alternately, with regard to what would prevent it from occurring).

Expectation amounts to "concerning ourselves with the actualization" of the possible event by "circumspectively looking away from the possible event to that for which it is possible" (*BT* 305/261). For instance, because I expect Abby to make dough, the situation made up of a dirty mixing bowl in the kitchen shows up as soliciting me to clean up. That is, I look away from the possible event – Abby making dough – to that for which this is a possibility – the affordance made up of the mixing bowl in the kitchen. By looking away from the possible event to the equipmental context for which the possible event stands as a possibility, *the present becomes determinative for my grasp of what is possible*.

Thus, a fully expectant relationship to death fixates on the demise that, given current actuality, is most likely to occur. Expectation transforms anxiety in the face of the possibility of death into a "fear in the face of an oncoming event" (*BT* 298/254), and thus creates the illusion that death can be restricted in its significance – as if death is only of concern when considering those events that will lead from the present situation to one's eventual demise. The most pressing issue for an "expectant concern" that "asks about death" is the question "When will it happen?"

> That the "When?" cannot in fact be determined changes nothing about the manner of questioning or the answer with which Dasein, having succumbed to the world, tends to console itself: "There is still plenty of time." It is in fact to the "not yet over" that one clings while expectantly posing questions concerning the "When?" of the "it's over," reckoning how long one has yet to live. (*GA* 64: 81)

By clinging to the present – the "not yet over" – and trying to reckon how and when the present state of affairs will lead to a particular demise, expectation fails to see or acknowledge that death is a possibility that alters the significance of every one of my possibilities. Expectation blinds me to the open character of my future horizon: "Expectant temporalness does not discern the 'it's over' as an indeterminate, certain possibility. It does not take itself into the future of that being which, in truth, it itself is" (*GA* 64: 81).

At the other end of the spectrum – the *running-ahead* end – we are "as far as possible from anything actual" (*BT* 306–307/262). Where expectation fixates on a specific particular happening that is the outcome of present activities, running ahead leaves behind what is happening now. It "uncovers the horizon of ... choice" by anticipating the entire range of "that which is available for choice" (*GA* 64: 54).

Take, for instance, a possibility like <being a parent>. The world as presently constituted affords us the opportunity to carry out a certain repertoire of parenting activities that are socially accepted as ways to actualize that possibility. Parents are socialized into these practices and, in the first instance and most of the time, they understand their role in terms of these conventionally accepted parenting activities. They have fairly clear and determinate expectations of what it means to be a parent. "Looking away" from their limited expectations to the present situation, they set about doing what one does when one is a parent in today's world. They "deliver themselves over," in other words, to prevailing expectations about how to be a parent.

Authentic parents, by contrast, realize that the possibility of being a parent is something that cannot be reduced to performing the actions on some list of socially accepted parental activities. An authentic parent understands that one can in fact do everything on that list and still fail as a parent. Conversely, sometimes being a parent is most authentically realized by a readiness to go off script. <Being a parent> is a possibility, then, that exceeds any fixed way of actualizing that possibility. A sense for the possibility in its full breadth allows authentic parents to respond in unexpected ways to the concrete situations they encounter.

The phrase "running ahead" is meant to capture this attitude of leaving behind any fixed, narrow understanding of the significance of a possibility, thereby opening oneself up to the full breadth of ways that possibilities can inform my response to the present situations. Thus, Heidegger says, in running ahead one "lets oneself be affected by indeterminacy as such" (*GA* 64: 55) – that is, the present determinate situation loses its hold on me. Instead of fixing on a particular conception of what counts as properly actualizing a possibility, an authentic understanding of a possibility opens up the range of what is available for choice because it expands my grasp of the open-ended ways in which any given possibility can be actualized.

Because a possibility by its very nature exceeds any particular way of representing or expecting its actualization, Heidegger argues that to even try to cognize the possibility as a possibility – to thematize it – "would take away from what is projected its very character as a possibility, and would reduce it to the given contents which we have in mind; whereas projection, in throwing, throws before itself the possibility as possibility, and lets it be as such" (*BT* 145).

So if we apply these observations to the possibility of death, we can say that running ahead toward death can shape my experience of the world without ever needing to be something that I "go through" or experience as actual. Running ahead

> does not tend towards a concernful making-available of something actual. Rather, in coming closer understandingly, the possibility of the possible [event] only becomes "greater." The closest proximity of being to death as a possibility is as far removed as possible from something actual. (*BT* 306–307/262)

Running ahead into death also opens us to the entire range of implications that death has for my other possibilities. In doing that, it tears me away from the normal set of socially approved attitudes toward death (cf. *BT* 297/253).

In understanding any possibility, I am not in a position to specify its meaning explicitly or exhaustively. Instead, I have a general grasp of its sense – of what it makes sense to do when confronting that possibility. We could think of this sense as a kind of intentional content that determines what would and would not count as the actualization of the possibility.

Heidegger describes the core content of the possibility of death as "the 'it's over'" (*das »Vorbei«*). The "it's over" is an intimation of being-in-the-world as a whole of both realized and unrealized possibilities – but a whole that has come to the moment where no further pursuit of possibilities is possible.

> This "it's over," as that toward which I run ahead, here makes a discovery in my running ahead to it: it is *my* "it's over." As my "it's over," it uncovers my Dasein as one day no longer there; one day I am no longer there amidst such and such things, amidst such and such people, amidst these vanities, these pretexts, this chattering. (*GA* 64: 116–117)

In running ahead to the "it's over," I come to the recognition that death is precisely that which I cannot live through or go beyond.

> In running ahead, the ultimate possibility becomes manifest as the "it's over" of being-in-the-world, as the possible "no-longer-there": there is no remaining within the world of concernful coping. (*GA* 64: 52)

Heidegger traces out in some detail the way that this content of the possibility of death – the intimation of the "it's over" – informs Dasein's mode of being-in-the-world. In describing the ontological character of the possibility of death, Heidegger focuses on four key "*moments of modalisation*" (*BT* 356/309; emphasis supplied) – that is, four ways in which death constitutes a modal structure that modulates other possibilities: "death [is] the [1] ownmost, [2] non-relational, [3] unsurpassable, [4] certain, and yet indefinite possibility"[6] (*BT* 356/309). Let's look at each of these briefly in turn. In explaining the transformative significance of running ahead into death, Heidegger mixes both existential/structural observations about the "content" of the possibility of death, and existentiell/psychological

---

[6] One might tease apart the certainty and indefiniteness of death and treat them as distinct moments. But Heidegger himself explains that the certainty of death is only properly recognized when it is seen as indefinite. To grasp death as certain in the right way is to understand that it "is indefinite as regards its certainty" (*BT* 310/265).

descriptions of authentic responses to death. In what follows, I'll try to tease apart the structural and psychological elements.

1. Ownmost

In running ahead into death – in anticipating *my* "it's over" – I discover an asymmetry that obtains between me and the world. I need the world to exist, but the world doesn't need me. The busy activity of worldly existence will continue without me when for me it's all over. Thus, in running-ahead into the "it's over" – into death – possibilities get sorted into two categories: my possibilities, and the *anyone's* possibilities (i.e., everyone else's possibilities and thus no particular individual's possibilities – the shared possibilities of the world). Running ahead into death brings into salience the possibilities that end when I end. It thus allows me to recognize the possibilities that I alone can actualize, the possibilities that determine what I can be individually responsible for. Running ahead into death reveals these possibilities as my own, because they are the possibilities that will be extinguished when "it's over" – when death as a possibility is actualized in some demise or other. The anyone's possibilities will continue on without me. Others will be able to fill those roles (cf. *BT* 284/240).

Once possibilities are sorted in this way, then the world's possibilities are shown to establish significance or bestow on me a status for which I am, at best, an accidental or contingent factor. The world's possibilities, one might say, are modalized as *contingent* possibilities, meaning I am a possibility of existence that is not reducible to public roles or conventional activities. Because death illuminates the distinction between my possibilities and the anyone's possibilities, it shows us that "Dasein is authentically itself only insofar as it ... primarily projects itself onto its ownmost ability-to-be, but not onto the possibility of the anyone-self" (*BT* 308–309/264). Because running ahead puts me in a position to recognize the specific finite chunk of modal space that is distinctive of me, it makes it possible, psychologically speaking, for me to be "wrenched away from the anyone" (*BT* 307/263).

2. Non-Relational

This moment of death's modalizing structure builds on the asymmetry disclosed by death's ownmost character. As we have seen, "death lays claim to Dasein as an individual" (*BT* 308/263). It follows that conforming to shared public norms, standards, and expectations will not protect me from going out of existence: "all being amidst the things we care about, and all being-with others will fail us when our ownmost ability-to-be is at stake" (*BT* 308/263). This does not mean that we can or should wholly repudiate those norms, standards, and expectations: "as essential structures of the constitution of Dasein, they belong to the condition of the possibility of existence as such" (*BT* 308/263). But running ahead into death shows me that public and conventional norms cannot determine what counts as success or failure when my existence as an individual is at stake. Others cannot define my "ownmost" possibility, and so they cannot determine what counts as a successful actualization of that ownmost possibility. Thus, death modalizes Dasein's existence because it "forces" Dasein "into the possibility of taking over from itself its ownmost being, and doing so on its own" (*BT* 307/263–264). Once that possibility is opened up, it makes it psychologically possible to understand myself as an individual.

3. Unsurpassable

In running ahead to death, we recognize that there is no getting around the possibility of death. No matter what other possibilities we pursue, running ahead "allows Dasein to understand that giving itself up is in store for it as the ultimate possibility of existence" (*BT* 308/264). But this "discloses also all the possibilities that precede it" in a specific light. Death modalizes them as "finite possibilities" – as "defined by their ending" (*BT* 308–309/264). This does not mean that the pursuit of every possibility will end in death – they can end for other reasons as well. But, to paraphrase Louis CK, no matter how important any given relationship or pursuit is to you, the best-case scenario is it ends with someone dead. Thus, the significance of every possibility is affected by death: because death is unsurpassable, we understand that, one way or another, all our pursuits will end.

Death as an unsurpassable "it's over" thus modalizes all our other possibilities by stripping them of the false appearance of being necessary. It shows that, necessarily, each possibility that structures my being in the world will end. One existentiell consequence of this might be to undermine my commitment to the form of life I happen to inhabit. When "running ahead discloses to existence that its ultimate possibility lies in giving itself up ... it shatters all one's tenaciousness to whatever existence one has reached" (*BT* 308/264). The undermining of commitments frees me to choose a different path:

> [O]ne is liberated from one's lostness in those possibilities which may accidentally thrust themselves upon one; one is liberated in such a way that for the first

time one can authentically understand and choose among the factical possibilities that precede the unsurpassable possibility. (*BT* 308/264)

4. Indefinite and Certain

Death is a possibility which is "indefinitely certain" (*BT* 310/265). That means that there is "a constant threat" to Dasein that arises from Dasein itself: "[I]n running ahead to an indefinitely certain death, Dasein opens itself up to a constant threat arising from its own 'there'" (*BT* 310/265). Where the unsurpassability of death modalizes my other possibilities as finite in the sense of necessarily coming to an end, the indefinite certainty of death modalizes my other possibilities as finite in the sense of being vulnerable – of being prone to fail at any moment. It is necessarily the case that I can fail in the pursuit of each possibility (or, conversely, that each possibility will fail to define me). We grasp this certainty in an existentiell sense only to the extent that we "maintain" ourselves in a state of constant anxiety – a constant responsiveness to the fragility and vulnerability of any given possibility.

* * *

In summary, then, death is a possibility that imposes significance on the field of all my other possibilities. Death makes those possibilities finite in a twofold sense: First, because of death, all of my other possibilities are doomed to come to an end, and, second, all of my possibilities are vulnerable in the sense of being prone to failure at any moment. Death sorts possibilities by differentiating my own possibilities from the world's possibilities. And running forward into death thus opens up the possibility of determining myself as an individual. With this description of the modalizing effect that death has on our possibilities, we've started to flesh out the transformative force of running ahead into death. I'll close with a few cursory observations about the significance of death for an authentic existence.

11.6 The Existential Transformative Force of Death

The distinction between authentic and inauthentic ways of relating to death has nothing to do with having a thematic understanding of death as a possibility. It is true that inauthentic Dasein has a non-thematic understanding of death. Dasein is "delivered over to its death" even though it "has initially and for the most part no express or indeed theoretical knowledge of death" (*BT* 295/251). As Heidegger explains, Dasein always "knows about death, but for the most part in the sense that 'I know about death, but I don't think about it.' Most of the time I know it in a sort of knowledge that recoils from it" (*GA* 64: 116). But authentic running ahead does not consist in replacing the immediacy of our everyday understanding of death with explicit thoughts about death. Running ahead does not involve "brooding over" death, or "thinking about death" and "pondering over when and how this possibility may perhaps be actualized" (*BT* 305/261). The authentic understanding of death that comes from running ahead necessarily "is not a kind of cognition" (*GA* 20: 334). Instead, it is "a primary kind of being of being-in-the-world itself" (*GA* 20: 334). To be more precise, it is "a way of disclosing the 'there' for existence" (*BT* 308/263).[7] The "there" is the actual situation in which we find ourselves at any given moment, a situation in which we experience attractions and repulsions that motivate us to act. In inauthentic existence, the "there" – the situation of present action – solicits us to act in terms of the concerns of everyday existence. The actuality of shared social life has priority in motivating us. In authentic existence, by contrast, the possibility of death re-attunes us to the situation of action and alters the pattern of attractions and repulsions.

So the *way* that an authentic relation to death discloses the situation of action is through effecting a change, not in *what I think* about existence, but rather in *how I am disposed*, in *how different possibilities matter* to me, and in *the way situations solicit me to respond*. What authentic anticipation of death makes immediately salient is how the various possibilities open to me allow me to either claim or disown responsibility for myself:

> Running ahead sets before us a choice; this mean it uncovers the horizon of this choice, and that which in the choice can be chosen: either to be a self through the "how" of assuming responsibility for itself, or to be in the mode of being lived by whatever it is occupied with at any given time. (*GA* 64: 54)

We can thus take up and pursue any other possibility in two different modes. Through running ahead into death, we encounter situations in "the 'how' of wanting-to-be-responsible-for-itself" (*GA* 64: 45).

---

[7] Authentically running ahead into death alters my "ability-to-be," and thus effects concrete changes in the way I actively engage with the world. In "the concrete structure of running ahead into death," Heidegger explains, we achieve a "pure understanding." But "it should be noted that understanding does not primarily mean just gazing at a meaning, but rather understanding oneself in the ability-to-be that is revealed in projection" (*BT* 307/263).

By inauthentically fleeing from death and losing ourselves in the routines of the everyday world, we encounter possibilities in the "falling how" – the how that conforms to public norms because it is "trained as a habit, as a routine, always with a view to the 'what' of [average] concerns" (*GA* 64: 44).

Keeping in mind these observations about death, one can now ask how, in particular, death can impel us toward an authentic existence. Death, like any other possibility, admits of an indeterminate number of different *existentiell* ways of taking it up. And so it should not surprise us that Heidegger offers a number of different descriptions of authentic ways of taking death as a modal structure up into existence. I will not attempt here to catalogue all the various existentiell ways of authentically incorporating death into existence. But a central aspect of authentic existentiell responses to death is the phenomenon of *disengagement* from the world. In running ahead into death, "the world recedes" in importance and "fades into the background" (*GA* 64: 53). Our social standing "fades away" along with it. Characteristics like "respectability and being different from the others" no longer motivate us to act (cf. *GA* 64: 52–53). "The world loses the possibility of defining [us] ... The world can no longer endow Dasein with being" (*GA* 64: 53). Psychologically speaking, in world-withdrawal, I find myself unmoved by social expectations.

Let's consider two contrasting accounts of the way disengagement contributes to our becoming authentically responsible for ourselves.

One interpretation of the existential significance of death runs like this: First, in running ahead into death, I see that there is no right answer to the question "what should I do with my life?" Death, it is said, discloses a *lack of fit* between me and any possible way of defining myself (see, e.g., Thomson 2013, 271). This lack of fit is an experience of disengagement as *detachment* from my usual standards for discriminating between what is important and unimportant. Norms and criteria of choice now show up as being radically internal to my projects. Once these projects lose their grip on me, I am deprived of any solid basis for caring about what I should do or who I should be. But this *detachment* from norms brings with it a possibility to choose my own project freely and reflexively. Detachment produces a fundamentally *decisionist* account of authenticity. To be authentic, then, consists in resolutely committing oneself to an intrinsically meaningless and arbitrary choice.

But there is another way of experiencing the existentiell significance of disengagement. Running ahead into death arguably shows me, not a lack of fit between me and all my possibilities, but rather merely the contingency of conventional worldly possibilities. In that case, my recognition of my own finitude does not necessarily lead to detachment from all mattering. Instead, it disentangles me from the deadening because habituatingly conformist effects of everyday activities. When liberated from the tendency to take worldly status seriously, a space is opened up to rediscover what really matters to me (given my disposedness and given the projects to which I am drawn). Running ahead into the "it's over" is a disengagement from the world that, far from depriving me of grounds for deciding what is important, allows what most matters to me to shine forth more intensely. In confronting the finitude of death, I discover that the transience of things makes me love them all the more. On this picture, then, authenticity is a resolute willingness to be thrown back onto my factical disposedness. Running ahead into death allows for a meaningful responsibility, because in it I own my thrownness and forge a coherent self by reconnecting to the projects that will allow me to realize my own individual commitments.[8]

***

I claimed at the outset that a complete account of Heideggerian death would do three things: First, it would explain the distinction Heidegger draws between death and demise; second, it would account for the existential import of death in Heidegger's account of authentic existence; third, it would explain the methodological role played by death in Heidegger's ontology.

With regard to the first task, I've argued that the distinction between death and demise is found in the distinction between possibilities and the events that actualize those possibilities. I've argued, further, that death is Dasein's distinctive possibility because it informs the significance of all our other possibilities.

With regard to the second task, I've reviewed Heidegger's claim that the existential import of death is found in the details of the way that death modalizes all our other possibilities. And I've suggested that running ahead into death transforms the character of existence – not by detaching me from all forms of mattering, but rather by allowing me to see more clearly what matters to me in the light of my individual thrownness into existence. But this is a claim that needs to be developed in considerably more detail than I've been able to do here.

---

[8] For attempts at developing this picture of authenticity, see Wrathall (2014a, 2014b, 2017a, and 2017b).

With regard to the third task, I've had very little to say directly. But I hope that I've laid the groundwork for understanding the fundamental role of modality in Heidegger's account of ontology. I claimed in passing that, for Heidegger, to be is to inhabit a specific chunk of modal space. The analysis of death in *Being and Time* offers an account of the specific way in which entities with Dasein's kind of being inhabit modal space. But it is a task for another time to work out the implications of the modal account of death for Heidegger's ontology more broadly.[9]

---

[9] I'm grateful to many people for their helpful suggestions on earlier versions of this chapter. These include participants at the meeting of the *American Society for Existential Phenomenology* at Barnard College on July 2nd, 2022; attendees at the University of Warwick's *Post-Kantian Seminar* on January 25th, 2022; members of Charles University where I presented a draft on April 21st, 2022; and students in my graduate courses on *Being and Time*. Comments by Nick Smith, Michael Nelson, Tobias Keiling, Aaron Wendland, Wanda von Knobelsdorff, Taylor Carman, Aryan Goenka, Erick Spahr, and Nikolas Land have significantly contributed to the development of the arguments in this chapter. Finally, I'm particularly indebted to Iain Thomson, with whom I've been discussing issues surrounding Heidegger's conception of death for many years.

CHAPTER 12

Heidegger on the Failure of Being and Time

Tobias Keiling

Despite its philosophical significance, Heidegger in retrospect thought his *magnum opus* failed in several ways. This chapter aims to elucidate the philosophical stakes of Heidegger's own critique of *Being and Time* (*BT*). Heidegger's self-criticism does not simply concern the fact that only about a third of the text announced in §8 of the introduction was published: Divisions One and Two, the text we now know as *BT*, were supposed to be supplemented by a third division on 'Time and Being', completing part one, which should have been followed by a second part, again consisting of three divisions, providing the '[b]asic contours of a phenomenological destruction of the history of ontology, guided by the problematic of temporality' (*BT* 63/39–40; translation altered). As Heidegger presents matters in his published writings, this failure to complete the book as planned would ultimately be vindicated by the further development of Heidegger's philosophy: it would have triggered what Heidegger calls a *turn* or *turning* (*Kehre*) in his thinking, a reorientation that he took to be both necessary and productive. As I argue in Section 12.1, this turn-narrative presents Heidegger's philosophy as evolving in a fundamentally continuous and coherent fashion, and therefore it covers over rather than explains the numerous philosophical difficulties and inconsistencies Heidegger came to see in *BT*. And this means one needs to look elsewhere than Heidegger's discussions of the turn to understand the specific problems that led Heidegger to abandon the project of *BT*.

The best source of Heidegger's self-criticism currently available is a set of recently published private notes that directly and quite harshly comment on the text of *BT*, identifying problems in various passages of the book and in key transitions of its overall argument. These problems include Heidegger's attempt to answer the question of being in view of Dasein's temporality, his reliance on the phenomenology of the everyday, and his account of hermeneutics and understanding. After offering my overview of the turn-narrative, I will discuss Heidegger's specific criticisms of *BT* in detail in Section 12.2. In the concluding Section 12.3, I consider how Heidegger's private notes have been taken up in the literature so far. Against Polt who sees Heidegger successfully responding to his own criticism in *Contributions to Philosophy*, I argue that the position Heidegger reaches in 1935/36 is still susceptible to the fundamental critique he levelled against *BT* and I explain how the standard account of the turn (that Polt relies upon) actually emerges in Heidegger's own critique of BT as an alternative to the circle of understanding.

12.1 Was There a Turn in Heidegger's Thought?

In the lectures and essays published by Heidegger during his lifetime, one finds only one explicit correction of the philosophical claims of *BT* concerning, on the face of it, a relatively minor issue. In 'Time and Being', Heidegger admits that 'the attempt made in *Being and Time*, §70 to base Dasein's spatiality on timeliness [*Zeitlichkeit*] is untenable' (*TB* 23; *GA* 14: 29). This retraction aside, the narrative Heidegger presents in published work as well as in late seminars is that of a specific continuity expressed by the idea of a *turn* occurring in his work after BT. Although this notion has been at the centre of debates in the literature on the continuities and breaks in Heidegger's philosophy (Braver 2015; Risser 1999; Sheehan 2014; Young 2015), one should be clear about its status. The idea is, first, Heidegger's own; it indicates how at some points in his career he wanted BT and subsequent texts to be read. Second, although recurring in Heidegger's unpublished writings and indeed key to manuscripts such as *Contributions to Philosophy* (1936; cf. *CP* 27, 322–324; *GA* 65: 31, 407–409), what gives this notion its prominence is that it appears in Heidegger's later writings to explain why the announced remainder of the text had still not been published nearly two decades after *BT's* initial publication. It offers a way to understand the failure of *BT* that avoids giving a detailed account of the sense in which the book failed to achieve its philosophical ambitions.

Consider how Heidegger presents the notion of the turn in the 'Letter on "Humanism"', the highly publicized essay that was the first of Heidegger's writings to appear after the Second World War. Although Heidegger admits the incompleteness of *BT*, the passage is also far from acknowledging the failure of his earlier philosophical project or detailing its reasons:

> If we understand what 'Being and Time' calls 'projection' [*Entwurf*] as a representational positing [*vorstellendes Setzen*], we take it as an achievement

of subjectivity and do not think it in the only way the 'understanding of being' in the context of an 'existential analysis' of 'being-in-the-world' can only be thought, namely as the ecstatic relation to the clearing of being. The adequate execution and completion of this other thinking that abandons subjectivity is surely made more difficult by the fact that in the publication of 'Being and Time' the third division of the first part, 'Time and Being' was held back ... Here, everything is turned about. [*Hier kehrt sich das Ganze um.*] The division in question was held back because thinking failed in the apt saying of this turn; the language of metaphysics did not help it to break through ... This turn is not a change from the position occupied by 'Being and Time'; rather, only in the turn did the attempted thinking reach the place of that dimension from out of which 'Being and Time' is experienced, experienced, that is, in the fundamental experience of the forgetfulness of being. (*BW* 231–232; *GA* 9: 327–328)

Though the passage is difficult to assess, what clearly emerges is that the point at which the text of *BT* breaks off is not primarily to be taken as indicating a problem or set of problems in the argumentative structure of the book. Rather, Heidegger's failure to complete the book as planned succeeds at making accessible its basic motivation, the 'fundamental experience' that being is at present not of genuine philosophical concern. The quotation marks Heidegger places around the terminology typical for *BT* (but not around the unfamiliar talk of 'the clearing', 'place', or 'dimension') indicate that this terminology is now taken as an instance of 'the language of metaphysics', contributing to rather than overcoming the 'forgetfulness of being'. That Heidegger 'held back' the third division after having published the first two further seems to imply that he intentionally let the text remain a fragment; the incompleteness of *BT* is to be understood as an indication of something more important and fundamental than what the project could have provided were it to have been completed as planned. The project of *BT* has become not an impasse, but a turn; its failure is remedied by further progress on the path of thinking.[1] In such a way, the turn-narrative urges on Heidegger's readers a quite charitable interpretation of the failure of *BT*.

But despite the crucial role this narrative plays in Heidegger's attempts to shape a favourable interpretation of *BT* in 1947, it is not Heidegger's last word. Between 1972 and 1975, Heidegger worked on a never-

---

[1] Heidegger similarly comments in (*BW* 231; *GA* 9: 328) and (*BW* 138; *GA* 9: 201), retrospectively defining as an intentional gesture the failure of earlier works. In 1941, Heidegger curiously ties the decision not to pursue the project of *BT* to the death of Rainer Maria Rilke, who died on December 26th, 1926. Heidegger learned of his death in January 1927. See *GA* 49: 39–40.

completed introduction to the entire *Gesamtausgabe*, composing a set of notes collected under the title 'The Legacy of the Question of Being' (*Vermächtnis der Seinsfrage*).[2] Among these notes is a short text titled '"Turn"? "Saying of the Turn"' (*'Kehre'? 'Sagen der Kehre'*), the quotation marks and an appended page reference making clear that the title is directly commenting on the passage from the 'Letter on "Humanism"' just discussed. Referring to the two notions in the title, Heidegger (2007, 9) continues:

> both, any talk of it, a grave error entrenched for a long time; motivated by the intention to make comprehensible the breaking-off of the publication of B. a. T. *before* a discussion of the all-sustaining centre, thus discussing it from the outside [and] not on the basis of the intuited matter [*erblickter Sachverhalt*] of how Dasein relates to being.

As Heidegger now sees it, the 'notion of a "turn" [*Vorstellung einer "Kehre"*]' formed 'a barrier to the path [*Wegsperre*] only slowly overcome ... For many years, leaping over the "turn" qua barrier to the path but never really setting it aside'. The substantial difficulty, Heidegger (2007) goes on to explain, is that 'with the misguided appeal to a turn, Dasein is in a certain, albeit unintended way again separated and set in opposition to being [*das Dasein wieder für sich dem Sein gegenübergesetzt*] ... It is not about a turn, but about the adequate characterization of Dasein as regards its belonging to the event' (10–11).

That Heidegger in private notes came to see the turn-narrative as an obstacle should make one resist the idea that it was his only or definitive way of locating the failure of *BT* in the development of his philosophy. Matters are further complicated, though, because the proposal was reiterated in public only a few years before. In 1969, during the *Seminar in Le Thor*, Heidegger distinguishes not two but 'three steps along the way of thinking', marked by different organizing conceptual centres: 'MEANING – TRUTH – PLACE (*topos*)'. Whereas these signal the discontinuity of Heidegger's philosophy, what remained constant, according to this version of the turn-narrative, was the motivation to make sense of being as such, moving from 'the question of the meaning

---

[2] The manuscript is preserved at the Deutsches Literaturarchiv Marbach (Sign. A: Heidegger 1, Inv.-Nr.: 2006.21.1–4) and published only in part (Heidegger 2011/12, 2013/14, 2009, 2010, 2015/16, 2008, 2007). Two paragraphs were published in the first volume of the *Gesamtausgabe* in place of Heidegger's own planned introduction (*GA* 1: 457–458, translated in *DS* 171–172). Heidegger (2013/14) is translated in Keiling and Moore (2022a and 2022b). McNeill (2020) translates material from Heidegger (2011/12).

of being' to 'the question concerning the truth of being' to 'the question concerning the place or location of being ... This signifies "the turn", in which thinking always more decisively turns to being as being' (*FS* 47; *GA* 15: 344–345). Although the narrative is here modified and extended to include a third position that Heidegger's thinking arrived at, only a few years later, Heidegger would, at least in private notes, take any appeal to the figure of the turn to be a hindrance to the progress of thinking.

At the same time, one should be clear that Heidegger's rejection of the turn-narrative is itself marked by a specific tension. On the one hand, rejecting it seems to imply that the development of Heidegger's philosophy should not be construed as a sequence of commitments: first to the philosophical system of BT, then to another and then possibly yet another – as Heidegger publicly stated in 1949 and 1969, respectively. On the other hand, when Heidegger suggests that the turn blocks the way, the rejection is presented in a form that continues to imply the idea of thinking as progress on a single path. Turning or not, likening thinking to a single path already stresses its continuity and coherence.

But as another fragment of the 'Legacy' manuscript, published in 1978 in the editor's afterword to the first *Gesamtausgabe* volume, reveals, Heidegger understood his thinking and philosophy generally to progress not on a single but on several paths. This is not only reflected in the motto Heidegger chose for the edition instead of including an extended introduction: 'Paths rather than works [*Wege, nicht Werke*]'. The first of the two fragments from the 'Legacy' manuscript in *GA* 1 elaborates this motto by offering an alternative to the image of the turn and to the idea of progress on a single path of thinking:

> The *Gesamtausgabe* shall show in different connections: a being-underway in the network of paths of the transforming questioning of the polysemous question of being [*ein Unterwegs im Wegfeld des sich wandelnden Fragens der mehrdeutigen Seinsfrage*]. The edition shall thus guide toward taking up the question, toward contributing to posing the question [*mitfragen*], and, most importantly, toward then asking the question more questioningly [*fragender fragen*]. (*DS* 172; *GA* 1: 437)

As Heidegger presents it here, the unity and coherence of his philosophy come from the normativity inherent in the activity of questioning. This normativity is of a peculiar structure: although the idea that questioning allows for varying degrees of intensity implies a single standard of the activity ('questioning more questioningly'), its content is inherently plural if the question of being is constitutively polysemous (*mehrdeutig*).³ To avoid a paradox in these conflicting demands, responding to them must be a matter of judgment, that is, of their context-responsive weighing. So although different paths of questioning can be identified, it is nonetheless a general feature of thinking that it orients itself among the possibilities of thinking, or in Heidegger's now preferred metaphor: thinking is not pursuing a path already laid out for it, it remains underway. As Heidegger adds in a second fragment also chosen by the editor to be published in 1978, the normativity of questioning also requires looking back critically at his work: 'The number of volumes ... provides many a cause for self-criticism' (*DS* 172; *GA* 1: 438). Although defining the position that the different fragments of the 'Legacy' manuscript develop is difficult, what clearly emerges is that Heidegger not only came to reject the turn-narrative, he also sketched a pluralist alternative to how it should be read: as several paths laid out for the reader to follow, cautioning that some will lead to aporia. Rather than commit to any definitive position or procedure, the only demand Heidegger's philosophy makes is that one not cease to ask the question of being, that is, that one remain underway.

Despite Heidegger's late rejection of the turn-narrative and the alternative image of a network of paths, that narrative has dominated much of Heidegger scholarship of the past decades and is accepted in most of it. In view of the material discussed above, this may have more to do with the availability of Heidegger's philosophy than with the exegetical plausibility of that narrative. In the first decades of research on Heidegger, only a few cryptic remarks on the failure of BT were publicly accessible; what Heidegger published in the 'Letter on "Humanism"' in particular seemed to be the definite take on how he saw his own philosophy. These remarks have only slowly been supplemented as Heidegger's unpublished writings became available over the years, with Heidegger's direct rejection of the turn-narrative becoming available only in 2007, in a limited edition outside the *Gesamtausgabe*. To see this point, consider a scenario in which the comment on the turn as a barrier to the path was among those fragments from 'Legacy of the Question of Being' chosen by the editor to be published in 1978. The mere availability of Heidegger's explicit rejection of the idea, contradicting the statement in the 'Letter on "Humanism"', would have certainly influenced the way in which scholars understood the failure of BT, which in turn would have shaped how newly

---

³ Elsewhere (Keiling 2018), I have argued that a tension between ontological monism and ontological pluralism is characteristic of Heidegger's later works as a whole.

available texts, such as *Contributions*, published in 1989, were interpreted. The turn-narrative is a product not only of Heidegger's own public attempts to shape the interpretation of his philosophy; it is also, at least to some extent, an artefact of Heidegger research.

It is still a different question if the turn indicates a structural feature of ontological questioning that, although first developed in this context, is not necessarily linked to Heidegger's self-interpretation. Commenting on the 'Letter on "Humanism"' in 1962 in a letter to William J. Richardson, Heidegger says as much ('The turn is in play within the matter itself.', *HR* 302; trans. mod.), and this is indeed how the notion is taken up in recent critical appropriations of Heidegger (Fried 2000, esp. 66–79). As I will discuss in Section 12.3, the idea of the turn emerges in a revision of the idea of the circle of understanding motivated by the problems Heidegger came to see with it. But this only confirms that one should be sceptical about the turn-narrative as an interpretive key to understanding the failure of *BT*. At his most critical, Heidegger presents a much more complex argument against the ambition and the argument of his first book.

12.2 Heidegger's 'Running Notes' on *BT*

Given the material now available to interpret Heidegger's later views on *BT*, Heidegger's sparse comments in published writings contrast sharply with texts that contain a much more direct and elaborate critique of the book's project. In this regard, a set of notes entitled 'Running Notes (R.N.) on "Being and Time"' (*Laufende Anmerkungen (L.A.) zu 'Sein und Zeit'*, GA 82: 3–136) stands out. These notes, which comprise approximately 130 pages of edited text, written in 1936 but published only in 2018, are dedicated to individual divisions, chapters, and sections of *BT*, relating Heidegger's self-criticism to specific passages.[4] Unsurprisingly, the longest commentary and most trenchant critiques are directed at passages that are crucial junctures in the argument of BT, such as the introduction running up to the sketch of the whole book in §8 as well as §32 on understanding, §44 on truth, and the transition from Division One to Division Two in §45. I will focus on these passages of the commentary to show that they develop several important points regarding how the specific methodology Heidegger envisages for ontology interacts with the content of the ontological knowledge to be gained with its help.

---

[4] The line of argument developed in the first half of the notes is parallel to that found in a 1941 lecture course on Schelling. See GA 49: 17–75.

Two points strike me as most important. First, Heidegger now considers it to be an unwarranted presupposition to say that genuine philosophical knowledge in ontology will have the form of an *answer* to the question of being. It is correct to determine Dasein and its ability to question as essential to the pursuit of ontology, but pursuing ontological knowledge is not like other forms of inquiry. It requires a deep transformation of Dasein's self-understanding as it comes to take more and more seriously the question of being, yet to presume that the answer to that question is, even in merely anticipatory form, already known would be to limit or undercut this growing questionability. As Heidegger writes in one of the comments on the last sections of *BT*, it is false to say that the book has failed because it hasn't provided an answer to the question of being:

> So it would seem. But in truth, it [the answer, T.K.] lays the foundation for the whole, it *precedes* the question, more to the point: questioning is presented as being merely an unfolding of this answer, namely that being 'is' understood in view of time ... The answer in 'Being and Time' is absent; yet not because it had not yet been found, but because it has been found *too much* [zu sehr *gefunden*]. (*GA* 82: 134)

Although several critical points Heidegger makes can also be found in other manuscripts and publications, a second radical claim in the 'Notes' is the explicit, repeated, and decisive rejection of time as explanatory paradigm. Since the explanatory power of Dasein's timeliness (*Zeitlichkeit*) and being's temporality (*Temporalität*) is central to the entire project, rejecting the paradigmatic status of *BT*'s temporal categories touches on all its core commitments. Sections 12.2.1–12.2.3 detail the critical implications of this rejection for different discussions in *BT*; Sections 12.2.4–12.2.5 focus on ways in which Heidegger is working towards an alternative.

12.2.1 *Understanding, Temporality, and the Question of Being*

One passage in which the rejection of time as paradigm for ontology is articulated directly is Heidegger's discussion of §5, the section anticipating the key result of the text's argument, that is, that '*the central problematic of all ontology is rooted in the phenomenon of time, if rightly seen and rightly explained*' (*BT* 40/18). Commenting on other lines from this section, Heidegger locates here 'the deepest error of it all' (*tiefster Irrtum des Ganzen*):

> To make being 'comprehensible' [*verständlich*] in view of 'time'; to make being 'visible in its 'temporal' character' (p. 18). Making

comprehensible – making visible – 'being' as regards the *horizon* of earlier understanding. Why *this* understanding; why *from out of time*? ... '*Exposition of the problematic of temporality*' (p. 18) – this the *answer* (p. 19) to the question of being. Here again the relapse [*Rückfall*] comes to the fore (the deepest error of it all). But 'temporality can at best be a preliminary finding – not a beginning or end – and this finding includes a decisive question (cf. already on p. 18): how does time come to be this measure for the *understanding* of being? (*GA* 82: 33)[5]

If *BT*'s methodological mistake is to assume that ontological knowledge has the form of an answer to the question of being, within the system of *BT*, this problem takes the form of a conjunction of ontological understanding and an account of time designed to provide such an answer. As Heidegger writes at the closing of §4, Dasein cannot but *understand* being, if even in the form of a 'pre-ontological understanding of being' (*BT* 35/15). To articulate such implicit knowledge becomes the ambition of the book, and according to the preview given in §5, such an articulation cannot but be given in view of the temporal nature of both being and understanding. To mark these points, Heidegger in the 'Notes' often refers to the *Seinsverständnisfrage* rather than the *Seinsfrage*, that is, to the 'question as to the understanding of being' rather than the 'question of being' (*GA* 82: 28, 35, 53, 79, 83, 102, 134); once, he even writes of the *Seinsverständnis-Temporalitätsfrage*, the 'understanding of being-temporality question', immediately adding: 'Here, the *prior question* has to be asked, the question as to the *basic experience of this projection*' (*GA* 82: 42). This is Heidegger's ambition to question more questioningly at work: asking this prior question calls into doubt the crucial notion *BT* offers for describing understanding, that is, that it has the form of Dasein projecting itself upon its possibilities, hence into its future. Heidegger makes the same point in the 'Letter on "Humanism"' when cautioning to understand *BT*'s notion of projection as 'representational positing', but only the 'Notes' show how much of *BT* hinges on this.

A first context in which the difficulty with projection emerges most clearly is in Heidegger's comments on *BT* as a project in *transcendental philosophy* (Crowell & Malpas 2007). The very notion of an understanding of being now appears to Heidegger as 'effectively still an offshoot of the

---

[5] The edition often contains an opening bracket or quotation mark that is not followed by a corresponding closing one. There are also some grammatical anomalies which, should they occur in the handwritten manuscript, have not been corrected by the editor. While I do not represent these in my translation, I cite the German text as it appears in the edition. Page references cited from *GA* 82 are Heidegger's and refer to the German pagination of *BT*. Asterisks mark illegible words.

Heidegger on the Failure of Being and Time　　　257

standpoint of consciousness ... and the Transcendental question' (*GA* 82: 34). What ties ontological understanding to the transcendental project is that the anticipated answer to the question of being gives understanding a determinate and specific form: '"temporality" [*Temporalität*]' is the 'transcendental *field of conditions* [Bedingungsfeld]' exposed in *BT*. The problem with identifying temporal categories as transcendental, Heidegger goes on to explain, is that it fails to generate an apt form of plausibility. Delimited or formatted in such a way, projection 'does not reach the origin – because this field of conditions [is] way too thin. The projection becomes, at best, "real" existentially, but not genuinely essential' (*GA* 82: 34). Rather than simply posit a specific set of transcendental conditions, genuine projection would have to explain 'why – in what way and for what reason – understanding of being "*belongs*" to Dasein' (*GA* 82: 34). As I discuss in Section 12.2.5 below, an important aspect of projection in its genuine or 'essential' form would be to retain its freedom to bind itself to another set of categories as transcendental.

Although the passages on §5 are particularly succinct, the rejection of tying understanding to temporal categories is a recurring theme in many of the notes. The idea is repeated in a long and particularly elaborate discussion of the transition from Division One to Division Two in §45. Heidegger here reiterates that the rejection is motivated by a phenomenological inadequacy, defining a second context in which *BT*'s notion of projection is inadequate. Rather than laying bare matters as they are, formatting projection as temporal understanding creates a form of self-deception:

> What in both an existentiell and a transcendental respect is a free projection (being-toward-death – conscience – timeliness [*Zeitlichkeit*]) is here presented as if it had been discovered by means of an appropriate existential analytic; yet the appropriateness consists only in the fact that the presupposed measure is suppressed as that which is being sought; it consists in the fact that the semblance is created that the investigation is moving gradually toward the originary when this is rather merely a presentation of what the projection opens up – a presentation that derives from the projection itself [*eine aus dem Entwurf zurückgehende Darstellung des mit dem Entwurf Eröffneten*]. / Yet this is no *intentional* deception but the erroneous phenomenological-existential self-deception as part of the methodology. / What is wanted is already decided: *time as horizon of the understanding of being*. (*GA* 82: 125)

Heidegger thus continues to uphold an idea characteristic of his approach to phenomenology, namely its effective merger with ontology (Figal 2010).

As he writes in a comment on §7, not only are ontology and phenomenology *'clamped together'* by the idea that being manifests itself in time; the *'clamp'* holding them together 'forces' the project of *BT* 'forward' (*GA* 82: 38). But Heidegger now believes that this merger skews the findings of phenomenological method. Accounts that are plausible when considered in isolation, that is, the 'free projection' of death, conscience, and the timeliness of Dasein, become distorted when integrated into the project of answering the question of being in view of temporality. As Heidegger sees it here, anticipating a specific answer to the question of being the phenomenological method of *BT* actively, albeit unintentionally, made entities seem to be as they are not; it turned their manifestation into a mere seeming. The mistake is similar to the one that Heidegger in the 1930s and 1940s finds in Hegel's understanding of phenomenology, in which the process of 'absolute representation' (*OBT* 139; *GA* 5: 186; cf. *HPS* 1–43) supersedes experience and its object. As Heidegger puts it in the above quote from the 'Notes': an illusion, a 'representation that derives from the projection itself' passes as an accurate representation of how things are. Or in the terms of the 'Letter', projection becomes 'representational positing'.

12.2.2 *The Phenomenology of World*

Heidegger continues this reasoning when he argues that the account of world provided in the third chapter of Division One (§§14–24), arguably one of the most innovative and influential parts of *BT*, in truth provides an example of how temporal categories distort phenomenology. As Heidegger now sees it, the description of everydayness prominent in this chapter is effectively occluding the genuine manifestation of world. By emphasizing the contrast between inauthentic and authentic being-in, the phenomenology of world in *BT* embodies 'an excess of the "worldly" self, in its reliance on itself [*Übersteigerung des "weltlichen" auf sich gestellten Selbst*]' (*GA* 82: 66). Because the motivation for overstating the role of the self is to reveal the temporal nature of Dasein, the explanatory paradigm of time is to fault for this:

> Because in the following – having in view existential timeliness [*Zeitlichkeit*] (cf. Division Two) – everything is geared toward authenticity, 'the world' and its meta-physical essence sinks – is lowered to the ambit of everydayness! ... World becomes a thin and empty system of references ... *World* – cannot at all be understood in the present context; neither by beginning with being-in-the world! ... nor with hammer and pliers! (*GA* 82: 66)

Heidegger on the Failure of Being and Time 259

This passage echoes a remark in the 1929/1930 lecture course *Fundamental Concepts of Metaphysics* (*FCM* 177; *GA* 29/30: 263), where Heidegger emphasises that in writing on everydayness in *BT*, 'It never occurred to me ... to try and claim or prove with this interpretation that the essence of man consists in the fact that he knows how to handle knives and forks or uses the tram'. In implicit reference to that lecture course, Heidegger in the 'Notes' adds a surprising and trenchant critical remark when he describes the world as analysed in Division One of *BT* as a manifestation of *Weltarmut* (*GA* 82: 65), the deficient mode of being-in-the-world associated with animal life in *Fundamental Concepts of Metaphysics*: 'Referential totality [*Verweisungsganzes*]; ultimately, that is what the animal, being securely at home *in its environment* [*Umgebung*], also has! – and yet doesn't' (*GA* 82: 66).

But the point is not that everyday Dasein is somehow assimilated to the way of being of animals. A more detailed analysis of what goes wrong here is provided when Heidegger discusses the poorness of the world of everydayness as *Weltverhüllung*, as a 'covering over of world' (*GA* 82: 63, 65, 69). Rather than its genuine manifestation, everyday existence is merely a semblance of worldhood:

> Completely misdirected in its procedure, wanting to make world 'visible' precisely where there is a *covering over* of world, where there is only the semblance that world would not world and only things existed. / *Worlding* as *arranging* the thingness of things [*Einrichtung der Dingheit der Dinge*]!, though not as temporal constitution but as letting them essentially hold sway [*Wesenlassen*] in their full earthly truth. (*GA* 82: 69)

Covering over the genuine manifestation of the world in worlding goes hand in hand with the ontological mistake of taking available or ready-to-hand being (*Zuhandenes*) as explanatorily basic for understanding intra-worldly entities. Heidegger now deems it necessary to 'step back even before availableness [*Zuhandenheit*]' (*GA* 82: 65). As a comment on the entire project of *BT* elaborates, to which Heidegger refers here, this means to set aside the dichotomy of availableness and extantness (*Vorhandenes*):

> 'Extantness' in particular does not arrive at the essence of *those* entities that are intended – *the things* ... Extantness [*Vor-handenheit*] ... [is] a type of relation within concern – a not-concerning-myself-with [*Unbesorgtheit*], but not the manifestation of the thing itself, which only appears from out of being as grounded in the there! (*GA* 82: 15)

Both here and in the above passage, the alternative to the phenomenology of world presented in Division One is defined by the idea that the world is, on the explanatorily basic level, made up of things (*Dinge*), an idea anticipated in *The Origin of the Work of Art* but explicitly articulated only much later (i.e. *BFL* 5–22). Whatever this means exactly, it clearly emerges that, already in 1936, Heidegger thought the notion of a thing should be given explanatory priority over the categories of both extant and available being.

12.2.3 *BT's 'Fundamental Deceptions' and the Failure of Hermeneutics*

The skewed phenomenology of world and the misleading ontology of intraworldly entities it leads to provide an example of how Heidegger thinks that the explanatory paradigm of time ultimately misdirects the project of *BT*. Heidegger further develops this point in a comment on §8, the section providing an overview of all the divisions *BT* was meant to include. As Heidegger now sees it, the faulty conception of what it means to question about being, that is, anticipating to answer the question in view of time, leads to three '*fundamental flaws*' (Grundmängel) and '*errors*' (Irrtümer) (*GA* 82: 41). Following the pattern described in the last section, Heidegger analyses these errors not as shortcomings of an otherwise correct approach but as theory-induced self-deceptions. Throughout the commentary, the three 'fundamental flaws' of *BT* are thus referred to as 'fundamental deceptions' (*Grundtäuschungen*, *GA* 82: 43, 44, 56, 92, 129).

As Heidegger recognizes, the status of these deceptions is ambivalent because they '*both support and at the same time mislead and strangle* the project [mißleiten und abbinden]' (*GA* 82: 45). Although the exact designations vary, Heidegger repeatedly calls these '*the phenomenological, the existentiell, and the ontological-transcendental*' deception. The following passage is the most extensive summary of what each consists of:

> The *phenomenological* intention aims to *come to a foundation and reach what is original* – in contrast to contemporary Neo-Kantianism that … had becomes baseless, only moving in 'theories' and leaning on historiography.
>
> The *existentiell* intention aims to pursue questioning not as a merely scholarly matter – not as an occupation, but *to make it the genuine concern of the acting self* and to face decisions. The *ontological-transcendental* intention went beyond description to an original *justifying and groundlaying* [Begründen] and then to constructing [*Bauen*] – the *systematic* presentation of the domains of what is originary.
>
> All three together were meant to enact a liberation – and a new constructing. (*GA* 82: 44)

Heidegger on the Failure of Being and Time 261

I will discuss each of these deceptions in order, before turning to how Heidegger details their unity in reference to the temporal nature of understanding.

Regarding the phenomenological method, Heidegger explains that it was driven by the 'addiction to pure givenness for description' (*GA* 82: 42), leading to several misconceptions. First, Dasein was 'presupposed as describable' (*GA* 82: 42). Although Heidegger identifies a passage in *BT* where that is explicitly denied, overall, 'it looks as if Da-sein were here described and dissected like something extant … That is the *phenomenological deception*' (*GA* 82: 45). The second aspect of the phenomenological deception is the prevalence granted to everydayness in the phenomenology of world already discussed in Section 12.2.2. The explanatory priority attributed to everydayness was 'motivated by "phenomenology"', and although the 'foreground of the everyday [*Vordergründigkeit des Alltäglichen*]' helped 'bring all sorts of "phenomena" to light – it also let questioning drift away from its metaphysical task' (*GA* 82: 42). A third element in the phenomenological deception is that treating something as an everyday phenomenon readily to be described denies its historical nature. 'Everydayness [is] the ahistorical in *historical* beyng [Seyn] that is grounded in Dasein' (*GA* 82: 42). Although these errors lead to describing matters merely as they seem, not as they are, Heidegger (*GA* 82: 42–43) attributes to the accounts in Division One greater overall plausibility than those in Division Two: '*Phenomenology* – as seeming! Worst in Division Two … The entire §63 an impossible mixture of existentiality and *phenomenology!*' The section concluding the phenomenology of authentic being-toward-death and the call of conscience thus presents the worst inversion of the phenomenological ambition. (I return below to why this should be the case.)

The second fundamental deception concerns the existentiell intention to conceive the understanding of being as the deepest concern of an authentic self. As Heidegger explains commenting on §8, this ambition led to the mistake of a 'one-sided preference for "possibility"', the 'danger of dissolving everything into the possibility of being oneself [*Selbstseinkönnen*]' (*GA* 82: 41). Heidegger finds this confirmed in §31, where the ontological implications of understanding are developed:

> *The proposition:* 'Possibility as an existential however is the most originary and ultimate positive ontological determination of Dasein' (p. 143/44) is the *fundamental error* in the interpretation of Dasein in 'Being and Time' – here one sees most clearly the influence of the existentiell. / In connection with this, 'understanding' is also understood existentially rather than

metaphysically and the intention to *understand being* is skewed in an existentiell fashion; but also, admittedly, [understanding, T.K.] was made a possible enactment in view of time (temporality). (*GA* 82: 80)

The third, 'ontological-transcendental', deception has also been broached in the above sections. Its mistake is to assume, as Heidegger (*GA* 82: 41) puts it in another summary of the three fundamental deceptions, that the question of being should take the form of a 'question of the possibility of understanding being [*Möglichkeitsfrage des Seinsverständnisses*] – as if one were ever to reach ground this way!' As discussed in Section 12.2.1 above, defining the question of being in such a way invests too much in the notion of an understanding of being ('*Understanding being* – as projection – projection upon temporality!', *GA* 82: 81). Heidegger here reiterates that this has the effect of overdetermining understanding in such a way that it can merely disclose its own conditions of possibility. Projection is 'merely seeming to find [*nur vermeintlich vorfindend*]', whereas in truth it only 'retroactively supposes' what it supposedly encounters (*GA* 82: 83).

Heidegger (*GA* 82: 83) brings this out most directly in a comment on the circular nature and the fore-structure of understanding as they are developed in §31: 'P. 152 – the complete errancy of the question of understanding being comes to light!' The ontological-transcendental deception here interlocks with the prevalence attributed to everydayness supposedly motivated by the phenomenological commitment to pure givenness. The phenomenology of everydayness leading up to the discussion of concern covers over the fact that understanding is not *necessarily* bound to temporal categories as transcendental conditions. Heidegger provides a counterexample:

> *Understanding* qua *projection* need not be concernful interpretation! Here the 'fatal mistake' of world as totality of meaning in reference to availableness. Freely creative projection [*frei schaffender Entwurf*], i.e. that of the *poet* (bringing things back from availableness etc. – everyday misuse and paleness – into their thingness). (*GA* 82: 87)

Given the importance of understanding for the overall setup of fundamental ontology, it is unsurprising that Heidegger sees the three deceptions coming together just here. As Heidegger elaborates, binding projection to the anticipation of a temporal answer to the question of being not only distorts phenomenological description. Rather than adding a hermeneutical dimension to the ontological project, the account of understanding and interpretation (*Auslegung*) contribute to its eventual collapse:

> The three fundamental deceptions combine in 'Hermeneutics'; here, interpretation – the interpreting projecting – becomes the principle of

philosophical knowing; namely, by its transposition to the being question itself – not only are entities to be interpreted with a view to being * but being with a view to time ... With such 'Hermeneutics', the will to understand is forced beyond beyng and into the temporality of timeliness [*Temporalität der Zeitlichkeit*] – such that it topples over [*so daß es sich selbst überschlägt*]! (*GA* 82: 43)

The key problem leading to all three deceptions, then, is that the anticipatory structure of ontological understanding is caught in a vicious circle. Heidegger does not reject the idea that Dasein's understanding is of a circular nature; progressively coming to understand a matter requires that one continuously revise one's pre-conception of it. However, if it is simply posited that the meaning of being is temporal, all understanding must be informed by temporal categories, and no matter how our understanding is going to be changed and might be improved in the future, this cannot be revised. The circle of understanding, rather than successively disclosing how things are, is bound to endlessly repeat in an identical fashion; it becomes vicious. This is the reason Heidegger singles out §63 as the worst phenomenology: it is in this section that the circularity of future-directed understanding is given ontological significance, supposedly confirming that time is the answer to the question of being. But that, as Heidegger sees it in the 'Notes', is an illusion created by the unwarranted presupposition that the question of being can be answered, and that it can be answered in view of temporality.

12.2.4 The Ontological Difference and the Problem of the Exemplary Entity

Heidegger's discussion of understanding is complemented by an awareness of a *problematic* tension between the ontical and the ontological level of analysis. One way to grasp this difficulty is in reference to Heidegger's comments on the idea of the ontological difference.[6] In the 'Notes', Heidegger insists that the ontological difference does not imply a kind of ascension from the meaning of entities to the meaning of being as the condition of their intelligibility. Instead of a 'unidirectional distinguishing [*einsinnige Unterscheidung*] of the ontic in the direction of the "condition" of *understanding*', the contrast between being and entities should be seen as a constitutive interaction or 'reciprocal essencing [*wechselseitiges Wesen*]' (*GA* 82: 35). Although this remark is made in the commentary on *BT* §5,

---

[6] Withy, in this volume.

it effectively rejects an idea explicitly articulated only in *Basic Problems of Phenomenology*, namely that showing how temporal categories sustain the distinction between being and entities will allow one to 'clear up' and 'unequivocally carry out' the ontological difference (*BP* 17/*GA* 24: 23). With the rejection of a unidirectional and unequivocal move from entities to being, the ambition to determine the ontological difference and hence the meaning of being becomes problematic: if there is a constitutive interaction between being and entities, the plurality and ambiguity of the ontic is bound to spill over into ontological meaning.

Interestingly, Heidegger's reaction to this problem in the 'Notes' is not to deny any relevance of entities for the question of being, an option explored much later in 'Time and Being' as the attempt to think 'Being without beings' (*TB* 2; *GA* 14: 2). But neither does Heidegger continue the project of a 'metontology' described in *Metaphysical Foundations of Logic* from 1928. In that lecture-course, Heidegger envisages basing ontology on an account of 'the possible totality of entities ... already there' (*MFL* 157; *GA* 26: 199) when ontological questioning sets in. In metontology, not only entities of a particular kind of being (i.e. Dasein) are relevant to the question of being but *all* entities in their supposed cosmological unity.

The idea of a reciprocal dependence between being and entities has important consequences for how to conceive of the ontological difference because it becomes impossible to oppose being to entities and disregard that the domain of entities (*das Seiende*) is inherently plural. Rather than abstract from their ontic particularity for the sake of conceiving a 'possible totality of entities', as in the metontological version of a return to the ontic, Heidegger now recognizes that every attempt to make entities count in ontology must heed their *specific* nature; a 'possible totality' is too thin a starting point for ontology. Some *concrete* entity must serve as 'our example' (*BT* 26/7) for ontology to be possible, but it is not a given that the inquiring Dasein will do. A version of this admission is articulated in the last section of *BT*, when Heidegger raises the question whether ontology needs an '*ontical* fundament? and *which* entity must take over the function of providing this foundation?' (*BT* 487/436). In the 'Notes', the comments on §8 press the point:

> Here it appears as if the analytic of Dasein would amount to an arbitrary or 'subject'-directed picking out of a particular entity within the 'universality' of entities, and thus it seems as if a prior decision has already been made regarding the concept of being in general – when this 'special beyng becomes authoritative for the *universal*! (*GA* 82: 40)

Although Heidegger allows that §8 need not be interpreted in a way that would 'thwart everything' (*GA* 82: 40), he admits that something like the above is 'said' in the section. With each inquirer as instance of Dasein,

> a *specific* entity comes into view and its specificity is that it is *not merely a case* – a species (with regard to formal logic) within a genus (which there is not) – rather, it 'is' as the process of constituting a horizon for the *understanding of being* as such ... In case one takes it to be a particular entity, then it must be a special 'particularity', one which includes universality not as a genus under which it is subsumed, but as a horizon that is supported and opened up only by *this* particular. (*GA* 82: 40)

Hence, despite the specific merger of the particular and the universal each Dasein is, attributing to this entity a paradigmatic status for ontology remains an unmotivated decision. As Heidegger sees it in the 'Notes', the perspective of ontological philosophizing and that of Dasein qua horizon-forming entity converge only in virtue of an intellectual operation Heidegger calls 'transposing' (*versetzen*): 'We transpose ourselves into that entity and its being, which is precisely being *open for* being as such and in general' (*GA* 82: 40). Heidegger here returns to another idea from the discussion of animal life in *Fundamental Concepts of Metaphysics*. Here, Heidegger glossed the 'self-transposition into another being' as 'a way of going along [*Mitgehen*] with this being' but cautioned that this way of speaking was 'liable to be misunderstood ... and ... quite inadequate with respect to the decisive aspect of the issue' (*FCM* 203; *GA* 29/30: 297–298). The context is the question of whether and how we can understand the way of being of non-human animals. When Heidegger takes up the idea of perspective-taking in the 'Notes', however, he is discussing the method of fundamental ontology. Relying on the idea of transposition in this context has much-farther-reaching consequences for Heidegger's ontological project.

The radical implication is that the ambitions of ontology, on the one hand, and the existential analytic, on the other, do not by themselves converge; trying to make sense of our own being does not directly lead to understanding the meaning of being in general. Yet that is what Heidegger explicitly stated in §2, citing the circular structure of understanding as evidence: discovering the meaning of being in general is ultimately the same as to 'make an entity – the inquirer – transparent in his own being' (*BT* 27/7). By contrast, the remark on §8 in the 'Notes' suggests that *BT* was able to answer the question of being not because self-transparency and ontological knowledge coincide but because it involved a successful transposition, an unacknowledged choice to understand being *from the perspective of* a particular instance of Dasein, that is, the entity that is in each case mine. The failure of *BT* therefore consists not only in the failure of temporality to explain the phenomena discussed in the first two divisions and hence the structure of being-in-the-world and the being of Dasein. Although this is a substantial shortcoming, it would still be possible to react to it by retaining the idea that individual Dasein is the exemplary entity. Arguably, Heidegger's interest in power (*Macht*) in the first half of the 1930s is an attempt to preserve the exemplary status of Dasein by turning to an alternative to time as the basic explanatory structure (Keiling 2017, 406–412). On the analysis provided in the 'Notes', the problem is not with the phenomenon considered as defining Dasein; the deeper mistake is to assume that the philosophical interests of ontology and that entity's understanding of itself necessarily converge.

12.2.5 'Domains of Projection' and the Issue of Ontological Pluralism

An implication of the idea that selecting an exemplary entity involves perspective-taking is that it is possible to choose different ontological paradigms. That several, alternative ways of understanding being are available is most explicitly addressed in the remainder of the passage on the transition from Division One to Division Two from which I quoted in Section 12.2.1. To recall, the most direct point of critique Heidegger voiced here concerns the vicious circularity of ontological understanding as conceived in *BT*: 'What is wanted is already decided: *Time as horizon of the understanding of being*' (GA 82: 125). Heidegger then continues by crediting the section of *BT* in question with harbouring an anticipation of ontological pluralism that runs counter to the stated ambition of fundamental ontology:

> *Yet*: precisely in this section the entire project all of a sudden advances *more carefully*. / P. 235: 'The projection of a (!) meaning of being as such can (!) proceed within the horizon of time.' / No longer 'the' meaning of being – no longer the only possible meaning – *a* meaning, hence other domains of projection [*Entwurfsbereiche*] for understanding being are admitted, even if not specified more closely. / No longer: time is *the* horizon for the understanding of being, but time *can* be the horizon – the domain of projection can thus be determined differently – *why* is not being said and neither, of course, is *how*. (GA 82: 125)

We can give an answer to the *how*-question drawing from the discussion in the last section: orienting ontology towards a different exemplary entity would amount to specifying another 'domain of projection' as paradigmatic for ontological understanding, what I have paraphrased as ontological perspective-taking.

Although Heidegger does not develop this explicitly, an answer to the question of *why* we can determine another domain of projection and take another entity than the one we in each case are as exemplary is also available to him. As early as 1928, Heidegger in 'On the Essence of Ground' described human freedom as the freedom to be the *'ground of ground'* (*PM* 134; *GA* 9: 174), that is, to be able to understand reasons and commit to taking these reasons as binding one's actions and beliefs. What Heidegger here and in *BT* calls Dasein's transcendence both enables and conditions how we use our being 'the ground of ground'. But whereas Heidegger in §73c, *BT* aimed to show that transcendence necessarily has a temporal form, in the 'On the Essence of Ground' he attributes explanatory priority not to time but to human freedom – it is the interplay of ground and abyss that ultimately defines "the *essence of finitude* in Dasein" (PM 135; GA 9:175).

Hence, one answer to the *why*-question in line with Heidegger's own work would be to reply that being able to determine our capacity for ontological understanding *differently* is just part of our freedom qua 'transcendence' (*PM* 109; *GA* 9: 164) towards the world. We transcend towards a world of many different entities, including the case of Dasein each one of us is, and each of these entities may yield to a projection of ontological understanding. The exemplary status fundamental ontology attributes to Dasein and, because the being of Dasein is temporal, to answering the question of being in the paradigm of temporality is then not merely a wrongheaded start to ontological theorizing. Because nothing forces us to 'transpose' our ontological understanding into an entity of the mode of being of Dasein to understand being in general, it restricts the freedom of world-disclosure in an unwarranted way. Recall that Heidegger acknowledged that *BT* has provided an answer to the question of being. As he adds in the comment on the end of *BT*, this has led to a limited yet lasting result: 'The relation of being to *time* will continue to hold, yet not as that which is essential, but only as *one* essential determination of being' (*GA* 82: 135). It is an implication of this comment that there are, that there have been, and that there always will be other answers to the question of being available, and giving each of these answers would equally be an exercise of ontological understanding. Genuine autonomy in ontological thought would then imply a specific form of ontological pluralism, namely the view that being has already been understood yet can always be understood or projected differently, beginning with each individual entity and its mode of being. [7]

12.3 Future Dasein: A Genealogy of the Turn

In the 'Notes', Heidegger clearly rejects the idea that ontological understanding is bound to the explanatory paradigm of time, and I have tried to argue that he does so in favour of a more basic notion of the freedom of ontological understanding. What is much less clear is what shape ontological normativity takes after its separation from temporality as the anticipated answer to the question of being and guiding thread of phenomenological analysis. Given that the 'Notes' are a work of self-critique, this is unsurprising. But the little Heidegger says about where to look for the genuine form for ontological understanding is interesting because it is indicative of what is problematic about Heidegger's positive account of ontology as it emerges in the 'Notes'. I close by arguing that the account he gives circa 1936 fails by the very criteria it introduces to argue against *BT*. Hence, Heidegger's immediate response to the problems he raises for *BT* isn't successful in avoiding them.

Central to the alternative account of ontological normativity that Heidegger lays out is 'the there' (*das Da*) or 'being-there' (*Da-sein*). Heidegger uses the idea that Dasein is or should be *Da* to express the thought that each case of Dasein can and should realise its proper way of being more fully. Every individual case of Dasein is in need of a transformation from its actual state of being; it can and must become genuine Dasein. This account of the normative dimension of Dasein as a way of being is quite thin, and it may appear empty and tautological. Throughout the 1930s, Heidegger reacts to this problem when he says that to be genuinely 'there' means to make use of the singular possibilities of the (historical) situation in which each Dasein finds itself and to respond to the contextually determined demands with which this situation confronts one's present being. This idea is anticipated in *BT*'s account of the situation (especially §§60–66, 79), where it relates to an authentic relation to history and, in the discussion of authentic temporality, to the moment (*Augenblick*) as genuine experience of the present.

Both in the 'Notes' and *Contributions*, the manuscript he composed the same year he rereads and comments on the sections of *BT*, Heidegger

---

[7] I tried to show this in Keiling (2017). For more on the notion of ontological pluralism in play here, see Keiling (2022).

draws from this discussion to develop a response to the problems he raises for *BT*. It is in this context that the notion of a turn is first introduced, as it is one way Heidegger describes what it means to exist as 'there' (*GA* 82: 592). To be clear, Heidegger here doesn't refer to the notion of the turn to provide an interpretation of his own philosophy. Rather, it is meant to indicate a version of the hermeneutical circle transposed from fundamental ontology to the philosophy of history. Because the function of understanding for ontology has become problematic, as we saw in Section 12.2.3, Heidegger attempts to describe a normativity that is intrinsic to Dasein but forgoes understanding, at least in its supposedly temporal form. As he explains in the 'Notes', being-there embodies the demand placed on existing Dasein and its efforts to respond to this alternative, genuine historical form of normativity:

> being-there is nothing given – it is also nothing to be *found* already there – it must be 'enacted' (created): the being of the there – hence impossible *to take apart*, no analytic. This enactment, initially as gathering in the persistent standing in the there [*Inständigkeit im Da*], through which insistence the there in its essence (always historical) is endured. (*GA* 82: 39)

Although Heidegger here clearly envisages Dasein as the locus of a radical but necessary self-transformation, its content and direction are only vaguely determined. The most he says emerges in his discussion of history. While *BT* took historical categories to be secondary to temporal ones, this priority is now rejected as part of Heidegger's rejection of the framework of temporal ontology. As Heidegger (*GA* 82: 36) says in a comment to §6, the framework is now seen as unsuited for the historical project of *BT*, the 'deconstruction of Greek ontology': '*Temporality* insufficient for this task!' Heidegger thus abandons the project planned for the second part of *BT* and to some extent executed in *Basic Problems of Phenomenology*. In the 'Notes', an alternative emerges when Heidegger credits the last lines of §6 (*BT* 49/26) with providing 'a hint of a possibility of "an even more originary horizon"'. This 'more originary' horizon, Heidegger comments, would 'no longer be a horizon for understanding being and this means: for the question of the *understanding of being* only', but would be the intimation of a '*second beginning*' (*GA* 82: 36).

On this brief account, then, it is intrinsic to Dasein qua being-there to anticipate a new beginning in philosophy coming out of a successful destruction of the history of being. But this project is independent from any concern for the role of temporal categories. Commenting on §10 *BT*, the section contrasting fundamental ontology to anthropology (now deemed 'totally skewed', *GA* 82: 50), Heidegger elaborates what would set a genuinely historical notion of Dasein apart from any account of the human being: 'The leap into *being-there* is something wholly different – it is also not fundamental ontology but philosophy itself, in the form of the second – *remembered beginning*' (*GA* 82: 50). When Heidegger adds that this second, remembered beginning of philosophy responds to the '*ceasing* first beginning' (*GA* 82: 50), he puts in place the outlines of the philosophy of history in *Contributions* (Polt 2006). This back and forth between first and second beginnings gives structure to the radical self-transformation demanded of Dasein in light of its intrinsic normativity. The reiterated turning between the two comes to replace the circle of understanding. Several passages address the notion of the turn, but the most explicit is attached to §31, the section on understanding:

> Being-there can never remain *present* and contract, so to speak, into a single point. It only manifests itself as something *gathered*... 'Circle' is a very bad characterization, beginning from 'method' and grasping – not from being! / Actually we should say: Dasein *as* 'circle' as the essential, returning inversion – the *essential turning* [*wesenhafte widerkehrende Ver-kehrung – die wesende Umkehr*]; this inversion as the innermost event of thrownness (errancy). (*GA* 82: 84)

The different figures of a turn that Heidegger here calls up indicate that the situation Dasein must and indeed should endure to realize its being is constitutively more complex than the 'fore-structure' (*BT* 192/151) of individual understanding identified in §32 and its anticipation of a fully transparent way of existing; this makes plausible why it must remain opaque to individual understanding. Nonetheless, as Heidegger (*GA* 82: 127) adds in a comment on the transition from Division One to Division Two, to gather while at the same time erring in the conflicting demands that define the present, each overturning the other, is what should define resolute Dasein: 'The decision into *being*-there as the transition from the first beginning to the other beginning!'

Responding to what he takes to be the crucial problem with *BT*, Heidegger thus replaces the expectation to answer the question of being in view of time with the anticipation of a new philosophical beginning emerging, in a way that fundamentally eschews individual understanding, from a transformation of philosophy's historical first beginning. As Heidegger sees it in 1936, although clarity of the present situation is ruled out by errancy, the confrontation with the intrinsic turning between the first and the second beginning is sufficient to allow Dasein to transform into what being-there genuinely means. I conclude by considering one way in which this picture of historico-ontological normativity has been interpreted in the literature. Drawing from this account, I argue that Heidegger's philosophy of history repeats rather than avoids the crucial error he finds in *BT*.

Richard Polt has argued that determining the 'there' as 'a new possibility for humanity, a possibility into which we are invited to "leap" to initiate a new epoch' is the 'paramount' theme of the 'Notes'. In line with *Contributions,* 'the point is that Dasein cannot be built on an existing human basis but requires a rupture in history – a qualitative displacement that inaugurates a new way to be' (Polt 2020, 55–56, 57). Polt goes on to identify several continuities of this project of radical transformation with *BT*, in particular the idea that the genuine mode of being-there is possibility rather than actuality, an idea *BT* cashes out in reference to the primacy of the future among Dasein's temporal ecstasies, most clearly emerging in our being-toward-death (Polt 2020, 61–63). As Polt sees it, despite the rejection of time as explanatory paradigm, the general scheme of describing Dasein as being-possible remains intact at least in Heidegger's 1936 philosophy of history. Even if genuinely being-there requires a break with the past in the hope of inaugurating a new epoch, our mode of being qua being-possible is still, as in *BT*, conceived as essentially 'future Dasein' (Polt 2020, 56).

The 'Notes' are a complex and ambivalent text. Attempting to fit the 'Notes' in with the philosophy of the 1930s, Polt provides a plausible interpretation of those strands of the text that indeed cohere with *Contributions*. But note that when Polt describes the revision of Heidegger's philosophy prompted by the failure of *BT*, he presents a version of the turn-narrative. In this narrative, Heidegger pursues the path set out in *BT*'s ambition to determine our being-possible but was forced to turn away from temporal understanding and towards a historical model for understanding the future, leading to the idea of a gathering and erring circling between the first and other beginning. Despite this modification, there is thus a deeper continuity in the project Heidegger pursues. But I think this underestimates how radical Heidegger's self-critique really is. As I want to show in the following, by adhering to the narrative Heidegger later proposed, Polt reduces the many complex problems Heidegger raises in the 'Notes'. In particular, Polt fails to notice that Heidegger's own response isn't successful in responding to them. Take the issue of conceiving projection as 'representational positing' identified in both the 'Notes' and the 'Letter'. Although the form and content of projective anticipation certainly change when placed not within the conceptual framework of fundamental ontology but in that of the philosophy of history, as Heidegger suggests in *Contributions* and in the 'Notes' themselves, this alternative way of conceiving of our being-possible overdetermines the form and content of projection in much the same ways as *BT*. Hence it is still vulnerable to the critique Heidegger directs at *BT*.

To see this, consider that Heidegger in his comments on the philosophy of history, on which Polt bases his reading, conceives of the future as *necessarily* emerging in a transformation of the first into the other beginning of philosophy. With a view to the understanding of ontology implied here, this idea overdetermines the meaning of being in much the same way Heidegger's temporal ontology did. Because it identifies a certain idea of being's historicality and some correspondence between the first and the second beginning as the single determinative ontological framework, the position emerging in Polt's reading continues to answer the question of being. The answer it gives is: being is what will have been understood by future Dasein as it remembers the first beginning of philosophy. Although the content of this answer is different from that given in *BT*, the argumentative structure around anticipation remains intact. Ontological understanding continues to take the form of an anticipation or intimation of an answer. As I have argued in Sections 12.2.4–12.2.5, a different reading of the 'Notes' and a more successful response can be given by emphasizing that ontological understanding is bound neither to a specific entity's way of being as exemplary nor to a single ontological paradigm.

Polt's reading is also problematic with a view to the account of our freedom it yields. The promise of a transformation of the first into the other beginning rests on the idea that the kind of normativity emerging from it will *necessarily* be binding on Dasein. Not one's temporal being, but one's historical fate is what one cannot and should not oppose. But the 'Notes' also allow for a reading that avoids this kind of historical fatalism: the freedom involved in Dasein's understanding of being is not such that it *must* respond to any specific kind of ontological normativity. Even in view of the ontological normativity Heidegger in the 'Notes' associates with the turn between first and other beginning to argue against the alternative described in *BT*, there can be neither a metaphysical necessity nor a necessarily compelling reason for me to commit to it. As I argued in Section 12.2.5, Dasein's ontological autonomy can motivate conceiving of ontological freedom as the capability to understand or project being in *different* ways and a corresponding commitment to ontological pluralism. Yet even if one doesn't follow this proposal, Heidegger clearly conceives of ontological freedom in such a way as to rule out determining a unified positive account of being, and that must include the one defined by his own philosophy of history. Settling on one definite answer, the question of being would lose its questionability; thinking would cease to remain underway. For this reason, Polt's reading and, to the extent that it outlines a positive (monistic) account of being, Heidegger's own ontology in 1935/36 falls short of the standards he raises and uses to argue against *BT*.

What does this leave us? I think Heidegger's discussion of the failure of *BT* in the 'Notes' can lead to a crucial but negative insight about what it means to question being and who is involved in such questioning: being-there is never a descriptive, but always a normative qualifier. There is no way Dasein must necessarily exist either now or in the future, or to put it in the form of a slogan: Dasein is normative all the way down. To say that it has the form of the being of the there is to say that to be *Da* simply means to respond to the demands it is confronted with, but it presupposes nothing about their general form. It is geared to the future but does not anticipate any future in particular. Projecting a definite answer to the question of being, be it in view of time or by way of an intimation of the other beginning, is an attempt to once again unburden oneself of the realization that Dasein has no essence structuring or limiting the demands of what has been, what there is now, and what the future might bring. If there is one lesson to learn from the failure of *BT*, it is this.[8]

---

[8] I thank Ian Moore for help with translations; I thank him, Taylor Carman, Steven Crowell, Sacha Golob, and Aaron James Wendland for critical comments to an earlier version of this chapter.

Bibliography

Adorno, Theodor. 1973. Aktualität der Philosophie (1931). In *Gesammelte Schriften Band 1: Philosophische Frühschriften*, 325–344. Frankfurt am Main: Suhrkamp.
Ahmed, Sara. 2004. *The Cultural Politics of Emotion*. Edinburgh: Edinburgh University Press.
Aho, Kevin. 2009. *Heidegger's Neglect of the Body*. Albany, NY: SUNY.
Alfano, Mark. 2013. The Most Agreeable of All Vices: Nietzsche as Virtue Epistemologist. *British Journal for the History of Philosophy* 21 (4): 767–790.
Angier, Tom P. S. 2018. Aristotle and the Charge of Egoism. *The Journal of Value Inquiry* 52 (4): 457–475.
Annas, Julia. 1981. *An Introduction to Plato's Republic*. Oxford: Oxford University Press.
Archer, Alfred, and Georgina Mills. 2019. Anger, Affective Injustice, and Emotion Regulation. *Philosophical Topics* 47 (2): 75–94.
Arendt, Hannah. 1994. *Essays in Understanding, 1930–1954: Formation, Exile, and Totalitarianism*. Ed. Jerome Kohn. New York: Shocken Books.
Aristotle. 1984. *The Complete Works of Aristotle: The Revised Oxford Translation, Vol. 2*. Ed. Jonathan Barnes. Princeton, NJ: Princeton University Press.
    1984a. Metaphysica. In *The Complete Works of Aristotle: The Revised Oxford Translation, Vol. 2*. Ed. Jonathan Barnes, trans. W. D. Ross. Oxford: Oxford University Press.
    1984b. Nichomachean Ethics. In *The Complete Works of Aristotle: The Revised Oxford Translation, Vol. 2*. Ed. Jonathan Barnes, trans. W. D. Ross. Oxford: Oxford University Press.
    1984c. Rhetoric. In *The Complete Works of Aristotle: The Revised Oxford Translation, Vol. 2*. Ed. Jonathan Barnes, trans. Rhys Roberts. Oxford: Oxford University Press.
    2001. Metaphysica. In *The Basic Works of Aristotle*. Ed. Richard McKeon, trans. W. D. Ross. London: Modern Library.
Arrien, Sophie-Jan. 2013. Faith's Knowledge: On Heidegger's Reading of Saint Paul. *Gatherings* 8: 30–49.
Augustine, Saint. 2008. *The Confessions*. Trans. Henry Chadwick. Oxford: Oxford University Press.

1982. *Eighty-Three Different Questions*. Trans. David L. Mosher. Washington, DC: The Catholic University of America Press.

1887a. *Augustin's City of God and Christian Doctrine*. Ed. Philip Schaff, rev. ed. Kevin Knight, trans. Marcus Dods. Buffalo, NY: Christian Literature Publishing Co.

1887b. *Expositions on the Psalm*. Ed. Philip Schaff, rev. ed. Kevin Knight, trans. James Tweed. Buffalo, NY: Christian Literature Publishing Co.

Baehr, Jason S. 2011. *The Inquiring Mind: On Intellectual Virtues and Virtue Epistemology*. Oxford: Oxford University Press.

Barash, Jeffrey. 2005. Historical Meaning in the Fundamental Ontology of *Being and Time*. In *Heidegger's Being and Time: Critical Essays*, 169–188. Ed. Richard Polt. Lanham, Boulder, NY: Roman & Littlefield.

Bartky, Sandra Lee. 1970. Originative Thinking in the Later Philosophy of Heidegger. *Philosophy and Phenomenological Research* 30 (3): 368–381.

1990. *Femininity and Domination: Studies in the Phenomenology of Oppression*. New York: Routledge.

Bauer, Nancy. 2006. Beauvoir's Heideggerean Ontology. In *The Philosophy of Simone de Beauvoir: Critical Essays*, 65–91. Ed. Margaret A. Simons. Bloomington, IN: Indiana University Press.

Beauvoir, Simone de. [1949] 2011. *The Second Sex*. Trans. Constance Borde and Sheila Malovany-Chavallier. New York: Vintage.

Bernasconi, Robert. 2002. Hannah Arendt, Phenomenology and Political Theory. In *Phenomenology World-Wide: Foundations, Expanding Dynamics, Life-Engagements*, 645–647. Ed. Anna-Teresa Tymieniecka. Dordrecht: Kluwer Academic Publishing.

Bigwood, Carol. 1993. *Earth Muse: Feminism, Nature and Art*. Philadelphia, PA: Temple University Press.

Blattner, William D. 1994a. Is Heidegger a Kantian Idealist? *Inquiry* 37 (2): 185–201.

1994b. The Concept of Death in *Being and Time*. *Man and World* 27: 49–70.

1999a. *Heidegger's Temporal Idealism*. Cambridge: Cambridge University Press.

1999b. Is Heidegger a Representationalist? *Philosophical Topics* 27 (2): 179–204.

2005. Temporality. In *A Companion to Heidegger*, 311–324. Eds. Hubert Dreyfus and Mark Wrathall. Malden, MA: Blackwell Publishing.

2006. *Heidegger's Being and Time*. London: Continuum.

2013. Authenticity and Resoluteness. In *The Cambridge Companion to Heidegger*, 320–337. Ed. Mark Wrathall. Cambridge: Cambridge University Press.

2014. Essential Guilt and Transcendental Conscience. In *Heidegger, Authenticity and the Self: Themes from Division Two of "Being and Time,"* 116–134. Ed. Denis McManus. London: Routledge.

Bornstein, Kate. 1994. *Gender Outlaw: On Men, Women and the Rest of Us*. New York: Routledge.

Brandom, Robert. 1994. *Making it Explicit*. London: Harvard University Press.
  1997. Dasein, the Being that Thematizes. *Epoché* 5 (1/2): 1–38.
Braver, Lee. 2007. *A Thing of This World: A History of Continental Anti-Realism*. Evanston, IL: North Western University Press.
  ed. 2015. *Division III of Heidegger's Being and Time: The Unanswered Question of Being*. Cambridge, MA: MIT Press.
Broadie, Sarah. 1991. *Ethics with Aristotle*. Oxford: Oxford University Press.
Brogan, Walter. 1990. A Response to Robert Bernasconi's *Heidegger's Destruction of Phronesis*. *The Southern Journal of Philosophy* 28 (S1): 149–153.
Burch, Matthew. 2020. Giving a Damn about Getting it Right: Heideggerian Constitutivism and Our Reasons to be Authentic. In *Transcending Reason: Heidegger on Rationality*, 99–122. Eds. Matthew Burch and Irene McMullin. Maryland: Rowman & Littlefield Publishers.
Butler, Judith. 1999. *Gender Trouble: Feminism and the Subversion of Identity*. New York: Routledge.
Caldwell, Anne. 2002. Transforming Sacrifice: Irigaray and the Politics of Sexual Difference. *Hypatia* 17 (4): 16–38.
Caputo, John D. 2001. The Absence of Monica: Heidegger, Derrida and Augustine's Confessions. In *Feminst Interpretations of Martin Heidegger*, 149–164. Eds. Nancy Holland and Patricia Huntington. Pennsylvania: Pennsylvania State University Press.
  2020. Being and Beings: The Ontological / Ontic Distinction. In *50 Concepts for a Critical Phenomenology*, 25–30. Eds. Gail Weiss, Ann Murphy, and Gayle Salamon 2020. Evanston: Northwestern University Press.
Carman, Taylor. 2003. *Heidegger's Analytic: Interpretation, Discourse, and Authenticity in Being and Time*. Cambridge: Cambridge University Press.
  2013. The Question of Being. In *The Cambridge Companion to Heidegger*, 84–99. Ed. Mark Wrathall. Cambridge: Cambridge University Press.
Carnap, Rudolf. 1932. The Elimination of Metaphysics Through Logical Analysis of Language. Trans. Arthur Pap. In *Logical Positivism*, 60–81. Ed. Alfred Jules Ayer, 1959. NY: Free Press
Cerbone, David R. 1996. World, World-Entry, and Realism. *Inquiry* 38 (4): 401–421.
  1999. Composition and Constitution: Heidegger's Hammer. *Philosophical Topics* 27 (2): 309–329.
  2007. Realism and Truth. In *A Companion to Heidegger*, 248–264. Eds. Hubert Dreyfus and Mark Wrathall. Malden, MA: Wiley-Blackwell.
  2015. Making Sense of Phenomenological Sense-Making: Moore on Husserl. *Philosophical Topics* 43 (1/2): 253–268.
  2016. Exile and Return: From Phenomenology to Naturalism (and Back Again). *International Journal of Philosophical Studies* 24 (3): 365–380.
  2017. Phenomenological Method and the Achievement of Recognition: Who's Been Waiting for Phenomenology? In *The Cambridge Companion to Philosophical Methodology*, 295–316. Eds. Giuseppina D'Oro and Soren Overgaard. Cambridge: Cambridge University Press.

2019. Essay Review: Social Epistemology Meets Heideggerian Ontology. *Studies in History and Philosophy of Science Part A* (76): 94–97.
Chang, Ruth. 2004. Putting Together Morality and Well-Being. In *Practical Conflicts: New Philosophical Essays*, 118–158. Eds. Peter Betzler and Monika Baumann. Cambridge: Cambridge University Press.
Chanter, Tina. 1995. *Ethics of Eros: Irigaray's Rewriting of the Philosophers*. New York: Routledge.
   2001. The Problematic Normative Assumptions of Heidegger's Ontology. In *Feminist Interpretations of Martin Heidegger*, 73–108. Eds. Nancy Holland and Patricia Huntington. Pennsylvania: Pennsylvania State University Press.
Chappell, Timothy. 2012. Varieties of Knowledge in Plato and Aristotle. *Topoi* 31 (2): 175–190.
Cooper, David E. 1997. Wittgenstein, Heidegger and Humility. *Philosophy* 72 (279): 105–123.
Correia, Fabrice, and Benjamin Schneider, eds. 2012. *Metaphysical Grounding: Understanding the Structure of Reality*. Cambridge: Cambridge University Press.
Crowe, Benjamin D. 2006. *Heidegger's Religious Origins*. Bloomington, IN: Indiana University Press.
Crowell, Steven G. 1984. Meaning and the Ontological Difference. *Tulane Studies in Philosophy* 32: 37–44.
   2000. Metaphysics, Metontology, and the End of *Being and Time*. *Philosophy and Phenomenological Research* 60 (2): 307–331.
   2001. Subjectivity: Locating the First-Person in Being and Time. *Inquiry* 44 (4): 433–454.
   2005. Heidegger and Husserl: The Matter and Method of Philosophy. In *A Companion to Heidegger*, 49–64. Eds. Hubert Dreyfus and Mark Wrathall. Malden, MA: Wiley-Blackwell.
   2007. *Sorge* or *Selbstbewusstsein*? Heidegger and Korsgaard on the Sources of Normativity. *European Journal of Philosophy* 15 (3): 315–333.
   2013. *Normativity and Phenomenology in Husserl and Heidegger*. Cambridge: Cambridge University Press.
   2013a. Being Answerable: Reason-Giving and the Ontological Meaning of Discourse. In *Normativity and Phenomenology in Husserl and Heidegger*, 214–236. Cambridge: Cambridge University Press.
   2013b. Conscience and Reason. In *Normativity and Phenomenology in Husserl and Heidegger*, 191–213. Cambridge: Cambridge University Press.
   2013c. The Existential Sources of Normativity. In *Normativity and Phenomenology in Husserl and Heidegger*, 239–260. Cambridge: Cambridge University Press.
   2013d. Making Meaning Thematic. In *Normativity and Phenomenology in Husserl and Heidegger*, 9–30. Cambridge: Cambridge University Press.
   2014. Responsibility, Autonomy, Affectivity: A Heideggerian Approach. In *Heidegger, Authenticity and the Self: Themes from Division Two of "Being and Time,"* 215–242. Ed. Denis McManus. London: Routledge.

2017. Exemplary Necessity: Heidegger, Pragmatism, and Reason. In *Pragmatic Perspectives in Phenomenology*, 242–256. Eds. Ondrej Švec and Jakub Capek. London: Routledge.

2018. The Middle Heidegger's Phenomenological Metaphysics. In *Phenomenology the Basics*, 229–250. Ed. Dan Zahavi. NY: Routledge.

2020. Transcending Reason Heidegger's Way. In *Transcending Reason: Heidegger on Rationality*, 17–52. Eds. Matthew Burch and Irene McMullin. Maryland: Rowman & Littlefield Publishers.

2022. Commitment: What is Self-Binding, and How is it Possible? In *Ways of Being Bound: Perspectives from post-Kantian Philosophy and Relational Sociology*, 29–46. Eds. Patricio Fernández, Alejandro Néstor García Martínez, and José Torralba. Basel: Springer.

Crowell, Steven, and Jeff Malpas, eds. 2007. *Transcendental Heidegger*. Stanford: Stanford University Press.

Dahlstrom, Daniel O. 1999. Time's Passing. *The Modern Schoolman* 76 (2/3): 141–162.

2009. Temptation, Self-Possession, and Resoluteness: Heidegger's Reading of *Confessions* X and What Is the Good of *Being and Time*? *Research in Phenomenology* 39 (2): 248–265.

2013. *The Heidegger Dictionary*. London: Bloomsbury Academic.

2021. The Topic of Sense in *Being and Time*. In *Heidegger and his Anglo-American Reception: A Comprehensive Approach*, 117–134. Eds. Pietro D'Oriano and John Rogove. Basel: Springer.

Dancy, Jonathan. 1995. Supervenience, Virtues and Consequences: A Commentary on *Knowledge in Perspective* by Ernest Sosa. *Philosophical Studies: An International Journal for Philosophy in the Analytic Tradition* 78 (3): 189–205.

DeGrazia, David. 2017. The Definition of Death. *Stanford Encyclopedia of Philosophy*. Ed. Edward N. Zalta. https://plato.stanford.edu/archives/spr2017/entries/death-definition/.

Derrida, Jaques. 1983. Geschlecht: Sexual Difference, Ontological Difference. *Research in Phenomenology* 13 (1): 65–83.

Devitt, Michael. 1997. *Realism and Truth*. 2nd ed. Princeton, NJ: Princeton University Press.

Diprose, Rosalyn. 1994. *The Bodies of Women: Ethics, Embodiment and Sexual Difference*. London: Routledge.

D'Oro, Giuseppina, and Søren Overgaard. 2017. *The Cambridge Companion to Philosophical Methodology*. New York: Cambridge University Press.

Dreyfus, Hubert L. 1991. *Being-in-the-World: A Commentary on Heidegger's Being and Time, Division I*. Cambridge, MA: MIT Press.

Dreyfus, Hubert L., and Jane Rubin. 1991. Appendix: Kierkegaard, Division II, and Later Heidegger. In *Being-in-the-World: A Commentary on Heidegger's Being and Time, Division I*, 283–340. Ed. Hubert Dreyfus. Cambridge: MIT Press.

Dreyfus, Hubert L., and Mark Wrathall, eds. 2007. *A Companion to Heidegger*. Oxford: Blackwell.

Edwards, Paul. 1976. Heidegger and Death: A Deflationary Critique. *The Monist* 59 (2): 161–186.
Engel, Pascal. 2018. The Epistemic Vice of Curiosity. In *The Moral Psychology of Curiosity,* 265–289. Eds. Ilhan Inan, Lani Watson, Dennis Whitcomb, and Safiye Yigit. Maryland: Rowman & Littlefield Publishers.
Evans, Gareth. 1982. *The Varieties of Reference.* Oxford: Clarendon Press.
Fernandez, Anthony Vincent. 2022. Feminist Phenomenology and Essentialism. *Presentation at Social and Political Philosophy Colloquium Series,* University of Groningen, Netherlands.
Figal, Günter. 1988. *Martin Heidegger. Phänomenologie der Freiheit.* Frankfurt am Main: Athenäum.
  2010. Phenomenology: Heidegger after Husserl and the Greeks. In *Martin Heidegger: Key Concepts,* 33–43. Ed. Bret Davis. London: Routledge.
Fink, Eugen. 1995. *Sixth Cartesian Meditation.* Bloomington, IN: Indiana University Press.
Fisher, Tony. 2010. Heidegger and the Narrativity Debate. *Continental Philosophy Review* 43 (2): 241–265.
Fleischer, Margot. 1991. *Die Zeitanalysen in Heidegger's Sein und Zeit: Aporien, Probleme und ein Ausblick.* Würzburg: Könighausen &Neumann.
Franzen, Winfried. 1975. *Von der Existenzialontologie zur Seinsgeschichte. Eine Untersuchung über die Entwicklung der Philosophie Martin Heideggers.* Meisenheim: Hain.
  1976. *Martin Heidegger.* Stuttgart: Metzler.
Frege, Gottlob. 1980. *The Foundations of Arithmetic.* Trans. John Langshaw Austin. Evanston, IL: Northwestern University Press.
Freeman, Lauren. 2011. Reconsidering Relational Autonomy: A Feminist Approach to Selfhood and the Other in the Thinking of Martin Heidegger. *Inquiry* 54 (4): 361–383.
Fricker, Miranda. 2007. *Epistemic Injustice: Power and the Ethics of Knowing.* Oxford: Oxford University Press.
Fried, Gregory. 2000. *Heidegger's Polemos: From Being to Politics.* New Haven: Yale University Press.
Friedman, Michael. 2000. *A Parting of the Ways: Carnap, Cassirer, and Heidegger.* Chicago, IL: Open Court.
Gallegos, Francisco. 2021. Affective Injustice and Fundamental Affective Goods. *Journals of Social Philosophy* 53 (2): 185–201.
Garcia, Manon. 2021. *We Are Not Born Submissive: How Patriarchy Shapes Women's Lives.* Princeton, NJ: Princeton University Press.
Golob, Sacha. 2014. *Heidegger on Concepts, Freedom and Normativity.* Cambridge: Cambridge University Press.
  2020. What Does it Mean to 'Act in the Light of' a Norm? In *Transcending Reason: Heidegger on Rationality,* 79–98. Eds. Matthew Burch and Irene McMullin. Maryland: Rowman & Littlefield Publishers.
  Forthcoming. Heidegger's Perversion of Virtue Ethics, 1924. In *Heidegger and the Classics.* Ed. Aaron Turner. NY: SUNY Press. forthcoming.

Gordon, Peter E. 2010. *Continental Divide: Heidegger, Cassirer, Davos*. Cambridge, MA: Harvard University Press.
  2018. *Adorno and Existence*. Cambridge, MA: Harvard University Press.
Gothlin, Eva. 2003. Reading Simone de Beauvoir with Martin Heidegger. In *The Cambridge Companion to Simone de Beauvoir*, 45–65. Ed. Claudia Card. Cambridge: Cambridge University Press.
Graybeal, Jean. 1990. *Language and "the Feminine" in Nietzsche and Heidegger*. Bloomington, IN: Indiana University Press.
Greco, John, and Jonathan Reibsamen. 2017. Reliabilist Virtue Epistemology. In *The Oxford Handbook of Virtue*, 725–746. Ed. Nancy Snow. Oxford: Oxford University Press.
Grisebach, Eberhard. 1928. *Gegenwart, eine kritische Ethik*. Halle-Saale: Niemeyer.
  1930. Interpretation oder Destruktion. Zum kritischen Verständnis von Martin Heideggers *Kant und das Problem der Metaphysik*. *Deutsche Vierteljahrschrift für Literaturwissenschaft und Geistesgeschichte* 8 (1): 199–232.
Guenther, Lisa. 2008. Being-From-Others: Reading Heidegger after Cavarero. *Hypatia* 23 (1): 99–118.
Guignon, Charles. 1993. Authenticity, Moral Values, and Psychotherapy. In *The Cambridge Companion to Heidegger*, 215–239. Ed. Charles Guignon. NY: Cambridge University Press.
  2000. Philosophy and Authenticity: Heidegger's Search for a Ground for Philosophizing. In *Heidegger, Authenticity, and Modernity: Essays in Honor of Hubert L. Dreyfus, Volume 1*, 79–102. Eds. Mark Wrathall and Jeff Malpas. Cambridge, MA: MIT Press.
  2013. In Search of Authenticity: A Heideggerian Quest. *The Humanistic Psychologist* 41 (3): 204–208.
Guignon, Charles, and Derk Pereboom. 2001. *Existentialism: Basic Writings*. Indianapolis, IN: Hackett.
Han-Pile, Béatrice. 2013. Freedom and the "Choice to Choose Oneself" in *Being and Time*. In *The Cambridge Companion to Heidegger's Being and Time*, 291–319. Ed. Mark Wrathall. NY: Cambridge University Press.
Haugeland, John. 1982. Heidegger on Being a Person. *Noûs* 16 (1): 15–26.
  1989. Dasein's Disclosedness. In *Dasein Disclosed: John Haugeland's Heidegger*. Ed. Joseph Rouse 2013, 17–39. Cambridge, MA: Harvard University Press.
  2000. Truth and Finitude: Heidegger's Transcendental Existentialism. In *Dasein Disclosed: John Haugeland's Heidegger*. Ed. Joseph Rouse 2013, 187–220. Cambridge, MA: Harvard University Press.
  2007. Letting Be. In *Dasein Disclosed: John Haugeland's Heidegger*. Ed. Joseph Rouse 2013, 167–178. Cambridge, MA: Harvard University Press.
  2013. *Dasein Disclosed: John Haugeland's Heidegger*. Ed. Joseph Rouse. Cambridge, MA: Harvard University Press.
  2013a. The Being Question. In *Dasein Disclosed: John Haugeland's Heidegger*. Ed. Joseph Rouse 2013, 51–63. Cambridge, MA: Harvard University Press.

2013b. Dasein. In *Dasein Disclosed: John Haugeland's Heidegger*. Ed. Joseph Rouse 2013, 76–82. Cambridge, MA: Harvard University Press.

2013c. Proposal for a Guggenheim Fellowship. In *Dasein Disclosed: John Haugeland's Heidegger*. Ed. Joseph Rouse 2013, 44–47. Cambridge, MA: Harvard University Press.

Heidegger, Martin. 2007. "Kehre"? "Sagen der Kehre". *Jahresgabe der Martin-Heidegger-Gesellschaft* 2007.

2008. "Eine gefährliche Irrnis". *Jahresgabe der Martin-Heidegger-Gesellschaft* 2008.

2009. Das Eigentümliche. *Jahresgabe der Martin-Heidegger-Gesellschaft* 2009.

2010. Das Geringe. *Jahresgabe der Martin-Heidegger-Gesellschaft* 2010.

2011/12. Auszüge zur Phänomenologie aus dem Manuskript *Vermächtnis der Seinsfrage*. *Jahresgabe der Martin-Heidegger-Gesellschaft* 2011/12.

2013/14. Das Argument gegen den Brauch (für das Ansichsein des Seienden). *Jahresgabe der Martin-Heidegger-Gesellschaft* 2013/14.

2015/16. Das Wegfeld des Denkens. Eds. Dietmar Koch and Klaus Neugebauer. *Jahresgabe der Martin-Heidegger-Gesellschaft* 2015/16.

Heinz, Marion. 2001. Das eigentliche Ganzseinkönnen des Daseins und die Zeitlichkeit als der ontologische Sinn der Sorge (§§ 61–66). In *Martin Heidegger: Sein und Zeit*, 161–188. Ed. Thomas Rentsch, 2015. Berlin: De Gruyter.

2019. Zeitlichkeit und Geschichtlichkeit. Zur Kritik von *Sein und Zeit* im Anschluß an Julius Kraft und Eberhard Grisebach. In Heinz and Bender 2019, 255–287.

Hepburn, Ronald W. 1980. The Inaugural Address: Wonder. *Proceedings of the Aristotelian Society, Supplementary Volumes* 54: 1–23.

Hibbs, Thomas S. 1999. Aquinas, Virtue, and Recent Epistemology. *The Review of Metaphysics* 52 (3): 573–594.

Hobbes, Thomas. 2008. *Leviathan*. Ed. John Charles Addison Gaskin. Oxford: Oxford University Press.

Hoffman, Piotr. 2000. Heidegger and the Problem of Idealism. *Inquiry* 43 (4): 403–411.

Holland, Nancy J. 2001. The Universe is Made of Stories, Not of Atoms: Heidegger and the Feminine They-Self. In *Feminst Interpretations of Martin Heidegger*, 128–148. Eds. Nancy Holland and Patricia Huntington. Pennsylvania: Pennsylvania State University Press.

hooks, bell. 1984. *Feminist Theory from Margin to Centre*. Boston, MA: Southend Press.

Huntington, Patricia. 2001. Introduction I – General Background: History of the Feminist Reception of Heidegger and a Guide to Heidegger's Thought. In *Feminst Interpretations of Martin Heidegger*, 1–42. Eds. Nancy Holland and Patricia Huntington. Pennsylvania: Pennsylvania State University Press.

Husserl, Edmund. 1965. Philosophy as Rigorous Science. In *Phenomenology and the Crisis of Philosophy*, 71–147. Trans. Quentin Lauer. New York: Harper & Row.

1989. *Ideas Pertaining to a Pure Phenomenology and to a Phenomenological Philosophy: Second Book*. Trans. Richard Rojcewicz and Frederick Kersten. Dordrecht: Springer.

1997. Phenomenology and Anthropology. In *Psychological and Transcendental Phenomenology and the Confrontation with Heidegger (1927–1931)*. Trans. and ed. Thomas Sheehan and Richard E. Palmer. Dordrecht: Springer.

2014. *Ideas for a Pure Phenomenology and Phenomenological Philosophy: First Book: General Introduction to Pure Phenomenology*. Trans. Daniel O. Dahlstrom. Indianapolis, IN: Hackett.

Inan, Ilhan. 2017. *The Philosophy of Curiosity*. New York: Routledge.

Kafka, Franz. [1925] 1998. *The Trial*. Trans. Breon Mitchell. New York: Schocken Books.

Kant, Immanuel. [1783] 1902. *Gesammelte Schriften, Bd. 4: Prolegomena zu einer jeden künftigen Metaphysik*. Eds. Rudolf Reicke and Preussische Akademie der Wissenschaften. Berlin: De Gruyter.

[1784] 1902. *Gesammelte Schriften, Bd. 4: Grundlegung zur Metaphysik der Sitten*. Eds. Benno Erdmann, Paul Menzer, Alois Höfler and Preussische Akademie der Wissenschaften. Berlin: De Gruyter.

.[1798] 1907. *Gesammelte Schriften, Bd. 7: Anthropologie in pragmatischer Hinsicht*. Eds. Karl Vorländer, Oswald Külpe and Preussische Akademie der Wissenschaften. Berlin: De Gruyter.

1900. *Gesammelte Schriften, Bd. 11: Briefe, 1789–1794*. Eds. Rudolf Reicke and Preussische Akademie der Wissenschaften. Berlin: De Gruyter.

[1781/87] 1968. *Critique of Pure Reason*. Trans. Norman Kemp Smith. London: Macmillan.

Kaplan, David. 2004. The Meaning of Ouch and Oops. Presentation at *Howison Lecture in Philosophy*, University of California, Berkeley. http://eecoppock.info/PragmaticsSoSe2012/kaplan.pdf.

Keiling, Tobias. 2017. Heidegger's Black Notebooks and the Logic of a History of Being. *Research in Phenomenology* 47 (3): 406–428.

2018. Phenomenology and Ontology in the Later Heidegger. In *Phenomenology the Basics*, 251–267. Ed. Dan Zahavi. NY: Routledge.

2022. Worlds, Worlding: Heidegger on Ontological Pluralism. *Epoché* 27 (2): 273–295.

Keiling, Tobias, and Ian Alexander Moore. 2022a. Martin Heidegger, *The argument against need (for the being-in-Itself of entities)*. *British Journal for the History of Philosophy* 30 (3): 519–534.

2022b. Martin Heidegger, *Das Argument gegen den Brauch (für das Ansichsein des Seienden)*. Eds. Dietmar Koch and Michael Ruppert. *British Journal for the History of Philosophy* 30 (3): 1–16.

Knowles, Charlotte. 2017. Das Man and Everydayness: A New Interpretation. In *From Conventionalism to Social Authenticity: Heidegger's Anyone and Contemporary Social Theory*, 29–52. Eds. Hans Bernhard Schmid and Gerhard Thonhauser. Cham: Springer.

2019. Beauvoir on Women's Complicity in their own Unfreedom. *Hypatia* 34 (2): 242–265.

2021a. Responsibility in Cases of Structural and Personal Complicity: A Phenomenological Analysis. *The Monist* 104 (2): 224–237.

2021b. Articulating Understanding: A Phenomenological Approach to Testimony on Gendered Violence. *International Journal of Philosophical Studies* 29 (4): 448–472.

2022. Beyond Adaptive Preferences: Rethinking Women's Complicity in Their own Subordination. *European Journal of Philosophy* 30 (4): 1317–1334.

Kochan, Jeff. 2017. *Science as Social Existence: Heidegger and the Sociology of Scientific Knowledge*. Cambridge: Open Book Publishers.

Korsgaard, Christine. 1996. *The Sources of Normativity*. Cambridge: Cambridge University Press.

Køster, Allan, and Anthony Vincent Fernandez. 2021. Investigating Modes of Being in the World: An Introduction to Phenomenologically Grounded Qualitative Research. *Phenomenology and the Cognitive Sciences* 22 (1): 149–169.

Kraft, Julius. 1932. *Von Husserl zu Heidegger: Kritik der phänomenologischen Philosophie*. Leipzig: Buske.

1941. The Philosophy of Existence. Its Structure and Significance. *Philosophy and Phenomenological Research* 1 (3): 339–358.

Kuhn, Thomas S. 1996. *The Structure of Scientific Revolutions*. 3rd ed. Chicago: University of Chicago Press.

Kukla, Rebecca. 2002. The Ontology and Temporality of Conscience. *Continental Philosophy Review* 35 (1): 1–34.

Lafont, Cristina. 2000. *Heidegger, Language, and World-Disclosure*. Trans. Graham Harman. Cambridge: Cambridge University Press.

Lear, Jonathan. 2011. *A Case for Irony*. Cambridge, MA: Harvard University Press.

2006. *Radical Hope*. Cambridge, MA: Harvard University Press.

Leland, Dorothy. 2001. Conflictual Culture and Authenticity: Deepening Heidegger's Account of the Social. In *Feminist Interpretations of Martin Heidegger*, 109–127. Eds. Nancy Holland and Patricia Huntington. Pennsylvania: Pennsylvania State University Press.

Lévinas, Emmanuel. 1995. *The Theory of Intuition in Husserl's Phenomenology*. Trans. Andre Orianne. Evanston, IL: Northwestern University Press.

Lewis, Michael. 2005. *Heidegger and the Place of Ethics: Being-With in the Crossing of Heidegger's Thought*. London: Continuum.

Lloyd, Genevieve. [1984] 1993. *The Man of Reason: "Male" and "Female" in Western Philosophy*. London: Routledge.

Marten, Rainer. 2017. Martin Heidegger: Das Sein selbst. In *Heideggers Weg in die Moderne: eine Verortung der 'Schwarzen Hefte,'* 229–241. Eds. Hans-Helmuth Gander and Magnus Striet. Frankfurt am Main: Klostermann.

McCall, Corey. 2011. Some Philosophical Ambiguities of Curiosity in the Work of Heidegger, Foucault, and Gadamer. *Journal of the British Society for Phenomenology* 42 (2): 176–193.

McDaniel, Kris. 2016. Heidegger and the "There Is" of Being. *Philosophy and Phenomenological Research* 93 (2): 306–320.

McDowell, John. 1998. *Mind, Value and Reality*. Cambridge, MA: Harvard University Press.

McManus, Denis. 2012. *Heidegger and the Measure of Truth*. Oxford: Oxford University Press.

  2013. Ontological Pluralism and the *Being and Time* Project. *Journal of the History of Philosophy* 51 (4): 651–673.

  2015. Being-Towards-Death and Owning One's Judgment. *Philosophy and Phenomenological Research* 91 (2): 245–272.

  2017. Beholdenness to Entities and the Concept of "Dasein": Phenomenology, Ontology and Idealism in the early Heidegger. *European Journal of Philosophy* 25 (2): 512–534.

  2018. Vision, Norm and Openness: Some Themes in Heidegger, Murdoch and Aristotle. In *Aspect Perception After Wittgenstein: Seeing-As and Novelty*, 173–198. Eds. Michael Beaney, Branden Harrington, and Dominic Shaw. NY: Routledge.

  2019. On a Judgment of One's Own: Heideggerian Authenticity, Standpoints, and All Things Considered. *Mind* 128 (512): 1181–1204.

  2020. Heidegger and Aristotle on Reason, Choice and Self-Expression: On Decisionists, Nihilists, and Pluralists. In *Transcending Reason: Heidegger on Rationality*, 125–150. Eds. Matthew Burch and Irene McMullin. Maryland: Rowman & Littlefield Publishers.

  2022a. Authenticity, Deliberation and Perception: On Heidegger's Reading and Appropriation of Aristotle's Concept of Phronêsis. *Journal of the History of Philosophy* 60 (1): 125–153.

  2022b. Heidegger, Being, and All That Is and Is So: On Paradoxes, and Questions, of Being. In *Heidegger on Logic*, 133–158. Eds. Filippo Casati and Daniel Dahlstrom. NY: Cambridge University Press.

  Forthcoming. Why Does Authenticity Matter in Being and Time? Heidegger and Aristotle on the Good, Being Oneself, and the Unity of Being. In Turner forthcoming.

McMullin, Irene. 2019. *Existential Flourishing: A Phenomenology of the Virtues*. Cambridge: Cambridge University Press.

  2013. *Time and the Shared World: Heidegger on Social Relations*. Evanston, IL: Northwestern University Press.

  Forthcoming. Patience and Virtuous Passivity. In *The Virtue of Patience*. Eds. Matthew Pianalto and Sarah A. Schnitker. Oxford University Press.

McNeill, William. 1999. *The Glance of the Eye: Heidegger, Aristotle, and the Ends of Theory*. Albany, NY: SUNY.

  2020. *The Fate of Phenomenology. Heidegger's Legacy*. Lanham/London: Rowman & Littlefield.

McTaggart, J. Ellis. 1908. The Unreality of Time. *Mind* 17 (68): 457–474.
Miščević, Nenad. 2020. *Curiosity as an Epistemic Virtue*. Palgrave Innovations in Philosophy. Switzerland: Palgrave Macmillan.
Moore, Adrian W. 2014. *The Evolution of Modern Metaphysics: Making Sense of Things*. Oxford: Oxford University Press.
Mulhall, Stephen. [1996] 2005. *Routledge Philosophy Guidebook to Heidegger and Being and Time*. New York: Routledge.
Müller-Lauter, Wolfgang. 1960. *Möglichkeit und Wirklichkeit bei Martin Heidegger*. Berlin: de Gruyter.
Murdoch, Iris. 2014. *The Sovereignty of Good*. London; New York: Routledge.
Nagel, Mechthild. 2001. Throwness, Playing-in-the-World. In *Feminist Interpretations of Martin Heidegger*, 289–308. Eds. Nancy Holland and Patricia Huntington. Pennsylvania: Pennsylvania State University Press.
Nicholson, Graeme. 1996. The Ontological Difference. *American Philosophical Quarterly* 33 (4): 357–374.
O'Brien, Mahon. 2010. Re-Assessing the 'Affair': The Heidegger Controversy Revisited. *The Social Science Journal* 47 (1): 1–20.
Philipse, Herman. 1998. *Heidegger's Philosophy of Being: A Critical Interpretation*. Princeton, NJ: Princeton University Press.
Plato. 1997. Republic. Trans. Georges Maximilien Antoine Grube, rev. Charles David Chanel Reeve. In *Complete Works*, 971–1223. Ed. J. M. Cooper. Indianapolis, IN: Hackett Publishing Co.
Plutarch. 1939. On Being a Busybody. In *Moralia Volume VI*, 469–517. Ed. Jeffrey Henderson, trans. W. C. Helmbold. London: Loeb Classical Library.
Pöggeler, Otto. 1972. *Philosophie und Politik bei Heidegger*. Freiburg/München: Alber.
  1983. Zeit und Sein bei Heidegger. In *Zeit und Zeitlichkeit bei Husserl und Heidegger*, 152–191. Ed. Ernst Wolfgang Orth. Freiburg/München: Alber.
Polt, Richard. 2006. *The Emergency of Being: On Heidegger's Contributions to Philosophy*. Ithaca, NY: Cornell University Press.
  2011. Meaning, Excess and Event. *Gatherings: The Heidegger Circle Annual* 1: 26–53.
  2020. A Running Leap into the There: Heidegger's *Running Notes on Being and Time*. *Graduate Faculty Philosophy Journal* 41 (1): 55–71.
Price, Anne Waldegrave. 2011. *Virtue and Reason in Plato and Aristotle*. Oxford: Oxford University Press.
Putnam, Hilary. 1981. *Reason, Truth, and History*. New York: Cambridge University Press.
  1988. *Representation and Reality*. Cambridge, MA: MIT Press.
Quine, William V. O. 1954. The Scope and Language of Science. In *The Ways of Paradox and Other Essays* 1976, 228–245. Rev. and enl. ed. Cambridge, MA: Harvard University Press.
  1955. Posits and Reality. In *The Ways of Paradox and Other Essays* 1976, 246–254. Rev. and enl. ed. Cambridge, MA: Harvard University Press.
  1960. *Word and Object*. Cambridge, MA: The MIT Press.

1969. Epistemology Naturalized. In *Ontological Relativity and Other Essays*, 69–91. New York: Columbia University Press.

Richardson, William J. 1963. Letter to William J. Richardson, April 1962. In *Through Phenomenology to Thought*, viii–xxiv. Trans. William J. Richardson. The Hague: Martinus Nijhoff.

Risser, James, ed. 1999. *Heidegger toward the Turn: Essays on the Work of the 1930s*. NY: SUNY Press.

Roberts, Robert Campbell, and William Jay Wood. 2007. *Intellectual Virtues: An Essay in Regulative Epistemology*. Oxford: Oxford University Press.

Ross, Lewis. 2020. The Virtue of Curiosity. *Episteme* 17 (1): 105–120.

Rouse, Joseph. 1990. *Knowledge and Power*. Ithaca, NY: Cornell University Press.

2013. Editor's Introduction. In *Dasein Disclosed: John Haugeland's Heidegger*, vii–xl. Ed. Joseph Rouse. Cambridge: Harvard University Press.

Sanford, Douglas. 1972. Begging the Question. *Analysis* 32 (6): 197–199.

Sartre, Jean-Paul. [1943] 2018. *Being and Nothingness*. Trans. Sarah Richmond. Abingdon, UK: Routledge.

Schalow, Frank. 2004. How Viable is Dreyfus's Interpretation of Heidegger? Anthropologism, Pragmatism, and Misunderstanding of Texts. *Heidegger Studies* 20: 17–33.

Schear, Joseph. 2015. Phenomenology and Metaphysics: On Moore's Heidegger. *Philosophical Topics* 43 (1/2): 269–278.

Schmid, Hans B. 2017. Authentic Role Play: A Political Solution to an Existential Paradox. In *From Conventionalism to Social Authenticity: Heidegger's Anyone and Contemporary Social Theory*, 261–274. Eds. Hans Bernhard Schmid and Gerhard Thonhauser. Cham: Springer.

Schmidt, Stefan W. 2016. *Grund und Freiheit. Eine phänomenologische Untersuchung des Freiheitsbegriffs Heideggers*. Switzerland: Springer.

Schmitz, Hermann. 1996. *Husserl und Heidegger*. Bonn: Bouvier.

Scott, Joan W. 1988. Deconstructing Equality-Versus-Difference: Or, the Uses of Poststructuralist Theory for Feminism. *Feminist Studies* 14 (1): 33–50.

Sedgwick, Eve Kosofsky. 2003. *Touching Feeling: Affect, Pedagogy and Performativity*. London: Duke University Press.

Sheehan, Thomas. 1984. Time and Being, 1925–27. In *Thinking about Being: Aspects of Heidegger's Thought*, 177–219. Eds. Robert Shahan and Jitendra Nath Mohanty. Norman, Oklahoma: Oklahoma University Press.

2014. *Making Sense of Heidegger: a Paradigm Shift*. London: Rowman & Littlefield.

Smith, Michael P. 1987. Virtuous Circles. *The Southern Journal of Philosophy* 25 (2): 207–222.

Sorenson, Roy A. 1991. 'P, Therefore P' Without Circularity. *Journal of Philosophy* 88 (5): 245–266.

Stone, Alison. 2004. On the Genealogy of Women: A Defence of Anti-Essentialism. In *Third Wave Feminism: A Critical Exploration*, 85–96. Eds. Stacy Gillis, Gillian Howie, and Rebecca Munford. London: Palgrave Macmillan.

Stroud, Barry. 1984. *The Significance of Philosophical Scepticism*. Oxford: Oxford University Press.
  2000. *Meaning, Understanding, and Practice: Philosophical Essays*. Oxford: Oxford University Press.
  2000a. Quine on Exile and Acquiescence. In *Meaning, Understanding, and Practice*, 151–169. Ed. Steward Candlish, 2002. Oxford: Oxford University Press.
Tengelyi, László. 2014. *Welt und Unendlichkeit. Zum Problem phänomenologischer Metaphysik*. Freiburg: Alber.
Thanassas, Panagiotis. 2012. Phronesis vs. Sophia: On Heidegger's Ambivalent Aristotelianism. *The Review of Metaphysics* 66 (1): 31–59.
Thomson, Iain. 2005. *Heidegger on Ontotheology: Technology and the Politics of Education*. Cambridge: Cambridge University Press.
  2013. Death and Demise in *Being and Time*. In *The Cambridge Companion to Being and Time*, 260–290. Ed. Mark Wrathall. NY: Cambridge University Press.
  2021. Death (*Tod*). In *The Cambridge Heidegger Lexicon*, 210–220. Ed. Mark Wrathall. Cambridge: Cambridge University Press.
Truwant, Simon. 2022. *Cassirer and Heidegger in Davos: The Philosophical Arguments*. Cambridge: Cambridge University Press.
Tugendhat, Ernst. 2001. *Aufsätze 1992–2000*. Frankfurt am Main: Suhrkamp.
Turner, Jason. 2010. Ontological Pluralism. *The Journal of Philosophy* 107 (1): 5–34.
Vigo, Alejandro G. 2010. Autoreferencia práctica y normatividad. In *Reflexion, Gefühl, Identität im Anschluß an Kant/Reflection, Emotion, Identity. From Kant Onwards*, 197–224. Eds. Ana Marta González and Alejandro Vigo. Berlin: Duncker & Humblot.
  2016. Practical Identity and Individuality. In *Action, Reason, and Truth: Studies in Aristotle's Conception of Practical Rationality*, 203–226. Louvain: Peeters.
Vlastos, Gregory. 1954. The Third Man Argument in the Parmenides. *The Philosophical Review* 63 (3): 319–349.
Volpi, Franco. 1989. *Sein und Zeit*: Homologien zur *Nikomachischen Ethik*. *Philosophisches Jahrbuch* 96: 225–240.
Walsh, Patrick G. 1988. The Rights and Wrongs of Curiosity (Plutarch to Augustine). *Greece & Rome* 35 (1): 73–85.
Whitcomb, Dennis, Heather Battaly, Jason Baehr, and Daniel Howard-Snyder. 2017. Intellectual Humility: Owning Our Limitations. *Philosophy and Phenomenological Research* 94 (3): 509–539.
Whiting, Jennifer. 2002. *Eudaimonia*, External Results, and Choosing Virtuous Actions for Themselves. *Philosophy and Phenomenological Research* 65 (2): 270–290.
Wiggins, David. 1987. *Needs, Values, Truth*. Oxford: Oxford University Press.
Withy, Katherine. 2015. Being and the Sea: Being as *Phusis*, and Time. In *Division III of Heidegger's Being and Time: The Unanswered Question of Being, 311–328*. Ed. Lee Braver. Cambridge, MA: MIT Press.
  2022. *Heidegger on Being Self-Concealing*. Oxford: Oxford University Press.

Witt, Charlotte. 2011. *The Metaphysics of Gender*. Oxford: Oxford University Press.
Woessner, Martin V. 2011. *Heidegger in America*. Cambridge: Cambridge University Press.
Wolin, Richard. 1990. *The Politics of Being*. New York: Columbia University Press.
Wrathall, Mark. 2011. *Heidegger on Unconcealment: Truth, Language, and History*. Cambridge: Cambridge University Press.
  2014a. Autonomy, Authenticity, and the Self. In *Heidegger, Authenticity and the Self: Themes From Division Two of Being and Time*, 193–214. Ed. Denis McManus. London: Routledge.
  2015. 'Demanding Authenticity of Ourselves': Heidegger on Authenticity as an Extra-Moral Ideal. In *Horizons of Authenticity in Phenomenology, Existentialism, and Moral Psychology: Essays in Honor of Charles Guignon*, 347–368. Eds. Megan Altman and Hans Pedersen. Dodrecht: Springer.
  2017a. Making Sense of Human Existence (Heidegger on the Limits of Practical Familiarity). In *Pragmatic Perspectives in Phenomenology*, 227–241. Eds. Ondrej Švec and Jakub Čapek. London: Routledge.
  2017b. Who is the Self of Everyday Existence? In *From Conventionalism to Social Authenticity: Heidegger's Anyone and Contemporary Social Theory*, 9–28. Eds. Hans Bernhard Schmid and Gerhard Thonhauser. Cham: Springer
Wrathall, Mark, and Max Murphy. 2013. An Overview of *Being and Time*. In *The Cambridge Companion to Being and Time*, 1–53. Ed. Mark Wrathall. NY: Cambridge University Press.
Wright, Sarah. 2017. Virtue Responsibilism. In *The Oxford Handbook of Virtue*, 747–764. Ed. Nancy Snow. Oxford: Oxford University Press.
Young, Julian. 2015. Was There a "Turn" in Heidegger's Philosophy? In *Division III of Heidegger's Being and Time: The Unanswered Question of Being*, 329–347. Ed. Lee Braver. Cambridge, MA: MIT Press.
Zagury-Orly, Raphael. 2015. D'une forclusion dans la phenomenology de la vie religieuse. In Cohen and Zagury-Orly 2015, 723–43. Paris: La règle du jeu.
Zagzebski, Linda T. 1996. *Virtues of the Mind: An Inquiry into the Nature of Virtue and the Ethical Foundations of Knowledge*. Cambridge: Cambridge University Press.
Zoller, David. 2021. Heidegger on Aristotelian *Phronêsis* and Moral Justification. *European Journal of Philosophy* 29 (4): 778–794.

Index

a priori, the, 106, 181–2, 184, 189
ability to be, 27, 120, 125, 127, 135, 146, 148–9, 152
agathon, 9, 16–19, 29, 195–6
agency, 175
all things considered judgment (ATCJ), 169–71
ambiguity, 87, 159, 191, 264
angst, *Angst*, 42–3, 189–91, 193, 195
answerability. *See* responsibility
anthropology, 7, 108, 269
anthropos, 16, 20–1
anticipation, 2, 27, 96, 200, 202, 244, 262, 266, 270–2
Antigone, 163
anxiety, 55–6, 66, 87, 118, 123, 127, 163–4, 169, 174–6, 184, 188, 227, 238, 243
anyone, the. *See* Man, das
apperception, 129, 182–3, 186–7
Aquinas, St. Thomas, 7, 85
Arendt, Hannah, 8, 104
Aristotle, 3, 7–9, 11–12, 14–22, 26, 80, 85, 97, 109, 169, 171, 180, 199
art, 40–1, 74, 103–4, 141, 149, 260
articulation, 57, 66, 73, 75–6, 79, 82, 108, 130, 176, 190
as, as-structure, 77
   apophantic, 77
   hermeneutic, 77, 190
assertion, 71, 73, 77–9, 171, 177, 180, 185, 190
attunement, 85, 87, 110, 117, 193
Augustine, Saint, 3, 7–9, 11, 13–15, 17–18, 21, 25, 29, 85, 88, 209
authenticity, 3–4, 10, 22, 24–6, 29, 87, 98, 104–5, 115–17, 119–23, 125–8, 131–4, 139–41, 145–6, 150, 152, 156–9, 161–4, 168–76, 191, 218, 245–6, 258
available, availableness (ready-to-hand, readiness-to-hand), 36, 77, 89, 95, 128, 171, 186–7, 194, 199, 239, 259–60, 262

background, 33–7, 45–8, 95, 148, 201, 236, 245
Bartky, Sandra Lee, 103, 105–6, 108–13, 119–20, 123
being, 3, 7, 9–14, 16–19, 22, 24–53, 63, 65, 68–9, 75, 81–3, 87, 90–102, 104–8, 111, 114, 118–23, 125–36, 139–52, 156–61, 163, 170–4, 176–96, 198–206, 209–16, 218–19, 223–30, 234–8, 241–2, 244–5, 247, 249–52, 255–9, 261–3, 266–73
   history of, 170, 175, 269
   human, 222
   modes of, 10, 51, 87, 115–17, 119–21, 259, 267–8, 271
   of entities, 4, 13, 31–47, 58, 60, 66, 125, 127–32, 138–9, 156, 202, 234
   question of, 6–8, 10–12, 26, 40, 108, 127, 146, 158, 248, 251–3, 255, 260, 262–5, 267–8, 270, 272–3
   regions of, 12
   sense of, 52, 251
   understanding of, 39–40, 45, 49–50, 53–61, 94–5, 99, 108, 128, 131, 137, 141, 143–4, 146–7, 152, 181, 183–6, 188, 202, 223, 250, 256–7, 261–2, 265–6, 269, 272
   unity of, 10
being toward, 95, 211. *See also* death, being towards
being-in, 46, 90, 107, 117
being-in-the-world, 24, 43, 72, 75, 79, 82–3, 86, 105, 109–11, 114, 116, 119–22, 221, 234, 237, 240–1, 244, 250, 258–9, 266
beingness, 47
being-with, 81–2, 105, 109, 115–16, 120–1, 149, 189, 242
Bergson, Henri, 199–200, 206
Bird, Larry, 162, 164
Blattner, William, 27, 50, 74–9, 117, 162–4, 190, 222–30
body, 112, 221
boredom, 87, 92, 175

289

Bornstein, Kate, 118, 123
Brandom, Robert, 68

care, 5, 66, 68, 85, 92, 98–9, 120, 143, 177–8, 182–5, 187–9, 192–7, 201, 209–10, 236
Carman, Taylor, 3, 35–6, 51–4, 71, 144, 172
Cassirer, Ernst, 180
Cerbone, David, 3, 49–50, 54, 61, 63–4
Chanter, Tina, 105–8, 111–12
choice, choosing, 27, 89, 125, 127, 135, 140, 149–52, 156, 168, 172, 193–6, 233, 236, 239, 244–5, 266
Christianity, 173, 199–201
circumspection, 95, 185, 189
clearing, 115, 120, 226, 250
cognition, 12, 35, 63, 71, 74, 77–8, 244
Cohen, Hermann, 180
concealment, 20, 115, 120–1
concern, 3, 8–9, 12, 14, 16–23, 25–8, 41, 84, 86, 120, 123, 130, 135, 150–1, 177, 203–8, 237–40, 244–5, 259–62
conformity, 81, 94, 96, 149, 163, 196, 241, 245–6
conscience, 4–5, 74, 80–2, 127, 161–2, 172, 176, 178, 185, 188, 191–3, 257–8, 261
consciousness, 4, 59, 69, 77, 92, 105–6, 119–22, 129, 183, 186–7, 211, 219, 257
coping, 45, 86, 162, 164, 184, 240
Crowell, Steven, 5, 33, 35, 37, 73, 78, 82, 96, 101, 158, 160–4, 171, 177–9, 181, 184, 187, 190, 194
curiosity, 4, 84, 87–94, 96–102

Dahlstrom, Daniel, 5, 15, 109, 198, 201, 212
Dasein, 3–4, 8–11, 14–16, 19–21, 23–9, 32, 42–7, 49–61, 65, 67–9, 72, 74, 80–1, 85–99, 101–2, 104–18, 120–2, 125, 127–9, 133–6, 139, 143–4, 146–7, 149–52, 158, 160–4, 170–8, 184–96, 217–21, 223–30, 232–6, 238, 240–4, 246–8, 251, 255–9, 261–73
  aloneness of, 7
  analytic of, 104, 107–8, 110, 127, 134, 174, 179, 184–5, 195, 264
  being of, 4, 8–9, 15–16, 20–1, 43–4, 116, 127, 139, 146–7, 150, 152, 174–5, 218, 234, 236, 266–7
  end of, 151
  ontological neutrality of, 114–15, 122
  temporality of, 5
  transcendental condition for, 161
  wholeness of, 218
  world of, 9, 12, 14–15, 52, 68, 160, 171
De Beauvoir, Simone, 104, 118–19

death, 5, 78, 127, 133–4, 150–1, 164, 185, 188, 190–1, 193, 200, 202, 207, 210–11, 214–15, 217–30, 235–47, 258
  being-towards, 128–9, 133, 139, 146, 151, 190, 211, 218, 220–2, 228–9, 257, 261, 271
  existential, 224–9
  existential death interpretation (EDI), 218, 222–30
  experience of, 214–15, 225, 236
  running ahead into, 217, 239–46
deception, 257, 260–3. *See also* self-deception
  phenomenological, 261
demise, 5, 215, 217–23, 226, 228–31, 235–8, 241, 246
Derrida, Jacques, 103, 113–14
Descartes, René, 7, 28
design *(Entwurf)*. *See* projection
destiny, 87, 149
Dilthey, Willhelm, 7
Diprose, Rosalyn, 112–13
disclosure, 59, 110, 125–6, 130–6, 138–45, 148–9, 152, 155–7, 188, 267
  of being, 125–36, 138–46, 148–9, 156–7
  of entities, 126, 145–6, 150, 156–7
  self, 129–32
discourse, 3–4, 71–6, 80–3, 105, 167, 177, 190–1
  of conscience, 81–2
discovery, 120, 129–32, 138–9, 141, 156, 240
dispersal, 98–9, 165
disposedness, 71–2. *See also* mood
Dreyfus, Hubert, 33, 45, 47, 74–7, 79, 125, 177, 184

ecstases, 90, 151
ecstasis, 202
Edwards, Paul, 221–2
Einstein, Albert, 133, 154
emotion, 110
enframing. *See* measurement
entities, 3–4, 8, 10–13, 15, 23–9, 31–54, 57–62, 66–8, 72, 75, 80, 125–52, 154–7, 160, 199, 202–3, 206, 218–20, 231, 233–4, 236, 247, 258–60, 263, 267
  totality of, 11–12, 264
environment, 75–6, 130, 155, 259
epistemology, 62, 67, 103, 107, 168
  Neo-Kantian, 181
equipment, 12–13, 36, 68, 128, 146–7, 199, 237
Ereignis, 211
es gibt, 204
essence, 21, 31, 33, 44, 48, 53, 58, 101, 104, 106–11, 116, 122, 128, 144, 159, 172, 181, 183, 196, 258–9, 269, 273

Index

ethics, 82, 93, 103, 168, 219
  ethical concern, 19
  ethical decision, 63
everydayness, 127, 150, 165, 185, 258–9, 261–2
existence, 4, 7–8, 13, 22, 27–8, 41, 44, 53, 58, 60–1, 63, 67, 72, 81–2, 102, 104–11, 113–22, 125–9, 131–6, 139–40, 143, 145–52, 155, 161, 172, 177, 183, 193, 198–9, 201–2, 204–5, 217–19, 221–4, 226–7, 229–30, 235, 237, 241–6, 259
  non-existence, 236
existentialism, 4, 7–8, 26, 115, 126–7, 145, 156
existentials, 199, 209

facticity, 81, 189, 192–4, 209
falling, 14, 135–6, 245
fear, 4, 54, 58, 65, 67, 84, 101–2, 238
feeling, 50, 65, 74, 76, 84, 118, 120, 183, 195
finitude, 26, 88, 91, 93, 98–9, 102, 128–9, 133, 139, 150, 165, 182, 184–5, 188–90, 194, 204, 207, 218, 222, 245–6
Fink, Eugen, 3, 63–7
for the sake of which, 15, 23, 187, 190
fore-
  conception (*Vor-griff*), 2
  having (*Vor-haben*), 2, 174
  sight (*Vor-sicht*), 2
  structure (*Vor-struktur*), 262, 270
foreground, 34, 45, 47, 261
formal indication, 32–3
freedom, 8–10, 22, 87, 89, 103, 110, 121, 125, 156, 192–3, 195–6, 257, 267–8
  existential, 121
  ontological, 87, 272
  radical, 115
Frege, Gottlob, 59, 79–80
Fritsche, Johannes, 177
future, 2, 5, 27–8, 89, 91–4, 97, 99, 101, 119, 123, 151–2, 155, 173, 199–205, 209–13, 215, 218, 234, 236–8, 256, 263, 268, 271–3. *See also* temporality

Gadamer, Hans-Georg, 93
gender, 4, 103–6, 108, 111–14, 118–19, 122
God, 14–15, 18, 38, 147–8
Golob, Sacha, 4–5, 72–3, 75, 79, 158
Guignon, Charles, 115, 125, 158, 165–6, 169, 174, 177
guilt, 5, 80–2, 127, 150–1, 174, 176, 185, 191–3, 220

Habermas, Jürgen, 177
Haugeland, John, 4, 8, 26, 74–6, 79, 93, 125–43, 145–6, 150, 152, 154–5, 222

Hegel, Georg Wilhelm Friedrich, 7, 112, 163, 258
Heraclitus, 80
hermeneutics, 248, 260, 262–3
hexis, 41, 97, 195
historicality, 272
history, 2, 11, 63, 92, 106, 125–6, 133, 152, 154, 156, 199, 268–73
  of being. *See* being
  of ontology, 178, 248
  of philosophy, 2, 40, 76
  of science, 57, 61
Hoffman, Piotr, 53–61, 63–7
hou heneka, 195
human, 7–9, 13, 41, 63, 68, 71, 78, 82, 105–6, 109, 112, 119, 125–6, 133, 151, 154–6, 159, 162–5, 173, 181–2, 185, 209, 211, 219–21, 232, 267, 271
  being, 5, 13, 15, 17–19, 21, 41, 80, 85, 87, 105, 107, 112, 125, 127–8, 140, 146, 150, 156, 177, 185, 198–200, 223, 228, 234, 270
  existence, 105–11, 120, 122, 198, 201, 204, 218, 226, 229
  life, 97
  nature, 102
  understanding, 1–3, 133
humanity, 96, 101, 271
Husserl, Edmund, 7–8, 35, 63, 86, 128, 180–1, 184

idealism, 3, 49–50, 53–61, 63–70, 158
identity, 18, 41, 89, 102–3, 112, 125, 131, 135–6, 140, 148, 150–2, 156, 163, 171, 187–94, 223–4, 226, 231–2
idle talk, idle chatter, 80, 87–8, 163–4
inauthenticity, 8, 25, 105, 113, 117, 132, 162–3, 165–8, 173–6
individual, 4, 7, 15, 20, 24–5, 80–3, 92–3, 96, 105, 111, 121, 138–9, 149, 165–6, 169, 171, 204, 217, 223, 233–4, 241–3, 246–7, 254, 266, 268, 270
individualistic, 115–16, 119, 122
individuality, 159, 217
individualization, 25
in-order-to, 13
intelligibility, 24, 33, 35–6, 48, 73, 75–6, 78–9, 82, 114, 120, 130, 135, 141, 145–6, 148–9, 157, 190, 201, 223, 229, 263
intentionality, 109, 116, 128, 163, 173, 182, 186
interpretation, 1–3, 5, 9, 47, 54, 66, 71, 76–9, 81, 99, 105, 112, 127, 141, 145, 149–50, 152–3, 157, 175, 178–9, 182, 185, 190, 195, 200–1, 208, 220, 230, 250–1, 259, 262–3, 269
  circle of, 216
  existential death. *See* death

interpretation (cont.)
  feminist, 103
  misinterpretation, 117
  self, 253–4
intuition, 73, 94, 180, 182–3, 188, 209
Irigaray, Luce, 105

Jaspers, Karl, 7
judgment, 10, 22, 27, 76, 88, 128, 142, 166–71, 176, 179–80, 253
  all things considered judgment model (ATCJM). *See* all things considered judgment model (ATCJM)
  propositional structure of, 71, 73

Kafka, Franz, 82
Kant, Immanuel, 7, 28, 50, 56, 77, 82, 112, 128–9, 133, 159–61, 163, 172–3, 177–89, 195–6, 207, 209
Keiling, Tobias, 5–6, 248, 268
Kierkegaard, Søren, 7, 125, 164, 173
knowledge, 1, 23, 29, 54–6, 59, 62–3, 75–7, 79–80, 84–8, 95–7, 99–102, 116, 123, 127–30, 133–4, 137–8, 140, 144, 152, 167, 179, 182, 184, 213–14, 243–4, 254–6, 263, 265
  self, 9, 22, 24–5, 28–9, 176
Knowles, Charlotte, 4, 103, 110, 115, 117, 120, 123
Kochan, Jeff, 54–7, 59, 66, 68
Korsgaard, Christine, 162, 187
Kuhn, Thomas, 126, 133, 135–7, 139–40, 145–6, 148, 152–7

Lafont, Cristina, 72
language, 3–4, 11, 40, 59, 71–8, 80, 82, 104, 227
  games, 213
  of metaphysics, 250
Lask, Emil, 7
Lear, Jonathan, 118, 225
legitimation *(Recht-gebung)*, 194–5
Levinas, Emmanuel, 86
life, 7, 9–11, 14–15, 21, 24–5, 28, 41, 64, 67, 78, 85–6, 88, 91–2, 97, 110–11, 117, 119, 121, 123, 125–8, 131–5, 137–40, 146, 148–52, 155–6, 159, 164–6, 172, 174–6, 187, 190, 196, 210, 219–28, 242, 244–5
  animal, 259, 265
logic, 8, 15, 115, 153, 160, 182, 185, 189, 223, 232, 265
  logically distinct, 33–4, 37
logos, 11, 179–80, 182, 185–6, 191, 196
  apophantikos, 177, 179
  legein, 101, 179–82
  logon didonai, 179, 185, 194, 196
Luther, Martin, 7

Man, das, 80, 104–5, 109, 114–17, 119–20, 149, 163, 174, 190, 241. *See also* the one, the anyone, the they
McManus, Denis, 3, 7, 12, 16, 24, 26, 28, 36, 98, 158, 165–71, 174–5, 194, 222
McMullin, Irene, 4, 84, 90, 98, 194
McTaggart, John McTaggart Ellis, 203, 208, 212, 214, 216
meaning, 3, 33–5, 37–9, 43, 46, 52, 54, 78, 85, 96, 100–1, 108, 115, 125, 127, 146, 150, 156, 165, 170, 186–7, 190–1, 196, 201, 203, 207, 210, 224, 232–4, 240–1, 244, 251–2, 262–6, 272. *See also* sense
measurement, enframing, 96
Meister Eckhart, 7
Merleau-Ponty, Maurice, 78
metaphysica generalis, 181
mineness, 105, 159, 163, 173–4
modality, 231, 247
modernity, 170
moment, 5, 14, 63, 74, 81, 86, 91, 93, 98, 163, 165, 177, 187, 199–200, 233, 240–1, 268
  of vision, 170
mood, 42–3, 53–7, 59, 66, 72–3, 78, 87, 105, 110–11, 116, 122–3, 189, 192
Moore, Adrian William, 60
Moore, George Edward, 55
Moore's paradox, 23
Mulhall, Stephen, 118

Natorp, Paul, 180
nature, 11, 52–3, 61, 63, 68, 81, 85–6, 103–4, 136–7, 141–3, 145, 154–5, 159, 162, 181, 198–202, 204, 210–11, 214–15
Neo-Kantianism, 179–82, 260
Newton, Isaac, 133, 136–7, 143–4, 154
Nietzsche, Friedrich, 7, 125
nihilism, 177, 196
normativity, 163, 172–4, 187, 252–3, 268–72
  normativity-first account of reason, 177–8, 183, 195–6
nothing, the, 42–3, 81, 87
nothingness, 224, 227
nous, 179–80, 182, 185–6, 188, 191, 196
noein, 101, 179–82
nullity, 224

occurrent, occurrentness, 51, 54, 77, 144, 218, 221. *See also* present-at-hand, presence-at-hand
one, the. *See* Man, das
ontic, 31, 80–1, 107–8, 111, 113–14, 138, 170–1, 220, 222, 263–4
  being-at-issue, 41–2
  comportment, 189–92, 195

knowledge, 179–81
realism, 50–2, 54, 144
transcendence, 45–7, 182–3, 185–90, 192
truth, 125–6, 129–33, 135
ontological, 4, 11, 38–42, 45, 69, 71–2, 80,
  87–8, 93–4, 104–5, 107, 111–16, 121–2,
  125–6, 129–30, 134–9, 141, 145, 156,
  158–9, 170, 177–81, 184, 186, 189,
  198–9, 201, 218, 220, 222, 225, 227, 240,
  254, 259, 261–8, 271–3
  being-at-issue, 41–2
  knowledge, 179–81, 254–6, 265
  pluralism, 11, 253, 266–7, 272
  pre-ontological difference, 44–5
  pre-ontological self-understanding, 43
  pre-ontological understanding, 40, 186
  transcendence, 181–3, 188–92, 194–5, 260,
    262
  truth, 125–6, 128–9, 132–5, 138–40, 143,
    145
  understanding, 130, 256–7, 263, 266–8, 272
ontological difference, 3, 31–48, 263–4
ontology, 3, 7–8, 11–12, 26, 31, 38–9, 44, 94–8,
  103, 105–15, 119, 122, 127–8, 134, 142,
  145–7, 150, 152, 156–8, 175, 185, 195,
  198, 217–18, 246–7, 254–5, 257–8, 260,
  264–6, 268–70, 272–3
  fundamental, 4, 108, 125–6, 131, 145–6, 150,
    157, 181, 198, 217, 262, 265–7, 269–70,
    272
ontotheology, 38

paradigm, 126, 135–7, 139–46, 148, 152–5,
  157, 255, 258, 260, 266–8, 271–2
Parmenides, 37
past, 5, 91–4, 99, 151, 199, 201–2, 204, 212–13,
  215, 234. See also temporality
Paul, Saint, 7
perception, 8, 33, 47, 77, 85–6, 94–5, 100, 128,
  180, 202
  perceptual background, 34
  perceptual model, 95
  perceptual object, 33
phenomenology, 5, 35, 63–5, 71, 82, 86, 101,
  106–7, 110, 170, 173, 178–80, 182,
  184–5, 188, 197, 200, 209, 248, 257–9,
  261–3
philosophy, 1–4, 8, 28, 30–1, 49, 58, 65, 70,
  104–6, 123, 159, 170, 172–3, 199, 209,
  248–9, 251–4, 269–72
  early modern, 55
  feminist, 103–4, 111, 119
  first, 12, 26, 62–3
  moral, 175
  of existence, 7

  of history, 270–3
  of science, 56–7
  political, 110
  practical, 186
  transcendental, 178, 256
phronêsis, 9, 16, 19–21, 23–4, 97–8, 176
Plato, 7, 29, 34, 37, 94, 195
poiesis, 16, 20
possibility, 1, 5, 11, 15, 20, 26–8, 31, 34–5, 46,
  54, 72, 80, 82, 84–7, 89, 91, 93, 97–100,
  102, 109, 113–22, 126–31, 133–4, 138–9,
  141–2, 147, 149–52, 154, 158, 161, 164,
  172, 174–5, 178, 185–6, 190, 192–3, 195,
  200–2, 207, 211, 214–15, 217, 220–46,
  261–2, 269, 271
potentiality-for-being. See ability to be
pragmatism, 7
presence, 89–91, 112, 199
present, 151
present, 2, 5, 10, 18–19, 21–3, 25–8, 69, 89–93,
  95–7, 99, 116, 119, 130, 150–2, 154, 165,
  171, 177, 188, 193, 199–208, 210,
  212–13, 215, 228, 230, 234, 237–9, 244,
  258, 268, 270–1, 273. See also temporality
present-at-hand, presence-at-hand, 95, 128, 144.
  See also occurrent, occurrentness
projection, 138, 149, 182–4, 187, 189–90,
  192–4, 196, 202, 225, 233–4, 239, 244,
  249, 256–8, 262, 266–7, 271–2
  self, 176
Putnam, Hilary, 140

Quine, Willard, 3, 61–8, 216

ready-to-hand, readiness-to-hand. See available,
  availableness
realism, 3, 49–50, 53–7, 66–70, 140–4
  minimal, 56–7, 66–8
  ontic, 51–2
  scientific, 56–7
reality, 7, 54–6, 59, 62–3, 66–7, 69, 94–5, 97–8,
  101, 118–20, 138–41, 143, 172, 202, 212
reference, 12–13, 29, 75, 79, 95, 160, 174,
  191–2, 210, 230, 232, 234, 251, 258–9,
  261–3, 271
referential context, 190
relativism, 139, 177
religion, 170
repetition, 27, 93, 97
resoluteness, 80, 127, 161–2, 165, 176, 202
responsibility, 4, 82, 87–8, 96, 98, 100, 102,
  117, 120, 125–9, 131–7, 139–40, 145–6,
  150–2, 156–7, 160, 162, 166–8, 174,
  191–2, 196, 217, 244, 246
reticence See silence

Rockmore, Tom, 177
Rousseau, Jean-Jacques, 112
Rubin, Jane, 125

Sartre, Jean-Paul, 159, 177, 222
Saussure, Ferdinand de, 72
Scheler, Max, 7
Schleiermacher, Friedrich, 7
Schurmann, Reiner, 177
science, 8, 10–12, 26, 31, 56–7, 61, 63–4, 67–8, 95–6, 136–7, 142, 152–5, 181–2
Scotus, John Duns, 7
selbst
  ownmost, 80
self, 4, 21–4, 74, 81, 84, 86–8, 90, 92–3, 95–102, 109–10, 119, 122, 159, 165, 167, 172–3, 175–7, 183–4, 186–7, 190–3, 195–6, 205, 209, 213, 225–6, 229–30, 241, 244, 246, 258, 260, 265–6, 269–70
  authentic, 261
  one-self, 161–3
  ownmost, 97, 120, 136, 176, 207, 210, 240–2
  self-concealing, 3, 48
  self-concern, 9, 21–3
  self-criticism, 248, 253–4, 268, 271
  self-determination, 9, 24–5, 28–9, 196
  self-disclosing, 46
  self-expression, 9, 21–2, 24–5, 28–9
  selfhood, 159, 174, 190, 192, 209
  self-importance, 22
  self-knowledge. See knowledge
  self-understanding. See understanding
self-deception, 170, 257, 260
sense, 67–8, 71
sense, 8–11, 17–18, 22–4, 26, 29–30, 40–1, 45–6, 52–6, 60–5, 79, 81, 111, 118, 126, 134, 139, 145, 148, 155–6, 159, 168–70, 174, 179–82, 195, 198, 200, 204–5, 209–13, 217–20, 222–34, 236, 240, 251, 265. See also meaning
Sheehan, Thomas, 7, 26
sight, 86, 88–9, 94, 116, 165, 185–6, 188, 192
sign, signs, 72, 140
  sign-structure, 72
significance, 14, 17, 25, 51, 67, 73, 75–6, 90–1, 99, 103, 105–6, 111, 119, 147, 150–1, 158, 169–70, 174, 188–90, 197, 218, 230, 232–6, 238–43, 245–6
signification, 188
silence, 74, 81, 90, 103, 115, 174
situation, 20–1, 24–5, 91, 110–11, 115, 123, 150–1, 165–6, 169, 202, 215, 217, 224–5, 227–8, 230, 232, 237–9, 244, 268, 270–1
  concrete, 110–11, 115, 130
  everyday, 113

existential, 54
hermeneutic, 39
situation-responsive, 97
structured, 194
universal, 63
skepticism, 50, 54–6, 177
  external-world, 54–6
solicitude, 120
sophia, 97–8
space, spatiality, 11, 55, 63, 74, 96, 162–4, 171–2, 180, 200, 206–7, 223, 231–2, 246–7
  modal, 231–2, 234–5, 241
  normative, 4, 159, 162
Stambaugh, Joan, 25, 174
structure, 8, 13, 15, 19, 27, 44, 51, 54, 65, 71–2, 76–81, 90, 93, 96, 100, 104–7, 109, 111, 113, 116, 160, 168, 172–3, 175–6, 183, 185, 189–90, 192, 194, 197, 205, 213, 218, 220–1, 223–4, 227, 241–2, 244, 252, 263, 265–6, 270, 272
  fundamental, 105, 109, 111
  modal, 237, 240–1, 245
  normative, 78, 90, 176
  of Dasein, 113, 175
  of understanding, 1, 73, 262, 265
  ontological, 107, 113, 220, 222
  temporal, 28
subject, 1–2, 24, 40, 66, 69, 71, 76, 95, 106–9, 119, 184, 264
  feminine, female, 106, 112
  human, 106–7
  masculine, 104, 106
  subjectivity of the, 183–4
  subject-predicate-structure, 71–3
substance, 11, 109, 112, 148, 199
summum bonum, 8, 14–17, 19, 22
sumpheron, 13, 23

technê, 16, 186
technology, 95–6, 103
telos, 9, 16–21
temporality, timeliness, 5, 27–30, 39, 90–1, 93, 99, 109, 116, 151, 173, 175, 198, 200–16, 218, 220, 248–9, 255–8, 261–3, 266–9
  authentic, 92, 268
  ecstases, 5, 202, 204–5, 207–9, 250, 271
  future *See* future
  now *See* present
  past *See* past
  present *See* present
  temporalizing, 90
they, the. *See* Man, das
Third Man Regress, 36–8
Thomson, Iain, 36, 222–8, 230, 235
thrownness, 97, 189, 192–3, 215, 246, 270

Tillich, Paul, 177
time, 2–3, 5–6, 10, 26–8, 39, 89–91, 98–9, 102, 151–2, 163, 173, 182, 187, 193, 198–216, 232, 235, 244, 255–8, 260, 262–3, 266–7, 270, 273
  authentic, 200–1
  clock, 5, 200, 203–7
  dispersed in, 99
  historical, 199–201
  measurement, 206
  natural, 212–13
  non-original, 203
  normal, 212–13
  objective, 200–1
  original, 201, 208–9, 211–16
  particular (*jeweilig*), 1, 194
  physical, 199–200
  religious, 200–1
  serial, 199, 201–2, 205–6, 208–11, 213–16
  space-time region, 231
  telling, 74, 76
  vulgar, 198, 205–8, 214
  world-time, 5, 198, 203–8, 214, 216
topos, 251
  hyperouranios, 195
transcendence, 42, 44–5, 63, 93, 172, 181–92, 194–5, 202, 267
truth, 4, 7, 22, 29, 90, 94, 101–2, 125–35, 138–41, 143–7, 150, 152, 154, 156–7, 159, 165, 177, 179–80, 220, 238, 251–2, 254–5, 258–9, 262
  criterion of, 66
  existential, 125–6, 129, 133, 135
  of existence, 127, 134
  ontic. *See* ontic
  ontological. *See* ontological
  primordial, 127, 161
  propositional, 185
  truth-testing, 126, 133–4, 137, 139–41, 143, 145, 156
Tugendhat, Ernst, 5, 177, 198, 208–16
turn/turning, the, 5–6, 248–54, 268–72

uncanniness, 81
uncoveredness, 20, 52–3, 117, 143–4
understanding, 1, 3, 11, 20, 28, 30, 32, 39, 44, 51, 53–61, 71–3, 76, 78, 80–1, 85–6, 89–90, 92, 99, 102, 105, 114–16, 119–23, 125, 129–31, 133–4, 139, 147, 154, 164, 170, 173, 182, 207, 209, 229, 232–4, 236–7, 239–40, 247–8, 255–7, 259, 261, 263, 266–72
  circle of, 1–2, 249, 263, 265, 270
  common, 149
  improper, 62
  of being. *See* being
  practical, 82, 86
  self, 43, 45, 60–1, 93, 99, 105, 109, 111, 115–22, 125, 127, 131, 149, 163, 171–3, 175, 187–8, 190–1, 193, 223–6, 229, 255

Wendland, Aaron James, 4, 125
White, Carol, 222
Withy, Katherine, 3, 31, 43, 48, 263
Wittgenstein, Ludwig, 74
Woessner, Martin, 177
Wolin, Richard, 125, 177
world, 1–2, 4–5, 7, 9–10, 12–13, 15–16, 21, 23–6, 30, 43, 46–7, 52–3, 58, 63–8, 73, 81–7, 89–91, 96–7, 100–2, 107–10, 112–14, 117, 119, 122–3, 125, 127–8, 132, 135, 140, 142, 144, 147–51, 153–4, 163, 166, 170, 172, 184, 188–91, 193, 200, 202, 218–19, 221, 223–4, 226–7, 230–41, 243, 245–6, 258–60, 262, 267
  disclosing, 45
  everyday, 67
  intraworldliness, 54, 68, 260
  openness to the, 27–8
  physical, 59, 67
  practical, 8
  prevailing of, 12
  social, 4, 54–5, 68, 103–4, 114–16, 119–22
  wholeness of, 26, 28–9
  worldhood, 43, 259
  worlding of, 46, 259
  worldless, 24
Wrathall, Mark, 5, 75–6, 79, 147–8, 217, 246

CAMBRIDGE CRITICAL GUIDES

Titles published in this series (continued):

Kant's *Metaphysics of Morals*
EDITED BY LARA DENIS
Spinoza's *Theological-Political Treatise*
EDITED BY YITZHAK Y. MELAMED AND MICHAEL A. ROSENTHAL
Plato's *Laws*
EDITED BY CHRISTOPHER BOBONICH
Plato's *Republic*
EDITED BY MARK L. MCPHERRAN
Kierkegaard's *Concluding Unscientific Postscript*
EDITED BY RICK ANTHONY FURTAK
Wittgenstein's *Philosophical Investigations*
EDITED BY ARIF AHMED
Kant's *Critique of Practical Reason*
EDITED BY ANDREWS REATH AND JENS TIMMERMANN
Kant's *Groundwork of the Metaphysics of Morals*
EDITED BY JENS TIMMERMANN
Kant's *Idea for a Universal History with a Cosmopolitan Aim*
EDITED BY AMÉLIE OKSENBERG RORTY AND JAMES SCHMIDT
Mill's *On Liberty*
EDITED BY C. L. TEN
Hegel's *Phenomenology of Spirit*
EDITED BY DEAN MOYAR AND MICHAEL QUANTE

For EU product safety concerns, contact us at Calle de José Abascal, 56–1°, 28003 Madrid, Spain or eugpsr@cambridge.org.